Pioneering Across America

The Families of Daniel B. Adlum and Patricia Reese 1620-2020

Pamela Adlum Vigil

Pioneering Across America
Copyright ©2020 by Pamela Adlum Vigil

ISBN 978-0-578-73848-2 (Hardcover edition)
      978-0-578-73849-9 (Paperback edition)

Library of Congress Control Number: 2020914291

Names: Vigil, Pamela, author.

Title: Pioneering across America : the families of Daniel B. Adlum and Patricia Reese / Pamela Vigil.

Description: Round Rock, TX : Pamela A. Vigil, 2020. | Includes bibliographical references and index.

Identifiers: ISBN 978-0-578-73848-2 (hardcover)

Subjects: LCSH: Families--History. | Genealogy. | Pioneers. | Pilgrims (New Plymouth Colony) | Mayflower (Ship) | United States--History--Colonial period, ca. 1600-1775. | BISAC: REFERENCE / Genealogy & Heraldry. | BIOGRAPHY & AUTOBIOGRAPHY / General. | HISTORY / United States / State & Local / General.

Classification: LCC CS71.A35 2020 (print) | LCC CS71.A35 (ebook) | DDC 929.20973--dc23.

All rights reserved. No part of this publication may be reproduced, distributed, or transmitted in any form or by any means, including photocopying, recording, or other electronic or mechanical methods, without the prior written permission of the publisher, except in the case of brief quotations embodied in critical reviews and certain other noncommercial uses permitted by copyright law.

Cover image credits:

"Mayflower in Plymouth Harbor," by William Halsall, 1882, at Pilgrim Hall Museum, Plymouth, Massachusetts
Wikipedia Commons

Emigrants Crossing the Plains or the Oregon Trail, by Albert Bierstadt, 1869, The Butler Institute of American Art, Youngstown, Ohio
Wikipedia Commons

Book design by StoriesToTellBooks.com

Contact the author at vigil.pamela@gmail.com

Pioneering Across America

The Families of Daniel B. Adlum and Patricia Reese 1620-2020

*Dedicated to the memory of my father, Daniel Bruce Adlum,
who taught me to love history
and to my grandchildren—
I hope learning about the people behind the events
will make history come alive for you.*

CONTENTS

PREFACE	ix
INTRODUCTION	xi
CHAPTER ONE: ON THE MOVE	1

The Adlum Family

Daniel B. Adlum's childhood and experiences in World War II, education and career

His grandfather's life in Iowa

Great grandfather's life in Altoona, PA

Adlum family roots in Northern Ireland and emigration to Pennsylvania Colony

Adlum family—American Revolution and beyond

Major John Adlum—experiences as a surveyor and as one of first winemakers in America

CHAPTER TWO: GAMBLING ON PROSPERITY	33

The Holman, Burnett, and Hardeman Families

The family of Ella Holman, Daniel B. Adlum's maternal grandmother, and root families, the Burnetts and Hardemans

Life in Oregon—Ella Holman's life in McMinnville and Portland

California gold—the Holmans and Peter Hardeman Burnett

Origins of Holmans in Virginia—Holmans pioneering west with Daniel Boone; some go to Texas

Origins of Burnett family in Virginia—pioneering west to Missouri

Origins of Hardeman family in Virginia—Life of Thomas Hardeman, Hardemans in Texas

Peter Hardeman Burnett leads 1843 Wagon Train to Oregon Country

CHAPTER THREE: EDUCATION	69

The Turner, Johnson, and Lee Families

The family of William B., Turner, Daniel B. Adlum's maternal grandfather

Story of Esther Ann Johnson—Daniel Adlum's great-grandmother and her parents

> *Origins of Johnson and Lee families in Connecticut*
>
> *Rev. Samuel Johnson and his son William Samuel Johnson*
>
> *Rev. Ralph Wheelock—seventh-great-grandfather of Daniel B. Adlum*
>
> *Mercy Standish Wheelock—granddaughter of Captain Myles Standish*

CHAPTER FOUR: FAITH 93
The Pilgrims of Plymouth

> *Story of the* Mayflower *and Daniel's and Patricia's ancestors who came to Plymouth*
>
> *History of the colony—Myles Standish and the Fullers and their descendants*

CHAPTER FIVE: FOR THE COMMON GOOD 125
The Puritans of Massachusetts Bay and Connecticut Colonies

> *Patricia Reese's Puritan ancestors in Massachusetts—William Paine, Sir Richard Saltonstall Jr. and Major Samuel Appleton*
>
> *Patricia Reese's Puritan ancestors in Connecticut—the Wolcotts and Governor Thomas Welles*
>
> *Daniel B. Adlum's Puritan ancestor—Governor William Leete and the Leete family*
>
> *Daniel B. Adlum's ninth-great grandfather—Rev. Henry Whitfield, founder of Guilford, CT*

CHAPTER SIX: REACHING FOR ZION 151
The Latter-day Saints

> *Ancestors of Patricia Reese, who joined the Mormon church—life in Utah*
>
> *History of Joseph Smith and the Church of LDS*
>
> *The Williams Family and their journey from Massachusetts to Utah through Nauvoo*
>
> *Origins of Samuel Comstock Snyder and his mother, Lovisa—descendants of Edward Fuller*
>
> *Snyder family journey to Utah—from Canada to Nauvoo to Salt Lake to Park City*
>
> *Immigration story of Watkin Rees and wife, Jane, in Utah*
>
> *Hyrum Williams, son Sylvester, and daughter Grace Williams Reese leave Utah for Oregon*
>
> *Grace Williams Reese's life with children in Oregon*

Chapter Seven: Wagons West 184
The Parvin, Parker, and Matthews Families

Ancestors of Patricia Reese's mother, Dorothy Agnes Parvin, and their trip west in 1853

Parvin, Parker, and Matthews families in Fulton County, Illinois

Origins of families in Virginia, Pennsylvania, and New Jersey

The Lost Wagon Train of 1853

Settlement in Lane County, OR

Chapter Eight: Unwavering Resolve 210
The Reese Family

Patricia Reese—growing up on cattle ranch in eastern Oregon with parents, Grover and Dorothy, during the Great Depression and World War Two

Chapter Nine: Still Restless After All These Years 225
The Adlum Family

Daniel Adlum and Patricia Reese's married life in Los Angeles
Conclusion

Pedigree Charts 244

Bibliography 258

Endnotes 267

Index 297

Author's great grandfather Hosea M. Parvin on his father's homestead land, Dexter, Oregon, c. 1890s, photo courtesy of Sharon and Larry Gilson

Preface

When my grandson Nikolay was born, I started to think about writing a family history for him so he would have a sense of belonging to something greater than himself. This book has evolved into something much larger than I imagined.

I developed my own sense of the importance of history at a young age. I grew up with a musket and powder horn, used by the Adlum family in the Revolutionary War, and a family document from 1774 hanging on the wall in our foyer. I was curious about the intense feelings in the family concerning politics and public affairs. The religiosity of our Protestant faith added a moral judgment as to how society and government should be formed. Constant searching for meaning and opportunity led the different factions of the family to be on the move beginning in the early seventeenth century, mostly in a western direction. Many of our ancestors seemed to hold a belief that whatever was over the next horizon would fulfill them. What was in our history that made us so curious and restless?

I believe I found some of the answers among our ancestors and the traits they passed on through the centuries. As I started my research, I was surprised by the close proximity between both sides of the family as they traveled parallel journeys. They have remarkably similar stories and struggles through adversity. It is the story of the trials all families go through, as well as the story of the formation and expansion of our nation.

This is a story about family, and I could not have written it without the assistance and previous work of many family members. I was fortunate to have a great deal of written documentation about my family on both sides from journals, personal letters, biographies, and autobiographies, as well as newspaper clippings and genealogy studies done prior to my work. I want to thank my cousin Virginia Adlum Houser for her work years ago on the Adlum family genealogy and Adlum cousin Gene Sharp and her husband, John Sharp, for their articles on Major John Adlum. Personal letters from the Adlum family dating from the eighteenth century, as well as John Adlum's memoirs and his books published on winemaking, helped fill in the family history. My great aunt Patricia Turner Shawver's charming tribute to her mother, Ella Holman, *Portrait of Mama*, painted a wonderful picture of her mother's life and personality. Cousin Elizabeth L. Smith, by editing and putting together her aunt Julia C. Turner's manuscript, *All the Years of Her Life*, on her mother, Esther Ann Johnson, provided valuable knowledge about my father's maternal grandfather's family. My father's cousin Dr. Nicholas Perkins Hardeman—who wrote

Wilderness Calling, chronicling his Hardeman ancestors—was coincidentally in graduate school at the University of California, Berkeley, in the early 1950s at the same time as my father, unknown to both to them. Dr. Hardeman's book was invaluable in tracing the history of my father's Hardeman ancestors.

My cousin Kathleen Stewart Baker was helpful in digging up the story of our great grandmother, Grace Williams Reese. Kathleen did a great deal of work researching the details of Grace's life in Drewsey, Oregon. The journal of my second-great-grandfather Watkin Rees, obtained from the LDS church, gave me a good picture of his immigration story. Stories on the Parvin family and the Lost Wagon Train of 1853 were provided to me by the Lane County Historical Society. My mother's cousin Wayne Burian did an extensive genealogy on the Parvin, Parker, and Matthews families. I am grateful to him and his wife, Charlene, for their enthusiasm in keeping the history alive. Wayne's sister Sharon and her husband, Larry Gilson, were also very helpful, providing helpful hints and fabulous early photographs.

I am very grateful to my husband, Joseph C. Vigil Jr., for both his encouragement and belief in me, as well as his patience for the mess my obsession has caused for three years. My siblings, Jeffrey Bruce Adlum and Ellen Adlum Pavlosek, have always offered loving support. My brother, Jeff, has been helpful by doing careful reading and any corrections of historical facts, for which I am grateful. When I wanted to quit, I thought of the work ethic of my daughter Kristin Kadar, who, like her ancestors, has tried to help the neglected members of society. My daughter Katherine Sasser has served as my editor, patiently reading and correcting the entire manuscript. She has made a huge difference in the finished product. I really appreciate her superior language skills and can't thank her enough for her interest and assistance.

To my mother, Patricia Reese Adlum, I owe all. She is my inspiration for this project and my inspiration for life. She has been invaluable, both in sharing her knowledge and her memoirs of her childhood, as well as reading the manuscript and offering suggestions. This book is for her.

Introduction

"May I have this dance?"

Patricia Reese 1948

Daniel B. Adlum 1948

My parents met in 1948 at a dance at the University of Oregon in Eugene. Highland House, the cooperative student house where my mother roomed, held a "ten cents a dance" affair to raise money. My father signed up for all the dances on my mother's dance card. My mother was a freshman, my father, Daniel Bruce Adlum, a dashing, older classman returning to college after serving in the Pacific Theatre in World War Two. It was the start of a wonderful love story. Unknown to them at the time, they had a connection from the very start of the colonization of America, as their families plotted similar courses through the centuries. Fate would bring them together in Oregon.

The struggles and triumphs of my family are part of that very great story of the building of the nation, from the first settlers at Plymouth, Massachusetts, and Jamestown, Virginia, to the establishment of towns, communities, schools, and government. They had the courage and fortitude to create and fight for a new nation. They were there at Plymouth in 1620, coming off the *Mayflower* after an arduous journey. One of my father's ancestors, Myles Standish, was the military captain at Plymouth. He knew my mother's ancestors on the *Mayflower*, one of whom was Edward Fuller, who came with his family and brother Dr. Samuel Fuller. Most of my mother's ancestors on the *Mayflower* succumbed to illness in Plymouth, as did over half the colony that first, harsh winter.

A large number of the ancestors of both my parents were Puritans. They left England during a period of great strife and political turmoil. Many of those who attempted reform of the Church of England were persecuted and became part of that Great Migration to the New World in the 1630s. They were well educated, many of them clergymen. Some, such as the Rev. John Lothrop, before immigrating to the New World, spent time in prison in England for their beliefs in church reform.

Cambridge University was a hotbed of Puritan thought in England in the early 1600s. Ancestors from both sides of the family attended Cambridge and brought their new ideas on religion and government with them to America. Cambridge alumni Rev. Ralph Wheelock, founder of Medfield (now New Denham), Massachusetts, was the first tax-supported public schoolteacher in America in the first free school founded in Denham in 1644. His great grandson Rev. Eleazer Wheelock founded Dartmouth College. My mother's ninth-great-grandfather, Nathaniel Dickinson, helped found Wethersfield, Connecticut, and then founded Hadley, Massachusetts. Nathaniel's grandson the Rev. Jonathan Dickinson became the first president of Princeton University and was one of the founders of the school. He was known for his scholarship, being thought only second to the Rev. Jonathan Edwards in his ability to argue religious theory.

Another educator—the descendant of a founder of New Haven, Connecticut—Rev. Dr. Samuel Johnson of Guilford, Connecticut was an important Enlightenment philosopher, pastor, and educator. Among his many accomplishments was the establishment of King's College, later renamed Columbia University. He served as the first president of King's College. One of his sons, William Samuel Johnson, went on to serve as the first senator from Connecticut as well as to work on and sign the U.S. Constitution.

My Adlum ancestors immigrated to the Pennsylvania Colony from County Antrim, Ireland. They immediately involved themselves in public affairs and government. The family pioneered in Pennsylvania and Maryland. The most well-known family member, Major John Adlum, after serving in the Revolutionary War as a youth, and having a successful career as a surveyor, became known as "The Father of American Viticulture" for his twenty years of work developing American grape varietals. He wrote the first book published in America on winemaking and developed a large circle of friends whom he corresponded with on winemaking, including Thomas Jefferson. His final vineyard was in the District of Columbia along the banks of Rock Creek.

Other ancestors came to Virginia as early as 1618, some serving in the House of Burgesses, Virginia's colonial legislature. They settled farms in Virginia and North Carolina and then restlessly moved on to Tennessee and Kentucky. They continued West, arriving on the West Coast in the first wave in 1843, on both sides of the family, Oregon pioneers came by wagon train to Oregon Country and then to California. Peter Hardeman

Burnett led one of the earliest and most significant wagon trains as first wagon master in 1843, helped develop Oregon, and then went on to become the first governor of California. All families were on the West Coast by 1910, having moved over a period of seventy years to end up near the Pacific.

All my ancestors, with the exception of one married couple who came from Wales in 1854, were here well before the American Revolution. They were mostly from England but also from Wales, Scotland, and Ireland. They were Protestants, mostly Calvinist Congregationalists and Presbyterians, but also some Baptists, Quakers, Methodists, Episcopalians, and a few who became Mormons. They came for religious freedom and economic opportunity with what must have been a great sense of curiosity and adventure. That curiosity and sense of adventure has characterized my family for 400 years.

They were a restless lot; seemingly dissatisfied with the status quo, they moved west through the wilderness time and time again. Over and over the new generations cleared land and established towns. They had a variety of occupations and were flexible in those choices, depending on opportunity. Many served in government, mostly at the local level, in addition to working as clergy, teachers, farmers, and businessmen. Generation after generation did their best, some doing very well financially, while others faced adversity and were put into precarious financial situations. Most lived at the middle-class level. They maintained their curiosity, drive, and search for new opportunities. My family has always been outer-directed, with an intensity of purpose. A strong theme of community responsibility and values has been maintained for centuries. The restless, hardworking spirit that defines American pioneers also defines my family.

The book is divided into different pioneering stories through my family's history during their 400 years in America. The first three chapters deal exclusively with my father's ancestors and their stories of western movement. Chapter One tells the story of my father's paternal ancestors, starting with my father's story in the twentieth century and tracing the Adlum family back to the early eighteenth century. Chapters Two and Three showcase my father's maternal ancestors. Chapter Two starts with my father's grandmother Mary Ellen Holman in nineteenth century Oregon and traces her root families back to seventeenth century Virginia. Chapter Three traces the family of Winifred Turner, my father's mother, back to their roots in colonial Connecticut. Chapters Four and Five tell the stories of my parents' Puritan ancestors. Chapter Four follows the *Mayflower* Pilgrims from Holland and through the history of the Plymouth Colony, while Chapter Five emphasizes my mother's Puritan ancestors in Connecticut and Massachusetts, as well as a few of my father's ancestors in the same area. Chapter Six follows my mother's paternal ancestors who became members of the Mormon Church and helped to develop Utah.

Chapter Seven is the story of my mother's maternal ancestors and their Oregon Trail odyssey. My mother's childhood growing up on a cattle ranch in eastern Oregon during the Great Depression is covered in Chapter Eight. The final chapter, Nine, concludes with my parents and our life as a family. Together these ancestors passed down their determination and curiosity about what is over the next hill to make the family what it is today.

Chapter One

On the Move

Family Cast of Characters

Daniel Bruce Adlum…(1921-1977) *father of author*
Helen Lee Adlum…(1913-2007) *sister of Daniel B. Adlum*

Henry Bruce Adlum…(1889-1955) *father of Daniel B. Adlum; grandfather of author*
Winifred Beatrice Turner…(1890-1956) *mother of Daniel B. and Helen Adlum*
Mildred E. Turner…(1886-1968) *married to Victor H. Allen; sister of Winifred Turner; aunt of Daniel B. Adlum*

Joseph Downs Adlum…(1886-1951) *older brother of Henry Adlum; uncle to Daniel B. Adlum*
Merle Daniel Adlum…(1919-1986) *son of Joseph Adlum; cousin to Daniel B. Adlum*

Daniel Joseph Adlum…(1860-1956) *father of Henry Bruce and Joseph Downs; grandfather of Daniel B. Adlum*
Carrie McKain…(1863-1956) *grandmother of Daniel B. Adlum*

Joseph Green Adlum…(1816-1893) *great-grandfather of Daniel B. Adlum; father of Daniel J. Adlum*
Evalyn Irwin…(1828-1908) *great-grandmother of Daniel B. Adlum; mother of Daniel J. Adlum*

Joseph Adlum…(1767-1846) *second-great-grandfather of Daniel B. Adlum; father of Joseph Green*
Anna McPhail…(1775-1851) *second-great-grandmother of Daniel B. Adlum; mother of Joseph Green*
Major John Adlum…(1759-1836) *second-great-uncle of Daniel B. Adlum; older brother of Joseph Adlum*

Joseph Adlum…(1727-1814) *third-great-grandfather of Daniel B. Adlum; father of Joseph and John Adlum*
Catherine Abbott…(1732-1822) *third-great-grandmother of Daniel B. Adlum; mother of Joseph and John Adlum*

John Abbott…(1700-1786) *emigrated from England, founder of Abbottstown, Pennsylvania; father of Catherine Abbott*

Alice Berwick…(1702-1742) *mother of Catherine Abbott; sister of Elizabeth Berwick; fourth-great-grandparents of Daniel B. Adlum*

John Adlum…(1701-1773) *emigrated from Ireland; fourth-great-grandfather of Daniel B. Adlum*
Elizabeth Berwick…(1705-1760) *emigrated from Ireland; fourth-great-grandmother of Daniel B. Adlum*
Captain John Adlum…(1725-1819) *son of John and Elizabeth; older brother of Joseph Adlum*

The Adlum Family

I stood in line at the market in West Los Angeles a few months after my father's death and wrote a check for my groceries. The checker glanced at my name and said "Adlum. That's an unusual name. Any relation to Professor Daniel Adlum at Pierce College?"

I said, "That's my father."

The checker replied, "He was the best teacher I ever had, and I learned so much American History from him."

I thanked him but could not bear to say my father had just died.

The sign over the main street in El Monte, California, in the 1920s proudly proclaimed it was *The End of the Santa Fe Trail*. It was certainly the end of the Old Spanish Trail, if not the actual Santa Fe Trail, and it was a destination for some of the people pouring into Los Angeles County during a population boom. One of the oldest cities in Los Angeles County, El Monte is situated in a fertile, sweet spot between the Rio Hondo and San Gabriel rivers in the San Gabriel Valley—perfect for the walnut groves and fruit crops grown there. In 1920 the population of El Monte was 1,283 and expanding. My grandfather Henry Bruce Adlum decided to take his wife, Winifred, and seven-year-old daughter, Helen Lee, there, moving more than 1,100 miles from their home in Seattle, Washington. They most likely traveled by ship down the coast but possibly came by rail. Travel by automobile from Seattle would have been quite difficult in 1920.[1]

After migrating to the west coast from Iowa at age twenty, Henry Bruce spent the years between 1910 and 1920 in a variety of sales jobs, moving many times within Portland, Oregon, and, in 1918, to Seattle, Washington, near his older brother, Jack Adlum. It was a big leap of faith for Henry Bruce to leave Seattle, go to California, and open his own business. He may have been following his brother Jack, who also went to Los Angeles County in the 1920s. Henry Bruce was thirty-one years old and full of optimism. It must have seemed like a great opportunity to be his own boss. It was here that my father, Daniel Bruce Adlum, was born on January 31, 1921. His father is listed as a confectioner on his birth certificate; Henry's candy store was right in the middle of town at 327 W. Main, El Monte, California. My father remembers his dad coming home with candy in his pockets when he was very young. They were happy memories, but it did not last.[2]

It is not clear what happened to the store or why they left California, but by 1924 the family was back in Portland and soon moved to Long Beach, Washington. The town of Long Beach is on Long Beach Peninsula, which sits just north of the mouth of the Columbia River, a long finger of land beside the Pacific Ocean, very near where the explorers Lewis and Clark got their first "full view of the Ocean" in 1805. It is full of breathtaking natural beauty, razor clams, salmon, cranberries, and a wide expanse of beach that appears endless.

Henry Bruce was determined to try a new venture here, partnering with his brother-in-law Victor Hugo Allen. They took over the Long Beach Natatorium. A natatorium is an indoor swimming pool—this one was filled with saltwater and was used as a place for beachgoers to swim.

The ocean in Washington State is too cold and dangerous to swim in. Long Beach was and still is a resort town. It was very popular with wealthy Portland residents in the late nineteenth and early twentieth centuries. There were many activities for tourists, including festivals, razor clam digs, the baths, and searching for items from the many shipwrecks in the area. The area around the mouth of the Columbia River and Long Beach Peninsula is known as the "Graveyard of the Pacific" because of the more than 2,000 vessels that wrecked or sank there. The dangerous sand bars, shifting winds, large waves, and currents made for a challenging voyage for sea captains.[3]

The Oregon coast was very difficult to get to from Portland in early days because there were very few roads built through to the coast, which made Long Beach more popular with Oregonians. Early on, vacationers would have to take a sternwheeler down the Columbia River and then take a stagecoach the rest of the way to get to Long Beach. Railroads were built in the 1920s, and eventually, roads were built to the interior of Washington, making the commute easier. The typical way to get from Portland to Long Beach in the 1920s was to come down the Columbia by boat or take the train to Astoria, Oregon, take a ferry

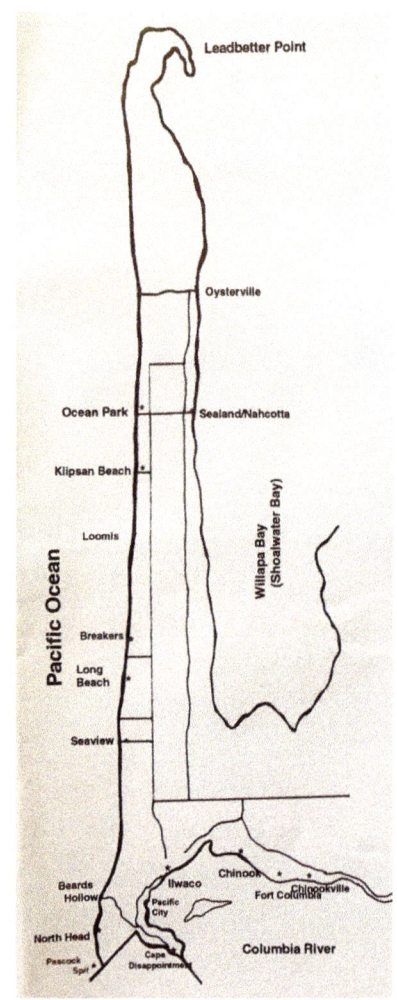

Map of Long Beach Peninsula, WA, image from The Long Beach Peninsula, p.65, D.J. Lucero, 2004, Charleston, NC, Arcadia Publishing, used with permission

across to Long Beach Peninsula, and then take the narrow-gauge railroad, nicknamed the *Clamshell Railroad*, up the peninsula to the town of Long Beach. The railroad also was called the *Irregular, Rambling, and Never Get There Railroad* for the relaxed way it was run.

Long Beach's claim to fame was the twenty-eight miles of beach, which residents boasted was the longest beach in the world. In the early 1920s they had car races on the wide expanse of beach. By 1925 some of the wealthier Portland residents started to go to Seaside, Oregon, instead, because transportation became easier. This caused Long Beach to lose some business.

Daniel remembered the joy of living at the beach when he was young. The family business evidently was not a success, because the Adlums were back in Portland by 1928. The 1930 census lists Henry Bruce as a wholesale coffee salesman, with him and the family living in a house he purchased on Couch Street in Portland.[4]

1923 Ad for Long Beach, WA, image from *The Long Beach Peninsula*, p. 94, D.J. Lucero, 2004, Charleston, NC, Arcadia Publishing, used with permission

The stock market crash of 1929 and subsequent, severe economic depression changed circumstances for the worse for Henry Bruce's family, as it did for many others. Oregon was already grappling with an economic slowdown in the 1920s. The two largest industries—timber and agriculture—were doing poorly prior to 1929. In Portland, business owners had trouble generating enough money to pay their business taxes. In the early 1930s the population of Portland was about 300,000. One third was receiving some kind of government aid, and about twenty-five percent of the men were unemployed. Many men had trouble supporting their families and some abandoned them.

Henry Bruce Adlum, who was said to be impatient and short tempered, felt the strain. His older brother, Jack, stayed with the family briefly in 1934. Daniel was thirteen at the time. He overheard his Uncle Jack tell his father that he did not have to stay, "He could just leave." In the morning they both were gone, and Daniel never saw his father again.

Daniel's life became very hard after his father disappeared. Creditors came and took all the furniture, and the family lost the house. Shortly afterwards, his mother, Winifred, had a bad accident and broke her back. She spent several months in the hospital and was unable to provide a home for him after that. Daniel's older sister, Helen, was able to move in with relatives in California, but there was no room for Daniel. He was left without a home at age thirteen. He moved into a room above a butcher shop owned by family friends and lived there while attempting to keep up with school. He had to work for his keep, making it difficult to get to school on time and maintain regular hours. Eventually, he left high school and joined the Civilian Conservation Corps.

The CCC was a government work program started by Franklin D. Roosevelt's administration for homeless, jobless, young men up to age twenty-eight. The CCC employed over three million young men like Daniel—87,000 in Oregon alone—until disbandment in 1942. They worked in forestry and built dams, roads, buildings, trails, parks, and camps. They also planted millions of trees, all while living in military-type accommodations with room and board. They earned $30 a month, of which they had to send $25 home to family. Daniel was so small when he went into the CCC—as well as being a little underage—that he worked in the kitchen at first. After growing several inches, he was then put to work on outside jobs. Some of the projects in Oregon that the CCC built include the spectacular Silver Falls State Park, Honeyman Memorial State Park, and the Timberline Lodge at Mount Hood.[5]

Daniel Bruce and Helen Lee Adlum, c. 1927, Portland, Oregon, author's collection

Daniel was able to return to high school at age nineteen, staying at his Auntie Mil's boarding house. Mildred Allen was his mother's sister, a wonderful woman who had suffered through her own hard times. At one point in her marriage to Victor Hugo Allen, her husband left her and their four children, Richard, Victor, Philip, and Patricia, and moved in with another woman, leaving Mildred struggling to make ends meet. She sent her son Victor to live with Daniel and his family for four years during that time. Daniel was close to Victor and to his cousin Patricia (Patty), who was like a sister. At the time his Aunt Mildred ran the boarding house, she was widowed, her husband having died at age fifty. Cousins Daniel and Patty had chores that included doing all of the dishes for the boarders.

Living at the boarding house allowed Daniel some stability while he finished high school. He graduated from Grant High School in Portland in June 1941. During his senior year, he joined the Oregon National Guard. They paid him a small stipend after graduation, which he needed to help with expenses. He was one of many young men who belonged to the National Guard in the ending years of the Depression.[6]

The Oregon National Guard's 41st Division was considered to be one of the best in the country and was the first to be called up during World War II. Daniel became an active-duty enlisted man right out of high school because the Guard was automatically made part of the army when the war started. The 41st was called up on December 10, 1941, three days after the attack on Pearl Harbor. They shipped out to Norfolk, Virginia, and then spent forty days on an ocean liner—to fool the enemy—traveling from the East Coast through the Panama Canal to Australia. They arrived in Australia to a thunderous welcome. Most of the Australian young men were in North Africa, fighting the Germans.

The Oregon National Guard was sent to protect Australia and to hold the line against the Japanese until the rest of the Army could organize to fight in the Pacific. They suffered tremendous causalities while doing so. Daniel's regiment trained in the bush country and in the northeastern, coastal tropical forests of Australia and were then deployed to New Guinea, the large island north of Australia, to help the Australians fight the Japanese.

Japan invaded New Guinea in an attempt to capture the capital port city, Port Moresby, and thus cut off Australia from its allies. In February 1943, Daniel's regiment set off for the war zone in an old Dutch ship. He wrote, "The well-polished brass plate in the engine room of the transport read Amsterdam 1902." Daniel described the ship as "slow, small with indescribable filth between decks. The Javanese crew scampering about the decks in sandaled feet with their live chickens and ducks merely added to the general filth."

The men of the 41st Division were the first American troops in the Southwest Pacific Theatre. Daniel's regiment, the 162nd Infantry, was the first to assist, landing at Nassau Bay in very dangerous conditions in their push to regain the important town of Salamaua.[7]

Daniel did not talk much about the war until he was ill and near the end of his life, at which point he reflected upon his experiences as part of the "Fighting Jungleers," as the 41st Division was called. They fought under terrible conditions. There was sauna-like humidity, endless rain, standing water, mud too thick to get equipment through the dense jungle, and almost no roads.

The 162nd Infantry of the 41st Division set a battle record of seventy-six days of continuous combat in the battle for Salamaua. It was a brutal conflict, with the Japanese sheltering in caves and dugouts and holding mountain ridges while receiving reinforcements, while, meanwhile, no ships could get through to reinforce the Americans. The 162nd received some supplies from air drops but often had to exist on half-rations or find their own food. The soldiers lost a tremendous amount of weight fighting tropical diseases such as malaria, dengue fever, and dysentery, while worrying about Japanese snipers hidden in trees.[8]

The conditions were so terrible in New Guinea that thousands of men on both sides collapsed, considerably thinning their ranks. Daniel posthumously received the Bronze Star for his participation in this battle. One bright spot was the help of some of the native tribes who had never been exposed to white men or modern warfare but went out of their way to help the Aussies and the U.S. soldiers against the brutality of the Japanese. They were fondly called "Fuzzy Wuzzy Angels" by the grateful Australian soldiers. Daniel wrote several articles about New Guinea for the Army newspaper at Camp McQuaide in California, describing the war and native people of New Guinea and some technical articles on Japanese machine guns.[9]

Cpl. Daniel B. Adlum describes the approach to battle in one of the articles he authored:

After four months in Papua, our battalion joined the remainder of the regiment, which was working its way along the coast in a north-westerly direction, neutralizing any enemy resistance found and securing various bays and harbors. We had by this time crossed into Northeastern New Guinea, which is the Australian-mandated territory. The main Jap forces were concentrated in the Lae-Salamaua area, district of Morobe, which is part of Northeast New Guinea. This is where the gold fields of New Guinea lie, Salamaua being a settlement which sprang up during the gold rush of the 1920s. On the 28th day of June 1943, our regiment established a beachhead at Nassau Bay, 15 miles below Salamaua, starting the main drive for that base. Each unit that was committed to action remained under fire continuously until Salamaua fell on September 12. In this area, as much of the island, steep mountains and hills slant down to the edge of the sea, forming small bays and inlets. The only flat land is found around these small indentations in the mountain chain. Our job was to make a frontal attack on the main Jap defenses in the ridges surrounding Salamaua while a force pushed inland. They as well as we met stiff opposition all the way. Nevertheless, within a few days we had pushed up the coast nine miles and gained control of Tambu Bay; that is to say, we controlled the beach.

In the steep ridges overlooking the bay, the Japs had organized their main lines of resistance. Near the crest and on the reverse slope of every commanding piece of ground, our enemies had constructed a series of defenses dug out of the earth and covered and reinforced with logs cut from the heavily wooded slopes. We dubbed these emplacements "pillboxes," but in every sense of the word they were really dugouts. At any rate they covered every possible approach by machine gun fire and they were well supported by mortars, light and heavy, as well as machine guns.

Worst of all, the Japs from their heights had direct observation of all our movements on the beach. Despite these difficulties, we managed to land our artillery, 105s and pack howitzers. Well supported by these, we gained each ridge successively by direct assault. In the weeks that followed, we pushed the Japs from their mountain strongholds. When we finally obtained the highest ground, it was only a short push downhill and Salamaua was ours.[10]

Daniel went on in further articles to describe the fear he and other soldiers felt in battle and how one did not know who could be counted on until that first baptism of fire. He had great praise for the medics—pill rollers, as they called them—and relayed the sad experience of seeing medics lose their lives while attempting to rescue wounded soldiers.

There were no roads, so the wounded had to be carried on litters over mountain passes. Daniel wrote of his admiration for the natives who carried the wounded down steep slopes. "The way they kept their balance in carrying our wounded down those steep muddy slopes without even jolting them was almost superhuman."

He wrote in a lighter note about the customs of the natives and described their notable system of valuation. "It seems to work for their needs. A man has three possessions on which he places considerable value. These are in order of their importance: first his pigs, second his garden, and last, strangely enough, his women."

Daniel B. Adlum U.S. Army, 1942, author's collection

The natives joined the soldiers when they started a new method of fishing. The men of the 162nd would throw a hand grenade in a stream. If there was a village nearby, the explosion would bring the entire able-bodied population on the run to retrieve the fish.

Throughout the heartache and tragedy of war, there were touching moments. When their mission was accomplished and the men of the 162nd were ready to leave Salamaua, their colonel had the remnants of the regiment assembled on the airstrip for a short speech. Daniel wrote, "We were a pitifully small band. Besides those killed and wounded, malaria, dengue, dysentery and other diseases had taken their toll." The colonel told them they had gained more miles of territory for the Allied cause than any other regiment, and he had not thought it possible for any force to remain in close contact with the enemy for as long as they had. When the 162nd arrived in Australia, their uniforms in rags, they were treated like heroes. The Australians were grateful to the Americans for helping hold the line against the Japanese.[11]

The war took its toll on those who fought under such brutal conditions. Daniel did not have a lot of use for guns after having to use machine guns on Japanese soldiers. He said, "You could not easily take them prisoner, because they would blow themselves up, and you as well." After two years in the field and several bouts of malaria that continued to bother him years later, he worked on a quadriplegic ward for wounded soldiers twelve hours a day, six days a week. Many years later, sitting in conversation with him when he was ill, he relayed that he had been so grateful to be alive without major wounds.[12]

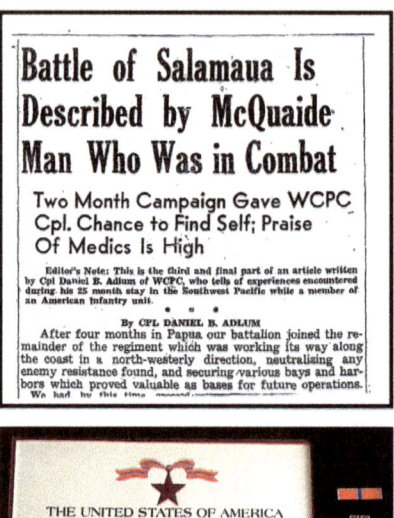

Bronze Star awarded to Daniel B. Adlum for Battle of Salamaua, newspaper clippings, describing battle, Unknown dates and paper, collection of Patricia Reese Adlum

Daniel was a positive and idealistic person who truly believed in the ability of mankind to improve. He was also practical and hardworking. He always had a love for history. After the war he went to school, using the GI Bill to help pay his way. He received his BA in history at the University of Oregon in 1949, followed by his graduate studies in history at the University of California, Berkley. He received his MA in history at Cal Berkley in 1950. His PhD dissertation choice on the first landscape architect of the U.S., Frederick Law Olmstead, demonstrated his passion for nature. He shared an ancestor with Olmstead—Captain Nicholas Olmstead of Hartford, Connecticut—but did not realize it at the time. Daniel felt that urban planning to preserve natural areas was very important. Shortly before he was to finish his PhD, his faculty advisor left the university and another PhD student at another university published on the same subject. Rather than start over as required by the circumstances, and since he had a family to support, he began to teach. He taught U.S. history, Russian History and Environmental Studies at Pierce College in Los Angeles for years.

In addition to his career, Daniel was involved in Democratic Party politics and public policy. When he first moved to Los Angeles, he took his family to live in Canoga Park in the San Fernando Valley. He was involved with the Party there and at the state level as a delegate to the Democratic State Convention. In the mid-1950s he was asked to run for U.S. Congressman for his district. Having small children and no significant campaign funds, he declined but continued to be involved. He also played an active role in his church, the Congregational Church of Northridge, serving as a parish leader.

As part of his interest in urban planning, Daniel had an important role in open-space planning for the San Fernando Valley in Los Angeles. He served as head of the Open Space and Parks Group of the planning committee Destination Ninety. Los Angeles, especially, the San Fernando Valley, was growing rapidly in the 1960s. Daniel felt it was important to preserve open space for parks within developments planned for the area. He had a passion for environmental causes and always supported thoughtful land use. In a *Los Angeles Times* article from 1967 about the work of Destination Ninety, he is quoted as saying, "From a personal standpoint, I'm finding it rewarding and stimulating to work with many people who, in the main, are devoted to the public interest. Every citizen, to be affective, needs competence in public problems broader in scope than his own particular specialty. Destination Ninety is helping fill that need for me." He would find it satisfying if he knew that one of his daughters, Ellen Suzanne, would go on to receive a degree in Landscape Architecture.[13]

Daniel's son, Jeffrey Bruce Adlum, when asked about his memories of his father, mentioned how much his father loved the sea. Daniel gave his two favorite books, *The Sea Scout Manuel* and Teddy Roosevelt's *Naval War of 1812*, to his son. Daniel passed on his love of the outdoors—especially, the sea—to his children, as well as the importance of preserving history, culture, and the natural beauty around us.

Although he was estranged from his own father, Daniel was fond of his grandfather Daniel Joseph Adlum, after whom he was named. Daniel Joseph shared a love of history and left him with heirlooms of the Adlum family. His grandfather shared his extensive collection of rare stamps collected when he was Postmaster in Missouri Valley, Iowa, as well as family letters dating from the late eighteenth and early nineteenth centuries and the Adlum family Bible. Other heirlooms are a document dating from 1774 swearing in his second-great-grandfather Joseph as coroner for York County, Pennsylvania, a musket and powder horn used in the American Revolution, and an eighteenth-century wineglass. This was a lot of history for a young man to take care of. Daniel understood his grandfather was trusting him to be the custodian of his family's history.

Daniel's paternal grandfather, Daniel Joseph Adlum, started the western movement of the Adlum family by moving from Pennsylvania to Iowa in 1880 at the age of twenty. It is not clear what prompted Daniel Joseph to move more than 1,000 miles from home, other than a job opportunity, but his hometown newspaper in Altoona made note of him leaving and taking a job with the railroad.

Missouri Valley, Iowa, was a railroad town, as was Daniel Joseph's hometown of Altoona. According to the 1880 census, he was working as a dry goods clerk in his father's store when he left home. His sisters and older brother, Wilford Downs, were still at home. Daniel was the first to leave, followed later by his brother, who moved to Missouri and then Minnesota.[14]

Missouri Valley was a new town in Harrison County, carved out of the frontier of southwestern Iowa, part of the land the United States gained from the Louisiana Purchase of 1803. In the early part of the 1800s, there were no white men settled there, although Lewis and Clark passed through on their epic exploration of the West for President Thomas Jefferson. French fur traders travelled in Iowa as well. The area teemed with elk and buffalo and served as an Indian hunting region for Pottawattamie, Sioux, and Omaha Indians. By the 1830s settlers began to move into Iowa, and it gained enough population to become a state in 1846. Fifteen years later, the entire state was covered with the farms of transplanted citizens. The miles of new railroads built connecting Iowa farms and towns to markets in Chicago encouraged more growth. New inventions, such as the telephone and electric lights, came about during this core period of the second Industrial Revolution.

Harrison County was organized by the state in 1853, and land was made available for $1.25 an acre. The county was rapidly populated as settlers moved in and established small farms. Many farmers grew corn, but wheat, barley, and rye were also grown. Hogs and cattle were a large part of agricultural outlays as well.

Missouri Valley was a rough frontier town with muddy streets full of teams of horses and wagons. The railroad was the primary reason for the rapid expansion of the town. Daniel Joseph was hired as a timekeeper by the Missouri Valley and Northwestern Railway Company. He worked for the railroad for seven years, advancing in his position as the town grew in size. Missouri Valley doubled in size from 1880 to 1884, mostly because of the convergence of three railroads: The Chicago and Northwestern (first known as the Cedar Rapids and Missouri), The Sioux City, and the Valley. This allowed the farmers in the area to have access to a number of markets for their goods. The railyard had large repair shops that employed almost 500 men at one point and had a place for hogs and cattle to feed on their way to market in Chicago.[15]

Daniel Joseph Adlum (Daniel B. Adlum's grandfather) c.1880s, Missouri Valley, Iowa, author's collection

At age twenty-seven Daniel Joseph took a gamble, left the railroad, and started his own mercantile business, drawing on his experience in his father's store. Along the way he fell in love and married a local girl, Carrie McKain, in 1884. They had two sons, Joseph Downs (born 1886) and Daniel Bruce's father, Henry Bruce (born 1889). Being active in public affairs and politics (Republican) led Daniel Joseph to be appointed Postmaster of Missouri Valley by President William McKinley in 1898. He was Postmaster for eighteen years. At the close of his long-held post, Daniel Joseph went back into business. According to the 1920 census, his occupation is listed as agent for real estate and loans.[16]

The 1920s were a time of great change for farm real estate and banking in Iowa. During World War I, farmers were pushed to produce record crops and livestock. They were encouraged by bankers and rising prices to expand, buy more land, and take on more debt. Land prices were rising, and things looked very promising for the productive Iowa farmers. Iowa farmland is some of the richest soil in the world.

When the War ended in 1921, a severe recession ravaged the general economy. There was a price depression in crop and farm goods, and suddenly, many farmers were unable to pay their mortgages. Many held huge amounts of debt on their land. Most of them banked in local banks in the nearest towns. These were small, state-chartered banks, some having capitalization of only around $25,000. Branch banks were looked upon with suspicion and were almost nonexistent. It was the age of "character loans" based on personal knowledge of borrowers, not unlike the film "It's a Wonderful Life." The banks were part of the community, and as the community suffered, so did the banks. Iowa led the nation in bank failures in the 1920s (87 a year), most being small town banks.[17]

The stock market crash of 1929 only increased the problems in Iowa. The two industries hit hardest in Iowa during the Great Depression were agriculture and banking. The 1920s had brought many foreclosures of farms, in addition to the bank failures. In the 1930s, things just got worse. The price of corn, the primary crop of many Iowa farmers, dropped so low that some farmers used it for heating instead of the more expensive coal, with the result that the area sometimes smelled like popcorn. Farmers became angry and frustrated and took out their frustrations by joining farm unions and joining protest movements. At one point in 1933, in a northwest Iowa county, farmers dragged a judge out of his courtroom, stripped him to his long johns, and threatened to lynch him if he foreclosed on any more farms.[18]

Daniel Joseph and his wife, Carrie, lived in Missouri Valley during this turbulent time, and their income waxed and waned with the economic situation. The 1930 census record shows they owned a house worth $10,000—more than the average value—and Daniel Joseph was still working in real estate and loans. According to family history, he ran a small local bank which failed in 1933, along with so many others in Iowa. There was no Federal Deposit Insurance for banks yet, and bank failures typically meant depositors lost all their money. Daniel Joseph stood by his financial commitments. He sold his house and liquidated his assets to pay off his bank depositors. He retired in 1934 at age 75 to Long Beach,

California. His two sons also went to California, leaving family in Portland and Seattle.[19]

The Iowa couple outlived the average lifespan. They were in Long Beach for twenty years, Carrie living until age ninety and Daniel Joseph living until age ninety-five. Daniel outlived his entire family: parents, siblings, and both sons. All his sisters died about thirty years before he did. Daniel's sister Mary was struck by a train, one of the dangers of living in her hometown of Altoona, which was crisscrossed by railroad tracks. His older brother, Wilford Downs, who married Carrie Mentzer in Missouri in 1888, had two sons, both of whom lived in Portland at the same time as Daniel's sons. Wilford, after divorcing his wife, went home to Pennsylvania and, sadly, developed early senility. He spent the last eighteen years of his life in the Blair County Hospital for the Insane. His death certificate in 1934 lists apoplexy and early senility as the causes of death.

Daniel Joseph and Carrie may have had trouble reconciling the lives of their two sons, Joseph Downs (Jack) and Henry Bruce. Both led very restless lives and had trouble with alcohol. Whatever combination of personality and circumstances led them to live as they did is not known. Had they lived at another time, perhaps, their lives would have been different. Their grandsons, however, were examples of lives well lived.[20]

Daniel Bruce did not know his first cousin from Seattle, Merle Daniel Adlum, but they surely would have bonded over their love of the sea. Merle grew up at Friday Harbor in the San Juan Islands off the coast of Washington. He always loved boats and built a career around them. His mother, the daughter of a Norwegian ship captain, was aptly named Oceana. His father, Joseph Downs Adlum (Uncle Jack), who worked as a ship's purser at the time Merle was born, left the family when Merle was one.

After living in West Seattle with his mother and stepfather, Merle joined an uncle when he was twelve and went to sea as a fisherman. At seventeen he joined the Navy but was discharged two years later after he broke his back in a storm. Recovering from his injury, he started his career working for the Washington State Ferry System and worked his way into leadership roles. Merle became Master of the Puget Sound Ferries, President of the Inland Boatman's Union, and a proponent and organizer of the Alaska State Ferries, among numerous other maritime accolades. He held the important position of Port of Seattle Commissioner for almost twenty years (1964-1983.) His civic activities included the Maritime Advisory Board and the Washington Committee for Responsible Environmental Policy.

Merle was a visionary when it came to the need for growth of the port and airport. He pushed for expansion of Seattle's Sea-Tac Airport. Like his cousin Daniel Bruce in Los Angeles, Merle was concerned with environmental and labor issues. Captain Merle Daniel Adlum led a full productive life and had a major impact on the development of Puget Sound's maritime economy.[21]

Daniel Bruce and Merle Daniel's grandfather, Daniel Joseph, saw expansive change in his lifetime. He was born in Pennsylvania just before the Civil War and grew up during the start of the new industrial revolution. Steel and iron industries gained prominence in Pennsylvania as the railroads used these materials to expand across the continent and change the face of the United States. Daniel Joseph was involved in the railroads at a time when they were rapidly growing, and he caught the wave of growth in Iowa to open a business and, eventually, became part of the local government. After a prosperous time in our nation's history, he lived through the instability of two World Wars and the Great Depression. He died in 1956 in California, in a completely changed nation that his father, Joseph Green Adlum, in Altoona could not have possibly imagined.

There was a well-established pattern in the Adlum family of sons moving to a new town to make their way in life. Joseph Green Adlum was no different. He left his father, Joseph, and mother, Anna, in Muncy, Lycoming County, Pennsylvania, in 1841, moving approximately 120 miles across the Allegheny Mountains to where the village of Bells Mills (now Bellwood) lay in the Logan Valley at the foot of Brush Mountain. He met the woman he would marry, Evalyn Irwin, the daughter of a local farmer, and built one of the first houses in what was to become the nearby city of Altoona in 1849. Adlum and Irwin—Irwin after his wife's family—was one of the first businesses in Altoona. Evalyn's younger brother Abraham Irwin lived with them and worked at the store. Joseph G. was the second justice of the peace of the county and was active in the affairs of the town. He and his wife raised six children: four daughters and two sons. Although the Adlums traditionally belonged to the Episcopal Church, Joseph Green and his wife spent some fifty-five years as members of the Bellwood First Methodist Church.[22]

The early 1800s in Pennsylvania were a time of growth in transportation and innovation of industries that would change the methods of transport. Early on, the best way to ship goods was by water, utilizing the many rivers in the state. Pennsylvania had the difficult problem of figuring out how to send goods more efficiently from Philadelphia to Pittsburg; the Allegheny Mountains were in the way. The mountains constituted a formidable barrier to east-west traffic until industrial advances in transportation were made. There were Indian trails across the Alleghenies and, later, the Braddock military road, but transporting goods across the mountains remained very difficult and slow, taking days with pack animals or ox and wagon.

There was competition between states for commerce and faster methods of transport. When the Erie Canal was planned and built in New York, and it became cheaper to send Philadelphia goods to Pittsburg via New York, the government in Philadelphia became concerned and authorized a $10 million transportation project involving canals and rail to connect the east and west sides of the state and provide better transport to other states. The project, called The Main Line of Public Works, connected Philadelphia and Pittsburg in 1834. It included the Philadelphia and Columbia Railroad, the Allegheny Portage Railroad, and the Pennsylvania Canal system. The western end of the canal system was located a few miles from present-day Altoona in a village called Hollidaysburg. This speeded up transport but was quickly surpassed by the building of a main line from Philadelphia to Pittsburg by the Pennsylvania Railroad Company. This cut a trip that normally took five to six days via the Main Line Canal to fifteen hours.[23]

Altoona, situated at the base of the Alleghenies, was the perfect place to establish a stopping point. The railroad's main shop complex was located there, as well as helper engines to push the trains over the mountains. Two major infrastructure projects west of Altoona were completed in 1854: The Horseshoe Curve and the Gallitzin Tunnels. The Horseshoe Curve was an engineering marvel that is still admired today. It is a 2,375-foot rail line that wraps around a valley and rises 122 feet from north to south. Workers cut through the mountain and filled two big ravines to build it.

The Horseshoe Curve, Mcdowell, A. P., photographer, The Horseshoe Curve, Altoona, Penna, from the Library of Congress, www.loc.gov/item/2002661523/

By 1857 the Main Canal system was out of business, and Altoona was booming from the railroads. The Pennsylvania Railroad grew into the largest in the world. Joseph Green Adlum was right in the middle of this dizzying change in industry and transportation in an area that became significant for both the railroads and the country for the rest of the century. From 1860 to 1870 the population tripled in Altoona. Railroads were the future.[24]

By 1860, when Joseph Green had a business and six children to support, Altoona was in the middle of arguments over slavery and states' rights. Pennsylvania was not sure how to feel about slavery but was greatly affected by the proximity of the southern states. The Democratic Party in Pennsylvania was split between pro-war and peace factions. Along with the Republican Party, no one was satisfied with the choices before them. The Constitutional Union Party sprang up out of the remnants of the conservative Whig Party, which died in 1856. In the pivotal presidential election of 1860, there were four candidates: two from the Democratic Party, north and south, Stephen A. Douglas and John C. Breckinridge, Abraham Lincoln for the new Republican Party, and John Bell for the

Constitutional Party. Lincoln won with forty percent of the vote, which led to the succession of eleven southern states.

In 1862 Altoona was chosen to host the Conference of Northern War Governors. They met at the famed Logan House Hotel, just steps from the railroad station, and publicly endorsed President Lincoln's efforts to free the slaves in the rebellious states. Joseph Green Adlum was involved in the politics of the time to the point that, in 1862, as a member of the short-lived Constitutional Union Party, he ran for representative to the Pennsylvania House of Representatives from Blair County.

The Constitutional Union Party sprang up as an alternative to the poor choices some border-state residents felt they had regarding the conflict between the North and South. The Party took no stand on slavery but wanted to foster "support of the Constitution, the union of the states and the enforcement of the laws." Joseph's feelings on slavery are not known, but he was a long-time member of a church which took a stand against slavery. For two year, in 1865 and 1866, Joseph Green served in the Pennsylvania House as a Republican Representative for Blair County.[25]

Involvement in public affairs and politics was a family tradition. His great grandfather John Adlum and his grandfather Joseph were involved in protesting the Stamp Act one hundred years earlier. One hundred and thirty years before Joseph Green Adlum became involved in the politics of the Civil War, his family made the fateful decision to leave the political and economic turmoil of Ulster and emigrate from Ireland.

Adlum—or Adlam, as it is sometimes spelled—is an old Saxon name derived from Adelhelm. The original bearer of the name was mostly likely a soldier who was honored. For many centuries the Adlum family was well established in southwest England. At some point some of the family immigrated to Ireland. The records are lost, but it is probable that it was in the seventeenth century, during or after the establishment of the Ulster Plantation.

The English struggled for years to conquer Ireland. Their efforts to unify and stabilize the area were strongly resisted by the Catholic natives. Tyrone's Rebellion or "The Nine Year's War," a major uprising led by an Irish chieftain, was brutally put down by the English in 1603 and led to all the major Ulster Irish lords being exiled by 1607 and their land confiscated.

Sir Arthur Chichester, the English Lord Deputy for Ireland, received a large land grant in County Antrim, Ulster, for services during the rebellion. He encouraged farmers from his native Devon County in southwest England, as well as Lancashire and Cheshire counties, to settle in Antrim. "They prospered so much, that much of southern Antrim became English in character."

The Adlums were among those from southwest England who immigrated to County Antrim. Chichester encouraged lowland Scots farmers to come as well. The idea was "to plant the area with Protestants" in order to push out the native Catholics and stabilize the region. The Scots Presbyterian farmers were poor, tough, and independent minded, having lived a marginal existence for years in a battle-worn area of Scotland, and they were eager for a new start. These Scotsmen constituted the majority of settlers to the Ulster Plantation and were well suited for the challenges of Northern Ireland.[26]

The Ulster Plantation was successful, but outside events during the century created political and economic strain. The English Civil War and its aftermath, as well as continued uprisings from the native Irish, tested the mettle of the transplanted Scots and Englishmen and made them even tougher. After Cromwell's Puritan five-year dictatorship (1653-1658), when the Crown (Charles II) regained power, they took no chances with dissident Protestant sects. The Crown began passing restrictive laws which would strengthen the alliance of the Anglican (Episcopal) church and the English government. These increasingly restrictive laws, called the "Test Acts," became intolerable in 1704 under Queen Ann. Unless one pledged allegiance to the Anglican church, one was shut out of legal procedures, serving in government, teaching, and acting as ministers, among other things. This disenfranchised the mostly Presbyterian Scots, disallowing validation of marriages in Presbyterian churches or full participation in public affairs. The Ulster Plantation was treated as a stepchild by England, with restrictive trade policies making it difficult to make a living.

Over time life in Ulster became more difficult for the Ulster Scots—or Scots-Irish, as they are now called—as well as everyone else in the area. Long, stable leases for property were raised to unaffordable prices in a policy called "rack-renting" where any improvements made by the farmers would raise their rent. Combined with several years of drought and bad harvests in the early 1700s, these tough Scots farmers were ready to leave and try their luck in the New World. The Adlums, who belonged to the Church of Ireland—the Irish version of the Episcopal Church of England—were ready to go with their Scots-Irish neighbors and joined the exodus as well.[27]

In 1724 John Adlum, Daniel Bruce's fourth-great-grandfather, married Elizabeth Berwick. In 1732 or 1734, depending on the source, he brought his wife and sons John (age seven) and Joseph (age five) to America. His grandson Major John Adlum, writing of his grandfather in his memoirs, describes him as "a poor Irish gentleman of liberal education." As a classic liberal education was hard to come by, he may have been more prosperous at one time, but conditions in Ulster encouraged a new start.

John Adlum and his family left County Antrim, mostly likely coming through the port of Philadelphia, stopping briefly in Chester and then Lancaster, and finally settling in York, Pennsylvania, in 1736. John's wife's family—her father was Simon Berwick—immigrated as well to the Lancaster, Pennsylvania, area.[28]

Map of Pennsylvania showing Adlum family locations, from www.freeworldmaps.net/united-states/pennsylvania/pennnsylvania-map.

William Penn's Quaker colony, established in 1682, welcomed immigrants of all religions. German refugees from the Palatinate region (the middle Rhine), persecuted and starving at home, felt welcome, as did the Scots-Irish Presbyterians coming from Ulster. Starting in the 1720s, both groups headed in increasing numbers to the frontier of the established colony: one hundred miles west of Philadelphia in lushly wooded land full of oak, hickory, yellow poplar, walnut, and elm trees. Here land was cheaper and it was easier to stake a claim but at the cost of conflict with Indians as part of their lives. The Germans, being excellent farmers, looked for limestone soil areas to establish farms on the west bank of the Susquehanna River in the Kreutz Creek area. The Scots-Irish, being more adventuresome in personality, pushed farther west to areas near streams with less fertile soil. The Adlum's town of York Springs in York County—established before 1741—was the first town established west of the Susquehanna River. The government in Philadelphia stimulated growth of the town by offering land warrants, payable at seven shillings a year, with the stipulation that the grantee build a building of at least sixteen square feet made of stone or brick within a year's time. In 1752 John Adlum's son Joseph, about age twenty, was granted such a land warrant by John Penn, one of William Penn's sons.[29]

York was a mostly German town with a few "English" residents. The Adlums got along well with their German neighbors and admired their industry and farming skills. John Adlum Sr. was voted in as the first high sheriff of York County in 1749, and was reelected in 1753, followed by justice of the peace in 1754 and coroner in 1763. The job of sheriff was an important one in colonial times. Not only was he responsible for law enforcement but also tax collection, supervising elections, serving legal documents (writs), and appearing in court; he was responsible for all the legal business of the county. Adlum was very active in affairs of the town, serving as vestryman for the Episcopal Church and, along with his son Joseph, was instrumental in getting a church built. John Adlum Sr. died on December 6, 1773. His obituary in the *Philadelphia Gazette*, December 15, 1773, starts as follows:

> **York Town: On Monday last died in this town, John Adlum, Esq. in the 74th year of his age. He was an affectionate Husband, a tender Parent, a kind Friend, a worthy Magistrate, and a good Christian. For the last years during the latter part of his life, he was concerned as one of the directors in the building of an Episcopal Church at that town, in which business he exerted himself to the utmost, it was the joy and pleasure of his sinking years.**

He did live to see the completion of the church and left a legacy for his descendants to follow.[30]

> ESCAPED from the sheriff of York county, on the 11th of this instant November, one Hanue Outmando, f. a Dutchman, a middle siz'd well set fellow, a baker by trade: Had on when he went away, a light colour'd half worn jacket, with red lining, short blue jacket, without sleeves, old felt hat, old shoes and stockings, and linen trowsers. It is supposed he is gone to his wife who lives near one of the brick yards between Philadelphia and Germantown. Whoever takes up and secures him in any county goal shall have Three Pounds reward; or if brought to York Three Pounds, and reasonable charges, paid by
>
> JOHN ADLUM, Sheriff.

Advertisement placed by John Adlum, sheriff of York County, PA for runaway prisoner, Philadelphia Gazette, Nov. 28, 1754, image, Ancestry.com

After John Adlum's term as sheriff expired, the county elected his son Joseph by a wide margin. They were popular citizens in the area. The people of York then elected Joseph to the post of coroner in 1764, and he held that position for sixteen years, through most of the American Revolution. Traditionally, in English society, the coroner monitored the integrity of public officials. They were called coroners because the represented the crown and the king's interest. Beginning in the twelfth century, they had the power to arrest the sheriff. In colonial times they were publicly elected to investigate deaths and had implied ability to monitor corruption. They would take over the sheriff's duties when necessary due to illness or other reasons.

Document declaring Joseph Adlum coroner of York County, PA, dated Oct. 6, 1774, signed by John Penn with the seal of King George III, author's collection

As well as serving as coroner, Joseph had a skin-dressing business, preparing deerskins for leather breeches. His older brother, John referred to as Captain John Adlum, moved to Frederick, Maryland, and was very successful in his skin-dressing business there.[31]

As coroner Joseph was a leading member of the York community and, along with his wife, was a member of the St. John Episcopal Church and trustee for the building of the church. He married his cousin Catherine Abbott of Abbottstown in June of 1758 in York. Catherine's father, John Abbott, was a very successful farmer who, with his sons, laid out the town of Abbottstown—formerly called Berwick—after emigrating from England in 1735. Abbottstown is about twelve miles from York Springs, as it was called then, and almost equal distance from Gettysburg in south central Pennsylvania. John Abbott's wife was Alice Berwick, sister of Joseph Adlum's mother Elizabeth. Major John Adlum said of the Berwick family: "the women were accomplished housewives, the men brilliant but somewhat eccentric."[32]

Joseph and his wife, Catherine, had nine children, including twins. They continued the often- repeated family names and had sons named John (1759-1836) and Joseph (1767-1846.) The oldest son, referred to as Major John Adlum, is an important source for information about the Adlum family through his letters, memoirs, and other writings.

The Adlums were interested in politics and, like most of the residents on the frontier, disliked the tone of the heavy-handed edicts coming from England. Major John Adlum wrote in his memoirs that his grandfather, John and father, Joseph, were strong supporters of the American cause. When the Stamp Act was repealed in 1766, the news spurred the local residents of York to celebrate with a bonfire. Adlum recalls the German residents of the town shooting off their muskets and shouting, *"Las uns der verflucht Staemp Kct, zu der defuel Schersen"* which he translated as, "Let us fire or shoot the cursed Stamp Act to the devil."[33]

At the same time, settlers on the frontier of Pennsylvania were affected by the French and Indian War, with raids by Indian allies of the French. The fighting was only a day's march from York. The war finally ended with the signing of the Treaty of Paris in 1763. The English victory helped keep the frontier more secure from the French, but the Indians did not give up and fought to keep the Americans out of the Ohio Territory, including heavy fighting in western Pennsylvania. Once peace with the Indians was declared in 1766, the king set forth a new proclamation that barred any Americans from settling west of the Appalachians and gave that territory to the Indian tribes. Nevertheless, there was continued friction and conflict between the settlers and the tribes in Pennsylvania until many years after the American Revolution ended.

The colonists became more restless in the early 1770s and believed they should choose how they were governed. Major John Adlum described in his memoirs how the lads of York, including himself at age fifteen, formed a boy's militia in 1774. After hearing the Declaration of Independence read aloud from the two-story brick town hall while standing in the crowd in the town square of York on July 6, 1776, Adlum, at age seventeen, along with some of the company, left for Philadelphia on July 7 to volunteer. The company was called to go to camp as part of the Pennsylvania Brigade of the Flying Camp of Colonel Michael Swope's Battalion. John Adlum was made a corporal in Captain Christian Stake's Company. They set out, marching to New Jersey as part of a mobile reserve force.[34]

Adlum witnessed the battle by which the British captured New York and in the aftermath was garrisoned at Fort Washington, which was unfortunately overrun by the British. David McCullough's book *1776* describes how the battle was not only a terrible defeat, but the capture of Fort Washington was an "utter catastrophe." McCullough quotes John

Adlum in the battle retreat and "how he ran uphill to the fort with hardly the breath to keep going." Adlum's company and all 2,837 soldiers garrisoned there were forced to surrender. Adlum was one of those put into the notorious Bridewell Prison. By intervention of a family friend, who asked the help of Col. McGraw, the unfortunate commander of Fort Washington when it was captured, Adlum was released and put on parole in New York. He earned his keep by being a servant to American officers, including Col. McGraw, who were quartered in private homes. At the time officers were routinely dealt with in this way. It's fortunate that he was not forced to remain in Bridewell or be imprisoned on a British ship. Many of those prisoners became ill and died. One of his uncles, his mother's brother John Berwick, was captured after the siege of Charleston and died after harsh treatment on a British prisoner of war ship.[35]

At Adlum's quarters in British-occupied New York, his young landlady, unhappy with her husband, began to take a personal interest in him and offered to buy him things and grant special favors. The American officers he was quartered with decided it was best for him to get away from her corrupting influences so "he would not be spoiled" as he put it. They managed to have him sent home in the first group of parolees in February 1777.

After a difficult journey to York and an illness—many released prisoners were ill when they got home—John Adlum helped his father in his business of dressing deerskins. The government had moved out of Philadelphia during the winter of 1777 and established a temporary capital in York, providing safe distance from the British army. The Continental Congress met there until June 1778. During this time that York was the center of political activity, John's father, Joseph, was active as an elected official. John was disappointed he could not return to the army with a commission because of the terms of his parole, which required exchange of a British soldier. He went to his uncle Captain John Adlum in Frederick, Maryland, and started to study mathematics and surveying. This is where he was when the war ended in 1781.[36]

After the war there was a need for surveying in many parts of Pennsylvania. Economic necessity created a tremendous push to develop transportation from Philadelphia to the rest of the state. Not only did Pennsylvania officials eye land west of the Allegheny River for distribution to veterans of the Revolutionary War as repayment for military service, they also needed a port on Lake Erie to allow Pennsylvania to compete in the western fur market so furs and other products could more easily be brought to Philadelphia. Carl B. Lechner, in his article "The Erie Triangle: The Final Link Between Philadelphia and the Great Lakes," points out that the trans-Appalachian fur trade that had been dominated by Philadelphia entrepreneurs before the War had moved west, following the Ohio River and leaving Philadelphia markets. If Pennsylvania was to compete for commerce and trade in western goods, they needed to improve their roads.

Lechner writes that:
… the state's road system in the late eighteenth century still consisted of primitive trail and horse routes that succeeded Indian paths through the forest with the exception of the two roads in southern Pennsylvania made during the French and Indian War for Generals Forbes and Braddock.

Along with planning roads and canals, there was a push to develop land in the northwest and north central parts of the state. There could not have been a better time for Adlum to head home.[37]

With $111 in his pocket, John Adlum headed to York to see his family and then headed to Carlisle, about forty miles northwest of York, to visit Col. McGraw. The colonel was glad to see him and offered to let him read for the law in his office. Adlum graciously declined but was grateful for the letters of introduction McGraw gave him. Adlum bought a horse for $32—half on credit—and some surveying equipment and headed to Northumberland, which was the center of surveying for the north and west branches of the Susquehanna River. He presented himself to Colonel Antes with his letter of introduction after failing to get a job with the deputy surveyor, Joseph Wallis. Col. Antes encouraged him and introduced him to his brother Henry, the sheriff of Northumberland County. Henry Antes gave him a temporary job as sub-sheriff. One morning he ran into an old friend of his father, Captain John Lowden. Upon hearing that John was Joseph Adlum's son, Captain Lowden proceeded to tell him how, "When they were young, your father could out shoot all trappers and marksmen with his 'long rifle' when shooting from 60 to 150 yards."[38]

The Pennsylvania long rifle, later called the Kentucky rifle after being used by Kentucky hunters such as Daniel Boone, was refined in York and Lancaster County. The rifles, designed by German gunsmiths and modified from the weapons they used in Germany, were a great improvement over the heavy muskets most men used at the time and were much more accurate at long distances. The rifles were improved starting in the 1750s, and some of the best were made in York. Joseph and his father, John as leading citizens of the town, may have had a hand in designing improvements. Not all could afford a rifle—the musket was standard fare. The fact that Joseph had one of these rifles in early days is evidence of his enthusiasm for them. Captain John Lowden, also an excellent shot, went on to lead a rifle company in the 1st Pennsylvania Rifle Battalion in the American Revolution.[39]

The surprise meeting with Captain Lowden led to a job offer to help the captain survey some land, and thus, Adlum started his career. He gained a reputation as an honest and accurate surveyor and began to get more projects. His first major job with the state was in 1787, when he was appointed commissioner to determine the state boundary between New York and Pennsylvania. This took him to the shores of Lake Erie and the lands of the Seneca Indians. In 1789 he was hired by Surveyor-General Lukens to survey the reserved tracts of land at Presque Isle (Erie), Pennsylvania was in negotiations with the federal government to buy the tract of land called the Erie Triangle—the harbor at Presque Isle was crucial for use as a river port to Lake Erie—which was finalized in 1792. Adlum was also "appointed by the state government in 1789 to examine the navigation of the Susquehanna River and then with Benjamin Rittenhouse and others to examine the Schuylkill River," according to Bessie Gahn, author of *Major John Adlum of Rock Creek*.

During this time, Adlum attended Indian conferences, became a friend of the Seneca chief Cornplanter, and used his keen eye to become familiar with the flora of the area. His map of 1791, created and drawn with associate John Wallis, son of Samuel Wallis, a large land owner in the Muncy area, and known as the Adlum-Wallis Map of Pennsylvania and Border States, was a magnificent piece of work showing exacting detail, including possible areas for canals to be built. The map was presented to Governor Thomas Mifflin in Philadelphia. Adlum was then appointed to the post of district surveyor in April of 1792.[40]

Land speculation fever had hit Pennsylvania by this time, and Adlum received several offers from speculators to survey land for them and to act as their agent. He contracted with speculator William Bingham of Philadelphia to acquire between one and two million acres of land. Norman B. Wilkinson writes in his article "The 'Philadelphia Fever' in Northern Pennsylvania that Adlum was allowed £500 a year for expenses and was to receive one third of the profits arising from the future sale of the lands, as well as a portion at the end of five years of the unsold land.

In 1793 Adlum gave up his job as district-surveyor but continued to work for Bingham and other speculators such as founding father and former Supreme Court Associate Justice James Wilson and Samuel Wallis. He may have done work for the Joseph Priestleys, father and son, as Adlum was a friend and correspondent to Dr. Joseph Priestley regarding scientific methods. His work for Bingham and others made Adlum a wealthy man.[41]

Land fever slowed for several months in August 1793 because of the outbreak of an actual fever which began killing many Philadelphia residents. All land warrants and business ceased at the land office in Philadelphia during the yellow fever epidemic which paralyzed the town, including the state and federal government. Philadelphia was the largest and most important city in the new nation; as the nation's capital it was filled with the leading thinkers in science, culture, and government. In 1793 it had a population of about 45,000, with a busy port bustling with trade.

Dr. Benjamin Rush, resident of Philadelphia and one of the most prominent physicians of the day, was the first to call the alarming deaths yellow fever. Summer fevers in steamy Philadelphia were not unusual; the streets were full of the stench of rotting sewage, garbage, and dead animals, leading to unhealthy living conditions. No one understood disease from microorganisms or the fact that mosquitoes were carriers of disease, but they understood yellow fever, with its fifty percent mortality rate, enough to panic when Dr. Rush urged people to "fly from it." Fly they did. Some 20,000 people abandoned Philadelphia, while the poor, who had nowhere to go, died in their beds and in the streets, and some of the remaining residents locked themselves up in their houses in panic. Governor Mifflin left, along with most of the state government. President George Washington left in a hurry to ride to Mount Vernon, leaving important papers behind. He left Secretary of War General Henry Knox in charge, but Knox lost his nerve and left as well. The renowned artist, inventor, and naturalist Charles Willson Peale locked himself and his family up in his house/museum, eventually resorting to eating his bird collection. They did not escape yellow fever. Both Charles Peale and his wife, Betsy, came down with yellow fever but survived. The mayor of Philadelphia, Matthew Clarkson, stayed in town and bravely attempted to deal with some 4,000 to 5,000 deaths in a city full of illness without the resources it needed to cope with such a disaster. Major John Adlum was, fortunately, in the countryside during the outbreak.[42]

Philadelphia in 1794 was a calmer and cleaner place. John Adlum took time to sit for a portrait by then-recovered Charles Willson Peale. Peale was the most celebrated painter of the time and had painted portraits of most of the founding fathers and leaders of the American Revolution, including George Washington, Thomas Jefferson, and the famous generals of the Revolution. Adlum's portrait shows a healthy, muscular man with a pleasant, intelligent expression, a handsome face with blue eyes and light hair, and the widow's peak hairline that every generation of Adlum men has shared since. Seventeen ninety-four was a banner year for Adlum, one that had him back in the woods with major contracts, negotiations with the Seneca Indians, and land purchases for himself.[43]

The previous year Governor Thomas Mifflin asked Adlum if he could find land for purchase for the Holland Land Company. European investors were now in on the land grab of Pennsylvania land. Authors Donald H. Kent and Merle H. Deardorff tell us, in their article about John Adlum's *Memoirs for 1794* for *The Pennsylvania Magazine of History and Biography*, how, in the spring of 1794, Adlum worked in the Allegheny Valley surveying land for James Wilson and the Holland Land Company, as well as William Bingham. Adlum's memoir of his work that year paints a vivid picture of his adventures and friendship with the

Portrait of Major John Adlum, by Charles Willson Peale, c. 1794, curtesy Pennsylvania Historical Society, painting is at the State Museum of Pennsylvania, Harrisburg, Pennsylvania

Seneca Indians, especially, the great Seneca chief Cornplanter. He admired Cornplanter, and the Seneca chief respected him as well. It was a tricky time to be surveying, as there were rumblings from the Six Nations of Indian tribes, who were angry that white men were pushing into the Erie Triangle area they considered their land.

Many of the Indian tribes were hostile to the Americans and did not want to sign treaties. They were encouraged by the British to antagonize the Americans. Pennsylvania sent an expedition to fortify their lake port, Presque Isle, which alarmed both the British—who wanted an Indian barrier state—and the Six Nations. At the same time, General Wayne's army was advancing against the western tribes of Indians. The Seneca, along with other tribes, squeezed by both the British and the Americans, were under great strain as they tried to maintain their lands. The Seneca of the Upper Allegheny traditionally sided with the Americans. Now, they were not sure which side to back. Adlum went to Cornplanter's village to talk to him and the major women of the tribe and convince them to hold off on joining the Six Nations in war. He had surveyed some land for Cornplanter in the past and was a trusted friend. As rumors of war intensified, Adlum convinced the Seneca chief to let him continue surveying. Cornplanter agreed, even sending some Indian guides with Adlum, including his own son at one point.[44]

Despite the reassurance of the Seneca, some of Adlum's men were too nervous to continue, and they quit. Surveying was quite a production, with fifty or sixty men, along with horses, guns, equipment and food, taken into the wilderness. Adlum wrote to Andrew Ellicott at Fort Le Boeuf on September 5, 1794, "I shall have about half my business done by the middle of this month, and as my hands are uneasy I have determined to order them home at that time." On August 31 he wrote to General William Wilson of Northumberland County, warning, "If the Indians attacked it would between the 25th of September, and the middle of October." Meanwhile, General Anthony Wayne was victorious on August 20 at the Battle of Fallen Timbers against the Northwest Indian Federation and the chief of the Shawnees, making the Northwest Territory safer for settlement.[45]

During this busy year, Adlum also bought land for himself in one of the beautiful areas he surveyed just north of the western branch of the Susquehanna. He bought a beautifully situated, large stone house on a piece of land on Wolf Creek in the township of Muncy in the newly designated Lycoming County.

Muncy is a little more than one hundred miles north of York and about 170 miles from Philadelphia. Tax records show Adlum had 400 acres here, among other property. His house of more than 3,500 square feet is lived in today and is still known as the John Adlum House. Adlum owned a lot of land in the area, and most of his extended family, including his brothers and sisters, moved there. He intended for his mother and father to retire there, and they moved from York to live the rest of their lives in Muncy.[46]

Adlum was finished surveying and was back at his home at Wolf Run in October when he was visited by William Davy, an Anglo-American businessman who described his genial host in his diary, *Mr. Davy's Dairy* by author Norman B. Wilkinson. "Mr. Adlum, a first-rate Surveyor, . . . is a sensible, pleasant intelligent Man, has been much with the Indians in their Settlements & particularly was several Days with their famous Chief Cornplanter who permitted his Son to accompany Adlum down to some of the American posts ...." Another entry reads: "Call'd on Mr. Adlum who entertained us with a sight of great a variety of curious presents, various articles of Dress & Weapons he & his party lately rec'd from the Indian Cornplanter."

John Adlum has been described by those who knew him as a kind, friendly man with a keen, inquiring mind that contributed to his success in scientific achievement. He was also a bit vain, but in a forgivable way, according to author Donald H. Kent. He and his family were active participants in the affairs of Muncy and Lycoming County. John Adlum became an associate judge of the county, appointed April 15, 1795 and serving through 1797, and was also commissioned a brigadier general in the Pennsylvania Militia.

John Adlum House, Muncy, PA, built c. 1790, currently occupied, photo from John Sharp, Ancestry.com

It was a journey of several days on horseback to get to Philadelphia, where he had frequent business. He was actively involved at the nation's capital in Philadelphia as part of The Commission on Inland Waterways of Pennsylvania, seeking ways to improve Pennsylvania's roads and canal systems. His years of surveying and life in the wilderness made him aware of the transportation issues and what roads and canals were needed to develop Pennsylvania. Plans were already underway to move the capital to the District of Columbia, and he often traveled back and forth between Maryland and Pennsylvania.[47]

By 1798 John Adlum was able to retire and concentrate on scientific endeavors. He had a keen eye for botany and wanted to establish an experimental farm. He resigned his positions in Muncy and moved to Maryland. He sent a proposal to President John Adams' administration for a Government Experimental Farm, which was rejected. He was before his time. It was not until 1887, after passage of the Hatch Act, that scientific stations were established in every state.

In 1805 Adlum married his cousin Margaret of Fredrick, Maryland, daughter of his uncle Captain John Adlum. He moved his new wife to Havre de Grace, Maryland, to a farm he bought in 1797 near the mouth of the Chesapeake Bay. He called it Wilton Farm. Today, it is called Swan Harbor Farm. At the farm he started experiments with grapevines, first with European and then native grapes. His younger brother, Joseph, worked with him and served as farm overseer. John made a wonderful wine from the Alexander grape there. In 1809 he sent a bottle of this wine to his friend Thomas Jefferson, who then ordered 165 cuttings from Adlum's vines to be planted at Monticello. Jefferson's letter to Adlum of October 7, 1809, states:

> This was a very fine wine, and so exactly resembling the red Burgundy of Chamberlin, (one of the best crops) that on a fair comparison with that, of which I had very good on the same table, imported by myself from the place where made: the company could not distinguish the one from the other.[48]

Eighteenth century Adlum wineglass, author's collection

James M. Grabler, in his book *Passions*, talks about Thomas Jefferson's correspondence with Adlum over the development of a truly American wine from native grapes. "While President, he became acquainted with John Adlum, who has been called the *Father of American Viticulture* for his early efforts with grape cultivation and wine-making."

Adlum was very busy with business and grape growing, while two daughters were born to him. Adlum was commissioned as a major in the Provisional Army by President John Adams in 1799 but resigned the next year because of business pressures when the threat of war with the French abated. He was at his farm when the War of 1812 started. As the British closed in and burned the new capital and also Havre de Grace, he moved his family to safety in Fredrick, Maryland, and assisted in the Army as a captain in the unsuccessful defense of Havre de Grace. After the war Adlum decided to sell Wilton Farm and move just outside the capital of Washington, with the burned ruins of the White House and other buildings a somber reminder of the war. He bought about 230 acres of land in several parcels along Rock Creek, stretching from Georgetown to the present day neighborhood of Cleveland Park in the District of Columbia, to establish a new vineyard. Here he spent more than twenty years studying and growing grapes and promoting American-made wine. In 1819 he first developed wine using the native Catawba grape, and by 1822 he had sent a bottle of what he would first call "Tokay wine" and then "Catawba" to Jefferson from his new vineyard.[49]

The Catawba grape developed by Adlum was called the first great American grape by the botanist Liberty Hyde Bailey. Nicholas Longworth of Ohio obtained cuttings from

Adlum in 1825 and planted the grape on a wide scale, becoming wealthy as a result. The Catawba grape is still popular in the vineyards of New York and Pennsylvania. Major John Adlum wrote the first book on winemaking, *A Memoir on the Cultivation of the Vine in America and the Best Mode of Making Wine*, published in the United States in 1823. In 1826 he published a pamphlet under the title *Adlum on Making Wine* in which he continued to list his types of stock and promote American winemaking as he continued his experiments with American grapes.

Adlum corresponded with the leaders of the day, including James Madison, Alexander Hamilton, and Thomas Jefferson. Being just outside the District of Columbia, he frequently advertised his wines in the newspapers to the influential people there. Despite failing to get the government interested in establishing an agricultural experimental farm on part of his land, he continued to write extensively in scientific journals and lobby the government to make viticulture a scientific discipline. Jefferson and he shared a love of wine and scientific method and corresponded for fifteen years. In addition, Adlum had correspondents all over the young United States. He was considered an expert in his field, although he did not make enough money from his experiments to support his projects.[50]

Money was tight in the last years of his life. The vineyard became a tourist attraction and had many visitors, but they only added to his expense. The great botanist of the day, Rafinesque, named a beautiful vine of the Alleghenies *Adlumia Fungosa* in honor of Adlum's work and surveying of the Allegheny.

Major John Adlum died in 1836 at his beloved vineyard. His wife, Margaret continued to live on the property until her death in 1852. John Adlum and his wife are buried in the Oak Hill Cemetery in Washington, DC. The Daughters of the American Revolution placed a bronze plaque on his grave, honoring him for his service.

The inscription reads:
Sacred to the memory of Major John Adlum native of Pennsylvania and a soldier
Of the American Revolution Who departed this life on the 14th day of March
Anno Domini 1836 in the 77 year of age, "he died and he lived an
Honest man the noblest work of God"

The vineyard is now mostly taken up by Rock Creek Park. The Federal Bureau of Standards building, complete with plaque noting his former home site, was built on the hill where John Adlum's house once stood.[51]

One of John's younger brothers, Joseph, worked with him for a number of years. The Adlums were letter writers, and we are fortunate to have copies of those letters, mostly from the late eighteenth and early nineteenth centuries. One letter John Adlum wrote to his younger brother Joseph, dated January 8, 1799, stated that President Adams had commissioned him a major of one of the twelve regiments being drawn up in anticipation of war. John wanted to know if Joseph could take over his business and act as overseer at the farm. The many family letters show an affectionate family concerned with each other, belief in God, and an enthusiasm for family business. Another letter is from Joseph Adlum (1727-1814), retired coroner of York then living in Muncy, addressed to his son Joseph (1767-1846), living at the farm at Havre de Grace, Maryland, and dated October 27, 1799. He mentions family affairs, including the marriage of a brother Thomas, success with their crops in Muncy, and other business, and asks his son to come visit him in Muncy.

John Adlum 's younger brother Joseph, at age thirty-one, married Anna McPhail on November 7, 1798, in Hartford County, Maryland, which was about seventeen miles from where the brothers worked at the Havre de Grace farm. Anna McPhail was most likely part of the prominent McPhail family of Baltimore. In the family collection of letters, there are letters written to Anna and Joseph from Anna's younger brother Daniel McPhail, describing his saddle and harness-making business in Baltimore. Daniel's sons would go on to be prominent in business and government in Baltimore. In his letter dated January 3, 1824, to his sister Anna, Daniel complained of cough and breast (lung) congestion. He died at age 48 on October 23, 1829.[52]

Joseph did go home to Muncy, as his father asked, taking his wife with him. Perhaps, that is why John Adlum had to resign his commission after a year and go home to Havre de Grace to take care of business. Joseph is listed on the 1810 census in Muncy. Their father, Joseph, died in 1814. In 1816 Joseph and Anna's son Joseph Green and daughter Ellen were born, boy-girl twins. Joseph Green Adlum was named after a prominent great uncle, Joseph Green, grandson of John Abbott and wife, Alice Berwick. His father, Joseph, and mother, Anna, were active in the community in farming and business, as well as the Episcopal Church, and were surrounded by other Adlum siblings in the area. They had eight children, most of who stayed in the area. A few years after Joseph Green Adlum left his family and moved to Altoona, his father, Joseph, died in Muncy in 1846. His mother, Anna, died in 1851 and was buried next to her husband in the Saint James Episcopal Cemetery in Muncy. By the time Joseph Green Adlum died forty-seven years later in 1893 in Bellwood outside Altoona, his obituaries in two local newspapers mention not only his accomplishments but those of his father, Joseph, and the Adlum family in the history of Pennsylvania. It was 160 some years since they first set foot in the Keystone state. The history of those pioneering years remains in the Adlum psyche.[53]

Chapter Two
Gambling on Prosperity

Family Cast of Characters

Mary Ellen "Ella" Holman...(1856-1928) *mother of Winifred Turner; grandmother of Daniel B. Adlum*
William Burke Turner...(1860-1924) *father of Winifred Turner; grandfather of Daniel B. Adlum*
Daniel Saunders Holman...(1822-1910) *came west on first wagon train, 1843; father of Ella Holman; great-grandfather of Daniel B. Adlum*
Martha Elizabeth Burnett...(1830-1913) *came west in 1846; mother of Ella Holman; great-grandmother of Daniel B. Adlum*

James Duval Holman...(1814-1882) *came west in 1846; son of John and Elizabeth; uncle of Ella Holman*
Frederick V. Holman...(1853-1927) *son of James Duval Holman; first cousin of Ella Holman*
John Holman...(1787-1864) *came west 1843; father of Daniel and James; second-great-grandfather of Daniel B. Adlum*
Elizabeth Duval...(1792-1841) *mother of Daniel and James; second-great-grandmother of Daniel*

Daniel L. Holman...(1750-1838) *father of Lt. Col. Isaac and John Holman; third-great-grandfather of Daniel B. Adlum*
Nancy Anne Saunders...(1758-1836) *third-great-grandmother of Daniel B. Adlum*
Lt. Col. Isaac Holman...(1795-1835) *oldest son of Daniel L. Holman; second-great-uncle of Daniel B. Adlum*
James Saunders Holman...(1804-1867) *first mayor of Houston, Texas; son of Isaac*

Glen Owen Burnett...(1809-1886) *came west 1846; grandfather of Ella Holman*
Sarah M Rogers...(1814-1889) *came west 1846; grandmother of Ella Holman*
Peter Hardeman Burnett...(1807-1895) *came west 1843; brother of Glen Owen*
Harriet W. Rogers...(1812-1879) *came west 1843; wife of Peter Burnett; sister of Sarah Rogers*

George William Burnet...(1776-1838) *father of Peter and Glen Owen; third-great-grandfather of Daniel B. Adlum*
Dorothy "Dolly" Hardeman...(1786-1842) *wife of George Burnett; daughter of Thomas Hardeman; third-great-grandmother of Daniel B. Adlum*

Thomas Hardeman…(1750-1833) *father of Dolly; fourth-great-grandfather of Daniel B. Adlum*
Mary Hardin Perkins…(1754-1728) *mother of Dolly; fourth-great-grandmother of Daniel B. Adlum*
Capt. Thomas Jones Hardeman…(1788-1867) *named Austin, Texas; son of Thomas*
Bailey Hardeman…(1795-1836) *signed Texas Constitution; youngest son of Thomas; brother of Thomas Jones*

John Hardeman I…(1654-1711) *seventh-great-grandfather of Daniel B. Adlum*
Maria Eppes…(1664-1728) *seventh-great-grandmother of Daniel B. Adlum*

The Holman, Burnett and Hardeman Families

Courage is resistance to fear, mastery of fear, not absence of fear

~Mark Twain

Daniel Adlum stood at attention at the gravesite of his ancestor John Holman with his mother, Winifred, at his side. It was Memorial Day 1929. Daniel was eight years old. The Daughters of the War of 1812 were honoring his second-great-grandfather with the placement of a plaque on his grave at the Masonic Cemetery in McMinnville to commemorate his service during the War of 1812. The stories his mother told him about his grandfather and the family pioneers filled him with admiration. What exciting lives they must have lived! His great-grandfather's family, the Holmans, had been pioneering across the country for generations, as well as his great-grandmother's family, the Burnetts and Hardemans. The culmination of their efforts ripened in McMinnville, Oregon. Their sacrifice and ultimate success allowed their children and grandchildren to have lives with more possibilities.

Daniel's mother, Winifred Turner, grew up mostly in Portland, other than a few years in California, but she spent some time at her maternal grandparents' farm outside of McMinnville and at their house in town. Her mother, Mary Ellen (Ella) Holman, often brought her four girls home for support from her parents and siblings while her husband was absent.[54]

Ella grew up as one of seven brothers and two sisters in the Daniel Holman clan. Her father had a prosperous farm of 640 acres just seven miles south of McMinnville for fifty-four years. Her parents' success in farming and business provided opportunities for Ella and her siblings. Ella grew up with a love of and talent for music. In the late 1860s her parents, Daniel Saunders Holman and Martha Elizabeth Burnett, bought her a beautiful rosewood piano costing $700—more than $15,000 in today's dollars. The tiny town of McMinnville, with no main roads or ports, was not easy to get to. The piano came "'round the Horn" from the east coast of the United States at additional cost. At the time, many ships came around Cape Horn at the tip of South America to bring supplies to the West Coast; the journey to Portland took months. Ella had music teachers who came to the house and helped her to become an accomplished singer and pianist. One of her brothers was a musician as well. Her brothers held a variety of careers: attorney, dentist, funeral home director, farmer, real estate agent, and engineer.[55]

Her parents were industrious and pious. They were members of the Disciples of Christ Church, sometimes called "Campbellites" after the founders, Thomas and Alexander Campbell, a Scots Presbyterian father and son duo who, among others, started the American Restoration Movement.

The Second Great Awakening in America led to rejection of traditional churches and a rise in emotionalism. The followers of the Campbells were just one of the many sects that started in the 1820s and '30s. There were frequent camp meetings with traveling preachers that attracted crowds. The Disciples of Christ were strongly committed to restoring early Christianity. They believed that all denominations should be swept away and all creeds abolished and replaced with faith based on the writings of the New Testament. They combined in 1832 with the Christian Church—followers of Barton Stone—as the revival movement gained traction in the U.S. They insisted followers must "be dipped or be damned," believing baptism was only valid by full emersion at the age of consent and awareness. Dancing and theatre going were frowned upon. Some Campbellites remarked how terrible it was that President Abraham Lincoln was shot while at the theatre. As an adult Ella still took her daughters to camp revival meetings but protested to the pastor that there was nothing wrong with dancing! He did not approve, but fun- and-music-loving Ella did not let him deter her. There were also pioneer meetings—opportunities for reminiscing by those who came to Oregon in the early days.[56]

Ella's father, Daniel, and grandfather John Holman came to Oregon in 1843, along with her maternal great uncle Peter Hardeman Burnett, who played a significant role in what is called the Great Migration of 1843. Peter brought his wife, Harriet W. Rogers, who was ill with consumption, and their six children, along with other relatives.

There were almost 1,000 pioneers on the first major wagon train to Oregon Country, a good portion of them young, unattached men. Peter was responsible for boosting and promoting Oregon to Americans—especially, Missourians—writing many newspaper articles and giving speeches about Oregon Country. He served as the first wagon master of the train of 1843. Three years later, in 1846, Ella's mother, Martha Elizabeth Burnett, came out to Oregon at age fifteen with her parents, Glen Owen Burnett and Sarah Rogers, and her brothers and sisters. She married Daniel Saunders Holman the next year. Her father's good friend, Dr. James McBride, married them. Daniel Holman's older brother James Duval Holman came west on the 1846 wagon train as well, with his wife, family, and younger brothers and sisters, including married sister Rhonda Holman Henderson and her family.[57]

Mary Ellen (Ella) Holman, c. 1874, about age 18, McMinnville, Oregon, from Shawver, Portrait of Mama

Oregon City, about eighteen miles south of present-day Portland, in 1843 was a collection of a couple dozen rough houses put up by the British-owned Hudson's Bay Company for their workers. It was the only area of civilization (so to speak), other than the missionary outposts and Fort Vancouver. The Daniel S. Holman family settled on land near the newly formed town of McMinnville, after first spending a few years in Polk County and Oregon City. Daniel's older brother James Duval Holman began trying to develop an area at the mouth of the Columbia River near Cape Disappointment after running a mercantile business for a few years in Oregon City. This beautiful land was on the north side of the Columbia at the start of the Long Beach Peninsula—now in the state of Washington.

Dr. Elijah White, a Methodist missionary turned land promoter, convinced James Duval Holman and other investors that the Baker's Bay area in Pacific County, Oregon, would become a major port on the Columbia. They called the town they were building Pacific City. James Duval Holman invested in lots and participated in the layout of the town. He bought a lot of land; he even brought a hotel from New York at a cost of $28,000, an enormous amount at the time. The hotel was disassembled, put on a ship, and then rebuilt by three carpenters who came on the ship from San Francisco.

Map of Oregon showing McMinnville and Long Beach, WA, source: National Atlas topo map of geography of Oregon, file: Map of OregonWA.png-Wikipedia Commons

Pacific City had an established post office in 1851 and started with a sawmill and grand hotel built by Holman. Holman's eldest son, Frederick, was born in the hotel and was the first white (non-native) child born in Pacific County. Unfortunately, Holman lost his investment when, the following year, the U.S. government decided to confiscate the land at Cape Disappointment and the adjacent land set aside for Pacific City to build a military fort. The government paid Holman twenty-eight years later for the hotel but not for the lots in Pacific City. There is no longer any sign of Pacific City.

The Holmans stayed in the area and moved to a land claim nearby at Baker's Bay. James became the first representative from Pacific County to the Territorial Legislature of Oregon. The family spent a few years in Baker's Bay, what they would later call Ilwaco, before moving to

Portland in 1856. James established a school there for his children in 1853 and built a few cabins, promoting the area as a summer resort. He later built a Presbyterian church in the area. James Duval had a small store on his land claim and grew a few crops; the main staple was salt salmon.[58]

One of his sons, Frederick V. Holman, who later became an influential attorney in Portland, told an interesting story about his early childhood years in the Ilwaco area. He said it was lonely and isolated, with few white men but some Chinook Indians. Chief Ilwaco, for whom his father named the town, and his wife, Yaclaw, daughter of the noted Chinook chief Concomly, built their cabin on his father's land claim with his blessing. The Chinook were the masters of the lower Columbia River and the Long Beach Peninsula for hundreds of years. Their skills in canoeing on the dangerous waters of the lower Columbia and fishing for salmon were much admired. The Chinook tribe had been decimated by earlier plagues of smallpox and a severe outbreak of malaria in the 1830s. Yaclaw's father died from smallpox during that time. Native residents had little immunity to these diseases and died off rapidly. The remaining tribe members mostly accepted the white men, as they had little choice.

In 1855 Frederick's father took a precarious journey in a whaleboat to Astoria for supplies for his little store. There were no steamers on the lower Columbia at that time. He came back with a pair of red-topped boots which Fred received for Christmas at age three and a half. Fred remembers this Christmas as his best Christmas ever. He immediately went down to Chief Ilwaco's cabin to show them off. Chief Ilwaco opened the door and exclaimed in Chinook, "*Na, six, Nanitch stickshoes tenas Holman*" ("Oh, see the boots of young Holman.") There were strings of razor clams hung in the cabin, smoked by the fire in the middle of the room. The chief cut some down with a knife and gave Fred some to eat. He never forgot the delicious, smoky flavor.

With the ocean so close, there was easy access to seafood. Living in such an isolated area was hard on the family, but it was a place of great beauty. Ilwaco became the jumping-off place for fishermen and beach goers in future years. It also became the starting point of the famous narrow-gauge railroad called "The Clamshell Railroad by the Tides," which began in the 1890s and ran up the Long Beach Peninsula. This is just a few miles from the resort of Long Beach where James Duval's grand-nieces Winifred Adlum and Mildred Allen would relocate with their husbands in the 1920s. There was a stop on the train called Holman, just north of present-day Ilwaco, Washington.[59]

All of the Holmans were civic minded and involved in supporting the public schools, as well as the arts. James D. Holman, after moving to Portland with his family from Ilwaco, was elected as one of three directors of the Portland public school and kept that position for four terms, advocating for the high school system of education. Two of his sons became prominent attorneys in Portland and were known throughout the state. As a son of Daniel S. Holman—also an attorney—said, "We Holmans go for the law and the arts."

Members of the Holman and Burnett families spread throughout Oregon and California. Many became attorneys and judges in California and Oregon.⁶⁰

When Ella was in her early twenties, she met William B. Turner, a promising young man in McMinnville. A big wedding was planned for June 1881. Ella's father, Daniel, hired a dressmaker to live at the house for weeks to sew the wedding clothes and complete trousseau for his first-to-wed daughter.

McMinnville is a charming, picturesque town at the western margin of the fertile Willamette Valley at the center of Oregon's wine country and is surrounded by acres of vineyards of pinot noir grapes. It is about thirty-three miles as the crow flies southwest from Portland and a leisurely country drive of about an hour on 99-W from Portland. In 1881 it was the principal town of Yamhill County. and "could boast of five general stores, two drug stores, two wagon shops, four blacksmiths, two cobblers, a furniture store, a barber, a saloon, a hotel, a livery stable, two boarding houses, a land agent, a jeweler/watchmaker, a butcher, a photographer, two doctors, a dentist, two lawyers, a tin store and a saddler. It had two flour mills, a college and several churches."

Mary Ellen (Ella) Holman, (far left of photo) with her girlfriends the day after her wedding, wearing her "2nd day dress" McMinnville, Oregon, from Shawver, Portrait of Mama

It was surrounded by fertile farmland, with wheat and other crops, a rapidly growing village, up from a population of 400 in 1880—when they put the rail line through—to 1.500 in 1886. At the time of Ella's wedding, there was much easier access to Portland for goods after the finalization of the railroad service to the town. It must have been a relief not to have to take a horse and wagon over rough roads to get there.⁶¹

There had been many changes and struggles since Ella's family first moved to the Oregon frontier, just short of forty years earlier. The Oregon pioneers of the 1840s migrated 2,000 miles to an area claimed by both Great Britain and the United States. They were beyond any organized civilization other than the outposts of the British-owned Hudson's Bay Company and some missionary settlements. It was a vast area covering all of present-day Oregon, Washington, Idaho, and parts of Wyoming, Montana, and British Columbia. This was beautiful land but required every bit of energy the pioneers had. They received assistance from Dr. John McLoughlin, the Canadian head of the British trading company located at Fort Vancouver. He was sympathetic and helpful to pioneers, even extending much-needed credit on goods to them. His job as a British subject and chief of the Hudson's Bay Company was to promote British interests and trade and discourage American settlers. Despite this, he was helpful and kind to them.

Dr. Marcus Whitman and his wife, Narcissa, established their mission in the Walla Walla Valley in 1836, preaching to the Cayuse Indians. The Whitmans were Methodist missionaries and served as a source of information and help for the pioneers as well. They were tragically murdered by the Cayuse in 1847, along with eleven others.

There was a steady increase in the number of pioneers coming to Oregon every year, even with the many hardships facing them once they got there. There was a shortage of everything, especially, clothes and shoes. Ella's great-uncle Peter Hardeman Burnett wrote in his autobiography that when his boots wore out he was embarrassed that he had to go barefoot to church. The first few years were very lean, often with not enough to eat. Ella's father, universally called "Uncle Dan" Holman, spent months in 1844, 1845, and 1846, travelling with supplies to meet pioneers, assisting them, giving them grain, etc. New settlers arrived in a depleted state with their oxen completely worn out, supplies almost gone, and families

Daniel S. Holman and Martha Elizabeth Burnett Holman, reprint from the Oregon Daily Journal, *Sunday, May 9, 1909, p. 60, Newspapers.com*

hungry as winter approached. After travelling some 2,000 miles, their arrival in the dark, drizzly Oregon winter weather must have been discouraging. Without help many would have been in a very dire situation. Daniel and his wife, Martha, were beloved by these pioneers for their assistance.

Daniel was a modest man who dismissed the tremendous effort he made for newly arriving pioneers. The wagon train of 1843 that carried Daniel to Oregon had abandoned their wagons at The Dalles, Oregon, and floated on boats or rafts down the Columbia the rest of the way. It was a precarious trip. Jesse Applegate, also on the 1843 train, lost a son to drowning on the Columbia, as well as a nephew. Because of this, great effort was made to construct a wagon trail over the mountains to the Willamette Valley, where most pioneers where headed, and avoid the Columbia all together. The Applegate brothers then forged a rough trail that future emigrants struggled to follow. The emigrants who took the southern Applegate route over the Cascades in 1846 had tremendous trouble getting over the trail with their wagons. The slow pace—eight months on the trail—meant they were running out of provisions and were close to starving towards the end of the journey. Daniel ended up rescuing his own sister's family.

Lucy Henderson Deady, Daniel's niece, in her journal of the trip, "Crossing the Plains in 1846," described the terrible hardships and how her Uncle Daniel came just in time with food and supplies to lead them to safety. Lucy, who later married William Deady, longtime U.S. District Judge for Oregon, relayed the terrible hardships her mother had to endure. Her little sister Salina accidently drank some of the emergency medicine—laudanum—hung on the side of the wagon and died. Laudanum is opium mixed in alcohol. They barely had time to bury her on the trail, and her mother delivered another child just three days later. Because of lack of food and the lateness of the season, they had to press on over very rough trail. Life on the trail could be brutal, especially, for women and children.[62]

Daniel Holman, slow to give himself credit, gave great praise to Dr. McLoughlin of the Hudson's Bay Company. In a letter to his nephew Frederick V. Holman, written when he was 83, he remembered the help of "The Father of Oregon." An excerpt from his letter of August 7, 1905, reads:

> It would take more time than I have to speak of all the very good things that Dr. John McLoughlin did, but I can say that he did all that was in his power to help the starving, worn-out and poverty-stricken immigrants that came to Oregon for the first three or four years. After I came, if he had not helped us we could have not lived in Oregon. At the time, he sent his boats to The Dalles, free of cost to help all that could not help themselves to go down the (Columbia) river. He also sent food and clothing to the destitute and gave it to them. He also furnished seed grain to everyone who wanted and waited for his pay until they raised wheat to pay. The fact is there was never a better man than he was. He did more than any other man to settle Oregon. History says Dr. Whitman was the man who saved Oregon to the United States but that is not true. It was Dr. John McLoughlin of the Hudson's Bay Company, so says every man that is a man that came to Oregon up to 1849.

The Holman and the Burnett families were most admiring of McLaughlin, a British subject and a Catholic who helped the mostly Protestant American pioneers in Oregon.[63]

Ella's grandfather Glen Owen Burnett settled in Polk County on a land grant and started farming. His passion was preaching the gospel, and he was one of the first circuit preachers in Oregon. He was instrumental in spreading religious education and even donated land and energies to start a Bible college, Bethel College. Bethel College was eventually merged into Western Oregon University at Monmouth. He was also responsible for starting Bethel Church in Polk County, named after a church he preached at in Missouri. Glen Owen married more young people than he could remember.

Glen Owen Burnett, (1809-1886) Ella Holman's grandfather, unknown date, www.findagrave.com

Dr. James McBride, the best friend of Ella's grandfather, was a preacher and physician who also came west from Missouri. McBride's son, Senator George W. McBride, would later end up hiring Ella's father, Wil Turner, for an important job in Congress.[64]

Ella's great-uncle Peter Hardeman Burnett played as large a role in the establishment of government in Oregon as he did in getting pioneers out to Oregon Country. When he first arrived in Oregon, he tried his hand at town building. He planned a town with a fellow emigrant, Morton McCarver. They called it Linnton after Senator Linn of Missouri and located it near the confluence of the Willamette and Columbia rivers. They believed it would be a major future port, but unfortunately, they miscalculated, as the port turned out to be Oregon City instead. Peter then turned to farming in Tualatin County, west of Portland, where he had a claim of 640 acres. He farmed this beautiful, productive land for five years. He called farming one of the most intellectually challenging of his careers. He appeared to love the land and had success with it.

Burnett was elected to the provisional government's Legislative Council in 1844 and wrote many of Oregon's first laws, including an adjustment to the anti-slavery law. The council threw out the organic laws by the 1843 committee, written before the great migration when Oregon had very few settlers. Burnett explained that no one on the small committee of 1843 was an attorney and that the laws as written would not hold up.

One of the committee members of 1843 was the future historian William Gray, who forever afterwards hated Burnett, although he did admit, "He was the smartest lawyer in the area at the time." He made significant improvements to the structure of government, including a way for government to receive revenue (lacking in the 1843 laws). Some of Burnett's laws turned out to be controversial. As a teetotaler he wanted to ban or regulate hard spirits. He also wanted to ban not only slaves but free blacks and proposed the severe punishment of whipping as a penalty for any blacks who stayed in Oregon after three years. The law was amended to remove the penalty, but it was not well thought out and generally condemned. He tried to explain, saying, "We wish to avoid most of those evils that have much afflicted the United States and other countries." He thought that the races needed to be segregated to prevent the degraded condition in which one race has power over another. Although he certainly was not enlightened, his thoughts were not unusual for those from slave states at the time.

Burnett was appointed Oregon's first Supreme Court Judge in 1845 and served until 1847. He was elected to the Territorial Legislature in 1848 and was also appointed to the Oregon Supreme Court by President James Polk in 1849, but he was already in California when the appointment came through.

The Burnetts and Holmans were actively engaged in building their new society when news came to Oregon in the summer of 1848 that gold had been discovered in California.[65]

"Oh, Susanna don't you cry for me, I've gone to California with my washbasin on my knee."

It seemed like everyone in Oregon dropped their plows and ran to California. Two thirds of the able-bodied men in Oregon Territory went to California. Half of the first elected 1848 Territorial Legislature left, leaving the Oregon government unable to get a quorum to meet until the following year. Oregon's first newspaper, *The Spectator*, shut down for a while because of gold fever. The newspaper issued this apology:

> *The Spectator* after a temporary sickness, greets its patrons, and hopes to serve them faithfully, and as heretofore, regularly. That 'gold fever' which has swept about 3,000 of her officers, lawyers, physicians, farmers, and mechanics of Oregon from the plains of Oregon into the mines of California, took away our printers."

The disease of gold fever was practically as contagious as the many virulent diseases of the day. Argonauts looking for their golden reward risked diseases such as cholera, typhoid, and malaria, as well as accidents, among other calamities. It was a very risky trip, no matter where one started. People came from all over the world: from Europe, which was in the throes of many rebellions and revolutions; from South America, Mexico, and Central America; from the Far East, China, Australia, and New Zealand. And of course, from the United States. Settlers in the Oregon Territory had an advantage; hearing the news before it reached the east coast of the U.S., they were in a better situation to make travel plans overland.

California was extraordinarily hard to get to in the days before railroads. One had to cross waterless deserts and high mountains or attempt to come from the sea. Oregonians had a difficult time cutting through timbered mountains with their wagons, but it was easier than coming overland from the U.S.[66]

Both Daniel S. Holman and James D. Holman went to California to mine for gold. Peter H. Burnett, along with his brother-in-law John P. Rogers, nephew Horace Burnett, and others, put together a group of 150 men and 40, oxen-pulled wagons and blazed a difficult trail. They left their wives at home to cope with the farms, children, and Indians. It was the first successful wagon trip from Oregon to California, which Burnett was understandably proud of.

The trip was difficult, with geographic challenges almost equal to the Oregon Trail, and it took more than a month, but Peter H. Burnett planned well and took six months of provisions and a good scout, Thomas McKay. They even managed to rescue Peter Lassen's group in the Sierras, who were lost and running out of food, and they were partly responsible for blazing a new trail in the California Sierras. It would be called the Burnett Cutoff.[67]

The Burnett wagon train started the trip in Oregon, using Jesse and Lindsay Applegate's rough trail, which had been laid out in 1846. The Applegate trail started at the Willamette Valley and continued down through Umpqua Canyon, where the going was so rough that the Oregon-bound immigrants who tried it in 1846 struggled to survive and had to abandon their wagons and continue on foot. The Burnett train took tools to improve and rebuild the trail. They followed the trail to Klamath Falls near the Oregon-California border and then blazed their own trail in California.

The gold fields were some forty miles east of present-day Sacramento, in the foothills of the Sierra Nevadas. When they got to the staging area for gold digging in the Sacramento Valley, Peter Burnett found friends and even relatives from Missouri. One of them was his sister Mary's husband, Dr. Benjamin Long. One of his Hardeman cousins, Dr. Glen O. Hardeman (Burnett's grandmother was Dorothy Hardeman), came from Missouri and journeyed through the Isthmus of Panama on the way to the California gold fields a couple years later. Travelling through the Isthmus and then catching a ship up the Pacific Coast to San Francisco was fraught with peril and disease—especially, the dreaded Chagres fever in Chagres, Panama—but it was faster than "coming 'round the horn" of South America.[68]

Burnett and his relatives arrived at John Sutter's fort, located in present day Sacramento, amidst general chaos. Prices for materials were high, and they were glad they had their own supplies. They headed to the North Fork of the Yuba River at Long's Bar, the property of one of the Long brothers whom Peter was acquainted with from Missouri, and bought a riverside claim of twenty by fifty feet for $300, to be paid in gold. Peter brought timber planks with him from Oregon and made himself a gold mining cradle (rocker), which was a big improvement over the washbasin to pan for gold. He and his brother-in-law and nephew were each making $20 a day within a few days and were able to quickly pay off their claim.

Burnett mined for gold for six weeks, made enough to give him living expenses for six months, then quit and rode forty miles for Sacramento, where he hung out his shingle as an attorney. One of his first clients was John Augustus Sutter Jr., commonly called August.[69]

August's father, John A. Sutter Sr., the most famous name in the gold rush, did not end up profiting from the discovery of gold on his land. In the end it destroyed him. Sutter came out to California when it was under Mexican rule. He left his wife, children, and debts behind in Switzerland and carved out a semi-feudal kingdom in the Sacramento Valley. Sutter managed to build up his large estate by using the labor of Hawaiians and Indians and even part of a troop of Mormons who had served under Frémont in the Mexican War. He had large amounts of cattle, horses, sheep, and swine, along with a fort, trading post, farm, and ranch land.

He convinced the Mexican governor to allow him to build up this estate, which was on the interior fringe of coastal California settlements, as a defense against foreigners. Sutter was appointed as an alcalde—major/sheriff—and called himself a captain. He had served in the military in Switzerland and fancied himself a military man. The Russians, through the Russian-American Company, who had built Fort Ross near Bodega Bay, Sonoma County, in 1812 to establish a foothold in California, decided to give up on it and sold the whole fort to Captain Sutter in 1841. The sale, mostly on credit, included a cannon, ammunition, and a huge amount of livestock, even a twenty-ton schooner. Sutter rebuilt his fort at the convergence of two rivers, the Sacramento and the American. It was the age of ranchos in California, and Sutter was the head of a powerful estate of 50,000 acres. He called it New Helvetia (New Switzerland.)[70]

When Mexico won its independence from Spain in 1831, California was ignored, for the most part. Just as the Spanish did not have the resources to deal with such a far-flung part of their empire, the Mexicans were preoccupied with internal matters, which distracted them.

The Spanish had known about California for quite some time—Juan Cabrillo had claimed it for Spain in 1542—but had great difficulty establishing permanent settlements. The vast coastline of 1,200 miles and the area's diversity of geography were challenges. But British and Russian fur traders making forays to the northern coast of California realized they needed more of a presence in Alta California. When the Spanish finally established their colonies in California, it was 1769, and when they did, they used their system of missions, presidios, and pueblos, as they had in other conquests.

The missions were the most successful. Starting in San Diego and moving north, at about thirty miles apart, they established twenty-one missions, nine of those by the determined Franciscan, Father Serra. The Franciscans were able to exploit local Indian labor and built up almost self-sustaining estates, with a lot of cattle, horses, and other livestock. The Indians in California were, for the most part, less aggressive and less organized than other Native Americans. This allowed them to be used as laborers fairly successfully. However, they frequently tried to run away and, understandably, were not happy with their situation. In the timespan of the Spanish occupation, from 1769 to 1833, there were 62,000 deaths of mission Indians and only 29,000 births.[71]

The Spanish also built well-planned pueblos, the largest of which was at Los Angeles; the provisional government was at Monterey. Their military forts—the presidios—were neglected and armed by lackluster, poorly trained soldiers and were not effective for defense.

When Mexico took over, it secularized the missions, as there were many elite citizens who coveted the mission lands. The military governor gave out land grants as he saw fit. John Sutter was one of the lucky, large landowners.

The Mexican War ended just after gold was discovered but before the discovery was widely known. The Treaty of Guadalupe Hidalgo transferred power to an American military governor in February 1848. The U.S. kept the Spanish system, which seemed satisfactory for the way of life there. Sutter, as a Mexican citizen, was not sure of his future in the new situation.

Sutter had hired a man, John W. Marshall, recently arrived from Missouri via Oregon in the fall of 1847, to build a water-powered sawmill. He planned to sell timber and ship it by river to San Francisco. Marshall set out to find a suitable spot on a river. He found one at Coloma. Coloma, in the foothills of the Sierra Nevadas, was on Indian land that Sutter had made a deal with the tribe to lease for three years. Marshall, after letting the river flow through his newly built sawmill, noticed a shiny glimmer in the water. He took his findings to Sutter. They were astonished they had found gold and slow to realize the ramifications. It was January 1848. Sutter tried to keep the discovery a secret, but as with most secrets of this magnitude, it did not stay secret for long.

The most memorable quote describing how the news got out is from Sam Brannon, president of the Mormon settlement in California and a very canny businessman. Brannon was working for Sutter as head of the Mormon contingent of workers at Sutter's Fort and had a store nearby when he heard the news. He bought enough gold dust to put in a jar, took it to the streets of Yerba Buena—later renamed San Francisco—and yelled, "Gold, Gold from the American River."[72]

The explosion that followed would forever change American history. The gold rush accelerated the settlement of California. As the Great Migration brought settlers to Oregon and led to it becoming a U.S. territory in 1848, so the gold rush accelerated the settlement of California, the population growth allowing California to become a state—in 1850—even more quickly. There was enough population in 1849 for California statehood, but Congress hesitated. Oregon Territory coming in as a free territory caused enough friction between the free and slave states. The idea of California coming in as a free state as well, when the balance stood at fifteen free states and fifteen slave states, put the South in an uproar. The hard-fought Compromise of 1850 was the result.

It was the age of orators in the Senate. Henry Clay of Kentucky, John Calhoun of South Carolina, and Daniel Webster of Massachusetts fiercely debated the issue. Although the compromise let California into the Union as a free state, organized New Mexico and Utah as territories without addressing slavery, and adjusted the western boundary of Texas, it added a very strict Fugitive Slave Law and other compromises to placate the South, which only increased the tension on both sides of the slavery issue.

President James Polk, the expansionist President elected in 1844, had had his eye on California for a very long time. He forced the issue by provoking a war with Mexico. In December 1848, when news reached him of the discovery of gold in California, months after the Oregonians heard it, he announced the discovery. This led to an even larger influx of people traveling to California; we could come to call those gold seekers the "49ers."

Within a year, San Francisco went from being a village of 800 to having 25,000 residents, and it soon quadrupled in size. People abandoned their jobs; at one point there were over 500 abandoned sailing schooners—that had no crews to sail them—in the San Francisco harbor. Some of these were sunk; others were pulled up to the dock and used for businesses or broken up for lumber. The influx of population changed the lives of native Indians in the state and, sadly, destroyed their way of life. In the 1840s there were about 150,000 native Indians of many different tribes in California. By 1880 only about 16,000 were left. If disease did not get them, starvation or murder did.[73]

The mix of people was chaotic, not only with different ethnicities, such as the many Chinese who came, but also with many young men who flooded the state. It was a wild, lawless society with vigilante committees taking the law into their own hands. Squatters trampled John Sutter's land, stole his horses, and ate his cattle; but worst of all, he could not find any workers. They would much rather be mining, gambling on striking it rich. Without labor he could not keep his empire going. His debts began to increase dramatically, as did his drinking habits.

To make matters worse, his wife—whom he had no intention of going back to—finally found out where he was via newspaper articles in Europe reporting how gold had been discovered on his property. She managed to scrape together enough money to send her son to California. Upon meeting his long-lost son, John Sutter at least pretended he was glad to see him.

Sutter, so in debt that he was about to lose everything, came up with a scheme to transfer ownership of everything to his twenty-one-year old son, August. The Russians were most persistent about getting their money back, as were his other creditors.[74]

This was the situation when August asked Peter Burnett to help him. An Oregon Pioneer article written about James Duval Holman states he recommended Peter Burnett to Sutter before he left for Oregon. A biography of Burnett's old partner McCarver, mentioned in R. Gregory Nokes's book on Peter Burnett, claims that McCarver helped August Sutter plan the layout of lots for Sacramento and that he expected to sell and profit from the sale of lots. Whatever the story, Peter Burnett was most capable and, being an attorney, probably, the most appropriate choice, and the two agreed Burnett would receive one quarter of the profits of all the lots sold in Sacramento.

He set out first of all to hold off the creditors while selling lots in Sacramento, personally guaranteeing that all debts would be paid. He had a lot of experience trying to build a town and knew how to avoid pitfalls. Unaware of animosity between father and son, he methodically went through Sutter's debts until he had them all paid off and had cleared his credit.

Sutter Sr., egged on by too much wine and resentment about his son's choice to sell lots in Sacramento in opposition to his own plan for a town three miles to the north, which he called Sutterville, schemed to get control back from his son and Burnett. While his son was ill, he convinced him to sign everything back over to him, and he dismissed Burnett just as Burnett was starting to make a profit for him. Peter Burnett was able to make a fortune on his portion and then pay off in full his own longstanding debts from Missouri. John Sutter Sr., very poor with money management, kept next to nothing. His son August, speaking about it later, said, "My father would have been a rich man had he not fired Burnett."[75]

As in Oregon, Peter Burnett was to play an active role in the new government of California. He and his family settled in when his wife and family came by ship to San Francisco in the spring of 1849. He was elected to the Legislative Assembly in San Francisco in March 1849 and then appointed one of four Superior Tribunal judges by the military governor, General Bennet Riley. It was clear that California needed more vigorous laws in the American style, as the Spanish system was not sufficient, given the population explosion.

California, like the Oregon Territory, voted in an antislavery clause. It was more from the fear of competing with slave labor than any sympathy for enslaved persons. Peter Burnett voted in favor of the antislavery law and again tried to encourage an exclusionary clause for blacks. This failed, but the legislators did include a disenfranchise law for dueling, which barred a person from voting if caught dueling. It was deemed necessary because, in the wild environment of California, duels were all too common.

Generally, Burnett was well known and well thought of. He made a great first impression, so much so that he received a large majority of votes as the first elected governor of California. Burnett was sworn in with high hopes but turned out to be a timid leader who did not take advice from others well. He resigned before his term was up. No one doubted his honesty or intellect, but he proved not up to the enormous job of governing a large and chaotic new state with many pressing issues while dealing with his own business and family illnesses.

He and his family stayed in California, as did many other members of the Burnett family. His wife regained her health in California and recovered from consumption, but sadly, they lost two children to this terrible disease. Burnett would go on to become a Supreme Court judge in California, followed by a successful banking career as head of Pacific Bank. Two of his sons would become attorneys as well.[76]

The California Gold Rush would change the nation's and even the world's economy. Seven hundred and fifty thousand pounds of gold were dug out of the "Golden State." Some 300,000 people descended on California, approximately half coming by sea and half overland. Fortunes were made, if not in gold, then in business. Levi Strauss would start his business here, as well as James Folger of Folger's Coffee. Sam Brannon, the brash businessman who would be excommunicated by the Mormon Church, became the first millionaire of the West. Peter Hardeman Burnett, who made significant contributions to government in both Oregon and California, made his fortune in California real estate. Most, however, were lucky just to survive the great adventure. The Holman brothers, Daniel and James, went back to Oregon. Daniel did not have great success at the mines, but James made thousands of dollars to take home.

Peter Hardeman Burnett, (1807-1885) first Governor of California, Ella Holman's great uncle, public domain, content.cdlib.org/ark:/13030hf4g5004g5/?orders+1

It seemed that much of Oregon and now California was interconnected with family, cousins, or friends. Everyone was connected. Ella's grandfather and great-uncle married sisters, daughters of Peter Rogers, a Missourian with roots in tidewater Virginia. Her mother, Martha, married into the large Holman family. After California opened up, her grandparents Glen Owen and Sarah Burnett moved to Santa Rosa, California, where her grandfather continued to preach for many more years. Her uncle Peter Burnett Holman would go to college there to become a minister like his father. There were cousins everywhere in Oregon and California who helped in good times and bad.

Ella grew up visiting the Portland cousins and continued as an adult. She had at least ten female cousins in the area. She especially liked going to Cousin Fred's house in the Goose Hollow section of Portland on Taylor Street, which was designed by architect Edgar M. Lazarus and built in 1892. Sadly, it was torn down in 2016, despite protests by preservationists.

Frederick V. Holman was a world traveler with a house of over 6,000 square feet filled with art, Chinese Ming vases three feet high, unusual furniture, and a yard filled with roses. As well as being influential in his law career, having protected the Oregon and Washington beaches for the public, among many other accomplishments, he was an avid gardener who helped start the Portland Rose Society and is credited with coining Portland "The Rose City" in 1905.

It was a life filled with opportunities. Ella was invited to many elaborate weddings of cousins, which she attended if she had the proper clothes. I am sure it would have been hard for her to imagine the extremely difficult, backbreaking life her parents and relatives endured in the small, hastily built log cabins in which they lived in the 1840s in Oregon Country.[77]

Ella's mother, Martha Elizabeth Burnett, did not like reminiscing about pioneer life or the difficult trip over the Oregon Trail she made when she was fifteen. She bore ten children under frontier situations—one died at age five—and not until later in her life did she have the comforts of civilization. The families were used to hardship. Martha's father-in-law, John Holman, lost three children and a wife by the time he went west and lost more sons and another wife soon after. They were a tough, determined people who continued to push themselves. Why did they go west and risk everything? Why had they been pioneering for generations? The answer starts in Virginia almost two centuries before.

John Holman, Unknown date, Ella Holman's grandfather, posted on ancestry.com

Three brothers came from England in the 1600s; one stayed in Virginia, one went north, and one went south, so says the Holman family history. The Holmans were vigorous people who had many children, including many sons. Isaac Holman, or Holeman as he spelled it, was born in Shenandoah, Page County, Virginia, in 1725. His father, Daniel, was one of the first settlers in Augusta County, Virginia, and is buried in the Shenandoah Old Cemetery in Shenandoah.

The Shenandoah Valley is a fertile area in the upper area of the Great Valley of the Appalachians. It is bordered by the Blue Mountains on the east and was populated in a large part by settlers moving down from Pennsylvania. Isaac and his family left the Shenandoah Valley in Virginia about 1752 for the frontier of North Carolina. There they established plantations after obtaining land grants in Rowan (later Davie) County. In the 1750s the Piedmont area of the Carolinas opened up with the best fertile land and prices. A square mile of that fertile, red-clay land of rolling hills cost only three shillings. Isaac had eleven sons, many with the same names as his brother's sons. They needed lots of land to support the large family. "Two of his younger brothers joined him and established themselves on adjoining plantations among the foothills of the Bushy Mountains on the headwaters of both Bear Creek and Dutchman Creek."[78]

The Holmans were slaveholders, and they most likely grew tobacco, as well as corn. Isaac and his wife were "Missionary Baptists," a sect that believed in evangelistic missionary work, unlike some of the other Baptist sects. Virginia was discouraging to faiths other than the Anglican Church, which was still the official state church. In the older Tidewater areas near the coast, there was prejudice against other Protestants. Non-Anglicans were refused meeting houses in Virginia until 1803, when church and state were finally separated. On the western frontier other denominations were left alone most of the time.

The Scots-Irish, German, and Welsh immigrants pushed to the interior frontier of Virginia, not only for cheaper land but also for freedom to practice their religion. After moving to Rowan County, North Carolina, the Holmans belonged to the Bear Creek Baptist Church, the oldest church in the area, which was built on the then-called Holeman Road. The Holmans acquired more land, buying and selling several plots. Isaac lived in the northwest corner of what is now Davie County, near Mocksville. Here, his story intersects with the famous frontiersman, Daniel Boone.

Daniel Boone's father, Squire Boone, moved the family from Pennsylvania to the Shenandoah Valley of Virginia and then kept moving south to the Piedmont area of North Carolina in 1750. Daniel Boone honed his skills as a backwoodsman and hunter in the frontier areas of Pennsylvania as a boy and in North Carolina as a young man. His father's estate was not far from the Holmans' many properties. It is probable that they knew each other.

Squire Boone is buried at Joppa Cemetery near Mocksville, five miles from the Holman homestead. Benjamin Boone, Daniel's cousin, was one of the witnesses for the signing of Isaac Holman's will. Later, James Holman would name his son after Daniel Boone. Daniel Boone Holman would end up in California in 1852, as well as a grandson of Daniel Boone, Alfonso Boone, who unfortunately died a premature death in the California gold fields, drowning in the Feather River Canyon.[79]

Daniel Boone would start his famous trip exploring Kentucky at Holeman's Ford, where a brother of Isaac Holman, Thomas Holman, established a foothold. Boone built a cabin there, five miles up the Yadkin River at the ford. He lived near Thomas Holman for approximately ten years. Boone was one of the most well-known of the "long hunters," frontiersmen who became extremely good hunters and trappers and as at home in the woods as the native Indians. The Kentucky rifle, with its amazing accuracy at long distances, was made famous by this group of hunters. This was the same Pennsylvania rifle, renamed, that was perfected in York in the time of the Adlums. It would be the most popular weapon of Americans for one hundred years.[80]

The frontiersmen of North Carolina and Kentucky would use this rifle to great effect in the Revolutionary War. Five of Isaac Holman's eleven sons were reputed to serve in the war, according to the Holman family history. Because of the large families that repeated names among brothers, it is difficult to ascertain who's who. The story goes that Isaac sent five of his eleven sons to fight for the American cause. All five of Isaac's sons came home from serving in the war, while a neighbor who also sent five sons lost all of them.

Isaac Sr. is listed in the North Carolina Revolutionary Army Accounts and in the Daughters of the American Revolution records as a patriot. Isaac Jr., one of his sons, enlisted as a private from Rowan County, North Carolina. They were close by Salisbury, the county seat where British troops were temporarily stationed as General Cornwallis pursued General Nathaniel Greene through the Carolinas. Half the troops from the famous battle of King's Mountain would be frontiersmen from Wilkes (Rowan) County.[81]

The Appalachian mountain range only had a few places to pass through. The "Overmountain Men," as the frontiersmen were called who went to Tennessee and Kentucky, found those trails, which had been used by the native Indians for years. There is a gap in Southwestern Pennsylvania and a gap in the Blue Ridge Mountains at Roanoke, Virginia. There is a notch in the mountains that intersect Virginia, Kentucky, and Tennessee that would come to be called The Cumberland Gap. A British naturalist and scientist, Dr. Thomas Walker, traveled through it in 1750 to the beautiful valleys of Kentucky in a trip funded by the Duke of Cumberland, King George II's son. Walker would name the Cumberland River after the Duke. Native Indians had used this Great Warrior's Path for years to get to their hunting grounds in Kentucky and Tennessee. The Cherokee and Shawnee fought over the area, known as "the dark and bloody ground."

Despite the Royal Proclamation of 1763 that established a line east of the Appalachians and decreed settlers would stay east of that line and allow the Indian tribes their hunting grounds, there were constant small encroachments of Indian lands by hunters and settlers looking for more land for their ever-growing families. The first permanent, white settler in what is now Tennessee was William Bean. He settled near the Watauga River on Boone's Creek in 1769 and was followed by other pioneers. This was technically Cherokee land past the Proclamation line. The settlers formed their own government, the Watauga Association, in 1772.

Daniel Boone and his followers were among those with wanderlust and a desire to push west for new land. Various treaties were signed by the governments of Virginia and North Carolina to attempt to settle the issue. In 1775 land promoter Judge Richard Henderson of North Carolina, in an attempt to obtain land for speculation in the beautiful Kentucky hunting lands, set up his own deal with some of the Cherokee Nation. He had the idea that he would make his own settlement, with his Transylvania Company handling sales. Daniel

Boone helped him explore and survey the land. An arrangement was signed in 1775 in Watauga with the Cherokee whereby they gave up their rights to the Cumberland River Valley and millions of acres in Kentucky in exchange for 10,000 pounds of goods. Neither side really had the rights to the land, but they proceeded as if they did. The Shawnee and breakaway Cherokee, the Chickamauga, disagreed and made life as difficult as they could for the pioneers coming onto their ancestral hunting grounds.

The two ways of life were incompatible. Once farms were plowed and settlers built their forts and homes, the Indians did not have access to the once-plentiful game they counted on for survival. Their only option was to try to force the settlers out, but the settlers kept coming and coming.

Historian Frederick Jackson Turner emphasizes the importance of this trail in his famous essay on the frontier. "Stand at the Cumberland Gap and watch the procession of civilization, marching single file-the buffalo following the trail to the salt springs, the Indian, the fur trader and hunter, the cattle-raiser, the farmer—and the frontier has passed by."

Daniel Boone's Wilderness Road through the mountains to Kentucky opened the west to pioneers willing to brave hostile Indians and start anew. Many members of the Holman family, including Isaac's son Daniel L. Holman and his brothers, followed Daniel Boone's lead. Daniel L. Holman, born June 20, 1751, in North Carolina, married Nancy Saunders, daughter of James Saunders, on Christmas Eve, 1772, when she was just shy of sixteen. They most likely went to Kentucky in 1779 in one of the first large groups with Daniel Boone.

Abraham Lincoln's grandfather, also named Abraham, would be one of the Virginians persuaded by Daniel Boone to follow him on this trip. Abraham Lincoln would, of course, be born on the Kentucky frontier in a log cabin in 1809. His grandfather lost his life to an Indian attack a few years after emigrating. The journey was very dangerous and rough, the trail not large enough for wagons, just single-file pack animals. It was a brutally cold winter that year and much of the livestock they brought froze to death. They had to eat the frozen carcasses to survive.

Nancy Saunders Holman, who had three children by this time—at about age 21—showed great bravery on this trip. Because the hostility of the Indians, mostly Shawnee, the settlers kept watch day and night. "One night one of Nancy Holman's children cried and could not be quieted. Fearing the child might attract the Indians, and that they would all be murdered, she carried the child into the thick brush, about 400 yards from the camp, and there remained alone with the child." Daniel Boone has been quoted as saying, "All you need for happiness is a good gun, a good horse and a good wife." Daniel L. Holman certainly had a good wife.[82]

There was always danger on the frontier. Frontier women, as well as the men, showed great courage. Some of the Holman family settled at Bryan's Station, an early settlement near Lexington, Kentucky. There were frequent Indian attacks, so they built a fort to withdraw to. The fort was in the shape of a parallelogram, with some forty cabins inside, four blockhouses on the corners, and twelve-foot logs with pointed tops as the walls of the fort.

During the American Revolution, in August 1782, they discovered they were surrounded by a large force—estimated to be almost 500 by Col. Daniel Boone, who was in the militia at the time—of Wyandot, Lake Indians, Shawnee, Delaware, and British Canadian Rangers. They did not want to let the enemy know they were aware of their positions, so they let the women out of the fort to get water from a nearby spring. Mrs. Holman and some other women, led by Polly Hawkins Craig, bravely stepped outside the fort with their water buckets to get water and then returned to the fort.

The siege began with the settlers and militia inside badly outnumbered and ill-prepared. The water the women fetched helped to douse flaming arrows shot at the fort. Unable to breach the walls of the fort and hearing the Kentucky Militia was near, the enemy finally retreated and the majority of the residents of Bryan's Station were saved. Unfortunately, the battle between the militia and the enemy force at nearby Blue Licks was a terrible loss for the Kentuckians. Daniel Boone lost his youngest son, Israel, in the Battle of Blue Licks.[83]

The first few years for pioneers trying to settle Kentucky were filled with almost constant threat of Indian attack. Daniel Boone was captured twice by the Shawnee and managed to escape both times. The natives admired his skills and bravery and tried to get him to stay with the tribe, but there was no mistaking they wanted to drive the other settlers away. Boone lost two sons—one was tortured to death—and a brother in the Indian Wars.

Henry Holeman (Holman), in 1776, settled in Fayette County—later called Woodford—which was still part of Virginia at the time. He had a plantation of 1,000 acres on Grier Creek near present day Versailles and in the neighborhood of Daniel L. Holman's plantation. He was tomahawked by the Indians in 1789, leaving a wife and fourteen children. Some pioneers gave up in fright and just went back to where they came from. The Holmans stubbornly persisted. They brought slaves with them to Kentucky Country, so they were most likely better off than a lot of pioneers. One out of five Kentucky pioneers was an African American slave. The Boone family also had slaves.

When they died, Isaac Holman and his wife, Mary Ann, owned several slaves at their plantation in Rowan County, North Carolina. Although Isaac Holman freed his faithful slave, Charles, in his will of 1807, the rest of his slaves were handed down to his children. His great-grandson, Daniel S. Holman, once he arrived in Oregon, would denounce slavery, even though his family had been slave owners.[84]

Isaac Sr. stayed in Rowan County and was buried with his wife on his plantation there, while many of his sons moved on to Kentucky and Tennessee. His son Daniel L. Holman lived more than twenty years in Woodford County, Kentucky. After his wife died, he moved to Fayetteville, Lincoln County, Tennessee, where he remarried and outlived a number of his children, including his eldest son, Lieutenant Colonel Isaac Holman, who would go to Texas with his sons some months prior to the Texas Revolution. Isaac Sr.'s son Daniel L. Holman, father of Isaac and John Holman, died in October 1838 at the age of eighty-eight after outliving a good portion of his family.[85]

Daniel's son John Holman, born in 1787 in Woodford County, Kentucky, married Elizabeth (Betsy) Duval in 1810 and served in the militia in the War of 1812, as did his older brother Lt Col. Isaac Holman. John and Betsy had fourteen children. As was common in the day, sons—and some daughters—were given the mother's or grandmother's maiden name as their middle name. James Duval Holman, born in Kentucky in 1814, had his mother's maiden name, while his younger brother Daniel Saunders Holman, born in Tennessee in 1822, was given the family name of his maternal grandmother. Other sons were named after admired persons. John named one son Thomas Jefferson Holman and another, Isaac Newton Holman.[86]

John Holman pioneered with his family in Kentucky until 1820, when he lived briefly in Gallatin, Kentucky, before moving on to Tennessee. There was a dispute with the Holman land grants which were tried up with Daniel Boone's grants. Both Daniel Boone and the Holmans lost their land in Kentucky in the chaos of conflicting land claims and poor practices by Virginia and North Carolina in handling those claims. By 1829 the Holmans were in Clay County, Missouri, where they stayed until John's wife, Betsy, died in 1841. John and one of his sons, Daniel Saunders Holman, then started to make plans to go to Oregon.[87] [88]

Lt. Col. Isaac Holman was John's older brother by twelve years. All the Holmans would be involved in community affairs. Isaac was one of the most prominent. Isaac was trained as an attorney in Henry Clay's law office and would go on to serve in the Kentucky Legislature in 1810 and 1816. In 1818 he moved his family to Lincoln County, Tennessee. Other family members would follow him, including his brother John. Isaac ran for office in Tennessee as well and served as a state senator. He knew General Andrew Jackson and offered the following toast at a banquet in his honor after the Battle of New Orleans. "Let us with one heart cleave to the support of our own government. It is one of our own forming, and ought to be administered by men of our choice."[89]

A credit squeeze put Isaac's family in a bind, and they decided to sell out and move to San Augustine, Texas. They moved in groups, two of his sons moving first, followed by the rest of the family in a large group that included their slaves. The Holmans became prominently involved in the Texas War for Independence. Three of Isaac's sons fought in the war. His son James Saunders Holman (1804-1867), along with his brother William W. Holman (1806-1873), served with Captain Bailey Anderson Jr.'s company as reinforcements at the Siege of Bexar.

William represented San Augustine in the first Congress of the Republic of Texas. James Saunders Holman would go on to become the first mayor of Houston. Holman Avenue in Houston is named after him. He spent his time advocating annexation to the United States and promoting railroads. After the Civil War, while supervising the construction of the Houston and Central Texas Railway, James became ill with yellow fever and then pneumonia and died near Bryan, Texas, in 1867.[90]

Another brother, William Sanford Holman (1816-1843), served in the Texas Army during the Texas Revolution and fought at the Battle of San Jacinto under Captain William Kimbro's San Augustine Company. Many of the Texas Holmans are buried in San Augustine County or Sabine County in private, family cemeteries. Other branches of the family spread far and wide across the country.[91]

Like the Holmans, the Burnett and Hardeman families also started in Virginia. James Burnett (1726-1797), of Scots ancestry, emigrated from Ireland and spent his life in Pittsylvania County, Virginia, growing tobacco. He married Mary Morrison (1750-1784) and had at least five sons and two daughters.

Pittsylvania was a rural county formed in 1767 from Halifax County and named for William Pitt, British Prime Minister, 1766-1768, who favored accommodation policies toward the colonists. There were no towns, just plantation stations on the major rivers, until Danville was finally developed. It was a hard life, despite the use of slave labor.

James Burnett served in the American Revolution as a lieutenant from Pittsylvania County. The census of 1782 for the county shows James and two of his sons, Henry and Gilbert, as heads of household. All of his children would eventually leave the area and head west, most likely through the Cumberland Gap, following the Wilderness Trail—Boone's Trace—to end up in Tennessee and Kentucky.[92]

His son George William Burnett would head out as a young man to Nashville, Tennessee, which was just a small village outpost at the time. George worked as a carpenter there, building many of the first buildings in Nashville, and met his future wife, Dorothy Hardeman, daughter of frontiersman Thomas Hardeman, there as well. On February 11, 1802, he married Dorothy, known as Dolly, in Davidson, Davidson County, Tennessee. Their first child out of thirteen who would live to adulthood was a daughter, Constantia Dudley Burnett, born in Nashville a year later. Peter Hardeman Burnett, their firstborn son, was born in 1807, followed by a brother, Glen Owen Burnett, two years later in 1809, as well as younger siblings in the years to come.

Peter Hardeman Burnett, in his autobiography, described the Burnett family as satisfied with a good living and not seekers of fortune. He described them as peaceful, just, sober, industrious, and pious. His father, George, was raised in poverty and only had three months of schooling but had a natural intellect and talent for literary pursuits—many of his cousins were attorneys—and extraordinary math ability. Peter stated that most of his aunts and uncles lived in Kentucky, working at a variety of occupations such as farmer, teacher, blacksmith, and cabinetmaker.

In 1804 George William Burnett bought 333 1/3 acres on the Harpeth River in Williamson County, Tennessee, for $1,000. George and Dolly lived in Davidson County until 1811, when they moved to Williamson County, four miles south of Franklin, Tennessee. Peter stated that his father was very industrious, knew his craft as a carpenter well, and was also a good farmer but easily taken advantage of.[93]

In 1817 George and Dolly Burnett followed Dolly's father, Thomas Hardeman, to Howard County, Missouri. The conditions were very rough. Their son Peter Hardeman Burnett described the hardships:

We spent the first winter there in a large camp with a dirt floor, boarded up on the sides with clapboard and covered with the same, leaving a hole in the center of the roof for the escape of smoke. All the family lived together in one room, the whites on one side and the blacks on the other.

The location of the farm in the sticky Missouri bottoms was unhealthy, especially, in 1821-22. Many of the family were frequently sick with fever and ague (as fever, such as from malaria), forcing them to finally give up on it and move to Clay County, Missouri, in 1822, where George bought a tract of 160 acres at $1.25 an acre. There, they started the hard work of clearing woods for fields to plow and building a home. The ability to be mostly self-sufficient was crucial on the frontier. The inventory of George Burnett's will in 1838 shows the extent of what was done at home, from homespun fabric—linen and cotton—and thread for clothes and shoes made at home, to emergency medicines, and large stores of staple goods as well as livestock. George, despite only having had three months of formal schooling, had a fair collection of books for a pioneer on the frontier. More than twenty-five books, including two Bibles and books on religion, but also geography, natural science, and philosophy were found on his estate.[94]

George's wife, Dolly Hardeman, like the Burnetts, also came from a family of Virginians. The Hardemans were of English and Welsh origin. The first ancestor to arrive in Virginia was Thomas Hardeman—he spelled it Hardyman—and he brought his son, also named Thomas Hardyman. Father and son died within three years of each other, 1657 and 1660, in Charles City, Charles, Virginia Colony. "The grandson of this tidewater Virginia gentleman, John Hardeman I, sailed from Virginia to England, perhaps to secure an education. He was jailed following his support of the Duke of Monmouth's unsuccessful rebellion."

He was fortunate to be exiled to the New World in 1685 instead being killed or left in prison in England. When he returned to Virginia, he married Maria Eppes of Henrico County. He would, like many of his ancestors and descendants, serve in the military and politics. He became a lieutenant colonel in the militia and served as a member of the House of Burgesses from Prince George County in 1710. "He died in 1711 after being kicked by his racehorse." His wife's family, the Eppes, were an old Tidewater Virginia family as well. Marie Eppes' father, Col. Frances Eppes II, Captain of the Guard and of Horse, served as a justice of the county there. Eppes planted some 927 acres in 1673, per land records. He had a mercantile business at Bermuda Hundred and was also the agent for a London firm. At the time he died of a wound in 1677, he was living with his second wife in Bermuda Hundred on the upperpart of the James River. Frances Eppes' father, Capt. Frances Wayless Eppes, arrived in Virginia Colony in 1625 and patented 1,700 acres on the James River in Charlestown. Married to Marie Pawlett, he served in the House of Burgesses in 1625 and also with his father-in-law, Capt. Thomas Pawlett, in 1639-40.

Captain Pawlett arrived in Virginia Colony in 1618 on the ship *The Neptune*, having received a "headright" land grant form King James I. He is listed on a plaque at the site of the Jamestown Colony as a member of the first Virginia House of Burgesses in 1619.[95]

The Hardeman family—spelling changed from Hardyman in later times—stayed in Virginia for several generations then slowly started moving out of the Tidewater region. The soil of the Tidewater area was wearing out and rapidly becoming unable to support future generations. John Hardeman III, after marrying an Irish woman, Dorothy Edwards, moved towards the frontier. They first went to Goochland County then to the rich Piedmont of Albemarle County.

Dr. Nicholas Perkins Hardeman's biography, *Wilderness Calling*, gives us many details of the Hardeman family, especially Thomas Hardeman. Thomas Hardeman was born in Albemarle County, Virginia, in January 1750. On a neighboring estate lived a very young Thomas Jefferson. The family then moved southwest to the Dan River and settled east of the Cumberland Gap in Pittsylvania County, Virginia. Their names were on the tax rolls of Pittsylvania County by 1767. It was from here that Thomas Hardeman, the future frontiersmen, would blaze a new path for his family and descendants. At age eighteen he went on his first "long hunt" past the forbidden line of demarcation of 1763, all the way to the French Lick area of Tennessee Country. He learned much about surviving in the wilderness on this trip. Nicholas Perkins and wife, Bethenia Hardin, were neighbors of the Hardemans. At age twenty, Thomas Hardeman married their sixteen-year-old daughter, Mary, and they set out on their own, taking a Bible given to Thomas by his pious Baptist father. The Burnetts lived in the county at the same time. George William Burnett, who would later marry Thomas's daughter, was born in 1770, the year Tom Hardeman married.[96]

After a few years of renting—his father had no land to give him—Thomas Hardeman became restless with the lack of economic opportunity, which at the time was very much tied to having sufficient land. He followed his former neighbor Captain William Bean to the Watauga area of frontier North Carolina on Boone's Creek. They settled on land in Washington County and built a cabin. Unfortunately, it was not safe, given the frequent attacks from Indians. His family had to flee back to Pittsylvania County. Indian problems in backwoods North Carolina increased during the American Revolution, as many of the tribes sided with the British. Thomas fought in several Indian campaigns. "Most likely he fought with William Bean and Col. Evan Shelby against the Chickamauga in 1779 and certainly commanded a group of Watauga backwoodsmen against a group of Cherokees a few months later."[97]

Hardeman's rank in one of the most famous battles of the Revolutionary War, The Battle of Kings Mountain, was lieutenant. The independent backwoodsmen of the North Carolina frontier were not too interested in the war until they realized the crucial need for their involvement. The victory of Lord Cornwallis and Colonel Tarleton at Camden, South Carolina, made the Americans realize their cause was in danger. Major Patrick Ferguson, in charge of the Tories at King's Mountain, warned the local Revolutionaries weeks before, "If they did not cease their rebellion he would march over the mountains, hang their leaders, and lay waste to their settlements with fire and sword."

This was all it took to rile up the backcountry militias. Cols. Isaac Shelby and John Sevier set up a conference and decided to go on the offense against the British and their Tory troops. Thomas Hardeman participated under the command of Capt. Bean. They collected "over-mountain men" as they marched, meeting up with more irregulars under Col. William Campbell. They marched 1,000 strong to the foot of King's Mountain, which lay at the border of North and South Carolina. Half of the American force would be frontiersmen from Tennessee. These riflemen were sharpshooters and experienced in Indian fighting.

Major Ferguson positioned himself and his loyalist troops of some 1,100 on the flat top of King's Mountain in a defensive position, thinking there was no way he could be driven off. On October 7, 1780, the Americans launched a fierce, four-pronged attack, with two columns on each side of the mountain. The Americans split into smaller groups, advancing under cover up the mountain to pick off the Tories. The enemy was totally surprised by the boldness of the attack. They had trouble accurately returning fire, misjudging by firing over the heads of their attackers—a common mistake when shooting downhill.

In a battle that lasted about an hour, Major Ferguson was cut down after trying a desperate charge down the mountain, as were 157 of his men, while 163 others were wounded and the rest (698) were captured. The Americans lost only 28 men. The over-mountain men were not to be underestimated again. This battle changed the course of the war in the South and gave momentum to the Rebels' cause. A British officer, writing at the close of the war, wrote, "The Americans had riflemen who could hit a man anywhere they liked at 200 paces ... At King's Mountain, they destroyed us."[98]

Thomas Hardeman was restless and had the urge to move on to a new frontier. After selling his 325 Watauga acres to a William Elles, in 1784, with a slave and a few cows and horses, he went over the Cumberland Gap to the French Lick area near present day Nashville. He used his military service payment to purchase 640 acres on the Little Harpeth River. He was also able to secure another 640 acres near the Cumberland River and decided to place a cabin there. He started a corn crop and then went back for his wife, Mary, and eight children. Instead of taking them overland the entire way through the Cumberland Gap, he decided to build a large flatboat and use the rivers to travel to Tennessee. In about 1786, in the middle of winter, he and his family, along with his sister Esther and her husband, John Everett, and their family and several slaves, and the family's livestock traveled down the Holston and Tennessee rivers and then up the Ohio and Cumberland rivers to French Lick. The overland trip was one of hardship, especially for a family.

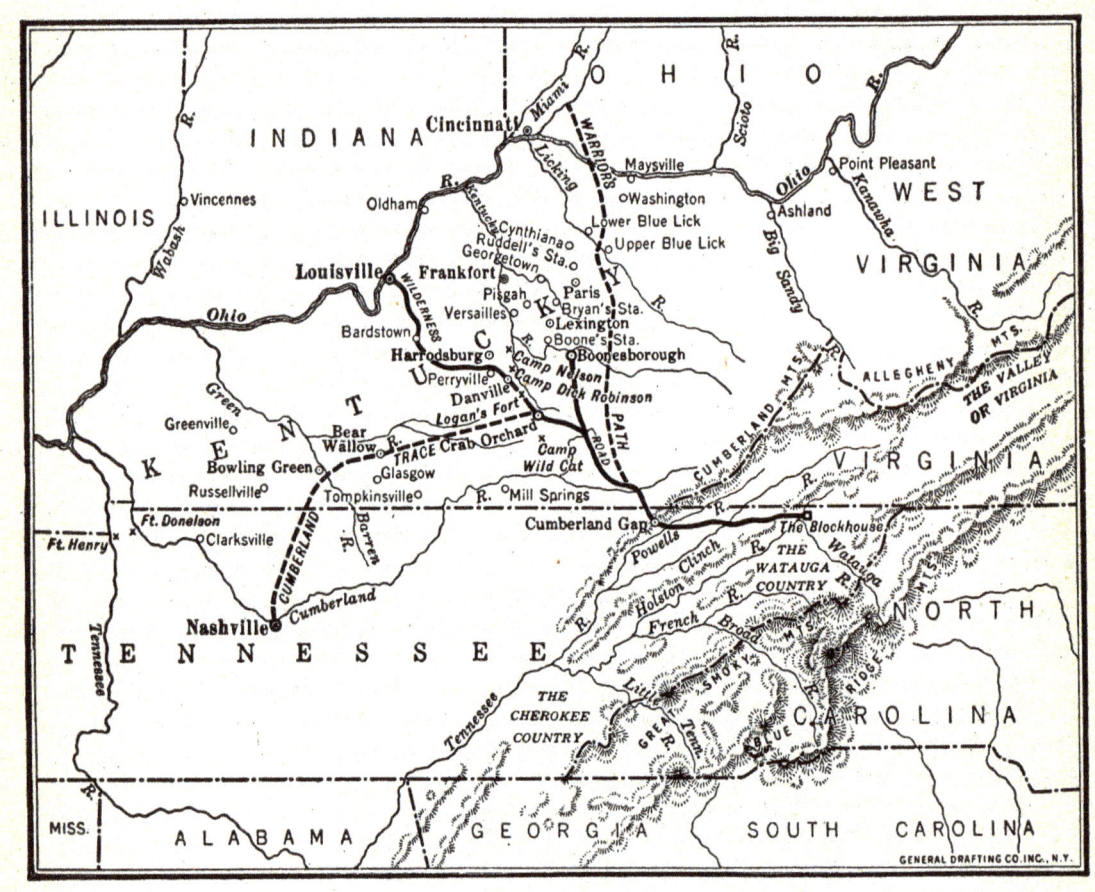

Daniel Boone and the Wilderness Road, (shows the exploration and settlement areas of the Holman, Burnett and Hardeman families) source: Tennessee State Library and Archives

The flatboat trip was precarious as well. They had a guide, the Chickasaw Chief Piomingo, but still faced many dangers from the rivers and threats from hostile Indians. Thomas Hardeman was gaining quite a reputation as a frontiersman, and soon other pioneers followed him.[99]

It was beautiful, lush land, with virgin forests teeming with wildlife. There were deer, bear, and buffalo, as well as wild turkey and many small animals, such as beaver and fox, which the settlers trapped for their fur. Woods had to be cleared to plant crops, and one had to keep an ever-watchful eye out for Indian attacks. As quickly as they could, the family built a fortified station to retreat to called Hardeman's Station. Every area with a collection of settlers needed a fort or station nearby because of constant threat of attack.

Over time the threat from Indian attacks subsided. By 1795 Thomas Hardeman was established with a manner of success and admiration of his peers. Over time he would obtain some 7,000 acres. A measure of a man's worth was in landholdings, and he had many children to hand land down to, as his father had not been able to do for him. Thomas and Mary had eight sons and five daughters who lived to adulthood. Thomas was able to give each of his sons many acres (400-640) and help his daughters as well.[100]

Thomas Hardeman became involved in politics. He was elected to the North Carolina State Legislature in 1788. There were some 700 miles of frontier between the Nashville area and the center of the North Carolina government that he traveled through to take part in the government. Mindful of his former neighbor, Thomas Jefferson, he was an anti-Federalist and strongly agreed with the Jeffersonian idea of democracy. During this time, his Baptist faith began to be tempered with the ideas of John Locke, and he became a deist.

Thomas was a friend and neighbor of Andrew Jackson. He became a member of the First Constitutional Convention of Tennessee, along with Jackson, and helped write the Constitution of Tennessee. In 1797 he was elected state senator of Davidson County in the new (1796) state of Tennessee. It was a two-week trip to Knoxville, close to 400 miles round trip. In November of 1798 Thomas received word that his wife, Mary, had died. He resigned his seat and went home to his plantation. His youngest son, Bailey, was only three.[101]

Thomas Jefferson described Tennessee as: "Tinassee is a good field for a man of industry, integrity and talents; and it is a good country to lay out advantageously the profits of business." Thomas Hardeman, as described by his grandson Peter, was a "man with a very fine constitution, a determined will and a naturally fine intellect," up to the task.

Life was terribly hard on women in the frontier, however, and they often went for long periods without their husbands at home. The frontier phase of Tennessee, lasting from 1768 to 1828, required daily work and, even with the help of slaves, was backbreaking. Corn was a priority crop and used for making whiskey as well as eating. With access to a lot of firewood, given all the forests, it was more profitable to make whiskey than to transport large amounts of corn to sell. This was the start of the Kentucky and Tennessee bourbon whiskey business that is so famous today.

Hogs were an important part of Hardeman's agricultural business as well. Settlers needed to have a variety of livestock and crops, as each plantation had to be largely self-sufficient. Access to a source of salt was important for preservation of meat and vegetables. Thus, the areas near French Lick and other salt licks were settled first.

Thomas expanded into the ferry business, built a sawmill, and encouraged his sons' mercantile businesses. After his wife died, he stopped running for office but always stayed involved with the issues of the day. He improved his literacy to the point that he was able to write articulate and persuasive letters later in his life. He studied with his children, for whom he provided a good education. Two of his sons, Bailey and John, passed the bar; another son, Blackstone, was a physician.[102]

The year after his wife died, Thomas Hardeman married her widowed sister, Susannah Perkins, on October 13, 1799. He took his new wife to reside in Williamson County, Tennessee, in 1803 and purchased a 2,160-acre tract of land on the Big Harpeth River. His new home, called Sugar Hill, was just five miles southeast of the county seat of Franklin. He built a three-story log home; not only did he still have children at home, but Susannah had seven of her own. His grist mill and sawmill on the Big Harpeth ground grain and produced lumber, and his nearby still produced whiskey and ale.

The Louisiana Purchase of 1805 opened more land to speculation and development and provided a faster way for cotton farmers—cotton was becoming an important crop in Tennessee—to get their product down the Mississippi River to New Orleans. Thomas Hardeman and his sons expanded their landholding to Louisiana; many of his sons were as restless for new frontiers as he was.[103]

The War of 1812 was a western war as well, which is a surprise. When we think of the War of 1812, we think of the naval battles. Those in the trans-Appalachian frontier were concerned with the English and their allies of different Indian tribes that made their lives difficult. Americans wanted to push into Spanish Florida and expand north into English territory. The Creek War against the "Red Sticks" would become intertwined with the War of 1812. Many of the Creeks intermarried with white settlers and accepted the agricultural practices of the settlers. The "traditional Creeks," the Red Sticks, did not. After a visit from the great Shawnee chief Tecumseh—his mother was a Creek—they began an anti-white campaign. Tecumseh knew the only chance for Indian nations to survive was for them to combine forces. Unfortunately for the Creeks, they were wiped out by an army led by Andrew Jackson, losing more than 800 warriors at the Battle of Horseshoe Bend on March 27, 1814. The Creek War elevated Andrew Jackson to major general in the army from the Tennessee militia in which he served during the Creek War.

Three of Hardeman's sons fought with General Andrew Jackson in the war against the English. All had known the general since they were children. Lt. Peter Hardeman fought in the Forty-fourth Regiment under Brigadier General John Coffee. Younger brother Bailey, at age eighteen, was a 1st Lieutenant in Capt. Ora Cantrell's artillery company. Their brother, Capt. Thomas Jones Hardeman, and brother-in-law Glen Owen fought in the Battle of New Orleans under General Jackson. Kentuckians and Tennessee militiamen formed a good portion of the soldiers in "Old Hickory" Jackson's army. Sixty-four percent of those killed in the War of 1812 were Kentuckians. Along with those tough frontiersmen from Tennessee, the "Volunteer" state, they made the difference in the war.

Thomas Jones Hardeman was captured during the Battle of New Orleans and wounded in the head by a sabre after refusing to divulge military secrets to the enemy. After the battle, which was a crushing defeat for the English, he was released. Even though the battle took place in January 1815, two weeks after the Treaty of Ghent was signed but before the news hit home, the significance of the English loss changed the nation. The War of 1812 eliminated English and Spanish influence in the Southwest and broke the power of the southern tribes, sadly ending their way of life. Andrew Jackson's stunning victory at the Battle of New Orleans showed the world we were ready to take our place at the table as a powerful nation.[104]

After the war, trans-Mississippi settlement picked up considerably. Thomas Hardeman started to consolidate some of his business and land in Tennessee and sell off or give land to his children. When he was sixty-five, his second wife, Susannah Perkins, died. He no longer had children at home, and he began to have the urge to wander again. In 1816 he set out to explore Missouri. He headed to Boon's Lick, about 150 miles west of the busy Spanish- and French-influenced trading center of St. Louis on the Mississippi. Here were beautiful, lush woods full of wildlife like the Tennessee of old. He called it "Elk Heaven." He went back to Tennessee and gave his attorney son John control of his business affairs there.

Thomas Hardeman started a new life in Missouri. In 1820 he paid taxes on 1,200 acres on the Missouri River, four slaves, and three horses. It was much smaller than his Sugar Hill, but he no longer needed an expansive estate. Thomas was still a leader and his sons John and Bailey, his daughter and son-in-law George, and Dorothy Burnett, as well as another son-in-law, Glen Owen, and family, eventually followed him to Missouri.[105]

A new generation of Hardemans and Burnetts tried to make their mark in the world. Two sons, Nicholas Perkins Hardeman and Peter Hardeman, who stayed in Tennessee, died early deaths by 1820. The remaining sons and daughters continued to explore new frontiers in Texas, Louisiana, New Mexico, and the Far West.

Peter H. Burnett described his Hardeman cousins as very different from the Burnetts in that they were brash and worldly seekers of fortune but still men of excellent character.

He said they were honest and frank in their opinions. One of the sons of Thomas, John Hardeman, was not only an attorney but multi-talented. He became known for his spectacular formal gardens and fruitage farm in Missouri, which showed what was possible to build out of wilderness. It goes without saying that slave labor contributed to the wealth and success of the Hardemans.

John was involved in the early Santa Fe trade. Old Franklin, the county seat, was the center of expeditions to the West. John Hardeman unfortunately died of yellow fever in New Orleans during an epidemic there while on business involving his Santa Fe trade.[106]

His father's plantation was only five miles outside the town of Franklin, Missouri. Most of the Hardemans owned lots in town, as well as mercantile businesses. Traders such as Kit Carson and the Becknell brothers lived in Franklin. Bailey, the youngest son of Thomas, went with William Becknell, "The Father of the Santa Fe Trail," on the Meredith Miles Marmaduke expedition to New Mexico in 1824-25. They trapped beaver along the Colorado River north and west of Santa Cruz and Taos, and despite almost losing his life from starvation, Bailey made quite a sum of money. He went back to Williamson County, Tennessee, opened a tavern and a store, endowed Hardeman Academy at Hardeman's Cross Roads, and donated land to build Wilson's Creek Baptist Church. His brother Thomas Jones used his legal training to settle and organize Hardeman County in southwest Tennessee in 1818. The Hardemans had an astonishing variety of careers: fur trappers, land promoters, farmers, merchants, lawyers, physicians, politicians, and military men.[107]

In the 1820s and early '30s, Mexico encouraged American settlers in Texas. Four of the Hardeman siblings, Bailey, Thomas Jones, Blackstone, and Julia, and their families moved to Texas in 1835 in a group, just as the Holmans had done. They moved to Carrey Creek in Matagorda County and later spread across Central Texas to Bastrop, Travis, and Williamson counties, among others. Like the Holmans, they became involved in the War for Texas Independence.

Thomas and his four sons were active in the move for independence. Son Thomas Monroe fought in the Battle of San Jacinto, where 800 Texans smashed a Mexican army of 2,500 men and clinched the war for the Texans. Perhaps, Thomas Monroe Hardeman knew William Sanford Holman, who was in the battle as well.

The lives of the Holmans and the Hardemans would parallel for years on the frontiers of different states until the families were finally joined by the marriage of Martha Elizabeth Burnett and Daniel Saunders Holman in Oregon. Thomas Jones Hardeman served in the Congress of the Republic of Texas from Matagorda County in 1837-39 and two terms in the State Legislature from Travis and Bastrop counties, in addition to serving as a judge from Bastrop County. He was responsible for the suggestion to name the capital city Austin.

Thomas Jones' brother Bailey helped secure a cannon at Dimmitt's landing and haul it to San Antonio, which encouraged General Martin Perfecto de Cos to surrender. Bailey preferred to stay in the military but was tapped for government. He served on the General Council of the Provisional Government, helped draft the Texas Declaration of Independence, which he signed, and then worked on the constitution. After the Battle of San Jacinto decided the war, Bailey negotiated the treaties with Mexico that ended the war. He was elected as the first Secretary of the Treasury of Texas. He would have no doubt been an even larger influence on Texas if he had not died prematurely of a fever at his home in Matagorda on September 15, 1836. Hardeman County, Texas, is named after Bailey and his brother Thomas. Bailey and Thomas Jones Hardeman are buried in the Texas State Cemetery in Austin.[108]

Three of the sons of Thomas Jones—Thomas Monroe, Owen Bailey, and William W. "Gotch"—became some of the earliest Texas Rangers and were involved in fighting the Cherokee. Their uncle Owen, of the Santa Fe Trail fame, had been killed by Cherokee Indians. Their long rifles were of little use to them, as they had to fight while galloping on a horse, so they turned to the Colt six-shooter and, later, the Walker-Colt pistol. Later generations would become Texas cattlemen, driving cattle north on the Chisholm Trail.[109]

The 1830s were a time of change and the passing of the pioneer torch. The generation of men and women who had pushed from Virginia to the frontiers of Kentucky, Tennessee, and Missouri would be in their twilight hours. "Old Tom" Hardeman left Missouri at the age of 81 and rode on horseback to Tennessee by himself to live with a daughter until he died in 1833. Daniel L. Holman died in Fayetteville, Lincoln County, Tennessee, in October 1838. George Burnett died in 1838, followed by his wife, and they are buried on their farm in Clay County, Missouri. The patriarchs of the Perkins and the Rogers families, also old Tidewater Virginia families that the Hardemans and Burnetts married into, died in Missouri as well. Many of their offspring would end up in the Far West.[110]

There were many old Tidewater Virginia families in Missouri, including that of Samuel Clemens (Mark Twain). Samuel Clemens was born in 1835 and grew up in Hannibal, Missouri, on the Mississippi, in a time of steamboats and increased focus on the West. His family, caught in the tough financial times of the 1830s, was very poor. He would later write of the tremendous change in travel and trade along the Missouri and Mississippi rivers during the time of the steamboats.

The new generation of pioneers found new challenges in the chaos of the 1830s. It was a time of great land speculation, credit and cash crunches, and finally, a bank crisis, the Panic of 1837. The Panic had many root causes. The Second Bank of the United States was up for re-chartering in 1836. Andrew Jackson vetoed it because he did not believe in Federal Banks. In 1832 he took $10 million out of the Bank of the United States and gave it to state banks.

After a brief downturn, banks began lending a lot of money for land, businesses, and western expansion. They also began printing more money, leading to high inflation. Foreign bankers, especially, the English, began to loan large amounts of money to American businessmen, hoping to profit from the expansion of the U.S. In 1836 President Jackson issued the Specie Circular Act which stated the government would only accept gold or silver in payment for federal land. The English bankers called in their loans and squeezed the U.S. banks so hard that the whole economic system took a tremendous hit. Some 800 banks in the U.S. failed.

In times of economic uncertainties, new religious fervor springs up. Peter Hardeman Burnett, once a deist, would become a Campbellite and, much later in his life, a Roman Catholic. Manifest Destiny would become part of this religious fervor and add to the idea of a Christian nation spreading from sea to sea. The Burnett brothers would try to make their living in this uncertain time. Peter, at times partners with two of his brothers, tried the mercantile business several times and failed. His brothers Glen Owen and Thomas became ministers and, at the same time, farmed in a time when the price for farm products dropped by half. The Hardeman clan would fare better, having started with more capital.

Peter's uncles tried to help him out; nevertheless, Peter became indebted from business failures. He abandoned the mercantile business, studied the law, and became an attorney, as well as an editor of a weekly paper in Liberty, Missouri, called *The Far West*. He was a prolific writer and quite persuasive. He served as district attorney of Platte County for three years and became quite busy while very slowly paying back his large debts from failures in business.[111]

Missouri was changing rapidly. Although it came into the Union as a slave state, there was still animosity between those who held slaves and those who did not. The immigration of a large group of Mormons starting in 1831 only increased the tension. Joseph Smith, their prophet, decided that Independence in Jackson County, Missouri, would be their new "Zion." Within a couple of years, the Mormons were one third of the population. There were bitter fights and suspicion between the independent, backwoods frontiersmen and the Mormons, who acted and voted as a group. These two groups would not be able to live near each other peacefully, as they had opposite views of life. The Mormons were driven out of Jackson County to Caldwell County, but the trouble increased. The Mormons were rapidly growing in population and rapidly becoming more and more hated. Conflict increased to the point that the Governor of Missouri, Lilburn Boggs, issued the Mormon Extermination order on October 17, 1838.

Peter Burnett would find himself on both sides of this issue. He served in the militia against the Mormon army, called "*the Danites*," and later defended Joseph Smith in a trial.[112]

In what would be called "The Hungry Forties," life became more difficult in the Mississippi Valley. Heavy rains caused the Mississippi and Missouri rivers to overflow, flooding low-lying farms and woodlands in the Missouri bottoms. Mosquitoes were a tremendous problem with an increase in malaria and other diseases. Farm product prices bottomed out, while the aftereffects of the Panic of 1837 left cash in short supply. The idea of pushing west for new land began to grow.

Senator Linn of Missouri introduced legislation that would give free land to settlers in the West. Although it would not pass at this time, insuring that, with enough settlers, Oregon Country became American became an important idea. Peter Burnett began to think that going to Oregon was the answer to his problems. It would be a chance to pay off his debts, which would never be paid off at the rate he was going. It would be a chance for a new start on new land and, perhaps, improve the health of his wife. The patriotic idea of settling Oregon Country for the United States appealed as well. He threw himself into the process of organizing a wagon train to the West.

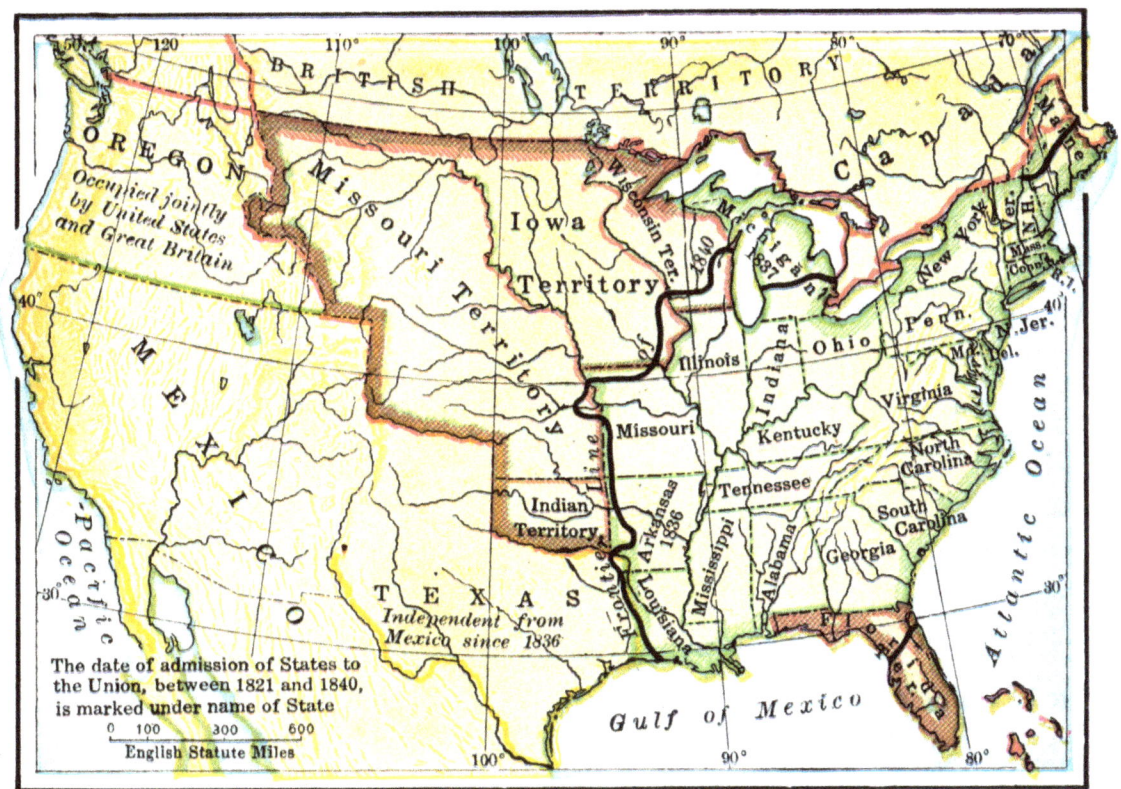

The United States in 1840, Forman, Advanced American History, NY, the Century Co. 1919, from Maps ETC, www.etc.usf.edu.amp

One man named Lennox, caught by the bug to go to Oregon Country, described the man who convinced him. A "rather striking-looking man" stepped up on a box in front of his store in 1842 and began to talk about the wonders of Oregon Country. Peter Burnett, with his folksy style, could always draw a crowd. With a twinkle in his eye, Peter said, "Out in Oregon the pigs are running about under the great acorn trees, round and fat, and already cooked, with knives and forks sticking in them so that you can cut off a slice whenever you are hungry."

The excitement began to build about a new frontier in the Far West. Many signed up to be part of this first large wagon train to Oregon. Peter convinced many Missourians, his own family, and two of the Holmans, who signed up as well.[113]

They started this great leap of faith in May of 1843, a few miles from Independence, Missouri, travelling across an unknown 2,000 miles to a new frontier. It took great courage to set foot on the trail and persevere through six months of danger and hardship. Patricia Turner Shawver, in her memoir of her mother, Ella Holman Turner, stated that her mother did not seem to be afraid of anything. Courage had been bred into her for generations.

Chapter Three

Education

Family Cast of Characters

Winifred Beatrice Turner…(1890-1956) *mother of Daniel B. Adlum*
Mary Ellen "Ella" Holman…(1856-1928) *mother of Winifred Turner; grandmother of Daniel B. Adlum*
William Burke Turner…(1860-1924) *father of Winifred; grandfather of Daniel B. Adlum*

James H. Turner…(1812-1895) *father of William; great-grandfather of Daniel B. Adlum*
Esther Ann Johnson…(1825-1910) *married to James H. Turner; great-grandmother of Daniel B. Adlum*

Gurdon Collins Johnson…(1786-1865) *father of Esther Ann; second-great-grandfather of Daniel B. Adlum*
Louisa Lee…(1787-1870) *mother of Esther Ann; second-great-grandmother of Daniel B. Adlum*

Gurdon Collins Johnson Sr.…(1759-1813) *third-great-grandfather of Daniel B. Adlum*
Esther Brainerd…(1757-1819) *third-great-grandmother of Daniel B. Adlum*

Samuel Johnson…(1727-1808) *father of Gurdon Collins Sr.; fourth-great-grandfather of Daniel B. Adlum*
Rev. Samuel Johnson…(1696-1772) *sixth-great-uncle of Daniel B. Adlum*
William Samuel Johnson…(1727-1819) *first cousin, 6 times removed, of Daniel B. Adlum*

Deacon Samuel Lee…(1754-1813) *father of Louisa Lee; third-great-grandfather of Daniel B. Adlum*
Mary Bingham…(1752-1791) *wife of Samuel Lee; third-great-grandmother of Daniel B. Adlum*

Jabez Bingham…(1724-1784) *father of Mary Bingham; fourth-great-grandfather of Daniel B. Adlum*
Mary Standish Wheelock…(1728-1809) *wife of Jabez Bingham; fourth-great-grandmother of Daniel B. Adlum*

Ralph Wheelock…(1682-1748) *father of Mary Standish*
Mercy Standish…(1685-1748) *wife of Ralph Wheelock; granddaughter of Capt. Myles Standish*

Rev. Ralph Wheelock Sr.…(1600-1684) *seventh-great-grandfather of Daniel B. Adlum*

The Turner, Johnson and Lee Families

"Learning is not attained by chance, it must be sought for with ardor and diligence."

~Abigail Adams

Winifred Turner not only inherited her mother's courage but also her love of music. When her parents' marriage broke up in 1910, and her mother, Ella, and younger sister, Patricia, moved to McMinnville, Oregon, to live with her grandmother Martha, she went with them and studied voice at the college there. This would be the same Linfield College where her great-granddaughter Kate Schmidt would come from Texas to major in English more than one hundred years later. Winifred didn't stay long in McMinnville. She moved to Portland for a job, and by June 1911 she was married to Henry Bruce Adlum.

The marriage of her parents had been a long-distance relationship for years because of her father's job in Washington, DC. The marriage had started well enough. Ella Holman, the charming daughter of one of the wealthy farmers in the area, was considered the belle of the town. William Burke Turner, whose family had been in Oregon only a couple of years when they met, had a distinguished and well-educated family background. Ella's father, William, and his brother Horatio were druggists at the Rogers Pharmacy in McMinnville, one of the first pharmacies in Oregon. The family of William's mother, Esther Ann Johnson (the Lees), had a long tradition of studying medicine and had many physicians in their family history.[114]

The field of pharmacy was just beginning to form in the last half of the nineteenth century. Before that, patent medicines were hawked by anyone who could get someone to believe the claims of whatever cure-all they were selling. Some of the drugs used in this timeframe were salicylic acid—made from willow bark (forerunner of aspirin)—quinine, and digitalis for heart disease. Opium derivatives as well as cocaine had been in use a long time, were unregulated, and often part of patent medicines.

In the late nineteenth century, an attempt to control these drugs and make a set formula mixed by pharmacists was the start of the realization that these drugs were addictive. It was common for the druggists, as they were called, to mix the formulas themselves in the back of drugstores, using prescriptions written in Latin.

William Turner found the chemistry of compounding medicines interesting, but over time he grew restless with the confinement of mixing chemicals and compounding drugs, thinking it was bad for his health. He tried his hand at farming. Times were hard in the early 1890s, and it was difficult to make a living farming. The family moved to the Los Angeles area in Southern California, near Ida Turner Narver, one of William's sisters. They stayed several years while he worked as a pharmacist again.[115]

Los Angeles had a tremendous land boom in the 1880s. Promoters described it as an ideal place to live, with pure air and civilized living. The ensuing enthusiasm resulted in as many as 1,700 new subdivisions planned in Los Angeles County during 1886-88, with a rapid increase in population. It was hyped as a healthy place for those with illness, especially tuberculosis.

Tuberculosis, formerly called consumption because it seemed to consume the body with severe wasting and painful bloody coughing, had killed one in seven people who had ever lived by the nineteenth century. By the 1890s awareness that Tb was a communicable disease led to promotion of not only sanitariums for patients but also the suggestion that climate change and wide-open spaces would help sufferers. The German scientist Dr. Robert Koch discovered the mycobacterium tuberculosis bacteria in 1884. His work earned him the Nobel Prize in 1905, but there was no cure available until antibiotic development in the 1940s.

Sick people headed west if they could. With so many ill people coming from the East, there was a need for pharmacists. Winifred's baby sister, Patricia, was born while the family lived in Los Angeles. The Turner family had four daughters in all: Pauline, Mildred, Winifred, and Patricia.[116]

William B. Turner was a distinguished, aristocratic-looking man. From his voter's registration information in Los Angeles in 1896, he is described as 5 feet, 10 inches tall, slender build, with light brown hair and blue eyes. A photograph of him in 1908 shows a good-looking man immaculately dressed. His career break came when a friend of the Holman family, Senator McBride of Oregon, asked him to be his aide in Washington, DC.

William went on to become the clerk of the senate, a position he held for a number of years. William was proud to be part of government in the tradition of his father, James Higgins Turner, who had been a state representative in Indiana, among other government positions. William moved to Washington, DC., while his wife and four girls eventually moved from California to

William Burke Turner, 1908, Washington D.C. (grandfather of Daniel B. Adlum) from Shawver, Portrait of Mama

Portland to establish Oregon residency. Ella and her girls settled near the Turner family in Portland, William's mother, Esther Ann Johnson, and his brother's and sister's families. William came home to Portland for summer break most of the time at first, but his life and thoughts were in Washington, DC.[117]

Portland in the early 1900s was an interesting place to live. In the second half of the nineteenth century, Portland emerged as the major northwest port, far surpassing Oregon City because of its location at the convergence of the Columbia and Willamette Rivers and the fact that deep-draft vessels could dock there. The port was busy shipping lumber, fish, wheat, and produce, while travel by rail was enhanced by the impressive new train station, Union Depot, built in 1893-4. There was constant building in a town that went from 800 people in 1850 to 90,000 by the close of the century.[118]

Starting in the 1890s, Seattle began competing with Portland as a port. Seattle grew because of the Alaska Gold Rush and railroads finally being built through to Seattle from Portland; the competition made Portland promote their city.

Portland began planning the 1905 World's Fair and Lewis and Clark Exposition that drew thousands of visitors. The house of Ella Holman and her daughters was filled with visitors. Family and friends who came to Portland for the World's Fair gave Ella a great deal of extra cooking and housework to do. Portland boosters beautified the city with roses and advertised it as the Rose City, increasing the population even more. A cable car system with 150 cars, the third largest in the world at the time, was built to get people around town, including a unique trolley that went up to the neighborhood of Portland Heights, which overlooked the city.[119]

Antique postcard of cable car running to Portland Heights, Portland, Oregon, early twentieth century, courtesy Portland Archives

Winifred's sister Patricia described their house in Portland Heights.

Our Portland Heights house was a very nice one. It still stands, a fine Victorian place with a large, landscaped, terraced lawn terminating in a street that went steeply to downtown Portland, about where Jefferson Street is. There was a unique cable car line like the famous one that San Francisco boasts. Our large lawn was kept beautifully by Chinese help. I remember so well our lovely roses! And the colored panes of glass around the windows. The house must have been very up to date for 1899: three floors and electric lights and a telephone.

The Turner girls were well loved by their cheerful mother, Ella, who would wake them up by playing the piano and make games out of cooking with them. In the Victorian era, ladies were always properly dressed. Their mother loved hats and considered white kid gloves an essential part of a ladies' wardrobe. Ella always insisted on good manners and setting a full, proper table, complete with snowy-white linen napkins with napkin rings. She cooked every day and even had tea after school with freshly baked bread or cookies and tea served in dainty, china cups. The house was full of music and fun. With many relatives nearby, they had a full social life, but checks from Washington were slow to come and money was tight.[120]

In 1903 the family moved to Washington, DC, to live for a year. The girls were happy to spend some time with their father, but it was obvious relations between their parents were strained. Their father was living with a distant female cousin, widowed, with three girls. It was a large, three-story house in the Petworth suburb—along Brightwood Ave. NW, now Georgia Ave. NW—just three miles from the White House. There were grand, tall ceilings and fireplaces in almost every room: in the library, the reception hall, the dining room, living room, and many of the bedrooms. Some of the bedrooms had tile fireplaces with coal grates, mostly for show, as the house had steam heat throughout. There was room for all, but their father maintained a separate bedroom. Their mother, as well as her girls, felt a sense of uneasiness being there in what appeared to be "the other woman's" household.

Washington, DC, which had been the nation's capital for one hundred years, still had growing pains, with almost a thirty percent growth in population between 1890 and 1900. During Theodore Roosevelt's administration, there was a push to beautify the city and finish the master plan of the cities' brilliant designer and architect, Pierre Charles L' Enfant. The McMillian Plan of 1901, named after Senator James McMillian, established the National Mall at the core of the city. The City Beautiful Movement Commission in 1902, with Frederick Law Olmsted Jr. among the members, drew up a park and parkway plan for the DC. area. The plan drew from the Metropolitan Park System of Greater Boston, which had been designed by Olmsted. The beautiful parkways were designed for carriage riding and were connected to the park system. Rock Creek Park, the first major urban park, was just a couple of miles from where Winifred and her sisters lived. She did not know at the time that her future husband's family, the Adlums, had owned land that had been integrated into the park where she walked.

The girls enjoyed seeing much of the capital city. The city had some electric streetcars, even one to Petworth. They went to President Lincoln's cottage at the Soldier's Home, where there was a beautiful view of the city. The Home was not too far from the church they attended, St. Paul's Episcopal Church, located on Rock Creek Church Road. On Sundays they rode a little streetcar line to get there.

William Turner's family was Episcopalian, and his girls were raised in their father's church. Their mother, Ella, found it too formal and preferred her own church, but she attended as well. William got tickets for them to see children's plays and took them sightseeing. On Easter Monday they rolled Easter eggs on the White House lawn and even saw President Roosevelt and his daughter Alice occasionally ride by their house on horseback. The girls were thrilled to see their mother dressed in a "ball gown of wool and silk trimmed with panels of tiny tucks and rich creamy lace and a stylish train" and their father in top hat and tails as they left in a carriage to attend a White House ball.[121]

When they went back to Portland the following year, checks from their father were often late, despite his salary being more than double that of the average white-collar worker at the time. Winifred's mother, Ella, decided to move them to McMinnville to a rented house owned by her brother. In 1910 William lost his position in DC due to a change in the political climate. It was announced in *The Oregonian* newspaper. Their father never came home again after that.

The year of 1910 was a fateful one for the family. William's mother, Esther Ann, died in Portland. Ella's father, Daniel S. Holman, living in McMinnville, also died that year. Daniel, being concerned for his daughter's welfare and that of his granddaughters, provided for them in his will. Ella and her younger daughters moved in with her mother, Martha, to take care of her. William B. Turner moved from DC to California and died in 1924 in Sacramento. A few months before William died, he sent a letter to his daughter Patricia, with a note enclosed for her mother, regretting the way he had treated her and their family. Winifred's and Patricia's mother, Ella, never said a word about her situation or complained in any way to any of her four girls but just tried to stay cheerful for them. After suffering a major stroke at age sixty, Ella had another stroke, this one fatal. In 1928 Ella Holman died in the home of her daughter Patricia, surrounded by her four beloved daughters as they sang to her for the last time.[122]

Winifred Turner Adlum and her sisters were all married with young children during their mother's last years. Winifred frequently moved up and down the West Coast during this time. She was living in Los Angeles in 1920 when women finally received the right to vote, and she proudly registered to vote there. She was still in Los Angeles in the early 1920s when her son, Daniel, was born.

She was an outgoing person who shared her love of music and would frequently sing the songs of her mother, sad old English folk songs such as "Sweet Belle Mahone" and "I'd Offer Thee This Hand of Mine." Her favorite was "Danny Boy," with her beloved son being named Daniel. She maintained contact with her father's family, the Turners, in Portland. Winifred's own husband abandoned her when she was forty-five, repeating her mother's experience. Ten years later, at age fifty-five, she married her cousin Roy G. Turner, the son of her father's brother Horatio. She explained that, still feeling badly that her son, Daniel, had no home as a teenager, she got married so that he would have a home to come to after serving in the war. Winifred lived long enough to see her daughter, Helen, married, her son married and successful, and to see her first two grandchildren. At age sixty-five, she died of a stroke, as had her mother.[123]

Winifred Beatrice Turner as a teenager, Portland, Oregon c.1906 (Daniel B. Adlum's mother) author's collection

Winifred Beatrice Turner (Adlum) with her firstborn, Helen Lee Adlum, 1913, Portland, Oregon, author's collection

Winifred's grandmother on her father's side was Esther Ann Johnson, a strong woman who had her own share of heartaches through the years. She and her husband, James H. Turner, did not make it to Oregon until 1878, although they had been thinking about going west since the 1850s when three of Esther's siblings headed to Oregon. They brought their entire family, fifteen in all, including son David, married son Grant and family, daughter Kate and her husband and baby, Ida, Nell, Jimmy, sons Will and Horatio, and younger sisters Ann and Clarissa. Esther Ann was fifty-three and her husband sixty-five as they started on this new adventure. Since the transcontinental railroad had been completed in May 1869, they had an easier trip than previous pioneers. They were able to take the train all the way from Indianapolis to San Francisco and then a steamer up to Portland. They then took a train to St. Joe's, a tiny community in Yamhill County, and finally, a stagecoach the remaining four miles to McMinnville, as the rail line to McMinnville was not finished yet.

Esther Ann Johnson, (brooch worn by her husband James H. Turner) great grandmother of Daniel B. Adlum, curtesy Elizabeth L. Smith

James H. Turner, State Representative, Marion, Indiana, "Biographical Sketches of Members of the 41st General Assembly of Indiana, 1861" from Turner, All the Days of her life, Esther Ann, courtesy Elizabeth L. Smith

Esther Ann hoped it would be the last move she would make. She was born in Dryden, New York, and moved to Ohio as a young child with her parents as they sought education for their children at the new "Episcopal College in the Wilderness," Kenyon College. She continued to move frequently as circumstances changed in her life. By 1878 she did not have much holding her in the East. Her parents, Gurdon Collins Johnson and Louisa Lee, had died, and her husband, James, was ready to leave Indiana and start again.[124]

Esther Ann and James had a full and busy life in Indianapolis. Esther Ann had eight children of her own, seven with James and two stepsons, so she had her hands full, especially, since her husband's business frequently took him out of town.

James Turner, trained as a carpenter, was in the milling business in Indiana. He also took government positions, serving as postmaster and a representative from Marion County to the Indiana State Legislature in 1861, just before the start of the Civil War. By 1862 James was in the Union Army as a major in the Commissary Department. He was a friend of Governor Morton of Indiana, who asked him to take care of Indiana's sick and wounded soldiers. James was commissioned by the state to do so.[125]

Gurdon Collins Johnson (1786-1864) from Turner, All the Days of Her Life, Esther Ann, courtesy Elizabeth L. Smith

Louisa Lee (1787-1870 wife of Gurdon Collins Johnson, from Turner, All the Years of Her Life, Esther Ann, courtesy Elizabeth L. Smith

Taking care of sick and wounded soldiers was a major problem in the Civil War. Before the war there were very few hospitals, and those were mostly used for sufferers of pestilence, who needed to be kept separate from the general population. Doctors were trained by apprenticeship, and there were only one hundred of them in the army at the start of the war; nurses (mostly men) at that time were not trained at all. The vast number of sick and wounded in battle overwhelmed the few hospitals. The challenge was to find places to serve as permanent hospitals, as well as field hospitals, and to supply them. The Union Government started the U.S. Sanitary Commission to monitor hospitals and collect and distribute supplies. The state of Indiana had its own State Sanitary Commission to deal with their wounded soldiers. There was a call for doctors and nurses. Some 10,000 heroic

Union women answered the call, some of them now famous for their service, such as Clara Barton, Dorothea Dix, and Mary Bickerdyke. Southern women answered the call as well.

Poor diet, lack of sanitation, and contaminated water, combined with lack of antibiotics or knowledge of how disease spread, led to widespread disease in the camps. The new bullets being used caused terrible, gaping wounds which posed additional challenges for surgeons and nurses. Too often the answer was amputation of an arm or leg if hit by a Minnie ball. According to Union records, there were about 29,980 amputations during the Civil War. There was such a large death toll—as many as twenty-five percent did not come home—and so many wounded that James was kept very busy. At times he was pressed into service to help surgeons in the field. At the 1862 Battle of Shiloh, fought in nearby Tennessee, the number of casualties was 23,000; it was one of the bloodiest battles of the Civil War. There were so many wounded soldiers that the surgeons and nurses could not keep up with treating them.

Lookout Mountain, Georgia (along the Tennessee state line) November 1863, L-R, Major James H. Turner, General Lew Wallace, Colonel Benjamin Harrison, General Paul J.A. Slocum, from Turner, All the Days of Her Life, Esther Ann, courtesy Elizabeth L. Smith

James' knowledge of surgery was helpful when he was given a set of instruments for surgery. He skillfully assisted when amputations were necessary. Esther Ann and other women in the city assisted the cause by knitting socks, rolling bandages, and making preserved foods for the soldiers in the field, who were grateful to get a break from eating dry hardtack. The preserved foods were important because scurvy was a problem due to lack of fruits and vegetables. The women of Indianapolis also rolled lint—a precursor to cotton balls—scraping it from worn cotton cloth for use in wound care.[126]

Although no battles were fought there, Indianapolis was heavily involved in the Civil War. Governor Oliver P. Morton, who was a major supporter of President Lincoln, turned Indianapolis into a gathering place for volunteer soldiers, and the city became an important railroad and transportation center for the Union cause. It was also an important stop for fleeing slaves on the Underground Railroad. There were twenty-four military camps established around the city, with some 4,000 men from Marion County—Indianapolis and surrounds—serving in the war.

Indianapolis had a small population of 20,000, yet they gave $1 million dollars to the cause, as well as supplies, clothing, and food, in a time of rising prices and personal hardship. Food and cloth became especially expensive, as the South was no longer able to grow cotton and the mills in the North and in England were closed; the cheapest cotton became unaffordable and thread was thirty cents a spool.[127]

Esther Ann found comfort in these hard times by reading the stories and poems of her childhood to her children. The books she read as a child, such as *The Fortunes of Nicholas Nickleby*, and poems such as "The Lady of the Lake," were enjoyed by her children. The families' love of education and books sustained them, as it had in the past. James and Esther Ann's marriage was one of good fortune and chance during a previous dark period in both their lives. Esther Ann's first marriage to Peter Koontz in 1850, brightened by the birth of their daughter Kate in 1851, ended in sorrow when her husband died of typhoid fever a few months later. Esther Ann faced an uncertain future.[128]

Esther Ann's income was insufficient after Peter died, so she decided to take a job teaching near family in Ohio. She was traveling on a canal boat back to Granville, Ohio, with her parents and her baby girl when a kindly stranger, James Turner, helped her with the baby. Although the manners of the time would not allow introductions to women by a strange man, James was able to get her father's name and track her down that way. He was a man with his own tragedy. His wife, Margaret McGregor, had died in 1850, leaving him with five- and three-year-old sons. He wrote to Esther Ann and asked for permission to court her, leaving information about character witnesses in Cincinnati and Fairfield, Iowa, where he had lived, so she would know what type of man he was. He won her with an articulate, beautifully written letter of June 22, 1852, asking for her hand in marriage.

Esther Ann Johnson and James Turner were married in Granville, Ohio, by Esther's brother-in-law Rev. William French on September 16, 1852. They started the marriage with three young children and the business affairs of Esther Ann, James, and their parents to tend to. James left soon after on a business trip, taking a boat on one of the many canals in Ohio in October 1852. He wrote to her about the journey:

Dear Ann,
We are lying in the Canal, in consequence of a breakage in one of the locks; as usual there is much dissatisfaction among the passengers, some talking and complaining of the captain. One supposes from the expressions, that the officers of the boat could lift over an embankment, thirty feet high… One Irishmen stole the bundle of another this morning

after a restless night on the boat…It will give you a faint idea of the manner in which we get along in a crowded boat, in a mass as varied in character as name,-Dutch, Irish, English, and native born; speculators, gamblers, actors, and actresses, all grades and all classes of society from the true gentleman and lady to the veriest sensualist that disgraces society by its presence; but such characters one will always meet with in a mixed mass of travelers; some on business, others for pleasure, and a few without any object but to prey on the others… I pray that God may have you in his Holy keeping together with our dear children, and that he will grant me a safe return. Then I hope it will never be necessary for me to leave you for so long a period. Kiss the babies for me.
Ever yours affectionately
J.H.T.[129]

The river canals in Ohio and Indiana were a major method of travel between the 1830s and 1860s before the railroads took off in the 1860s. They were the interstate highways of their age. It took a tremendous amount of ingenuity, hard work, and money to build the canals. The state of New York spent over $7 million to build the Erie Canal.

Before the Erie Canal was finished in 1825, Ohio could see the need to develop their own canals to more easily move goods and people. The Ohio and Erie Canal project was

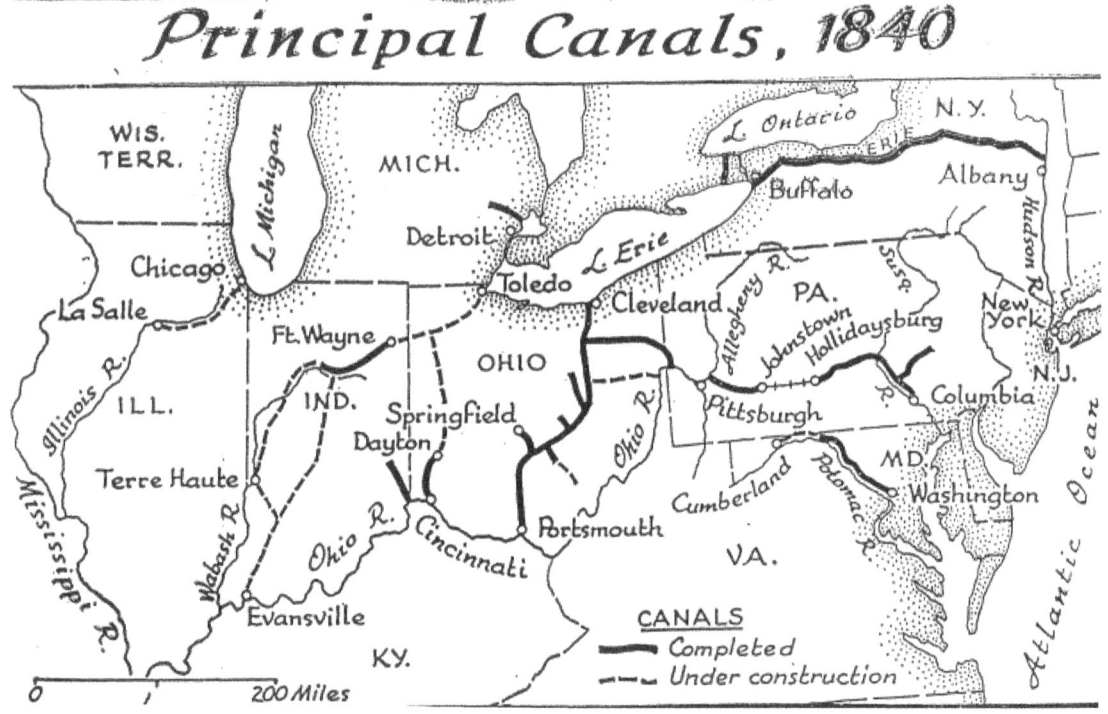

Principal Canals of 1840, public domain, accessed from www.4.bp.blogspot.com

started, and by 1827 the first section from Cleveland to Akron was open. It cost about $10,000 a mile to build and rapidly changed the character and expansion of the state by allowing farmers to get their goods to large markets less expensively. It was called "The Ditch That Brought the World to the Wilderness."

By 1832 the state had 308 miles of canal open—with 146 locks necessary for the changes in elevation—as well as smaller feeder canals. Irish and German immigrants did a lot of the work of digging the canals and often got sick from the stagnant water. Cholera became a major public health problem in a series of epidemics in the 1840s. The canals were a portal for people carrying the disease, as the contaminated water spread the disease among canal workers and then the general population.

As James described, being a passenger on the very crowded canal boats was quite an experience. Usually, the large passenger boats had a separate cabin for men and women, with berths stacked high, but not all paid for a berth. The boats were pulled by ropes attached to two or three horses or mules, with a mule skinner directing them along the canal. Large boats could not pass but had to wait for each other, as well as wait to pass through the locks. When a lock malfunctioned, it caused great delay.

Twenty-plus years earlier, Esther Ann's parents, Gurdon Collins Johnson and Louisa Lee, had used the newly built Erie Canal to move their family to Ohio from New York. Gurdon Collins and Louisa had built a pleasant life for themselves and their children on their farm in Dryden, New York. Dryden was a small farming community twelve miles from Ithaca in the central Finger Lake district of New York. Dryden was part of the Central New York Military Tract, where land was given to soldiers who fought in the American Revolution as compensation for their service. Raising sheep and milling lumber (pine) were major industries at the time in Dryden.

Gurdon Collins and Louisa had eight living children; they had lost three at birth or shortly after. As their children grew older, Gurdon and Louisa began to realize they would not have the educational opportunities they wanted for them in that small village. Samuel Lee Johnson, their eldest, named after Louisa's brother Dr. Samuel Lee, was a very serious student, as were his younger brothers and sisters. Dr. Lee hoped Samuel would follow him into medicine, but his nephew chose the ministry as many of his Johnson ancestors had done. A visit from his Uncle Samuel, who lived in Coshocton, Ohio, gave him the idea of going west to a new college—Kenyon College—an Anglican school being built by Bishop Chase of Ohio. His mother, Louisa, being rather frail, wanted to be closer to her physician brother as well. The family sold the farm and set out.[130]

The finished Erie Canal was not too far from their home in Dryden; it began a little more than fifty miles from them. The canal started north of Syracuse at the east shore of Oneida Lake where the Hudson River met the canal. In 1830 they may have taken a stage the twelve miles to Ithaca, which sat at the lower edge of Lake Cayuga, one of the Finger Lakes, and then taken a boat up the lake and then the river to the canal. They travelled on the Erie Canal to Buffalo, New York, where they changed to a larger boat that took them across Lake Erie. When they arrived in Cleveland, Ohio, the family changed to a smaller canal boat to Dover/New Philadelphia, Ohio, where they then took a stagecoach to Coshocton, where Dr. Samuel Lee and his family lived. It took them seventeen days to travel 300 miles. Some treasured belongings were lost, but they were ever so glad to arrive safely and have family to stay with.

When the Johnson family arrived in Ohio in 1830, the frontier stage was over. Almost all of the Americans who immigrated to Ohio did so prior to mid-nineteenth century. In 1800, Ohio was sparsely populated, with one white settler per square mile. By 1820, Cincinnati had developed as a great capitalist and manufacturing center, but most Ohioans lived in small towns of one hundred or less people or on farms. By 1825 the population of Ohio grew to 800,000; it was the fourth-most-populous state in the nation. Although the roads were still poor, the National Road, which went from Maryland to Ohio, as well as the new, expanding canal system, were continually being worked on and improved

The Northwest Territory, which included Ohio, had been fiercely fought over for centuries. Not only did the many native Indian tribes fight each other for control of the land, but the French, English, and then the Americans aligned with various tribes to fight each other as well. The Iroquois Confederacy of Five Nations—the Cayuga, Mohawk, Oneida, Onondaga, and Seneca—and later, a sixth tribe, the Tuscarora, was the most powerful organization of tribes in what is now present-day New York. The French traders traditionally sided with the Wyandot (Huron), in the Ohio Territory, while the Dutch sided with the Iroquois Nations. The Dutch sold the Iroquois superior weapons that allowed them to almost completely wipe out the Wyandot and other native tribes to their west in Ohio Country in the bloody Beaver Wars that began in the 1640s. The tribes fled and mostly abandoned the Northwest Territory.

During the seventeenth and eighteenth centuries, with the Dutch out of the picture, both France and England claimed Ohio Country. They faced fierce opposition from the tribes that had migrated to and repopulated the area—the Delaware (Lenape), Shawnee, Mingo, and Wyandot. England tried to close the Northwest Territory to settlers with the Royal Proclamation of 1763 in an effort to make peace with the tribes west of the Appalachians. At the time of the Revolution, four of the Iroquois tribes sided with the English. Under the Treaty of Paris of 1783 that ended the Revolutionary War, England nominally withdrew from the Northwest Territory. Many native Indian tribes still lived in the area and were hostile to the idea, having not been part of the treaty. The English gave weapons to the native tribes, bought American scalps from them, and maintained some of their forts, hoping the tribes would hold the border of the United States and prevent the expansion of American settlers into the area.

The continued push west by Americans, many with land grants in the Ohio Valley, awarded for their service in the Revolutionary War, created conflict with the tribes that claimed the area. There were frequent conflicts between tribes and between tribes and settlers. The Shawnee and the Chickamauga, a faction of the Cherokee, had started war against the settlers in 1776. The Chickamauga Wars merged into the Northwest Indian Wars—also called the Ohio Indian or Border Wars—of 1785-1793. The Treaty of Granville in 1785 forced the tribes to give up much of the present-day land of Ohio. The Battle of Fallen Timbers in 1794, with General Anthony Wayne leading the Americans, was a decisive victory after many previous losses to the Native tribes. There was still unrest through the War of 1812 and beyond, but by 1830 most conflict was a thing of the past. The Wyandot were the last to go, a sad remnant of the great tribe they once were as they headed west to reservation land.[131]

Louisa's brother Dr. Samuel Lee was one of the large group of settlers who settled in Ohio Country. By the time Esther Ann's mother Louisa and her family arrived, Ohio was calm. Louisa's husband found a farm to buy in the village of Keene, just six miles from Louisa's brother in Coshocton. The small village had an adequate school for the young children. Gambier, where the Episcopal Bishop of Ohio, Philander Chase, established Kenyon College in 1824, was thirty-two miles away. Their eldest, Samuel Lee Johnson, was eager to attend but decided to teach for a year, giving him additional time to study for the challenging entrance exams. Samuel and Esther Ann's father, Gurdon Collins Johnson, became a lay reader at the Episcopal mission at Mill Creek, which was five miles north of the farm. Every Sunday he would take the farm wagon to the mission to read to the congregation.

The family was happy and busy on the farm, and all hands were needed for all the chores. Esther Ann and younger brother Horatio would feed the sheep. Her older brothers would help their father in the fields, and the girls would help with the livestock, sheep, cows, hogs, and chickens. The smokehouse was put to use in the fall, smoking hams, while fruits were peeled and dried, and butters and preserves were mixed. Over time the family's life revolved more around the college and education as the children grew up.[132]

Gurdon Collins Johnson decided to sell the farm and move the family to Gambier. His eldest, Samuel, was offered a job as tutor at Kenyon when he graduated from the college and went on to the seminary, so he would be in Gambier for a number of years. Gurdon bought a large lot close to the college campus. They rented while he had a house built. There were a wide variety of ages in his family; Samuel Lee, his oldest son, was seventeen years older than his youngest child. Gurdon Brainerd, his second son, was born in 1814, followed by sister Clarissa (Clara) in 1816 and Mary Cordelia in 1820. Horatio Van V., born in 1823, was followed by Esther Ann, born in 1825. Esther Ann had two younger brothers, Hiram Sobieski, born in 1827, and William Vittz, the youngest child, born in 1829. Gurdon felt it was important for his children to be around the intellectual atmosphere of the nearby college and Episcopal church.

Gurdon and Louisa decided to make their living taking in college boarders but found that providing room and board for hungry college students was a tough way to make money. Esther Ann and her siblings were surrounded by the intellectual atmosphere and got to know many of the students, including a future President, Rutherford B. Hayes. Ohio, called the "mother of presidents," sent eight native sons to the White House. Hayes was one of a group that included William Henry Harrison, Ulysses S. Grant, Warren B. Harding, James A. Garfield, Benjamin Harrison, William McKinley and William Howard Taft. Hayes was known for playing his flute beautifully in the mornings while he was a student at Kenyon. Esther Ann enjoyed listening to the "First Morning Hymn" in the fall of 1838, which Hayes played almost every morning.

When Ann was seventeen, she was still in public school but taking Latin and mathematics from one of the college professors. Her parents sent her to the Granville Female Seminary, where both her older sisters, Clara and Mary were then teaching. Her brother Horatio decided to study medicine with one of the local physicians, Dr. Thrall. Esther Ann's mother, Louisa, was frail and sometimes in bed for weeks, which added to Esther's responsibilities, as she was left to care for the family.

Gurdon Collins and Louisa realized it would be hard to keep their family together as they grew up and started their own lives.[133] Reverend Samuel Lee Johnson, the oldest son of Gurdon and Louisa, received a call from Indianapolis to become the rector of Christ Church, the Episcopal church in Indianapolis. It took three days by horseback on muddy roads to reach Indianapolis. He accepted the position and also became the head of the new boarding and day school they were building called St. Mary's. Samuel married the same year and took his bride to Indianapolis.

His younger brother Gurdon was married and settled in Granville, Ohio. Esther Ann's sister Mary married Rev. William French, whom she had met while he was a student at Kenyon, and they moved to Indianapolis. Brother Horatio went to Indianapolis for a position in medicine, resulting in several of the Johnson siblings moving to Indianapolis together.

In the 1840s the settlement of Indianapolis was about twenty years old, with a population of about 6,000 and very few streets, many filled with stumps left by the hurried clearing of trees. Founded in 1820, the original site of the city was the former home of the Lenape (Delaware) tribe, who lived along the White River. Indianapolis was laid out in a square of one mile on the banks of the White River at the mouth of Fall Creek. It became the county seat of Marion County and eventually, in 1825, the state capital of Indiana. By 1847 the railroads reached the city, as well as a hub of roads connecting the city to other towns. Although the area had fertile farmland, many low-lying areas near the river were subject to flooding, creating a set-up for water-borne illnesses due to poor drainage and sanitation. In the 1820s malaria from mosquitoes, influenza, cholera, and smallpox were already causing public health problems. The government set up an Indiana Central Medical Society in 1823 and a board of public health in 1831 to deal with these health issues.

A series of epidemics caused great sorrow in the 1840s, not only for Indiana and Ohio but for those travelling west as well. Indianapolis had a severe outbreak of scarlet fever in the winter of '46. Esther Ann was now living in Indianapolis. Her brother Samuel had written to her asking her to assist him in teaching at St. Mary's. The scarlet fever spread through the school, and Esther Ann helped nurse the patients, students and teachers alike. There were no antibiotics or knowledge that the disease was contagious. Esther Ann became very ill, as did many others, but she recovered, with her brother Horatio attending her. Esther Ann's sister Mary moved back to Granville, Ohio, with her husband, William French, when he took a position in the church there.

In 1848 Samuel became busier and busier at Christ Church, and he asked his sister Clara to take over for him as principal at St. Mary's, with Esther Ann as an assistant. It was a time of illness for the family. Esther's brother Vittz, never strong, came down with tuberculosis in Granville, and a severe outbreak of typhoid hit Indianapolis. Esther Ann's older brother Rev. Samuel Lee Johnson, beloved by his parishioners and his family, succumbed to typhoid on Christmas Eve 1848. They called for his uncle Dr. Samuel Lee to come from Coshocton, Ohio, but it was too late.[134]

In the spring of 1849, there was a religious awakening in Indianapolis, no doubt from all the death and sorrow caused by the epidemics. Churches started holding daily services. Not only had typhoid hit, but they were in the midst of a severe cholera outbreak that spring that hit Indiana, Ohio, and other states. Typhoid fever and cholera were just two of the bacterially caused diseases that were responsible for several pandemics in the nineteenth century.

Typhoid fever, caused by Salmonella typhi, is spread though fecal-contaminated food or water or direct contact with an ill individual. Symptoms include high fever, rash on chest or back, severe headache, and muscle aches. It had a twenty percent or higher mortality rate at the time, usually caused by infection, pneumonia, or intestinal bleeding. Cholera, from the waterborne bacterium vibrio cholerae, caused by drinking contaminated water, has a very rapid onset. It is a disease of the small intestine that causes severe diarrhea and rapid death from dehydration. It had a high mortality rate in the years before antibiotics and IV fluids.

Cincinnati lost 8,000 to cholera. President Polk was still a relatively young man when he died of the disease just four years after leaving the White House. Many people heading west on the Oregon Trail died of cholera as well. The stagnant water of the canals and water sources, combined with the poor sanitation of the times, led to the rapid spread of the deadly diseases.

The Johnson family went on despite their sadness and found comfort in their role in expanding education in the area where many local farmers did not see the need for much schooling for their children. A new teacher, Mary Bushnell, came to the school and caught the eye of Esther Ann's brother Horatio. Mary and Horatio married, and then Horatio introduced Esther Ann to a friend, Peter Koontz, the owner of the local flour mill. Esther Ann and Peter fell in love and were married by Rev. William French, her brother-in-law.

The happiness the family had was short lived, for in the summer of '51 came the worst typhoid epidemic they had ever seen. There were not enough nurses to help the ill. Esther Ann's husband, Peter, and her brother Sobieski both helped take care of a poor family who worked at the mill, and both fell ill themselves. On July 25 her brother died and then in August her husband, Peter, died as well. Her brother Sobieski was only twenty-four when he died, her husband, Peter, thirty-four. The income from the mill was not enough to support Esther Ann and her baby now that she had to hire a superintendent to run it.

Her sister Clara gave up being principal of St. Mary's and married Isaac Woods, who was considering leaving the area and joining family in the west. Esther Ann had lost two brothers and a husband, and a third brother, Vittz, was not well. Vittz was considering a move to the west along with Clara and her husband and Horatio and his wife, Mary. The year 1851 was a time of great uncertainty for the family.[135]

The next fifteen years or so found Esther Ann very busy—after marrying her new husband, James Turner, in 1852—with their children and the care of elderly parents. Her parents had seen so much, having lost six of their children before they themselves died. (Daughter Mary French died in 1861 at age forty-one.) Esther Ann's father, Gurdon Collins Johnson, worked at a variety of careers, as did many Americans of the time. Nineteenth-century Americans often had to be jack of all trades to be successful in changing circumstances. Gurdon was one of the first merchants in Marion County and also served as postmaster of his community. Not only did he farm, but he was part owner of the local mill, where he used his knowledge of fulling. Gurdon, who died in 1864, and his wife, Louisa, who died in 1870, are buried in Green Lawn Cemetery in Indianapolis, next to two of their sons. They passed on the importance of education to their children, as well as the long history of their family in Connecticut, and told their children many stories of the Johnson family of Guilford and the Brainerds of East Haddam. The children heard stories of their ancestor, Connecticut Colonial Governor William Leete, whose granddaughter married into the Johnson family, as well as stories about the Lees and the Wheelocks. Esther Ann would think of these strong people in her history and it would help her carry on.[136]

Esther Ann's grandfather, also named Gurdon C. Johnson, continued the long family history of working as a fulling miller and being involved in Episcopal Church education. He was born in Guilford, Connecticut, the hometown of generations of his ancestors, on February 2, 1759. The town of Guilford is on the Connecticut coast in New Haven County. Gurdon's third great grandfather Robert Johnson emigrated from Kingston Upon Hull, Yorkshire, England, to New Haven in 1641 and was one of its founders.

His descendant Gurdon is listed in the U.S. Revolutionary War Rolls as having served at age sixteen in the 33rd Regiment of Foot in 1775 in Connecticut. At age twenty-two he married Esther Brainerd, daughter of Daniel Brainerd of East Haddam in Killingworth, New Haven, Connecticut, on May 8, 1781.

The Brainerds had been established in East Haddam for as long as the Johnsons had in Guilford. No doubt they compromised on their marriage site of Killingsworth as a town approximately between the two families. Although Guilford and East Haddam are only about thirty miles apart, fifteen miles would still be a day's ride to the wedding. Both families were loyalists before the Revolutionary War. Esther Ann was named for her brave grandmother Esther Brainerd of East Haddam, who as a child had been accused of hiding British spies in their house. Despite having her fingers pinched in iron pincers by the local smithy, she refused to say a word. As the Revolution progressed, they were won over to the cause.[137]

Gurdon and Esther had moved to Granville, Washington County, New York, by 1790, according to census records. Washington County lies just adjacent to Connecticut; possibly, he received a land grant there. Gurdon served as a captain in the New York militia in Washington County, commissioned in New York City on March 8, 1791. By 1802 he had moved his family some fourteen or fifteen miles across the border to Fair Haven, Vermont, and set up a fulling mill near the river there. By the mid-nineteenth century, this area would be known as "The Slate Valley," running twenty-four miles along the New York-Vermont border from Granville to Fair Haven. The valley's six-mile-wide vein of slate would lead to many quarries being built there.

At the time Gurdon and his family lived there, conditions and roads were very primitive. In 1805 a rough, muddy toll road to Fair Haven opened up. Average tolls for taking livestock were one cent for a sheep or hog; cattle, oxen, and horses were as much as six cents per eleven miles of the road. Fair Haven first prospered as a mill town, with many mills set at the falls of the Castleton River. Land records show Gurdon purchased several acres of land from a General Orms at the foot of the old Dry Falls. Gurdon mortgaged the land to his father, Samuel Johnson, of Guilford. He was a fuller and clothier dealing in woolen cloth, as was the family tradition. The many Merino sheep in the area provided the wool.[138]

Fulling is an ancient trade involving cleansing and treating woolen cloth to make it thicker and eliminate the oils and dirt. In Roman times fulling was done by men stomping their feet in tubs full of wool ankle-deep with urine. It was difficult, exhausting work. Stale urine was so important to the process that it was taxed. The odious process of using urine was eventually replaced by using soap instead. Using water power from mills improved the process tremendously. Thickening carding wool gave the fabric strength and waterproofing (felting.)

Gurdon, as businessmen often do, had trouble getting some of his clients to pay their bills. He composed a little ditty addressed to Enoch Wright, dated March 19, 1806, for a bill a year overdue.

The above account, if you pay in wheat
I and my family will eat:
But if you don't I'll tell you what,
I and my family must go to pot;
But if you pay in wheat at large,
I and my family will you discharge.

Gurdon was driven out of his house and property by a great freshet (flood) in July of 1811 and died a little more than a year later. One of his daughters, Esther, became a poet and his son Gurdon Collins emphasized education and the church for all his children, continuing the family traditions. The family was no doubt greatly influenced by Gurdon's uncle Reverend Doctor Samuel Johnson DD., one of the most important intellectuals of his generation.[139]

Reverend Samuel Johnson, born in 1696 in Guilford, Connecticut, was a clergyman, educator, philosopher, historian, and encyclopedist. A graduate of Yale, he wrote volumes of books on philosophy and religion. Samuel, son of Samuel Johnson Sr., a fulling miller, was greatly influenced by his grandfather William Johnson at a very early age. He was a precocious child; his grandfather taught him English at four and Hebrew at five. His grandfather, who was a church deacon, teacher, judge, militia leader, and state assemblyman, would take him around to his friends and have Samuel recite passages of memorized scriptures. William Johnson died when his grandson was six; from then on, Samuel studied with a variety of tutors, some better than others. He entered the Collegiate School at Saybrook—later renamed Yale and relocated to New Haven—at age thirteen. He studied Puritan orthodoxy and the classics that were taught there and graduated in 1714 with a bachelor's degree. He received his master's in 1717.

Johnson's first love was teaching. He taught grammar school in Guilford, even while he was a student at Yale. He taught both adults and children for almost sixty years. At Yale he began to write, starting a work on the Puritan mind and natural philosophy. He then wrote—in Latin—an encyclopedia of all knowledge, using the methods of the Reformation logician Petrus Ramus. He cataloged all the books at Yale, and his library catalog scheme was used by other colleges until the Dewey Decimal Classification came into being in 1876. He is known as the "Father of American Library Classification." When a collection of some 800 books arrived from England for the Yale library—which he cataloged—he discovered the works of Enlightenment thinkers such as Francis Bacon, John Locke, and Isaac Newton, which opened a new world of thought to him.

Johnson began to rethink the stern Calvinist ideology of the Puritans. He used what he learned from these sources to write the *Revised Encyclopedia of Philosophy* in 1716. At this time he was appointed the senior tutor at Yale, joined later by his good friend Daniel Brown, who was appointed tutor in 1718. In 1720 he became the Congregationalist minister of a church in West Haven, Connecticut, but softened the strict Calvinist doctrines in his sermons. In 1722 he and some others, including Daniel Brown, decided the Episcopal Church better fit their idea of theology. The Puritans in charge of Yale and the churches in Connecticut did not take kindly to this change in faith and expelled Johnson and others who converted. Johnson sailed to England, and on March 31, 1723, he was ordained as an Episcopal priest and given a missionary assignment in Connecticut. While in England he received honorary master's degrees from both Cambridge and Oxford. He was the first man born in America to receive an honorary master's from Oxford.

Johnson returned to Connecticut and opened the first Anglican church built in the colony, Christ Church, in Stratford. By 1752 he had founded twenty-five churches—all staffed by his disciples—in the colony. He has been called "The Father of the Episcopal Church in America."

Of course, there was argument with the Puritan theologians. He had a long-running pamphlet war with the leading Puritans. One of his main antagonists was Jonathan Dickinson, President of Princeton. Johnson was a minority fighting for minority religious rights in a Congregationalist Church state. He presented the Anglican position against both the Old Light and New Light Puritans in vigorous defense of a need for an Episcopal bishop in Connecticut and freedom from the taxes for Puritan churches. Ironically, it was the opposite fight of what the Puritans had dealt with a century before in England. At the same time, he opened a common school in Stratford and boarded and tutored sons of prominent New York families.

Dr. Johnson began to talk with Dr. Benjamin Franklin and Dr. William Smith in 1753 about establishing a "new model of college" that would be profession oriented, with classes in English instead of Latin and experts in subject matter as professors instead of just one tutor. The Puritan schools, Harvard and Yale, were based on the classics and emphasized studying Greek, Latin, and theology. Dr. Franklin wanted Johnson to come to Philadelphia to help start a college there, but Johnson preferred to stay near home and work with the Anglican Trinity Church in New York to raise money for a new college in New York.

Johnson, Franklin, and Smith replaced the study of theology as taught in the Puritan colleges with moral philosophy based on Dr. Johnson's "new system of morality" and his philosophy textbook titled *Elementa Philosophica* as the core of the curriculum. Johnson had started to replace the Puritan ideas of sin and predestination, starting with in his sermons back in 1715. Now, in his book of philosophy, he defined philosophy as, "The Pursuit of True Happiness in the Knowledge of things being what they really are and acting or practicing according to that Knowledge."

Dr. Franklin and Dr. Smith would eventually open the College of Philadelphia, which became the University of Pennsylvania. Dr. Johnson opened an Anglican college in New York called King's College, now Columbia University, in July of 1754. He served as its first president. It was diverse, public spirited, with no religious test for admission, and taught not only English literature and moral philosophy but a wide scope of subjects, including math and science. The Enlightenment idea of the pursuit of happiness and usefulness as citizens was a core philosophy. It was the first "new model" college in the New World.

Smallpox was a major curse at the time, and Johnson had to leave the college for periods of time during outbreaks. He lost his wife, Charity Floyd Nicoll, his beloved son William "Billy," and a grandson to smallpox between 1756 and 1758. He married Sarah Beach, the widow of an old friend. His oldest son, William Samuel Johnson, who had been in London for a few years, returned to Connecticut in 1771, giving him great joy. Rev. Samuel Johnson finished his autobiography and died on January 6, 1772. There is a monument to him at Christ Church in Stratford, where he served as minister for most of the forty-seven years between the founding of the church and his death. (He spent eight and a half years at King's College.)

Johnson left us a large volume of work on religion, philosophy, history and education. Samuel Johnson was one of the first tutors at Yale to teach the famed Puritan Minister Jonathan Edwards and introduced him to the ideas of John Locke and other Enlightenment thinkers. Samuel does not get the attention of his famous student, although he was very well known and respected in England among the leading theologians and philosophers of the day including Bishop George Berkley. His contributions were enormous in religious philosophy, history and education. *"The Founder of American Philosophy"* wrote the first philosophy textbook printed in America and can be considered the first important philosopher of the colonial period. His emphasis on education and missionary work provided a beacon for those that followed.[140]

Samuel Johnson's eldest son, William Samuel Johnson, born in Stratford, Connecticut in 1727, would follow in his father's footsteps and graduate from Yale in 1744. His father wanted him to follow in his career as a clergyman, but his talent and heart lay in law and government. He studied law and became prominent in his field and famous in his own right as one of the signers of the U.S. Constitution. He represented the colony at the Stamp Act Congress, served on the colony Supreme Court, and served in Connecticut's militia for twenty years, rising to the rank of colonel. He followed his father as the third president of Columbia University (1787-1800) and also received an honorary master's from Oxford University, as had his father. He was a very close friend of the famous English author Dr. Samuel Johnson—author of the first English dictionary—and had many other British friends. He disapproved of the king's government and attitude towards the colonies. While he served in London for five years as the Connecticut Colony's agent for Indian affairs, he was in charge of settling land titles for the colony for land obtained from the Mohegan Indians. Returning to Connecticut, he had difficulty breaking with England and felt that revolution was not the answer; he favored negotiations, instead. He would go on after the war to serve in the Congress of the Confederation, where he was a major influence and much beloved by the southern delegates, as well as those from Vermont who granted him his own town—Johnson, Vermont—in thanks.

In 1787 he played an important role at the Philadelphia Constitutional Convention. Johnson had an active role in the framing of the Constitution and was a strong supporter of the New Jersey Plan that called for equal representation of the states in the national legislature. He called for a separate senate. He chaired the Committee of Style, which edited and framed the final version of the Constitution. Edits to a draft copy exist in his handwriting at the Library of Congress. He served as a U.S. senator from Connecticut from 1789-1791 and lived a long, productive life, dying at age ninety-two in 1819 in Stratford, Connecticut. The importance of democratic government, education, and the church were shared with future Johnson generations.[141]

Esther Ann's mother, Louisa Lee, had stories of her own to pass down to her children. Tiny, frail Louisa was a tower of mental strength. She knew what she wanted for her children and was active in their education. The Lees were also long-time residents of colonial Connecticut. Her grandfather Dr. Samuel Lee was born in Canaan, Litchfield County, Connecticut about 1729 and married Silence Fletcher on March 28, 1754, in Canaan. Litchfield County, in the extreme northwest of the state, was the last county in Connecticut to be developed. Samuel Lee died on November 19, 1781, according to family history. A Samuel Lee is listed on the honor roll of Litchfield County Revolutionary soldiers. It was probably his son. His son Samuel Lee (Deacon Lee), born in 1754 in Canaan, married Mary Bingham in Windham, Connecticut and by 1790 had moved to Poultney, Vermont, where his children, who included Dr. Samuel Lee and Louisa Lee, were born. Poultney is just six miles from where Louisa's future husband, Gurdon Collins Johnson, would grow up in Fair Haven.[142]

Louisa's mother, Mary Bingham, told her stories of her grandfather and grandmother on the maternal side: Jabez Bingham (1724-1784) and Mary Standish Wheelock (1728-1809). Before they were married, Jabez made his bride a beautiful chest of drawers made of cherry wood that the family passed down and lovingly cared for through many moves. Mary Standish Wheelock's great-grandfather was Rev. Ralph Wheelock, Puritan minister and teacher educated at Cambridge.

Wheelock was born in Shropshire, England, in 1600. He received his bachelor's degree in 1623 and his master's in 1631 at a time of religious dissent and the rise of Puritan beliefs at Cambridge. John Milton and John Eliot were his contemporaries. He came to America as part of the Great Migration, sailing in 1636 with his wife, Rebecca Clarke, and three children, to join the Massachusetts Bay Colony. They briefly settled in Watertown then moved to Dedham in 1637, where Rev. Wheelock had a major role as one of the founders of the town.

Rev. Wheelock and Rev. John Allin (1596-1671), who had also attended Cambridge, started a gathered church in Dedham. Thirty families agreed on a set of principles and let the two ministers plan the rules of the congregation. They started with eight men and expanded their congregation to include seventy percent of the town. Wheelock signed the Dedham Covenant, which was the founding constitution of the town. After becoming a "freeman" about 1638, he was appointed as the clerk of writs at the General Court of Massachusetts Bay Colony in 1642, as well as commissioner to solemnize marriages, which were civil not religious ceremonies in the time of the Puritans. In February 1644 a Dedham town meeting voted for the first free public school in America. Ralph Wheelock was the first teacher at this school and, thus, became the first tax-supported public school teacher in the colonies.[143]

Dedham began to run out of space for growing families. Rev. Wheelock founded the town of Medfield—less than ten miles away—in 1651. The first lot of twelve acres in the town was granted to him. Rev. Wheelock moved his family there and lived there the rest of his life. He most likely wrote the document called "The Agreement," which all residents had to sign, promising to abide by the laws and to settle differences peacefully. He was active in the affairs of both towns and served the towns in a variety of official positions. There is still a Ralph Wheelock School in Medfield.

Rev. Wheelock died on January 11, 1684, having played a role in the establishment of two towns and in education for residents of those towns. His descendants include a significant number of educators. His great-grandson Eleazer Wheelock would go on to found Dartmouth University. Other descendants include Benjamin I. Wheeler, a president of the University of California, Lucy Wheelock, founder of Wheelock College, Colonel Eleazer Louis Ripley Wheelock, founder of Wheelock, Texas, and organizer of the University of Texas, poet Emily Dickinson and actor/screenwriter Matt Damon.[144]

It was no wonder that Gurdon Collins Johnson and Louisa Lee emphasized education to their children. One story that Esther Ann Johnson would never forget was that of the important book that was lost on the move to Ohio so many years before. Her father carefully wrote the date of her birth in this family Bible, as so many ancestors had done before. It was gently wrapped for the trip to Ohio, but the box of books that it was wrapped in disappeared. Esther Ann would not forget the name of the original owner of the Bible. It was the Bible of Mercy Standish, the granddaughter of that feisty military captain, who came on the *Mayflower*.

Chapter Four

Faith

Family Cast of Characters

Captain Myles Standish…(1584-1656) *came on the* Mayflower; *seventh-great-grandfather of Daniel B. Adlum*

Barbara Mullins…(1584-1659) *wife of Myles Standish; seventh-great-grandmother of Daniel B. Adlum*

Loara Standish…(1627-1656) *daughter of Myles and Barbara Standish*

Captain Josiah Standish…(1633-1690) *son of Myles and Barbara; sixth-great-grandfather of Daniel B. Adlum*

Sarah Allen…(1639-1690) *wife of Josiah Standish; sixth-great-grandmother of Daniel B. Adlum*

Mercy Standish…(1685-1748) *daughter of Josiah and Sarah; fifth-great-grandmother of Daniel B. Adlum*

Dr. Samuel Fuller…(1580-1633) *came on the* Mayflower; *brother of Edward; ninth-great-uncle of Patricia Reese*

Edward Fuller…(1575-1621) *came on the* Mayflower; *ninth-great-grandfather of Patricia Reese*

Ann Fuller…(1575-1621) *came on the* Mayflower; *ninth-great-grandmother of Patricia Reese*

Captain Matthew Fuller…(1603-1678) *came in 1640; son of Edward and Ann; eighth-great-grandfather Patricia Reese,*

Samuel Fuller…(1612-1683) *came on the* Mayflower; *son of Edward and Ann; eighth-great-grandfather of Patricia Reese*

Jane Lothrop…(1614-1658) *wife of Samuel Fuller; eighth-great-grandmother of Patricia Reese*

Rev. John Lothrop…(1584-1653) *father of Jane; ninth-great-grandfather of Patricia Reese*

John Fuller…(1656-1726) *son of Samuel Fuller; husband of cousin Elizabeth Fuller; seventh-great-grandfather of Patricia Reese*

Elizabeth Fuller…(1626-1714) *daughter of Matthew Fuller; wife of John Fuller; seventh-great-grandmother of Patricia Reese*

The Pilgrims of Plymouth

"We are all, in all places, strangers and pilgrims"

~Robert Cushman

In early seventeenth century Holland, two English expatriates forged a remarkable friendship that would last their lifetimes. Myles Standish was a fiery professional soldier hired by the Dutch to help protect the Low Countries from the Catholic Spanish Empire. He had been in Holland for years when he met Reverend John Robinson, the charismatic, intellectual minister exiled from England along with his flock. They both had roots in the English gentry that converted to Calvinism and became known as Puritans. Although very different in appearance and style—Standish was short, red haired, and powerfully built with a bit of a short temper, while Robinson was tall and dark with a calm, persuasive manner—they were both leaders of men. John Robinson's spiritual guidance and congregational ideas would go to America with the Pilgrims and greatly influence their community from Holland. The military and organizational skills of Myles Standish would protect and strengthen the tiny Separatist settlement at Plymouth, Massachusetts. Their contributions, along with the steadfast leadership of William Bradford, William Brewster, and fellow pilgrims such as Edward Winslow and Dr. Samuel Fuller, would change the history of America.

Myles Standish was brought into the romantic American folklore of the Pilgrims in the poem "The Courtship of Myles Standish," written by *Mayflower* descendent Henry Wadsworth Longfellow. Longfellow's description of Myles stays with us.

His lyric poem starts:

In the Old Colony days, in Plymouth the land of the Pilgrims,
To and fro in a room of his simple and primitive dwelling,
Clad in doublet and hose and boots of Cordovan leather,
Strode, with a martial air, Miles Standish, the Puritan Captain.
Buried in thought he seemed, with his hands behind him, and Pausing
Ever and anon to behold his glittering weapons of warfare,
Hanging in shining array along the walls of the chamber, --
Cutlass and corselet of steel, and his trusty sword of Damascus,
Curved at the point and inscribed with its mystical Arabic sentence,
While underneath, in a corner, were fowling piece, musket, and Matchlock.

Chapter Four: Faith

Short of stature he was, but strongly built and athletic,
Broad in the shoulders, deep chested, with muscles and sinews of iron;
Brown as a nut was his face, but his russet beard was already
Flaked with patches of snow, as hedges sometimes in November…

There has been endless debate about Myles Standish and his family origins. The latest research indicates he was probably born in Lancashire, England, about 1584, as a gentleman of the large Standish family. He was well read and well educated. Standish owned a book titled *Allegations against Bishop Pilkington of Durham*. Pilkington was the founder of Rivington Grammar School in Chorley, Lancashire. This is evidence that he probably attended the school, as had other Standishes in the area. There were many branches of the family; many had been Roman Catholic, but the members of his branch were early converts to Protestantism. His probable Great-grandfather Alexander was a Standish of both Standish and Duxbury, thus giving Myles' claim that he had been denied his birthright more validity. Myles' will of 1656 states:

"I give unto my son & heire. they apparent Alexander Standish all my lands as heire apparent by lawfull decent in Ormskirke Borscouge Wrightington Maudsley Newburrow Crowston and in the Isla of man and given to mee as Right Heire by lawful decent but Surruptuously drained from mee My great grandfather being a 2cond or younger brother from the house Standish of Standish."

Captain Myles Standish, from a painting done by Mike Haywood based on a 1626 likeness done in London source: NY Public Library

Neither Myles nor his descendants ever inherited the famous Duxbury Hall with attached lands in England, having been cheated out of it during the English Civil War, but we now have a Duxbury, Massachusetts, founded by Myles.[145]

Standish served in Queen Elizabeth's army at a very young age, starting as a drummer and reportedly working his way up to lieutenant. His father was a soldier as well, following a distinguished military heritage in the Standish family. Captain John Smith wrote of him that he was a "bred soldier in Holland." It is assumed that he was one of the soldiers under the English commander Sir Horace Vere that fought the Spanish in the Netherlands during the Eighty Year War for Dutch independence. Standish stayed during the twelve-year truce—signed in April 1609—preserving the peace under the Dutch. That is where he became acquainted with Rev. John Robinson and his Puritan church in Leiden.[146]

John Robinson was one of the leading theologians of his day. He is considered to be one of the founders of the Congregational Church, along with Robert Browne. He was such a charismatic minister that not only did the congregation of Scrooby, England, follow him to Holland, but the size of the congregation in Leiden grew to almost 400, attracted by his preaching.

Robinson was born at Stourton-Le-Steeple, Nottinghamshire, England, in 1576. He attended Corpus Christi College at the University of Cambridge, obtaining his Bachelor of Arts degree in 1596 and Master of Arts degree in 1599. He was ordained a priest of the Church of England and in 1599 was both a dean of the college and serving a lectureship in Greek. Cambridge was a center of Puritanism; dissenters from the Church of England felt it was still too "Catholic" and wanted "to purify the church."[147]

The sixteenth century was one of religious turmoil caused by the corruption within the Catholic Church and conflict caused by the new ideas of the Protestant Reformation. The economic pressures of the time and resentment by the gentry of the power and wealth of the church that was beyond the reach of the law added to the turmoil. In England, King Henry VIII cared only about divorcing his wife, Catherine of Aragon, which Pope Clement VII would not let him do. This dispute caused Henry to break with the Catholic Church and establish the Church of England, also known as the Anglican Church. The Anglican Church replaced the Catholic Church in England, but the new church kept most of the traditions and rituals of the Catholic Church, as well as the religious bureaucracy.

As the ideas of Martin Luther and John Calvin spread across England and the rest of Europe, more and more people agreed with the idea that one could have a personal relationship with God by reading the Bible and practicing faith in what they thought was a pure, uncorrupted form. In 1572, during religious wars in France, the French Calvinist Protestants—Huguenots—were murdered by the thousands during the St. Bartholomew's Day Massacre.

English Protestants were smart to be nervous at home. The monarch was considered the supreme leader of the Church of England. At the time, all subjects, no matter what country, worshiped as their ruler wanted them to. During the reign of Queen Elizabeth, laws were passed to pressure dissenters and separatist congregations who left the Church of England. The Separatists were sometimes called Brownists, after one of the first ministers of separatist Puritan churches in England, Robert Browne, who established a separatist church in Norwich in 1580. The Separatists despaired that the Church of England would reform enough to their satisfaction and decided to hold their own private services.

The objections of the Puritans regarding Anglican services involved the emphasis on traditional liturgy instead of the Bible, wearing of vestments, making the sign of the cross, and the hierarchy of the church with too much unelected power invested in bishops. They felt that these were manmade additions, not original to the Bible and, therefore, served only to glorify man instead of God, as well as taking a great deal of money from the general populace for the extravagant lifestyle of the bishops. Puritans felt that the services should be simplified and focused on the Bible instead of rote liturgy.

The Separatists developed the Congregational form of church governing in that each church was its own entity with a democratic process to elect elders and ministers. They wanted a righteous, honest society and a religious hierarchy that reflected them and their values. The sermon became the most important feature of the service, delivering knowledge as well as moral guidance.

A well-educated clergy was essential. England, including the Anglican Church, was in economic and social turmoil at the time. Many positions in the Anglican Church were bought through patronage, with some priests barely literate in theology and others corrupt and degenerate. The common man longed for spiritual guidance, which he found in the well-educated Puritan ministers who focused on sermons based on the Bible. People were abandoning their local church and travelling miles to hear Puritan ministers in private services.[148]

When Queen Elizabeth I died in 1603 and James I of Scotland came to the throne, the situation for dissident Protestants changed for the worse. They were hopeful that King James would be sympathetic to their cause, having been raised a Scotch Presbyterian; however, he hated the strict way he had been raised and was uninterested in cutting any slack to the Puritans. He had no intention of letting Puritans worship outside the law and began to crack down harshly. He made it illegal for Separatists to hold their own services and strictly enforced The Act Against Puritans of 1593. Anyone who did not attend the services of the Church of England for forty days was subject to arrest and imprisonment or banishment from England. He felt a strong Church of England was tied to his power as king. "No Bishops, No King," was his mantra. There were no politics outside religion. Religion was politics.

During this time, John Robinson resigned his position from Cambridge—college fellows were forbidden to marry—to marry Bridget White. He took a position at St. Andrew's Church in Norwich. Shortly after, James I issued a proclamation requiring that all ministers conform to the new book of canons. John Robinson, who truly believed in the Puritan cause, was forced to resign and privately preached in Nottinghamshire until he joined with his friend William Brewster and his group, who were secretly meeting at Scrooby Manor. William Brewster allowed John Robinson to hide out at the Scrooby Manor estate. Robinson's devoted parishioners from Norwich followed him there.[149]

William Brewster had gone to Cambridge, as had John Robinson. Brewster's distinguished family had been in Nottinghamshire for over 200 years. He was postmaster and bailiff, as his father had been, and was in charge of the Archbishop of York's property, Scrooby Manor.

The village of Scrooby is in northwest Nottinghamshire, not too far from the Sherwood Forest made famous by Robin Hood. It is about 150 miles north of London in an area that was filled with intellectual Puritan ministers at the time. Rev. Richard Clifton was serving as the minister at Scrooby while Brewster served as deacon.

William Bradford, who gave us the most significant book in seventeenth-century America, *Of Plymouth Plantation*, the story of the Pilgrims in America, was a young but important member of the congregation as well. Bradford was the son of a nearby, well-off farming family who were struck by tragedy. Bradford lost both parents and the majority of his family, one after another, from illness, with the exception of his uncles. At the age of twelve, he was bedridden for months and began to study the Bible. He joined the Puritan congregation as a teenager. John Robinson became an associate pastor and preached to Bradford and the growing congregation.[150]

By 1607 the congregation decided it was too dangerous to stay in England and set about immigrating to Holland. It was necessary to get permission from the government to leave England. They doubted it would be granted, so they made their plans in secret. They had to walk some sixty miles to the port of Boston in Lincolnshire. They were betrayed by the ship captain, arrested, put on display for ridicule, their money and belongings stolen. After a month they were released, and they made another attempt, finally arriving in Amsterdam in August of 1608.

By 1609 they were in Leiden, a city about thirty miles away, with Robinson as their pastor. Rev. Clifton stayed in Amsterdam. Leiden, a densely built commercial city of tall, red brick buildings and carefully constructed canals, was the center of the textile industry in Holland. It could have not been more different than the rolling green hills and pastoral environment they had come from in England. The population of Leiden was about 40,000. Most importantly, it was one of Europe's most important centers of learning, with the famed University of Leiden; there, the Puritans finally had freedom to worship as they chose.[151]

Leiden had been through terrible hardships in the fight against Holland's Spanish overlords. They experienced a long siege by the armies of Phillip II, resulting in more than 6,000 citizens dying of starvation and disease.

Seventeen Protestant provinces of the Netherlands revolted in 1566. The city of Leiden was part of the Reformed Movement led by the great Protestant leader William the Silent in the revolt against the Spanish. They managed to hold off the Spanish Hapsburgs, and William rewarded the city with the (Calvinist) University of Leiden in 1575. It was at the forefront of Christian scholarship.

Thirty some years later, Robinson joined the university and was active in the great theological debates of the day. He was a prolific writer and excellent debater. Leiden was full of political and religious refugees—about one quarter of the population—and had more freedom and tolerance than anywhere in Europe at the time.

Holland was an economic powerhouse, rich with commerce, and the Spanish hated to give up control. The Dutch finally signed a truce with the Spanish in 1609, but they still needed the help of the English to protect their country. This had a sobering effect on the Pilgrims and their activities there due to King James and his government trying to reach into Holland to influence them.[152]

About half the Pilgrims took jobs in Holland's important textile industry. As foreigners, their economic opportunities were limited. William Bradford was a wool merchant and member of the serge-weavers guild and could then employ other Pilgrims who were not guild members. It was hard work with long hours. They toiled all day, six days a week, with their children working beside them. It was vastly different work than the farms they were used to. Although farm work is laborious, there are periods of rest, which they did not get in the textile factories.

Samuel Fuller, who was a deacon in the church and, ultimately, the Pilgrim doctor, was employed as a serge weaver. Other Pilgrim occupations included carpenter, shoemaker, hat maker, tailor, mason, midwife, and watchmaker, among others. Some Pilgrims were poor, but others were well-connected merchants and/or academics. William Brewster, who gave up a highly respected position in England to go to Holland, was paid by Brewer—a prosperous merchant friend of John Robinson—to publish Puritan books. Many of these were smuggled into England and secretly distributed.

Edward Winslow, a young man who would become well known in both Plymouth and Massachusetts Bay Colony, was Brewster's assistant and typesetter. The Brewster Press, now known as the Pilgrim Press, had a distinctive type which ultimately led to the English government figuring out where the subversive texts were coming from.[153]

Brewster and Winslow bunked together in a small house full of printing press materials in what was called Rubbish Alley. The Dutch now honor the memory of William Brewster with the street name, William Brewster Steeg.

Rev. John Robinson and his extended family bought property nearby in the southwest corner of Leiden near St. Peter's Church—Pieterskerk—where the Pilgrims would live and worship. There were twenty or so small houses built in the garden behind Robinson's house for members of the church to live in. Perhaps, Dr. Samuel Fuller and wife and child, or his brother Edward Fuller and family, lived in one of them.

The Fuller brothers were originally from Redenhall, Norwich, near Scrooby. They were the sons of Robert Fuller, a butcher, and Sarah Dunkhorn, his wife. Samuel was baptized on

January 20, 1580/1 at Redenhall Parish in Norfolk County. By 1611 he was noted to be residing in Leiden. His older brother Edward was baptized on September 4, 1575, at Redenhall. They were both named in their father's will of 1614. Edward was listed in Leiden records shortly after this. Most of the Puritans, including the Fullers, were from eastern England. There was a core group from Nottinghamshire/Norwich and East Anglia.[154]

Rev. John Robinson was a sympathetic leader and broadminded—for the day—regarding women's roles in the church. Perhaps because he was surrounded by strong women, they were free to speak their mind in worship and study. He said they were equal in the eyes of the Lord. Gender roles were very well defined at the time. Certainly, it was a patriarchal system, but Puritan women were seen as important partners to their husbands.

Despite the Puritans' relative freedom to worship, life in Holland was very hard. After almost twelve years there, they began to think about immigrating to the New World. They could not go back to England, because they would be imprisoned or killed. Religious and social unrest in Europe led to the Thirty Years' War, starting in 1618, which made them fear for their safety. Their children were working too hard; many were in the ribbon-making trade, which required small, nimble fingers. They were afraid of losing their English heritage if they stayed too long in Holland, and the fact that the truce with the Spanish was close to being over led them to think it was time for a move.[155]

In the University of Leiden's library, there were several books describing the New World. Champlain had explored the area in 1605 and Captain John Smith of Jamestown mapped the coast of New England in 1614 and described the environment in his book *A Description of New England*, published in 1616. The essays describing Indian torture practices gave them pause. Early explorers left accounts of how the Indians "delight to torment men in the most bloody manner that may be; flaying some alive with the shells of fishes, cutting off the members and joints of others by piecemeal and broiling on the coals."

Despite their fear of the Indian torture practices, and the risks of such a bold move, the Puritans started to petition the English government for permission to go to America to join the Virginia settlement. John Carver, Robinson's beloved brother-in-law, and the well-respected Robert Cushman, wool merchant and devout deacon of the church, were selected to petition the court in England. Dr. Samuel Fuller, as deacon in the Leiden church, was active in the negotiations as well, writing letters to London.[156]

They asked the Court of King James I for permission to settle at the mouth of the Hudson River, which was at the northern end of the Virginia Colony charter. The petition was just about approved when Brewster went too far with his anti-royal tracts. He sent a missive to England denouncing five articles in the new liturgy imposed on Scotland, which enraged the king. Immediate demands for Brewster's arrest and that of Brewer were made. Agents of the king found the printing press in Leiden and smashed it. Brewer went to prison and, ultimately, died there. William Brewster evaded the authorities and slipped into hiding for almost a year. He mostly likely went to the northern part of England—he and his wife hidden by friends—not to reappear until July 1620. His substantial library in Leiden was carefully packed up by members of the congregation and taken to England.[157]

Robert Cushman and John Carver found a solution by having a group of about fifty-plus London adventurers—investors—led by merchant Thomas Weston finance a joint stock venture to send the Leiden community to plant a new settlement in America. The investors hoped to make money off the fishing and fur trade in America, as their profits were decreasing in the European wool trade. The adventurers put the deal together with a third party, Christopher Martin, a ruthless merchant who made life miserable for the Pilgrims. The members of the Separatist congregation were somewhat naive and were cheated and conned by the savvy businessmen they were dealing with. The adventurers added some people who had practical trades who were willing to go to the New World. Some of them, such as the Billington family, were nothing but trouble. John Billington would eventually be convicted of murder in Plymouth Colony after causing much grief in the community.[158]

The Merchant Adventurers, as the investors' group was called, demanded that the Pilgrims commit to working six days a week and to have no individual property until the debt was paid off. It was a very expensive venture and cost about one year's wages per person. The congregation decided only the strongest families would go first—about sixty-six in total. Rev. John Robinson and the rest of the congregation could go later. The families sold their houses and gathered their belongings. They were ready to go in the spring but discovered Weston had not procured a ship for them. The Pilgrims knew they would have to work very hard to repay the debts they incurred to finance this trip and were anxious about all the delays.

Robinson, and the rest of the congregation, accompanied the brave Pilgrims, traveled by canal boat to Delfts Haven, the Dutch port town they were to sail to England from, to say goodbye. The Pilgrims loaded all the belongings and supplies they could onto the small ship *Speedwell*, which they had purchased and intended to keep for a year in the New World. They expected Christopher Martin to purchase more supplies in England and hire a second, larger ship for the crossing. They had an emotional farewell, with Robinson admonishing them to remember to look to the Bible for strength and answers. His farewell was so memorable that Edward Winslow, years later, could still remember large portions of it. Robinson's thoughts and language can be found in the Mayflower Compact, drawn up by the passengers on the *Mayflower*, which shows his profound effect on his congregation.[159]

The *Mayflower* was hired in London, along with its master, Christopher Jones, who was one quarter owner of the ship, and his crew of about thirty. Master Jones and his crew sailed it to Southampton, where they started loading the *Mayflower* with supplies. The Pilgrims and their fellow travelers who were forced upon them by the Merchant Adventurers—they called them strangers—intended to take both ships across the Atlantic.

The *Mayflower* was what was called a sweet ship, mostly used in the wine trade, shipping goods to Europe and returning with sometimes as much as 180 tons of Bordeaux wine in casks. The spillage of the wine helped mask the odors from the bilge. The ships were not really meant for passengers, so fitting in their belongings and having some measure of privacy was next to impossible for many. The Pilgrims were anxious about the journey and the extreme sacrifices expected.[160]

Before they left Holland, it had to be decided if they should even take their wives on such a difficult trip. Four of the group, including Samuel Fuller, decided their wives should stay in Holland for the time being. Samuel left his wife, Bridget, and child behind where he thought they would be safe until the community was built. This was his third wife, his first two having died, so he wanted to be cautious. His brother Edward Fuller brought his wife and twelve-year-old son, also named Samuel. Edward had another son, Matthew Fuller—about age sixteen—who stayed in England with family friends. Matthew is thought to have been born in 1603, as there is a record of a Matthew Fuller being baptized on October 16, 1603, in Redenhall. Some, including William Brewster, left their daughters and took their sons, thinking that building a new colony would be too hard on the daughters.

Eighteen women ended up on the trip, including three—Elizabeth Hopkins, Susanna White, and Mary Allerton—who were very pregnant. William Bradford's wife, Dorothy, came with him but had to say an anguished goodbye to their three-year-old son, whom they left with her parents. Others wondered if they had any chance of ever seeing family again.[161]

They brought food, tools, personal belongings, books, and many Bibles. Myles Standish, who boarded the *Mayflower* with his wife, Rose, brought his diverse collection of books, a beautiful sword from Damascus inscribed with Arabic verse, full armor he had used when fighting the Spanish, and weapons such as matchlock guns and a precursor to the flintlock.

The *Mayflower* was heavily armed with cannon, including extra cannon to be used for defense of the colony. Dr. Samuel Fuller brought his surgeon's box and as many herbal medicines as he could, along with medical and botany books. His twenty-one-year-old assistant, William Butten, came with him. William Brewster's large library made it aboard, along with his chest, which was used as a table on which to sign the Mayflower Compact. Brewster's chest can be seen in the Pilgrim Hall Museum in Plymouth, Massachusetts, along with other artifacts such as an iron cooking pot probably used by Myles and Rose Standish.

Shoemaker William Mullins is estimated to have brought 250 pairs of shoes and 13 pairs of boots. Mullins and Peter Browne may have brought Dorkin chickens, a historic breed of bird from their home parish recorded in Plymouth early on. The pilgrims brought large amounts of Edam and Gouda Dutch cheeses and butter. The cylinder-shaped Edam cheese with flattened ends stacked well and, wrapped in its coat of red wax, didn't spoil; it just got drier. [162]

The Pilgrims took an enormous amount of butter from Holland. (Holland's reclaimed marshland was not so good for crops but perfect for dairy farms.) When the Merchant Adventurers refused to pay the harbor master the £100 due while the ships sat at the dock, waiting to leave, the Pilgrims had to sell some of their provisions. They had to offload between 60 and 80 firkins—3,300 and 4,720 pounds—from the ships to pay the debt, so it was fortunate they had so much.

The most important provision onboard was the beer. Everyone drank beer, even children, because the water frequently was not safe to drink. The beer they drank had a low alcohol content—it was called small beer—and sometimes had pine or spruce needles added to the barrels for flavor and scurvy prevention. Additionally, lemons or lemon juice would have been very important for prevention of scurvy, although they may not have brought any.[163]

The *Mayflower* itself was not in great shape and, as it turned out, neither was the *Speedwell*. The living space on the low-ceilinged gun deck—five and a half feet—on the *Mayflower* was about 58 feet by 24 feet for all 102 passengers and two dogs, one a giant mastiff. The passengers put up makeshift partitions for privacy. The exact size of the *Mayflower* is not known, but it is estimated to have been about 100 feet long by 24 feet wide. It was miserably cramped. Fortunately, some of the passengers were children. William Brewster was hidden from authorities onboard the *Mayflower*, along with his wife and two sons.

After much haggling with the investors led by Weston and Christopher Martin and many more delays—somehow £700 of goods that were supposed to be bought by Weston didn't materialize—the two ships set sail. Their sister ship, the *Speedwell*, almost immediately began leaking, which it had previously done on the trip from the Netherlands to London. They patched it up after pulling into port at Dartmouth and set sail again around August 21, 1620. Another 300 miles out, the *Speedwell* again began leaking, and they had to return to port at Plymouth.[164]

By now everyone was beside themselves with anxiety. The trip itself was going to be extremely difficult at best. After selling everything, going into debt, and leaving their loved ones, now they had missed the best season for sailing. News reached them of another group of 180 Puritans who had set sail from Holland to America. They heard that 130 died on the ship before they even reached land. About two dozen of the pilgrims who were on the *Speedwell* gave up on the trip after it was decided that the ship could not make it. As many as could squeezed onto the already over-crowded *Mayflower*, where the passengers had already been living for a month and a half, eating up the supplies. Robert Cushman, who was on the *Speedwell*, began to have heart palpitations and a sense of doom. He decided to stay behind.[165]

On a sunny September day in 1620, they set sail again, after prayers, on a very crowded old ship with a captain who had never sailed across the Atlantic, a somewhat disgruntled crew, less provisions than they expected, and missing a good number of their church who had to stay behind. They brought their faith and tremendous courage. They believed they had a covenant with God, like the Jews of old, and were determined to succeed. The odds were very great that they would fail. The historian Samuel Eliot Morison called the Pilgrims, "the spiritual ancestors of all Americans," all pioneers, because of their "ardent faith in God, a dauntless courage in danger, a boundless resourcefulness in the face of difficulties, an impregnable fortitude in adversity."[166]

The journey of sixty-six days and almost 3,000 miles went very slowly, at a pace of two miles per hour. There was miserable seasickness, especially during the second half of the trip when they ran into terrible storms that frightened passengers and crew alike. During one of these storms, one of the main beams cracked in half. Master Jones and his officers were debating turning back to England, but the Pilgrims saved the day by using a large iron screw they had brought from Holland for house building to strengthen the mast, and they were able to sail on. Passenger Stephen Howland fell overboard and was miraculously rescued. Two died of disease on the voyage: a crew member who was bitterly cruel to the Pilgrims and Samuel Fuller's young apprentice. Many were sick and weakened, especially as they started to ration beer and early signs of scurvy appeared. Elizabeth Hopkins gave birth to a baby boy she appropriately named Oceanus. It is hard to imagine much worse circumstances in which to give birth. Everything was wet, even their clothes that were packed away. They were out of firewood and the weather was getting colder. Wearing moldy, wet clothing just added to their discomfort.[167]

Finally, land was sighted off Cape Cod on November 9. They were well north of their destination, the mouth of the Hudson River. Master Jones attempted to head south but very rough seas nearly wrecked the *Mayflower*, so they decided to turn back north and explore Cape Cod. They anchored in what would become Provincetown harbor. The reduced rations of beer had started to take its toll, and the crew wished to get rid of the passengers as soon as possible. There was restlessness among the passengers as well. The strangers—those passengers forced upon the Puritans by the Merchant Adventurers—who were not bound by any sense of community or purpose, realized they were not within the bounds of the original patent since they were not in Virginia. The mouth of the

Hudson marked the northern edge of the Virginia Company patent. The Pilgrims decided they needed a socially binding contract until they could form a colony government.[168]

The Mayflower Compact that was drawn up by the leaders of the Leiden congregation, including William Brewster, William Bradford, John Carver, and Edward Winslow, showed some understanding of early contract law theory. Acclaimed historian and biographer Rebecca Fraser points out that it is a very significant part of our democratic social history in that "it was the first time in Western history that a contract was made among a group of individuals forming a colony, not with a monarch." On November 11, 1620, forty-one adult males over age twenty-one, including Myles Standish, the two Fuller brothers, Edward and Samuel, and the servants aboard, signed the compact. As historian Nathaniel Philbrick notes, "The Mayflower Compact bears the unmistakable signs of Robinson's influence."[169]

Mayflower Compact

Having undertaken, for the glory of God and advancement of the Christian faith and honor of our King and country, a voyage to plant the first colony in the northern parts of Virginia, do these present solemnly and mutually in the presence of God and one of other, covenant and combine ourselves together into a civil body politic, for our better ordering and preservation, and furtherance of the ends foresaid; and by virtue hereof to enact, constitute and frame such just and equal laws, ordinances, acts, constitutions and office, from time to time, as shall be thought most meet convenient for the general good of the colony, unto which we promise all due submission and obedience. In witness whereof we have hereunder subscribed our names at Cape Cod, the 11th of November, in the year of the reign of our Sovereign Lord King James, of England, France and Ireland the eighteen, and of Scotland the fifty-fourth, Anno Domini 1620.

The Leiden congregation did not want Christopher Martin as the governor of their new colony under any circumstances and voted as a bloc to elect John Carver as their governor. It was said about him that, "He was a gentleman of singular piety and rare humility." William Brewster would serve as Elder.

Myles Standish was eager to set out on his mission of exploration and assessing the dangers facing the safety of the colony. The congregation had hired Standish as their military commander upon the recommendation of John Robinson after first considering Captain John Smith for the job.[170]

Standish led sixteen men from the Mayflower on the first exploration of the Cape. They wore armor, carried muskets, and had Dutch cheese and hardtack for nourishment. They were looking for natives and any possible settlement site. The land was forbidding—miles of sand dunes—not the best area for a plantation. They did find shellfish and fresh water, which they drank with relief. William Bradford wrote that, "He and his companions were hastened ashore (by Master Jones) and made to drink water, that the seamen might have the more beer." Mourt's Relations quotes, "Our victuals was only biscuit and Holland cheese, and a little bottle of aquavitae (strong liquor) so we were sore athirst."

Standish and his men spent a month and a half exploring Cape Cod in a series of expeditions. They had a brief encounter with Indians, who ran away. Standish and his men found several graves, as well as dried Indian corn that had been buried. They "borrowed" half the amount in desperation, intending to make amends later. When the shallop was assembled, they took it out with more men. The shallop a sailboat with a center mast, had been transported in four pieces on the voyage and then put back together by the ship's carpenter once they made anchor. During one expedition, Myles Standish and the men with him were attacked by arrows from a group of Indians hidden in the woods, but luckily, none were injured. They named that place First Encounter; it was near modern day Eastham. Upon further exploration they discovered Plymouth Bay and thought perhaps it was a better choice than the cape for settlement.[171]

Many on the ship were sick. The conditions were not good for staying well with such close quarters as they continued to live on board. It was colder than they expected, and they were not prepared. They were experiencing brutally cold weather during what has been called "The Little Ice Age." While the men were searching on land, there was an epidemic of illness and death on the ship. With no access to vitamin C from fresh fruit and vegetables, scurvy symptoms—bleeding gums and loose teeth—became worse and led to extreme weakness. A sense of doom and inability to fight off pneumonia, TB, and other illnesses were pervasive. The women and children cooped up on the ship began to die. It must have been very hard not to fall into despair.

On December 7, 1620, William Bradford's twenty-three-year old wife, Dorothy, slipped from the icy deck of the ship into the water and drowned. There is no evidence that it was suicide, but it certainly was a desperate time. With snow on the ground and increasing illnesses, they needed to find a permanent place and decided to set sail for Plymouth Harbor. They anchored in the shallow harbor, three quarters of a mile out, on December 16, 1620. The men who were well enough went ashore to select a good spot for their colony.[172]

By Christmas Day, with extreme effort by those who were not ill, they had erected most of the first building at their settlement site on the bay at what they called New Plimouth. It was eerily empty land, although signs that people had lived there were everywhere. There were many skeletons left out bleaching in the sun, signs of planted corn fields, and evidence that the area had been abandoned. It was obvious there had been an Indian settlement there but no sign of where the inhabitants had gone.

Keeping a nervous eye out for hostile Indians, the Pilgrims slowly started to build homes. There were so few able-bodied men, and it was so bitterly cold, that it was extraordinarily difficult work. By now, people were dying daily. During that first terrible winter, half the settlers died. More than three fourths of the women died, making the men who didn't bring their wives glad their wives had stayed in Holland. By the end of the winter, only five women were left, one of them Governor Carver's wife, who would die of a broken heart a month after her husband died of a stroke in the spring. Edward Winslow lost his wife, Elizabeth, William Bradford his wife, and Myles Standish his beloved wife, Rose. Young Samuel Fuller lost both his parents, Edward and Ann, but thankfully, he still had his uncle Dr. Samuel Fuller. Surprisingly, the girls fared the best, with only two out of eighteen dying.

William Bradford was voted in as governor and kept that position the majority of his life. Bradford, writing about that terrible time of sickness, said there were only six or so on their feet able to care for the rest. He singled out Myles Standish and William Brewster as tending to the sick in a most loving manner. "A rare example and worthy to be remembered; two of these were Mr. William Brewster, their reverend Elder, and Myles Standish, their Captain and military commander, unto whom myself and many others, were much beholden in our low and sick condition."[173]

During the winter when the pilgrims were busy just trying to survive, they had seen occasional glimpses of Indians in the woods. On March 16th, when they were busy planting crops, they were surprised by a tall, majestic Indian, naked except for his fringed leather belt, who came out of the woods and causally greeted them with, "Hello, English." Samoset stayed with them a few days and the pilgrims fed him mallard duck, cheese, and beer and gave him a horseman's coat to wear to ward off the chill. Samoset explained that the area they were settling was known by the Indians as Pawtuxet. The tribe that lived there had been wiped out by a plague of some sort.

His friend Squanto, who was an emissary of Massasoit, the sachem—chief—of the Pokanokets of the Wampanoag Federation of tribes, and who would become important to the English settlers, was the last survivor of the tribe at Pawtuxet of about two thousand living there. Ironically, he had been saved by being captured by an English slaver before the epidemic swept through the coast. Squanto spent five years in England and was very savvy about the politics of both cultures. Squanto led them to relations with Massasoit, acting as an interpreter, and a peace treaty between the Pilgrims and the Wampanoag Federation was signed that would last fifty years. He famously helped them plant their first crop of corn. Squanto would die of an illness only two years later, after some controversy and double dealing regarding his loyalty to Massasoit.[174]

The Pilgrims' dramatic first meeting with Massasoit occurred on March 22, 1621, when Massasoit and his brother Quadequina were seen standing with sixty armed braves at the top of the hill overlooking the new colony. The sachem had traveled from his home at Mount Hope, about forty miles away in what is now Rhode Island. Edward Winslow was sent to him with gifts and told him that the Pilgrims wanted peace and trading. Winslow told him that King James saluted him with love and peace and wanted him as an ally. This suited Massasoit very well. He needed an ally against his adversaries, the Narragansett tribe. The Narragansett had become his overlords, since they were not affected by the plague of a few years back that shrank Massasoit's people from an estimated 15,000 to 1,000.

Peace negotiations began, with Standish and Brewster meeting Massasoit at the river and taking him to William Bradford's house for negotiations, where they provided food and drink. They agreed to support each other if attacked, not bring weapons to trade, and support their mutual survival.

Edward Winslow wrote a description of the chief, who was in his prime:
In his person he is a very lusty man, in his best years, an able body, grave of countenance, and spare of speech. In his attire little or nothing differing from the rest of his followers, only in a great chain of white bone beads about his neck, (wampum) and at it behind his neck hangs a little bag of tobacco, which he drank and gave us to drink; his face was painted with a sad red like murry, and oiled both head and face, that he looked greasily. All of his followers likewise, were in their faces, part or in whole painted, some black, some red, some yellow, some white, some with crosses, and other antic works; some had skins on them, and some naked, all strong, all tall, all men of appearance…

Myles Standish and Edward Winslow were the Pilgrims' best linguists, and both were close friends with various Indians. They would travel back and forth, sometimes spending the night in a wigwam in an Indian village.[175]

The Pilgrims did not come to America with oppressive ideas about the Indians. Europeans were enthralled with stories of the Native Americans. Princess Pocahontas, of Jamestown and Captain John Smith fame, had been presented to the court of King James I in 1616 with all pomp and circumstance. The Pilgrims, who hoped to live peacefully, were somewhat apprehensive after reading about Indian torture, but they were very interested in the native people. The bravery and dignity of the natives was much admired. They respected the chiefs, considering them to be as important as their king at home. They were, however, somewhat disconcerted about the way Indian women were treated—the women did most of the agricultural work—and the easy sexuality among the Indians. The settlers rationalized that ancient Britons, before the Romans came, had painted their bodies like the Indians did.

The Pilgrim's minister, John Robinson, had been emphatic that the Indians had souls. They felt it was their duty to teach them Christianity, which was complicated by the fact that the tribe did not have a written language. The Pilgrims felt reading the Bible was essential to understanding God's word. The Wampanoag spoke a language belonging to the Algonquian family, closely related to the Pequot, Mohican, and Narragansett. We have borrowed many of their words, such as moose, chipmunk, raccoon, opossum, skunk, squash, squaw, and moccasin.

Edward Winslow made a great effort to understand and phonetically write down the language of the Wampanoag. Eventually, an Indian Bible in the Massachusetts dialect of Wampanoag was transcribed and printed by a later settler and missionary, "the Apostle to the Indians," John Eliot of Duxbury.[176]

There were conflicts and misunderstandings due to the vast differences in culture. The New England Indian tribes were much less advanced than those of the Southwest and other areas of America. They were living as hunter-gatherers with some simple farming and led a semi-nomadic lifestyle. They did not understand much of the Western concept of land or rights, and the settlers did not understand that the Indians did not have permanent homes but operated by season. They rapidly adapted to the tools and materials the Pilgrims brought with them, as it made their lives much easier. They had no domesticated animals other than dogs, no wheel, and no metal tools, but they were eager and quick to learn.

The relationship changed the culture and living patterns of the both native tribes and the Pilgrims. The Pilgrims used the Indian method for planting corn and were helped by this knowledge, as well as other adaptations to the new land, such as new foods, but the Indian culture was affected the most by the newcomers.

When the Mayflower finally left for England in April 1621, the Pilgrims were very sorry to see it go. They were on their own in this strange new land. Master Jones had not intended to stay so long, but he and his crew had been in no shape to depart earlier. The Pilgrims intended to send both furs and timber on the trip back, but with so many in a state of semi-starvation, it was hard to accomplish. The ship carried stones from the harbor for weight instead. With a mostly empty hull, Master Jones sailed back in half the time it had taken to come across the Atlantic, even with a sickly, smaller crew. The starvation and illness of that terrible winter in Plymouth probably shortened the life of Master Jones, who died the next year. The battered old *Mayflower* was left in the Thames River to rot and was sold for scrap a few years later.[177]

By the fall of 1621, after almost a year in the New World, the Pilgrims were still building their town and fort. A letter written by Edward Winslow states, "We have built seven dwelling houses, and four for use of the plantation." Fire caused them to lose some of the houses. The original thatched roofs were eventually banned because of fire hazard.

By the following year, they had built a fence eight to nine feet high around the half-mile perimeter of the town.

Myles Standish had a great deal to do with the placement and layout of the colony. Historian Nathaniel Philbrick thinks it is probable that Standish had training in military engineering from the University of Leiden and decided the layout of the settlement. The two-story fort, which also served as the meeting house for church services, was at the west end of the main street at the highest point overlooking the bay. It was fortified with several large cannons. Standish was responsible for training the men and organizing the watch shifts. They had to worry not just about possible hostilities from Indians but also the Dutch and French.[178]

The colony rejoiced to see the *Fortune* sailing into the harbor in November 1621, after at first worrying that it might be an enemy ship. It brought thirty-five young men, as well as Deacon Robert Cushman, who finally made it to the colony.

Cushman was known for his extensive study of the Bible. He stayed only two weeks but preached a sermon to the Pilgrims, urging them to be faithful to their best instincts. He also brought a new patent, as the original for the mouth of the Hudson was no longer valid. The *Fortune* also brought a letter from Weston, scolding them for not sending the Mayflower back with more goods. He obviously did not realize their dire straits, as very few supplies came with the men on the ship.

With new people to feed, the Pilgrims were forced to tighten their belts even more, but that month they celebrated what is now called the First Thanksgiving. Both natives and Pilgrims alike were grateful for having come though extremely difficult times of sorrow and death. So many women had died that there were only four in the colony at that first Thanksgiving.[179]

Myles Standish and Edward Winslow both were influenced by their personal relationships with the Indians. Winslow saved Massasoit's life in March 1623 at a low time for both the tribe and the Pilgrims, caring for him when he was sick, treating him with fruit preserves and chicken broth from the Plymouth chickens, and staying with him to minister to him. Massasoit may have had typhus. By the time Winslow got to him, he could not see, was in terrible pain with constipation of almost a week and had not swallowed anything for two days.

This became an important event in the story of the Pilgrims. Because Massasoit was so grateful for his care, he told Edward of a plot by the neighboring tribe, the Massachusetts, to do away with the settlement of Weston's men at Wessagussett—Weymouth—as well as Plymouth. Massasoit urged the Pilgrims to take action.

The plot was foiled by Captain Standish and his men, including the Indian Hobbamock. Standish became close friends with Hobbamock. He was considered a special warrior and advisor to sachem Massasoit, was called a pniese, and was thought to be invincible in battle. He was also responsible for collecting tribute for his sachem. Hobbamock moved to land near Standish early on and was devoted to both Standish and Massasoit. The two warriors lived near each other for the rest of their lives. Hobbamock converted to Christianity and was one of what were called the "Praying Indians."[180]

Standish led two major raids on Indian villages, the first to find and punish Corbitant, sachem of the Narragansett, for an attempted coup and kidnapping of Squanto, which Hobbamock had discovered. This raid earned Standish much respect. The second raid, at Wessagussett, to punish the Massachusetts tribe after Massasoit informed the Pilgrims of the plan for annihilation of the colonies, seems to have backfired. It so frightened the Indians away from trading that the Pilgrims had to use the Wampanoag as middlemen.

Thomas Weston, while pretending to back the success of the Pilgrims, sent sixty men to form a competing settlement near the Massachusetts Indians at Wessagussett. Unlike the highly disciplined Pilgrims, who had a moral code to live by, these men lived in disorder, constantly stole from the Indians, and caused general havoc. They were eventually desperate and starving.

The Indians soon had enough of them and hatched a plot to get rid of them but realized they would have to get rid of Plymouth as well. Standish and his men, including Hobbamock, led a preemptive strike, killing several Indians and bringing the head of the Massachusetts priest, Wituwamat, back to Plymouth, where it was raised on a pike and stood as a grim reminder for years. The Pilgrims were grateful, but it was thought too violent by Standish's dear friend John Robinson, who was distressed when the news reached him in Holland.[181]

Another event in 1623 would change the colony. The ships *Anne* and *Little James* brought family from Leiden, including Samuel Fuller's wife, Bridget, and their child, other wives and children who had been left behind, and a new wife, Barbara, for Myles Standish. After three long years without a partner, Standish married Barbara late in 1623 in a civil ceremony. Bradford and Winslow, as well as other widowers and widows, remarried as quickly as they could. They considered marriage a civil ceremony as it was in Holland. This was the beginning of the idea of separation of church and state, which the Pilgrims practiced in their community.[182]

Slowly, the community was growing in size. Edward Winslow made a trip to London in 1624, bringing back the first cattle: a bull and three cows. "Plymouth now had one hundred and eighty inhabitants, thirty-two houses, a grain store and plenty of cattle pigs and poultry." The original idea of fishing for profit did not pan out, but the Pilgrims did become heavily involved in the fur trade. They established their first trading post at Buzzard Bay on the Manomet River and, eventually, had posts up and down the coast, including up the Kennebec River in Maine. The European craze for broad-brimmed felt hats led to a boom in the beaver fur trade. The beaver's thick fur made excellent felt. With the Wampanoag as intermediaries, the Pilgrims sent tons of beaver fur to England.

Standish continued to try to keep the colony safe during its expansion. The massacre of 380 settlers by Indians in Jamestown, Virginia, in 1622, was at the back of his mind.[183]

Although criticized by his enemies as hotheaded—a little cannon quickly fired—Standish was much loved and respected by the colony. He had a warm and loving manner and helped care for both colonists and Indians. He sent many wounded Indians to Dr. Samuel Fuller to be cared for. He was reelected over and over as commander of the militia and was later sent to neighboring settlements to help with disputes. He served in many capacities in the colony, serving as assistant governor and treasurer of Plymouth.

Standish made several trips back to London to bring trading goods and to negotiate a settlement with the Merchant Adventurers, who were difficult to deal with regarding their debt. Despite sending thousands of pounds of beaver skins and timber to the investors, they were not able to pay off what they owed—one ship was seized by the French, another by the Turks—and the merchant group finally declared bankruptcy. Isaac Allerton, one of the Pilgrims who had been doing a lot of the trading, had pocketed some of the money, so they sent Myles to trade instead. Finally, with Allerton's assistance, an agreement was reached where Myles Standish, William Bradford, and the other leaders of the colony, including Dr. Samuel Fuller, bought out the Merchant Adventurers and assumed the colony's debt.[184]

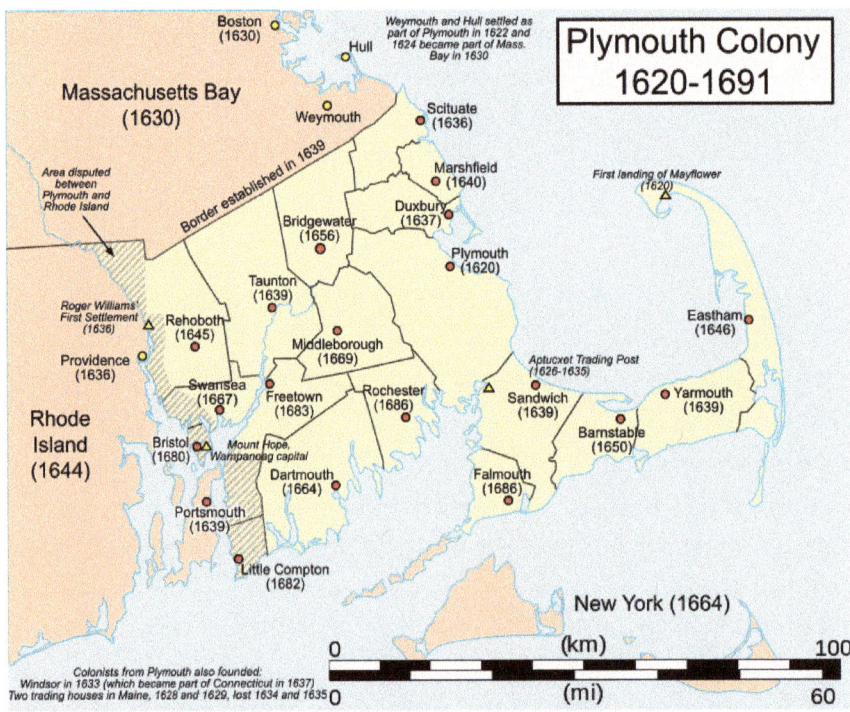

Map of Plymouth Colony, source: www.colonialamerica.thinkport.org

One of the final letters from Pastor John Robinson in Leiden to Plymouth refers to Standish as, "The Captain that I love and am persuaded the Lord in great mercy and for much good has sent. He is a man humble and meek amongst you, and towards all in ordinary course." After a trip to London in 1625, Myles brought back the terrible news that their beloved pastor had died in Leiden. Robinson was only forty-nine. It devastated all. They had never given up hope that their spiritual leader would make it to the colony. That same year Robert Cushman died in London during a bubonic plague outbreak, adding to the Pilgrim's sorrow.

Myles never forgot his dear friend John Robinson, and in his will years later, he left money to Robinson's granddaughter, "Whom I tenderly love for her grandfather's sake." Robinson planned to come to Plymouth once the majority of his church had emigrated, but the backers of the venture never supported his passage. His influence lingered, with one colonist, Elizabeth Tilly Howland, leaving her most precious possession, one of his books, *Observations Divine and Mortal,* to her family in her will.[185]

By 1627 the Plymouth colony was considered a modest success. Puritan Englishmen thought they could have a new life in New England. Over time, as more Puritans came to the colony, it became harder to maintain the core group of Pilgrims in Plymouth. New towns were settled nearby, across the bay, and up the Cape. Duxbury, Marshfield, and Scituate were settled to the north. To the south they formed Sandwich, Barnstable, and Yarmouth on Cape Cod.

In 1630 John Winthrop and the newly formed Massachusetts Bay Colony brought Puritans who were not Separatists to settle just north and south of Boston harbor and on the rivers nearby.

John Alden and Myles Standish were the first to move away from Plymouth and establish Duxbury, which was located just north of Plymouth. They intended to come back for church services on Sundays, but that proved infeasible in bad weather, and eventually, the new towns all had their own meeting houses.

The first division of property occurred in 1623 and again in 1627, assigning individual lots in Plymouth and division of the livestock. Although the company insisted houses and property belonged to them until the debts were paid, it was impractical to hold everything communally. The community also had trouble holding some of the strangers to the rules. People understandably work harder on their own property.

While serving Plymouth Colony in many government roles, Myles and his wife raised five sons who lived to adulthood—Alexander, John Myles, Josiah, and Charles—as well as a daughter, Loara. Myles' daughter made a sampler with silk embroidery that still survives. At the time, samplers were done by well-educated, young English ladies to show their skill in embroidery.

Loara Standish is my name
Lord guide my heart that
I may do thy will also
My hands with such
Convenient skill as may
Conduce to virtue void of
Shame and I will give
The glory to thy name.

One of Loara's brothers, Josiah Standish, would become a soldier like his father. He would also serve in government. The Pilgrims in Plymouth Colony first proclaimed their laws in a General Assembly. By 1636 the General Fundamentals were written, including a bill of rights, trial by jury, right of the government to levy taxes, distribution of land, and punishment for crimes. They relied on English Common Law and Biblical laws for their framework. Women had more rights than their English counterparts. They could not be written out of their husband's will and in some cases served on juries.

In 1658 Josiah was made a member of the Council of War. He then moved to Bridgewater and was elected lieutenant on June 6, 1660. Moving back to Duxbury in 1663, he held a number of positions: member of the Grand Inquest, 1664; deputy to the General Court, 1665; and selectman, 1666. Later, he was elected again to various posts, including deputy to the General Court, 1671-1682. Elections were held yearly for many posts in the colony, and he was repeatedly reelected. His daughter Mercy was the owner of the Bible that Daniel Adlum's great grandmother kept safe for so long until, sadly, it was lost in 1830.[186]

Dr. Samuel Fuller faithfully served his community as well. He was a self-trained healer, as was the case in the day. It is possible that he attended medical lectures at the University of Leiden before coming to Plymouth. He was sent by Plymouth to help sick and dying newcomers at the Salem settlement led by John Endicott in 1629 and to help Salem establish a church, since he had experience as an active deacon in the Plymouth church. He attempted to alleviate suffering when he could and was much appreciated by the community, as he was by the settlement at Charlestown that he helped the following year. Dr. Fuller wrote a letter to William Bradford on August 2, 1630, from Charlestown that said, "The sad news here is, that many are sick, and many are dead. The Lord in mercy look upon them! I can do them little good, for I want drugs, and things fitting to work with." Seventeenth-century medicine could not do much for the scourges of the day such as smallpox.[187]

Thomas Morton, who established an undisciplined trading post he called Merrymount, a few miles north from Plymouth, and whose behavior with Indians would cause grief for the Pilgrims, had nothing nice to say about either Capt. Myles Standish or Dr. Fuller.

He called Standish, "Captain Shrimpe" and ridiculed the appearance of Dr. Fuller. He describes Dr. Fuller as follows: "He wears a long beard and a garment like the Greek that begged in Paul's church." Morton was scornful of Fuller's care, stating: "He did a great cure for Captain Littleworth (his mocking nickname for John Endicott) he cured him of a disease called a wife."[188]

In 1633 there was another round of illness in Plymouth—probably, smallpox—that killed twenty of the Pilgrims and very many of the Indians. Dr. Fuller became ill, caring for the sick, as did his wife. He made out his will on July 30, 1633, to provide for his children, his nephew Samuel, and the other children he had taken in, not knowing if his wife would survive him or not. His nephew Samuel was one of the executers of the will, which was proved on October 28, 1633. The exact date of his death is not known. He gave Samuel his share of stock and swine, as well as a garment, and provided for all his children and his wife. He had the most livestock of anyone in the colony at the time and two houses, one in town and one in the country. He had a large number of books: probably, at least ten to twenty medical texts, as well as religious books. He was the first physician to settle in New England. His son Samuel and nephew Matthew would follow in his footsteps in medicine. William Bradford called him, "A man godly, and forward to doe good, being missed after his death."[189]

After the death of his uncle, Samuel Fuller set out with his livestock for the town of Scituate. He became a freeman of the colony in 1634, joining the church in Scituate in November 1636 and elected constable in 1641. He had twenty acres of land there and built what was the fifteenth house in town. There he met Jane Lothrop, daughter of the famed Rev. John Lothrop (sometimes spelled Lothropp or Lathrop), minister of Scituate. Captain Myles Standish—the seventh-great-grandfather of Daniel B. Adlum—Magistrate of Plymouth Colony, performed the marriage ceremony of Samuel Fuller and Jane Lothrop on the eighth of April of 1635 in Scituate. (They became the eighth-great-grandparents of Patricia Reese.)

The ceremony was held in the house of Mr. Cudworth and can be imagined to have been observed by the leading citizens of the town. Samuel and Jane no doubt shared a bond in the tragic history of their families. Samuel was orphaned as a child; Jane lost her mother while her father was imprisoned in England, leaving her and her siblings practically orphaned.

Jane's father, John Lothrop, was a prominent Puritan voice in England. He was an Anglican clergyman who became a Congregationalist minister at a dangerous time in England's history. William Laud, who became Bishop of London in 1628, was an autocratic ruler of the Anglican Church and very much opposed Calvinism. As Charles I began his rule in 1629, Laud became more powerful, leading to him becoming Archbishop of Canterbury in 1633. Laud had Lothrop, along with fellow Puritan ministers, thrown into Newgate Prison and the Clink, the notorious medieval prison located in the Tower of London. We still use the term "thrown in the clink" to mean "sent to prison."[190]

Lothrop was born in Etton of Yorkshire County and was baptized on December 20, 1584. He attended Queen's College at Cambridge, where he finished his BA in 1605 and MA in 1609. He was ordained in the Church of England and appointed to a local parish in Kent. By 1623 he had renounced his orders and joined the Independents. In 1624 he was called to London to replace Rev. Henry Jacob as the pastor of the First Independent Church, which based its practices on those established by Rev. John Robinson in Leiden. The church met in Southwark—just across the Thames from London—in secret. They were discovered and arrested for failure to take the oath of loyalty to the Church of England. Most were released after some time in prison, but Lothrop was thought too dangerous to let out. Lothrop's wife, Hannah House—also from a prominent Puritan family—died while he was in prison. Finally, Laud agreed to free him if he would agree to leave the country and sail for the New World, taking his congregation with him.[191]

Lothrop sailed on the *Griffin* with his family and members of his congregation, landing in Boston on September 18, 1634. Anne Hutchinson, who would become a famous religious dissenter in the Massachusetts Bay Colony, was on the ship as well. Lothrop moved to Scituate, which was founded by men from Kent County, England, with whom he was familiar, including Henry Rowley, whose son Moses would marry into the Fuller family when he married Elizabeth Fuller, Samuel's niece.

Lothrop described the houses in Scituate as "meane." The walls were made of poles filled with stone and clay, with thatched roofs, oiled-paper windows, and rough plank floors. He described them as mere "booths" because they were open and the occupants had to have a fire piled high at all times to stay warm in winter. Lothrop built a large meeting house and home, finished in 1644, that is still in use as a library in Barnstable. It was a pioneer town for these pilgrims with new ideas about how to worship. Lothrop was a strong proponent of the idea of separation of church and state.

Plaque at Lothrop Hill Cemetery, Rev. John Lothrop, Barnstable, MA, Ancestry.com

Governor John Winthrop recorded in his journal Lothrop's statement on arrival, rejoicing in finding, "a church without a bishop… and a state without a king."

Lothrop died in 1653, leaving a large number of accomplished descendants, including six presidents, notables in education, government, and arts. He is buried in Barnstable on Lothrop's Hill near the Meeting House with other family members, including Jane and her husband, Samuel Fuller, nearby.[192]

Scituate had a rough start with its rocky soil that proved difficult to farm or to raise cattle on. There were fields lying fallow for years, abandoned as a result of the native deaths from epidemics. The new residents used these fields to plant crops but needed to supplement their incomes with fishing and ship building. The men from Kent who started the town were more businessmen than farmers. Eventually, ship building became a large industry in Scituate. Historian Jeremy Bangs claims that by 1650 Scituate was double the size of Plymouth and was wealthier.[193]

The large increase in English settlers to both Plymouth Colony and the Massachusetts Bay Colony put increasing pressure on relations with the native Indian tribes. Combined with competition from the Dutch and French for the beaver fur trade, there was jockeying for economic position among the Indians and the Europeans. Control of the fur trade was the main goal of all parties involved. Misunderstandings and upsets escalated between the different parties, leading to the Pequot War of 1637. Although most of the fighting was in Connecticut, all of Plymouth Colony, Massachusetts Bay Colony, and Saybrook Colony united to fight the Pequot.

The Pequot were a fierce, aggressive tribe with a lot of power over the fur trade and currency in the form of wampum with their ideal location at the lower Connecticut River and head of the Thames and Mystic rivers. They ignored their agreement to allow other tribes access to fur trading posts on the rivers. The years of disease weakened all the tribes and increased economic insecurities. The influx of settlers into the Connecticut River Valley pressured them as well.

The Mohegan split from the Pequot, who then became their enemies. Uncas, sachem of the Mohegan, kept the English in a state of anxiety about the Pequot's intentions towards them. There were several incidences that inflamed tensions. The Niantic, a subtribe of the Pequot, killed a trader, Captain John Stone, and some of his men in 1634. Everyone hated Stone, as he was a terrible man. He had been banned from Massachusetts Bay Colony for misbehavior, but he was English, so his death needed to be protested. Another trader, John Oldham, was killed in 1636, his head and hands chopped off—although by the Block Island Indians, not by the Pequots—and the English sought retribution.

After many attempts at diplomacy, tensions increased. Led by Capt. John Endecott, the English retaliated against the Pequot at the Pequot village near Fort Saybrook by burning the village and killing one Indian. The Indians retaliated with a long siege of Fort Saybrook that led to desperation and starvation among the settlers inside, and then they attacked Wethersfield, killing many settlers and capturing two girls. The Pequot tried to get other tribes to join with them, but the Mohegan, Wampanoag, and Mohawk sided with the English. The Narragansett to the north stayed neutral, thanks to the intervention of Roger Williams. Finally, the militia of the colonies, with their Indian allies, surrounded the Pequot settlement at Mystic. After a terrible massacre, where some 500 Pequot lost their lives—many burned to death after fires broke out—the Pequot were defeated. Some survivors were sold into slavery in the West Indies. The 200 Pequot remaining were forced to join other Indian tribes and no longer use the name Pequot.

The Indian allies of the English were shocked by the brutality of the battle. They supposedly said, "Why must you be so furious?" The native Indians were used to a constant state of warfare between tribes, but it was very different from European warfare. According to Scott Weidensaul, author of *The First Frontier,* "Indian warfare included small scale raids, ritual torture and a tit for tat type constant testing of the warriors of their enemy tribes." They also took captives to sometimes use as slaves or to replace family members. They would make captured enemies run the gauntlet and routinely used slow, ritual torturing to death of their enemies as part of their framework of war. "They could extend war for years in this manner, but typically, large numbers were not killed." The results of this war were sobering for all sides but especially, for the Indian tribes. There was a shift in power now that the powerful Pequot had been vanquished. The Narragansett became the dominant tribe. Uncas, the scheming sachem of the Mohegan, had his influence increased as well.[194]

Captain Myles Standish did not appear to take part in the Pequot War, but he was called upon soon after to defend Massasoit from enemies, as per their treaty of 1621. A Narragansett sachem called Miantonomo led an attack against Massasoit, which Standish countered with a threat for the sachem to make restitution to Massasoit or face vengeance. The threat worked and Miantonomo returned every stolen item to Massasoit and made restitution.[195]

Soon after the Pequot War, Rev. Lothrop and his congregation started the town of Barnstable on Cape Cod in 1639, taking half the town of Scituate with them. There had been disagreements about baptisms in the church and lack of arable land in Scituate, so his church made a fresh start. Samuel Fuller and his wife, Jane, followed him and spent the rest of their lives in Barnstable. A welcome newcomer was Samuel's brother Matthew and his wife, Francis, and family, who moved from England about 1640. Samuel had not seen his brother since he was a child, twenty years earlier. Matthew Fuller quickly became an active member of the community.[196]

By 1643 Matthew Fuller was a sergeant in a military company of the colony headed by Captain Standish. In 1650 Matthew established himself as the first physician in Barnstable, following the profession of his uncle and cousin. In 1653 he represented Barnstable at the Plymouth Colony Court. He had liberal views and took a stand on the side of the unpopular Quakers—who were mostly condemned in the colony—for which he was fined. One of his daughters, Mary later married Quaker Ralph Jones in Barnstable. Matthew's daughter Anne married her cousin Samuel Fuller, grandson of Edward Fuller and son of Samuel and Jane. [197]

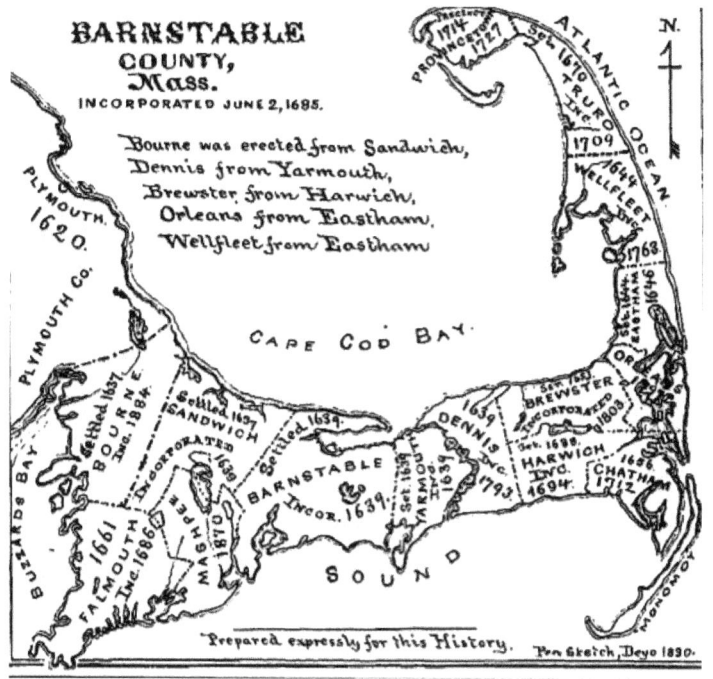

Map of Barnstable County, MA 1890, image www.en.wikipedia.org

The 1650s solidified the English colonists' hold on the coast of New England. By some estimates, there were some 23,000 settlers up and down the coast, straining the native people's ability to hold onto their land and way of life. As the fur trade slowed, Indians had no way to pay for the English goods they desired, and they increasingly sold land, leaving them in a more and more desperate situation.

The old guard who tried to maintain a fragile truce and coexistence was dying out. William Brewster, the faithful spiritual advisor to the Pilgrims, died in 1644. He left a library of some 400 books he had collected during his lifetime. On October 3, 1656, Captain Myles Standish died after suffering from some kind of kidney disease, perhaps kidney stones. He was active to the end in his loyal defense of the Pilgrim colony. He had some interesting books in his collection, including a history of the world, Turkish, German, and Swedish histories, Homer's *Iliad*, Caesar's *Commentaries*, and Barriffe's *Artillery*. He also had a history of Queen Elizabeth, as well as practical books and religious books. His estate in Duxbury was valued at about £140. William Bradford, the strong leader of the colony for so many years, and source of most of our information about the Pilgrims, became ill in the fall of 1656 and died on May 6, 1657. Edward Winslow, who had been an important part of the story of the Pilgrims, died at sea in the West Indies in 1656 after some years as Plymouth's diplomat in London. Massasoit, slowing down and diminished in his power, died in 1660. The new generations of both sides were facing different circumstances than their parents had, and they now had to make different decisions.[198]

Massasoit's oldest son, Wamsutta—English name, Alexander—died in 1662, just two years after his father. His younger brother Metacomet—Philip—became sachem of the Pokanoket and Grand Sachem of the Wampanoag. Metacomet had a great dislike for Josiah Winslow, son of Edward Winslow, who had been such a friend to his father. Josiah, who was now governor of Plymouth Colony, had Metacomet's brother Wamsutta arrested for selling land to Roger Williams in Rhode Island, even though Wampanoag outside of Plymouth were not subject to Plymouth's laws. His brother died shortly after this, and Metacomet wondered if he had been poisoned. Most likely, he died of a disease to which he had no immunity. Metacomet, who did not have the talents of his father and was thought to be vain and impulsive, felt increasingly pressured to find a way out of the situation of having to sell lands for his support. Grumbling among his braves led him to start preparing for confrontation. He began to stockpile guns and ammunition.[199]

When the Pilgrims first started trading with the Indians, they set down laws about selling them liquor or guns. They saw that many "dranke themselves drunke," with sad results for all around them. One of the problems the Pilgrims had with Thomas Morton was that he plied the Indians with liquor and sold them arms, along with his parties with Indian women. The Pilgrims tried to make sure the Indians had proper titles to their land and were not selling it away under the influence of liquor.

The Indians had a strong desire for the superior English goods and tools and, increasingly, used wampum as currency to trade. These small white beads made from shells and woven into belts and other items become an important currency for Pilgrims as well. The Pilgrims recorded sales of land from the Indians and tried to document every purchase. Some of the Indians began to think they had a clear disadvantage. Pilgrim and Puritan families were having seven to eight children, while the birthrate for Indians was less, creating more pressure. Historian David Brainerd states that, "although the Pilgrims generally treated the natives as a race apart, they made a conscious effort to treat them fairly." However, since the Indians were not really considered equal in the society, they came out on the short end. Brainerd goes on to say, "The end result was mostly because of the introduction of new diseases and a societal system to which the Indians could not fully adjust for several generations."[200]

There was suspicion that King Philip, as the English called Metacomet, was planning an attack against them. The lives of the English settlers and the various Indian tribes were intertwined in many ways. Indians sought recourse in colony courts for many matters, even murder. In Plymouth three Englishmen were hung after being convicted of murdering an Indian. With missionary efforts, about 1,000 Indians converted to Christianity and were settled in villages of Praying Indians in Plymouth Colony. The Mohegan and Mohawk tribes were traditionally aligned with Plymouth, as were the Wampanoag with their long-standing treaty with the Pilgrims. All the different colonies such as Massachusetts Bay Colony, Connecticut, New Haven, and Rhode Island established separate relations with the different tribes—the Wampanoag, Nipmuc, Narragansett, Mohegan, Pequot, and other tribes of New England—many of which were traditional enemies of each other. Diplomacy failed to calm the competing interests, and what we now call King Phillip's War blazed with terrible consequences.

The spark that ignited the war started with the story of a "praying Indian" called John Sassamon, who was a protégé of John Eliot, the missionary. Eliot sent Sassamon to Harvard—established in 1636—to study, and he became well versed in both cultures. He served as an interpreter to King Philip. In January of 1675 he came to Gov. Josiah Winslow with the news that Philip planned to gather allies to attack the English. Winslow sat on the news until late January when Sassamon's body was found in the ice-covered Assawompset Pond. After an inquest, it appeared it was murder. Based on testimony of an Indian witness, Plymouth Colony authorities arrested three of Philip's men, tried them with a jury of twelve members of Plymouth Colony and six elders of the Praying Indians, and hung them.

Two weeks later, on June 20, 1675, the attacks on English settlements began, first destroying the small Plymouth settlement of Swansea. Philip tried to draw other tribes into the fight. The Praying Indians stayed loyal to the English, as did the Mohegan and the Mohawk. The Nipmuc, the Narragansett and Pocumtuc tribes all became allies of the Wampanoag, but they did not necessarily follow Philip. Their sachems called the shots for their tribes. It was a civil war that would rip apart intertwined relationships between tribes and settlers.

Other attacks came fast and furious, with the Indians hitting town after town, destroying what they could, forcing Gov. Winslow to call up a militia in Plymouth Colony of 1,000 men and about 2,00 Indian allies. An alliance was eventually formed between the colonies of Massachusetts Bay, Connecticut, New Haven, and Plymouth to provide assistance for the war.[201]

The Standish and Fuller families were drawn into the fight. Myles' son Josiah, who had been a lieutenant of the militia in Bridgewater since 1660, was promoted to captain during the war. His father, Myles, had been one of the original purchasers of land, buying the land from Massasoit. Matthew Fuller had been surgeon general of the Plymouth military since 1673, earning four shillings a day for his work. He was appointed captain and was in charge of the Plymouth troops in the war. His son, Lieutenant Samuel Fuller, fell fighting Indians at Rehoboth on March 25, 1676.

Captain Matthew Fuller knew of the military talent of Captain Benjamin Church, considered to be "America's first Ranger," having been appointed by Governor Winslow to form the first American Ranger Company, incorporating native Indians and their methods of fighting into his force. Church—Daniel Adlum's seventh-great-uncle—was a frontiersman living near the Saconnet Indians in Rhode Island. Captain Fuller asked Church to go with him to Pocasset to flush out Philip and end the war. Fuller said he was "too ancient and heavy" to be chasing Indians.

Church was more than ready to be in the fight. Church and thirty-six men transferred by boat to the shores of Pocasset. Fuller and Church split up the men, Fuller heading north and Church heading south towards his home area of Sakonnet—now Little Compton, Rhode Island. Church and his men were ambushed in a field where they could only crouch

Colonel Benjamin Church, first American Ranger, image www.enwikipedia.org

behind a small crumbling wall while 300 Indians shot at them. Church and twenty men held off the enemy for six hours before they were able to sneak away via canoes on the Sakonnet River. The battle is known as the Pease Field Fight. Church attributed their escape without casualties to "the glory of god and His protecting Providence." Church and his men were eventually responsible for cornering Philip. He and his men chased Philip into the Miery swamp. An Indian militia member named John Alderman shot Philip on August 12, 1676. This ended fighting in the south but fighting would continue in northern New England until a treaty was signed in April of 1678.[202]

King Philip's War is considered to be the deadliest war per capita in the history of America. In a little more than a year, at least twelve towns were completely destroyed and many more ruined, with Indians attacking at least half the towns in New England. The economies of Plymouth and Rhode Island suffered terribly. There was a great loss of life on the colonist side and even greater loss on the Indian side. More than 1,000 colonists died, and an estimated 2,000 Indians were killed, with another 3,000 Indians dying of sickness and starvation. The towns of Praying Indians suffered much, even though they had been on the side of the English. There was widespread destruction, including the death of 8,000 cattle. The economy suffered such losses that there was no expansion for fifty years. There were excesses on both sides; the colonists were so horrified by the destruction and torture done by the Indians that they responded with fury.

There was much anxiety and discussion about what to do with the captive Indians. Church and Eliot were among those who thought they should be treated with care. Nevertheless, many were sold as slaves and sent to the West Indies, including Philip's wife and child.

King Phillip, Philip, King of Mount Hope, image by Paul Revere, Yale University Art Gallery, public domain via Wikipedia Commons

The war changed New England forever. It was the last attempt of the Indian tribes to drive the English out and the first time the colonists had felt truly American. They had defended themselves and survived.[203]

Captain Matthew Fuller lived to see the treaty signed, but he was in his seventies and exhausted. He had given his all to Plymouth Colony. He made out his will, dated July 25, 1678, and then closed his eyes for the last time. His property was handed down to his wife and children. His estate lay in the northwest corner of Barnstable at Scorton Neck. He and his brother Samuel both had estates in this part of Barnstable that bordered the town of Sandwich. Matthew also owned land in Falmouth and Middleboro that been given to him by the colony for distinguished service. He died a wealthy man with a large estate of £667, including pearls, precious jewels, and diamonds. His brother Samuel died in Barnstable on October 31, 1683, and was buried next to his beloved wife, Jane. Samuel was one of the very last remaining passengers of the *Mayflower* when he died. He left a more modest estate than his brother but still did well and was considered a man of fine character and ability. Captain Josiah Standish moved his family to New London, Connecticut, in 1686, having bought land there. He died in 1690, followed a few months later by his wife, just as the influence of Plymouth Colony was fading. The 3,000 residents of Plymouth Colony were annexed into Massachusetts Bay Colony in 1691.[204]

The Pilgrims of Plymouth Colony who started the colonization of New England were eventually overshadowed by the much larger settlements of Puritans in Massachusetts Bay Colony and Connecticut. These radical Separatists, who suffered so much for their beliefs, never achieved their Zion of a perfect, godly community in the New World, but they strove to live by their commandments and sense of duty. They had optimism and buoyancy about the future. When the new church at Salem began, William Bradford had this to say. "As one small candle may light thousands, so the light kindled here hath shone unto many, yea in some sort of our whole nation." They managed to maintain a fragile peace for fifty years and succeed as a colony against all odds. Their strength of character and self-discipline under duress set the stage for continuing growth in self-government and democracy for their many descendants, including those of Myles Standish and the Fullers. The Puritans of Massachusetts and Connecticut, along with the rest of New England, would carry on what they began so courageously.[205]

Chapter Five

For the Common Good

Family Cast of Characters

William Paine…(1600-1660) *ninth-great-grandfather of Patricia Reese*
Anna North…(1563-1645) *ninth-great-grandmother of Patricia Reese*
Robert Paine…(1601-1684) *ninth-great-uncle of Patricia Reese*
John Paine…(1632-1675?) *eldest son of William Paine and Anna North*
Hannah Paine…(1630-1656) *daughter of William; wife of Major Samuel Appleton; eighth-great-grandmother of Patricia Reese*

Major Samuel Appleton…(1624-1696) *married Hannah Paine; eighth-great-grandfather of Patricia Reese*
Judith Appleton…(1653-1741) *daughter of Samuel and Hannah Paine Appleton; seventh-great-grandmother of Patricia Reese*

Henry Wolcott Sr.…(1584-1655) *ninth-great-grandfather of Patricia Reese*
Elizabeth Saunders…(1584-1655) *ninth-great-grandmother of Patricia of Patricia Reese*
Henry Wolcott Jr.…(1610-1680) *lived in Wethersfield, CT; son of Henry Sr.; eighth-great-grandfather of Patricia Reese*
Sarah Wolcott…(1622-1684) *wife of Henry Wolcott Jr.; eighth-great-grandmother of Patricia Reese*
Samuel Wolcott…(1656-1695) *married Judith Appleton; son of Henry Wolcott Jr.*
Sarah Wolcott…(1686-1738) *married Richard Welles Jr.; daughter of Samuel and Judith; sixth-great-grandmother of Patricia Reese*
General Oliver Wolcott Sr.…(1726-1797) *Governor of Connecticut cousin, 8 times removed, of Patricia Reese*

Sir Richard Saltonstall…(1521-1601) *Lord Mayor of London; twelfth-great-grandfather of Patricia Reese*
Sir Richard Saltonstall Jr.…(1586-1661) *nephew of Sir Richard; cousin of Patricia Reese*

Governor Thomas Welles…(1590-1660) *Colonial Governor of Connecticut; ninth-great-grandfather of Patricia Reese*
Alice Tomes…(1593-1646) *wife of Governor Welles; ninth-great-grandmother of Patricia Reese*

John Welles...(1621-1659) *son of Thomas Welles; eighth-great-grandfather of Patricia Reese*
Captain Richard Welles Jr....(1684-1738) *married Sarah Wolcott; great-grandson of Thomas Welles; sixth-great-grandfather of Patricia Reese*

Governor William Leete...(1613-1683) *Governor of New Haven and Connecticut; eighth-great-grandfather of Daniel B. Adlum*
Anne Payne...(1621-1668) *wife of Governor Leete; eighth-great-grandmother of Daniel B. Adlum*
Andrew Leete...(1643-1702) *magistrate; youngest son of William Leete; seventh-great-grandfather of Daniel B. Adlum*
Elizabeth Jordan...(1650-1701) *wife of Andrew Leete; seventh-great-grandmother of Daniel B. Adlum*

Rev. Henry Whitfield...(1597-1657) *founder of Guilford, CT; ninth-great-grandfather of Daniel B. Adlum*
Dorothy Scheafe...(1601-1669) *wife of Rev. Whitfield; ninth-great-grandmother of Daniel B. Adlum*

The Puritans
in Massachusetts Bay and Connecticut Colonies

Any person who chooses to enter a society "must willingly bind and engage himself to each member of that society to promote the good of the whole."

~ **Thomas Hooker**

Puritans in England during the 1620s and '30s were becoming more apprehensive about the future of their country. As they became more outspoken about the policies of the government of Charles I, they began to lose their livelihoods in increasing numbers. Prominent ministers such as Thomas Shepard, John Cotton, and John Davenport lost their positions, while Rev. Thomas Hooker was forced to leave England and go to Holland. John Winthrop, an attorney and wealthy member of the gentry, lost his position at court. He joined the Massachusetts Bay Colony—formed in 1629 in Cambridge, England as a trading company—which started as a colony at Salem with John Endicott as Governor. Winthrop found investors and likeminded individuals to follow him to Massachusetts. He was convinced that he was called to create a new, godly society that would be an example for all to follow. His sermon, "A Model of Christian Charity, given on the ship *Arbella* while sailing to Massachusetts, inspired the Puritans to think of their calling to create a model Christian community in the New World. Their shining example of "A City on a Hill" would light the way for others. Patricia Reese's Puritan ancestors William Paine and Samuel Appleton of Ipswich, Massachusetts, as well as Gov. Thomas Welles and Henry Wolcott Jr. of Connecticut, were a part of this group of committed Puritans who sought to form an improved Christian society and civil government.

The 21,000 Puritans who came to New England during the decade between 1630 and 1640 were well educated and highly skilled compared to the immigrants in Virginia Colony. At home in England they were a small, persecuted minority, perhaps only ten percent of England's population, and were radicals in both religion and politics. Close to half the immigrants to the New World were skilled artisans, and many were literate, more than twice as much as England as a whole. One historian claims there was never such an educated group of individuals as the Puritan society of Massachusetts and Connecticut up to that point in history. Over one hundred university graduates were in this group, many of them ministers. They came in family groups of like-minded people, friends, and neighbors, many of whom followed their ministers, such as the congregation at Chelmsford, the former church of Rev. Thomas Hooker. [206]

The inspiring leader of the Puritans, John Winthrop, settled at Charlestown (Boston) and took over as governor of the colony from John Endicott. Some emigrants such as Winthrop's son, John Winthrop the Younger, William Paine, and Sir Richard Saltonstall Jr., were wealthy landowners who invested their time, money, and energy as original proprietors of towns. Because Massachusetts Bay Colony was set up in organized towns as opposed to individual efforts, it was focused from the start on community.

Forming a just, Christian community that was effective, with proper limits on power, was of primary importance. Puritans believed clergy should not serve as government officials. They struggled with how to balance the rights of the individual against the interests of the community as a whole. They argued among themselves how to create a godly community, with the result that some separated from Massachusetts Bay, taking their church communities to Connecticut and developing their own towns and government there.

William Paine, a Puritan merchant of Ipswich and Boston, was a man of great enthusiasm and energy who left a legacy in Ipswich, Massachusetts, that lasted hundreds of years. He was part of the Great Migration of Englishmen starting with John Winthrop's flotilla of ships that carried non-Separatist Puritans to the New World in 1630.

When he arrived in Boston in April of 1635, stepping off the ship *Increase* with his wife, Anna North, and five children, he was already on the list of landowners in nearby Watertown, starting with seventy acres and rapidly acquiring more. Paine was friends with John Winthrop the Younger—they both came from Suffolk County in England—and Sir Richard Saltonstall Jr., who developed the town.

Sir Richard is also in the family tree of Patricia Reese. His uncle, Sir Richard Saltonstall (1521-1601), who was Lord Mayor of London in 1598, is Patricia's twelfth-great-grandfather. Saltonstall Jr. was one of the original members of the Massachusetts Bay Colony and signed the Cambridge Agreement in 1629, along with John Winthrop, before coming to the New World. He was appointed an assistant to the colony that year. Saltonstall, who came to Massachusetts in 1630 with Winthrop, put a lot of energy into establishing Watertown and, later, Fort Saybrook with John Winthrop the Younger. He left New England in 1631 but continued to work on colony affairs from England.

Not all colonists stayed. It was brutally hard the first few years. There were a lot of deaths and about one in ten returned to England for a variety of reasons.

William Paine was one of the earliest colonists to realize that manufacturing needed to be developed to provide jobs and sustain the colony. He obtained a controlling interest in Thomas Dudley's mill on the Charles River in Watertown, which he operated as a fulling mill until his death. After acquiring the interest in the mill, he then turned his interest to the town of Ipswich, which his friend John Winthrop the Younger founded in 1633.[207]

Ipswich is a coastal town on the Massachusetts north shore, about twenty-five miles from Boston, with good land for pastures and excellent fishing. Originally called Agawam from its Indian name, it was bought by John Winthrop the Younger from Metacomet, the sagamore of the Pawtucket Indians. The deed was finalized on June 28, 1638, with a purchase price of £20.

Encouraged by Winthrop, William Paine and his brother Robert procured a grant of land in Ipswich. It was an attractive, prosperous town with many merchants from East Anglia, such as the Paines, who had revenue from their land holdings in England. Many ancestors of Patricia Reese were settlers in Ipswich, including Samuel Appleton, Matthew Whipple, Thomas Burnham, and Robert Andrews, master of the ship *Angel Gabriel*. Richard Saltonstall, eldest son of Sir Richard settled there after his father went back to England. It was a more-mercantile town than its agrarian neighbors and became the second-most prosperous town in Massachusetts Bay after Boston until the mid-eighteenth century. When ships became larger in later years, they were not able to dock at Ipswich because of the many sand bars on the Ipswich River.[208]

In 1641 Ipswich was a busy river port, with Paine obtaining permission from the town to build a wharf on the river for his warehouse there. A town wharf was completed a few years later. Paine had become a freeman in 1640, which meant he was a church member in good standing and able to vote. William Paine and his brother Robert served on many commissions and committees, with an enthusiasm for public service and support for education.

Puritans felt very strongly about the importance of education. Their theology required educated minds to read the Bible for themselves, as every person had an obligation to maintain a covenant with God. They were strong supporters of liberal arts education and believed all knowledge was God's truth. In Europe only the privileged minority was educated, but the Puritans knew that an educated populace was important for a civil society to succeed. They intended to diffuse knowledge as broadly as possible. The fact that they established Harvard only six years after landing on the shores of Massachusetts, while struggling to build communities, was evidence of their commitment to establishing a "second Cambridge" for training Puritan ministers. John Harvard, who was newly arrived, donated £777 and a library of 400 books to start the university. It was common for Puritan businessmen in New England to donate money, land, or even crops to the university, and many of Patricia's Puritan ancestors did so.[209]

William and Robert Paine left their own legacy of commitment to education in Massachusetts. The Massachusetts legislature passed a law in 1647 that required all towns with fifty or more families to hire a teacher to instruct their male children how to read and write. When the number of families reached one hundred, they were required to set up a grammar school. Robert Paine offered to erect a building for use as a school in 1649 if the town would set apart certain lands. On January 11, 1650, the Paine brothers, along with Major Daniel Denison and William Bartholomew, granted certain lands in trust for the school. On January 26, 1652, the town created a formal trust, with William and Robert Paine among the trustees—called *feoffees*. Robert provided a house and two acres for use of a school, which would be used for more than two centuries, on Paine Street in Ipswich. William left a unique piece of land, thirty-five seaside acres called Jeffrey's Neck—now called Little Neck—to the school in trust in his 1660 will, intending for the land to provide income for the Ipswich schools forever.

I giue unto the free scoole of Ipswitch, the little neck of land at Ipswitch, commonly knowne by the name of Jeferrys neck. The which is to bee, and remaine, to the benifitt of the said scoole of Ipswitch, for ever, as I have formerly Intended, and therefore the sayd land not to bee sould nor wasted.

William Paine, 1660[210]

Antique postcard showing Little Neck, Ipswich, Massachusetts, early twentieth century, www. Historicipswich.org

William Paine was well acquainted with the Winthrops. Both father and eldest son were talented men. John Winthrop the Elder was educated at Trinity College, Cambridge, then studied law, later serving as a justice of the peace and court attorney. He was a country squire in England—Lord of the Manor at Groton Manor—and a devout Puritan when he decided to immigrate to Massachusetts. As governor of Massachusetts Bay Colony, he concerned himself with keeping the colony together with religion, laws, and Christian charity. He was known for his charity and devotion. When Massachusetts Bay ran out of funds, he used the proceeds of the sale of Groton Manor to assist the colony. His son John Winthrop the Younger was educated at Trinity College in Dublin, then studied law and was admitted as a barrister in London, but he was more concerned with matters of science, industry building, and doctoring. He would later serve as governor of Saybrook Colony and then Connecticut Colony. He was not as strict a Puritan as his father and allowed loosening of restrictions on other faiths.[211]

In 1631 John Winthrop the Younger followed his father to Massachusetts Bay Colony and was one of the assistants there in 1635, 1640, and 1641, as well as 1644-1649. He founded Agawam—Ipswich—in 1633 then went back to England, returning in 1635 as governor of lands granted to Lord Say and Sele and Lord Brooke at the mouth of the Connecticut River, which he named Fort Saybrook. In the 1640s he founded New London, an important center for shipbuilding, where Patricia's ancestor John Elderkin built ships.

Winthrop's father, John knew that exploration for future mines and industry would be important to the survival of the colony. As a scientist, John Winthrop the Younger was interested in developing mineral resources and took on the job. He was instrumental in developing the iron works at Lynn (Saugus) after a first attempt at Braintree (Quincy), Massachusetts. This was the first integrated iron works in America. William Paine was a major investor in both ventures.[212]

The English Civil War, which started in 1642, caused immigration to the New World to drop off drastically as Puritans stayed in England to fight. It was thought that the colony needed to develop its own manufacture of iron goods, as goods were in short supply and, with less ships coming in, increasingly expensive to import. Winthrop was able to raise £15,000, an astonishing amount of money, from twenty investors in England and four in Massachusetts. They were called The Company of Undertakers of The Iron Works in New England.

Chair made by John Elderkin (1614-1687) prominent ship builder in New London, CT and ancestor of Patricia Reese, Milwaukee Museum of Art, posted by Rhomfield, Ancestry.com

After disappointing results in Braintree, William Leader, a man experienced with iron works, was hired to pick a good site and run the iron works built there. A 600-acre site near the Saugus River turned out to be an excellent place for this massive undertaking of heavy industry. The development included a blast furnace, forge, and a rolling and slitting mill, which made it one of only a dozen such advanced mills in the world at the time. Originally called Hammersmith, after the English village that was the hometown to a lot of the iron workers, it included two blacksmith shops, a coal house, warehouse, and dock on the river, as well as houses for the workers. However, it was difficult to find enough workers. Managers relied on indentured servants, as well as some Scottish prisoners of war shipped to America after being captured by Cromwell in the Battle of Dunbar and the Battle of Worcester.[213]

The Saugus Iron Works produced iron from 1646 to about 1670. It provided critical commodities of cast and wrought iron goods for the expanding colony. Paine became more involved with the Saugus Iron Works, eventually owning two thirds of the stock in an attempt to rescue it from mismanagement. It functioned more profitably after his intervention in 1658, but after his death in 1660, problems with mismanagement and labor resumed. The high cost of labor was a deterrent and the iron works eventually ceased functions, spreading skilled iron workers out to other areas to continue what the Saugus Iron works had begun.[214]

Paine was interested in home manufacturing throughout his life. He had his hand in many commercial ventures that supported jobs for the community and was frequently asked by John Winthrop the Younger to get involved in commercial ventures for the sake of the colony. He was part of a company known as the Free Adventurers, who supported settlement of western Massachusetts and the development of Sturbridge, eventually operating the lead mines there.

After fifteen years in Ipswich, Paine developed a large mercantile business in Boston and made his home there. The inventory of his will, done October 22, 1660, showed a net worth of £4,239—an enormous amount in 1660—a large amount of it in real estate and industry investment. He left control of the Saugus Mines, as well as other businesses, to his son John with additional help from his son-in-law Samuel Appleton as one of the executors. His daughter Hannah had married Appleton on April 2, 1651, and had three children—Hannah, Judith, and Samuel—but sadly died as a young mother just a few years later. Paine wanted to make sure he provided for his grandchildren in his will, leaving £1,500 to the three children of Hannah and Samuel. In addition to leaving means of support for his family, and land for the support of Ipswich schools, Paine left money: £20 to Harvard, and £100 to general charity, as well as gifts to several clergymen and others.[215]

As was the Puritan way, men with wealth were not generally ostentatious but lived their lives to show benefit to their community. Puritans believed wealth was a gift from God and not to be squandered. Moderation, setting limits to one's spending and indulgences, was a core Puritan belief. Leland Ryken, professor of English emeritus at Wheaton College in Wheaton, Illinois, in his book *Worthy Saints,* points out that excessive profiteering by merchants was frowned upon. One example in the Massachusetts Bay Courts involved Robert Keanye, a merchant in Boston.

Chapter Five: For the Common Good 133

He was fined £200 for charging excessive prices. Rev. John Cotton of Boston pointed out that this was not the Christian way to behave.[216]

Paine had great faith in his son-in-law Samuel Appleton. Appleton, born in 1624, came to Ipswich as an eleven-year-old child from England with his father—also named Samuel—and family. As did the Paine family, the Appleton family originated from Suffolk County. Both Samuel Appleton and his father were descended from the ancient family of Appulton of Waldingfield, Suffolk. Like the Paines, the Appletons were members of the gentry and familiar with the Winthrops from their home county.

Samuel Appleton Sr. arrived in New England in 1635 with his family, including eldest son, John and younger son, Samuel. By 1636 the elder Samuel Appleton was settled in Ipswich and admitted as a freeman. He went on to be a prominent member of the town and was chosen deputy to the General Court on May 17, 1637. He died in Rowley, Massachusetts, in 1670. His sons John and Samuel became influential members of their community, both serving in the militia. John was deputy to the General Court for fifteen years between 1656 and 1678, as well as rising to the rank of captain and then major in the militia. He was vigorous in his defense of home rule for Massachusetts Bay Colony, as was his younger brother.[217]

The younger Samuel Appleton was successful in his own right. After being left a widower with three children under five, he quickly married Mary Oliver on December 8, 1656. Mary Oliver was a carrier of hemophilia and passed this gene down to the five children she had with Samuel. Samuel set out to regain his first three children's inheritance, named in his father-in-law's will, successfully suing Saugus Iron Works for their portion of the estate. He ended up with the 600 acres and the iron master's house, which was given to his son Samuel Appleton Jr.

After Samuel Appleton's father died, he inherited the fertile 460 acres of farmland next to Ipswich originally granted to the Appletons in 1638 by the colony. As well as this property, Samuel Appleton owned a sawmill in Ipswich. Like his brother John he served in government and the militia. In 1668 he served as commissioner of Essex County. He increased his responsibilities, becoming a deputy to the Massachusetts General Court, serving from 1668-1671, 1673-1675, and 1679-1681. Samuel served as a lieutenant in the company of his brother Captain John Appleton from 1669-1671.

When King Philp's War broke out, Samuel was promoted to captain on September 24, 1675. He was placed in charge of one hundred men marching to the frontier towns of the Connecticut River Valley after Thomas Lothrop's company had been destroyed by Indians on September 18 and the town of Springfield burned to the ground. After the resignation of the commander, Major William Pynchon—founder of Springfield—Samuel was promoted to major on October 4, 1675 and was the commander in chief of all the troops in that section of Massachusetts. The 17th-century historian William Hubbard praised his command. "By his industry, skill and courage, those towns were preserved from running the same fate with the rest, wholly, or in part, so lately turned into ashes." An attack was made on Hatfield by 700-800 Indians, and Major Appleton's men bravely repelled them. His sergeant died next to him, while Appleton himself barely escaped with his life, a bullet having gone through his hat.[218]

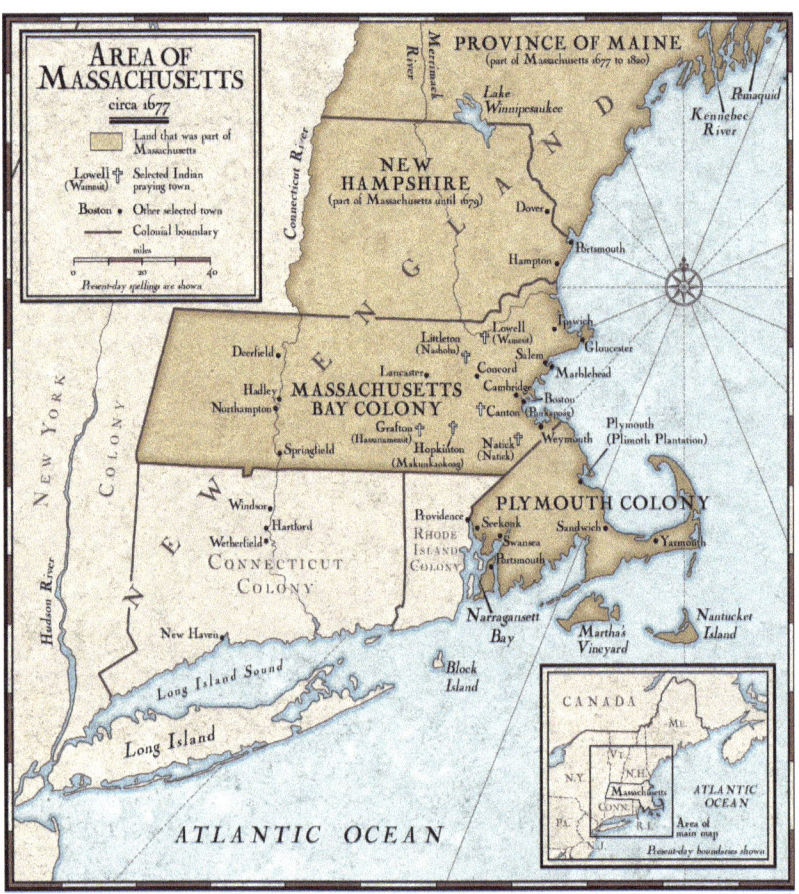

Massachusetts Bay Colony Map, source: New England Colonies in 1677, National Geographic Society.org

In December the united colonies made a determined attempt to defeat the Narragansett Indians. Appleton was in charge of 527 men from Massachusetts, 159 men under William Bradford from Plymouth, and 300 men from Connecticut under the command of Robert Treat, along with 150 Mohegan warriors. With Gov. Josiah Winslow of Plymouth as commander in chief, a fierce bloody battle commenced. Appleton lost 110 of his brave men, but the Narragansett Fort was finally captured on December 19, 1675, in what would be called The Great Swamp Fight. Appleton, by now in his early fifties, returned to Ipswich after the war and retired from active military service.[219]

Along with the brutal destruction of the war and a great fire that destroyed much of Boston in 1676, political uneasiness was developing. After King Charles I was beheaded in 1649, the English Civil War left Oliver Cromwell established as Lord Protector in charge of a Puritan-controlled England. In 1653 Puritans thought they might breathe a sigh of relief, and they expected politics in the home country would be settled. Just seven years later, in 1660, after the death of Cromwell in 1658, Parliament invited Charles Stuart—the son of Charles I—to become king. Charles II assumed the throne and the monarchy was restored, along with tighter control of the colonies.

The English court began to interfere more with the government of the colonies. In 1677 a pamphlet written by Andrew Marvell expressed this view: "There has now for diverse Years a design been carried out to change the Lawfull Government of England into an Absolute Tyranny and convert the established Protestant Religion into downright Popery." The view of the general public after the English Civil War was that the monarchy could not be above the state and the will of the people.[220]

In 1685 Charles II died and was succeeded by his son James II, who appointed Sir Edmond Andros to be the royal governor of the Dominion of New England. This destroyed local control and essential self-rule that the colonists had been used to. The colony had been operating as a commonwealth with little interference from England. The original charter neglected to state that the governor and officers of the colony were to remain in England, and the colony had taken advantage of that fact, setting up their government in Boston with an idea not to stray too far from English Common Law.

Samuel Appleton fiercely opposed the government of Andros. In 1687 he refused to pay taxes that had been levied by Andros without the approval of the local council. The idea of no taxation without representation was already firmly entrenched in the minds of many of the colony. Andros, furious at this rebellion against his power, issued a warrant for Appleton's arrest on September 19, 1687. Appleton is said to have gone to his son's house, who was then living at Saugus, to deliver a fiery address from a rocky cliff near the iron works. The spot became known as Appleton's Pulpit from that day on.[221]

Appleton's Pulpit, Saugus, MA, (where Major Samuel Appleton made his speech against tyranny) photo from Ancestry.com

The next day Appleton was arrested and brought to court, remaining in prison until March 7, 1688, when he was finally released on a £1,000 bond. By April 18, 1689, colonists had had enough of Governor Andros and wrestled control of the government from him. Major Samuel Appleton was given the honor of handling Andros into the boat that took him to prison on Castle Island in Boston Harbor. Appleton went on to serve on the new council and continued to serve in government. When the witchcraft frenzy hit Massachusetts in 1692, he was serving as a judge on the Court of Oyer and Terminer, held in Ipswich on April 16, 1692.[222]

There had been widespread belief in witchcraft over much of Europe as well as the colonies. Africans and Native American Indians also had traditional beliefs in the occult. It was thought that the devil had a physical presence and witches assisted him. Witches had been put to death in Sweden, Germany, and England for unexplained catastrophes or illnesses and unusual behavior. It was hard to find anyone in the seventeenth century who did not believe in the supernatural to explain the unexplainable. Stacy Schiff, in her book *The Witches, Salem 1692*, tells us about Rev. Cotton Mather's diary of the Salem witch trials and his belief in spectral evidence. Unlike physical evidence, spectral evidence depended on the accusation of the witnesses, who would claim the defendant appeared to them in evil form, invisible to anyone but themselves, and, "The word of an accuser could be enough to convict." The well-educated were not immune to fear of the supernatural. Schiff writes, "Rev. Cotton Mather, one of the best-read men in New England, at one point thought diabolical agents had stolen his sermon notes, which eventually showed up scattered on the streets of a neighboring town." Even though much of our physical world is explainable now, there are still events that we are superstitious and fearful about, resulting in wildly irrational thoughts.[223]

Massachusetts Bay Colony had put a few witches to death before 1692, as had Connecticut. Henry Wolcott—an Adlum-family ancestor—then Magistrate of Windsor, Connecticut, presided at a witch trail in Hartford on December 28, 1662. Connecticut hanged its share of witches but stopped forty years before the famous trials in Salem. In Massachusetts in 1692, at the height of the hysteria, between 144 and 185 witches and wizards were accused in twenty-five towns. The dreary, dark, ice-cold Massachusetts winter of 1691-92, with constant fear of Indian attack and catastrophe around every corner, led to a panic that started with two, hysterical young girls. By the time they finished, "Massachusetts had executed fourteen women, five men, and two dogs for witchcraft." After the hangings, the Puritans caught their breath and stopped the madness.[224]

Ipswich fared better. Unlike its neighboring town of Salem, no witches were convicted at the court that Appleton served on. Judge Appleton died at the age of 71 on May 15, 1696. He passed down his Ipswich farm to his four sons, having done all he could for the common good of his colony. He is buried in the Old North Burial in Ipswich and is memorialized on a mural at the Ipswich Post Office, where he is pictured, along with Reverend John Wise, protesting Andros and taxation without representation. Ipswich proudly calls itself "The Birthplace of American Independence 1687."[225]

Judith Appleton, one of Major Appleton's daughters with Hannah Paine, married into the Wolcott family of Connecticut. Judith married Samuel Wolcott in Wethersfield, Connecticut on March 6, 1678. Born in nearby Windsor, Samuel was a merchant and farmer in Wethersfield, one of the towns on the Connecticut River settled by colonists moving down the Connecticut River Valley from Massachusetts. Samuel Wolcott's grandfather Henry Wolcott, at age fifty, emigrated with his family, including son Henry Wolcott Jr., from Somerset, England, after a conversion to the Puritan faith.

Henry Wolcott, born in 1578, the second of three sons of John Wolcott of Golden Manor, had property in Tolland, Somerset, and a prosperous country life when he found religion as a result as his association with minister Edward Elton. After coming to New England in 1628 to get settled, he returned to England in 1630, sold his property, and returned on the *Mary and John* with his wife, Elizabeth Saunders, and their children. Wolcott was a freeman in Boston by October 19, 1630, and by 1637 was a member of the first legislature of Connecticut, having settled in Windsor. He was a prominent member of the town, serving as magistrate for years. Wolcott died on May 30, 1655, followed shortly after by his wife on July 7, 1655. His son Henry Wolcott Jr. also comes into the story as a magistrate in Windsor. He was important in documenting the words of Rev. Thomas Hooker, founder of Hartford. The shorthand notes that Wolcott made while listening to Hooker's sermons and lectures are the only written record of thirty-eight of the famous minister's sermons in Connecticut.[226]

When John Winthrop pictured the Puritan community of Massachusetts Bay, he envisioned a tightly knit community of like-minded individuals all working together to make a godly community. Once men start thinking for themselves, as Puritans were expected to do in their own study of the Bible, differences were bound to come up. Dissenters such as Roger Williams and Anne Hutchinson, as well as the Quakers, caused argument and, therefore, were banished from the colony. Religion was of the utmost importance to people in the seventeenth century, and few people thought that a society with people of different beliefs could be successfully maintained.

There was great excitement in the colony when the two famous Puritan ministers and friends from Cambridge, Rev. John Cotton and Rev. Thomas Hooker, arrived in 1633 after sailing together to Massachusetts on the *Griffin*. A fellow minister, Thomas Shepard, remarked upon seeing them leave England, "I saw the Lord departing from England when Mr. Hooker and Mr. Cotton were gone." Rev. Cotton became the primary minister in

Charlestown (Boston), while Rev. Hooker, with his assistant, Rev. Samuel Stone, settled at Newtown (Cambridge), across the Charles River from Boston, where some of his former congregation who called themselves "Mr. Hooker's Company" had settled. Cotton and Hooker were both very talented theologians but with different styles, which soon led to conflict and Hooker's departure.[227]

Both agreed with basic Calvinist theory that man was sinful and was saved by the grace of God. Predestination means that God decides who is going to heaven; you can't be saved by good works alone. The ministers differed in their approach as to who should be given church membership.

Massachusetts Bay Colony, led by Winthrop and Rev. Cotton, felt that only church members in good standing and, therefore, freemen, should be allowed to vote in the colony and must show evidence of conversion. Rev. Cotton emphasized grace in his sermons and felt that membership should be restricted to the elect. As Rev. Nathaniel Ward in *The Simple Cobbler of Agawam* said, "Others shall have free liberty to stay away from us." When the brilliant but difficult Roger Williams disagreed with the colony's restrictive practices and treatment of the Indians, he was banished, in large part by the efforts of Rev. Cotton. Anne Hutchinson, who had followed Rev. Cotton to Massachusetts, began to hold her own meetings in her home, attracting many followers with her belief that individuals had a personal covenant with God, and there was no need for clergy and government. Cotton and Winthrop found this an affront to the colony, especially since she was a woman, and banished her as well. Both Roger Williams and Anne Hutchinson ended up in what was to become Rhode Island.[228]

Rev. Hooker did not go as far as Roger Williams and Anne Hutchinson did later, but he had less restrictive ideas towards church membership and voting rights in the colony than Cotton and Winthrop. In a letter to Winthrop he stated his position: "In matters which concern the common good, a general council chosen by all, to transact business which concern all, I conceive most suitable to rule and most safe for relief of the whole." His plain but lively sermons emphasized the practical, the process of encouraging good works, and becoming one of the true believers of Christ. He felt it was better to err on the side of inclusiveness regarding church membership, and he focused on teaching a Christian way of life in his sermons.

The theological arguments with Cotton, and lack of adequate pasture in Cambridge, led Hooker and his congregation to petition the colony to leave. Winthrop was reluctant to grant the removal, as he was a friend of Hooker and thought the colony would be stronger if they stayed together. But as the historian William Hubbard wrote, "Two such eminent stars, such as Mr. Cotton and Mr. Hooker, both of the first magnitude, though of differing influence, could not well continue in one and the same orb."[229]

On May 31, 1636, Rev. Hooker and his assistant, Rev. Stone, led one hundred members of their congregation, along with some 160 head of cattle, goats, and sheep, over the old Connecticut Path, an Indian trail through the wilderness by the banks of the Connecticut and Little (Hog) rivers, to a place the Indians called Suckiaug in the fertile Connecticut River Valley. Rev. Stone and a few men had explored the place six months before and spent a miserably cold winter in huts they built there.

Hooker and his pilgrims camped along the two-week, one-hundred-mile journey, with the infirm Mrs. Hooker carried by stretcher, and cows that provided milk for nourishment. Mr. Hooker's company sold their homes in Cambridge (Newtowne) to members of Rev. Thomas Shepard's congregation who had just arrived from England. They called their new town in Connecticut Newtowne, first, and then Hartford. There were a few settlers just seven miles away north of them in Windsor, as well as a few settlers in Wethersfield, five miles south of them. Windsor and Wethersfield still argue about which town was established first, but the truth is that all three towns

Map of Connecticut River Colonies, source: National Geographic Society.org

were established at almost the same time between 1634 and 1636, Hartford coming last but with the most people and the prominent minister Rev. Hooker.[230]

The settlers were in an area outside the jurisdiction of the Massachusetts Court and claimed by three different groups. Plymouth had established a trading post near Windsor and insisted they had rights to the area. Some Indian tribes also still claimed the area, and the Dutch had established a fort on the south side of the Little River they called House of Good Hope. The three towns on the Connecticut River were established by February 1637 as a commonwealth of Connecticut Colony. They were ruled by a group of eight magistrates from Massachusetts for one year, after which the plantation was free to set up their own government. John Winthrop the Younger was to give guidance for one year while serving as governor of Saybrook Colony.

On March 28, 1637, the magistrates made a new plan for self-governance and elected a new group of eight magistrates: Two men were elected from each town (deputies), comprising a General Court, plus two others for more urgent business. They dealt with the Suckiaug Indians by making deals to buy land. They ignored Plymouth and the Dutch because they had superior numbers and could intimidate them. There were about 250 men and 160 families in the three towns. One of the first items on the list of the new magistrates was to devise laws for voting. They decided no church membership or religious test was necessary, only minimal property ownership. A few months later, the Pequot War broke out and they declared war against the Pequot.

Connecticut declared war partially as an accommodation to the Suckiaug Indian tribe, who were under the thumb of the Pequot. The Suckiaug were grateful after the defeat of the Pequot and ceded land to Hartford in the North Meadows. Hartford developed in typical, New England-town fashion with a central meeting house and town square surrounded by homes and then farmland farther out. Cows were held in a common yard, while sheep were tended by the town shepherd. All residents farmed some land, no matter what other jobs they held, as it was necessary for survival. Most homes had very simple furnishings with very few chairs; stools were mostly used. Pewter spoons and wooden plates were used to eat with. Forks were not in general use. The few prosperous residents had silverware to use. Church services in the meeting house were mandatory for all residents, members or not, with two services held on Sunday in addition to a lecture on Thursdays. The meeting house was the center of life in the town; it was where residents got their news and held town meetings in addition to church services.

Hooker's congregation had been together for several years, and they were devoted to their minister. Several of Patricia Reese's ancestors were among the founding townsmen of Hartford that followed Rev. Hooker. William Andrews was the first paid schoolteacher in Hartford, receiving £16 a year from the town as well as tuition charged from his students. Future governor Thomas Welles was active from the start in the government of Hartford and the only official to hold all four top positions in Connecticut Colony government.[231]

Thomas Welles arrived in Boston prior to June 9, 1636, with his wife, Alice Tomes, and six children. He had a house in Boston—possibly, another in Cambridge—at that time, before he left for Hartford with Rev. Hooker. There is some suggestion that he was secretary to Lord Say and Sele; he had a close association with the lord's family and had a good education. He was born about 1590 in Stourton, Warwickshire, England, son of Robert and Alice Welles. He had property in Burmington, Warwick County, England, and owned one share in the Piscataqua patent of lands—now in Dover, Durham, Stratham, and parts of New Hampshire—along with Lord Say and Sele, Lord Brook, Sir Richard Saltonstall, and others.

When he settled in Hartford, he was a member of the first court of magistrates, elected on March 28, 1637. He was reelected as a member of the court of magistrates and served from 1638 to 1654. He served in government every year until his death in 1660. His name is on almost every page of the Connecticut Colony Record, including work on the committees to complete the Fundamental Orders, the first written constitution of Connecticut, as well as criminal laws and relations between colonies and the Dutch. He was considered one of twelve most important men in the start of Connecticut Colony. He not only served as magistrate every year until his death, but he was elected the first treasurer of the colony in 1639, serving until 1641, as well as secretary from 1640 to 1649. Most assuredly, he was in the audience for Rev. Hooker's famous sermon delivered to the Connecticut General Court on May 31, 1638, along with the twenty-eight-year old magistrate Henry Wolcott Jr., who took notes in his journal.[232]

Rev. Thomas Hooker, who is called "The Father of Connecticut" is said to have inspired the Fundamental Orders of Connecticut with his sermon that day that emphasized the right of the governed to choose their leaders. This was of major significance in the early seventeenth century, when most of the world was ruled by kings, emperors, and tsars. Puritan sermons followed a certain format: a quote from the Bible followed by statements and reasons for those statements. The text of Hooker's famous sermon was from Deuteronomy 1:13 and 1:15: *"Take you wise men, and understanding, and known among your tribes, and I will make them rulers over you."*—and—*"So I took the chief of your tribes, wise men, and known, and made them heads over you, captains over thousands, and captains over hundreds, and captains over fifties, and captains over tens, and officers among your tribes."*

His statements as translated included three doctrinal statements and three reasons:

Doctrinal statements:

1) The choice of public magistrates belongs unto the people by God's own allowance

2) The privilege of election which belongs to the people must not be exercised according to their whims but according to the blessed will and law of God

3) Those who have power to appoint officers and magistrates have it in their power also to set the bounds and limits of the power and places unto which they call them.

Reasons:

1) Because the foundation of authority is laid firstly in the free consent of people.

2) Because by a free choice the hearts of the people will be more inclined to the love of the persons and more ready to yield obedience.

3) Because of that duty and engagement of the people."[233]

The essence of these thoughts is evident in the first Charter of Connecticut, The Fundamental Orders, written mostly by attorney Roger Ludlow of Windsor and adopted by the colony on January 14, 1649. It was the most advanced government charter the world had seen to date, and it emphasized the voluntary nature of the covenant: that the purpose of government was not to rule but serve in an orderly fashion. "The Word of God requires that to maintain the peace and union of such people there should be an orderly and decent government established according to God, in order to dispose of the affairs of the people." This constitution, as transcribed and documented by Secretary Thomas Welles, was in use in Connecticut for 180 years and was a prototype of our present U.S. Constitution, providing for divided legislative, judicial, and administrative powers. Historian Johnston's *Connecticut* states, "The birthplace of American democracy is Connecticut.

We would not have discovered the sermons of Rev. Hooker, written in shorthand notes in a small book belonging to Henry Wolcott Jr., but for the work of a scholar, Dr. J. Hammond Trumball, who discovered the manuscript book in the Massachusetts Archives two and one quarter centuries later and transcribed Henry Wolcott's documentation. Wolcott's little, leather-bound book is now in the procession of the Connecticut Historical Society.[234]

John Winthrop understood finally that Massachusetts, like Connecticut, must draw up its own laws to limit the powers of the magistrates. Rev. Nathaniel Ward of Ipswich drew up the Body of Liberties in 1641 to protect life, liberty, property, and reputation. There was to be no taxation without representation, no cruel and unusual punishment or beating of one's wife or abuse of animals. It was a precursor to our Bill of Rights in that there was to be freedom of speech, due process of law, and the right to a jury trial. The Puritans of both Massachusetts and Connecticut wanted a godly commonwealth but also showed early concerns for individual rights and a more just society. They sought to perfect society in what they believed was a virtuous Christian fellowship. However, they still treated outsiders harshly, with what we now consider draconian laws, if they tried to argue theology.[235]

The churches of the new settlements, although they were not originally separatists, modelled themselves after Plymouth, with a Congregational system called the New England Way. Meanwhile, England leaned towards Presbyterianism as conflict between the king and Parliament continued. The Connecticut Colony continued to grow, with Rev. Hooker in Hartford, and the new government of the colony settled there with Thomas Welles an active participant. Other settlements came soon after.

Rev. John Davenport started New Haven Colony in 1637. Rev. Henry Whitfield, an ancestor of Daniel Bruce Adlum, brought over colonists at his own expense and started Guilford, Connecticut, in 1639. Henry Whitfield, born in Greenwich, Kent, in 1592, was from a prominent family. His father, Thomas, was a lawyer in London, and his mother, Mildred Manning, was descended from the family of the "Father of English Literature," the poet Geoffrey Chaucer. Henry studied at New College, Oxford, where he became a friend of the future founder of Saybrook Colony, George Fenwick. After studying religion, Whitfield became the vicar of St. Margaret's Church in Surrey. He married Dorothy Sheaffe of Kent and fathered nine children. When Thomas Hooker and John Cotton decided they should emigrate, Henry Whitfield tried to convince them to stay in England. Instead, he became convinced of their cause and eventually followed them to the New World. Ancestors of both Daniel and Patricia, William Leete, future governor of both New Haven and Connecticut colonies, and Francis Bushnell came to Guilford with Rev. Whitfield.[236]

Influential ministers such as Cotton, Hooker, and Davenport were invited back to England during and after England's Civil War to help decide theological questions but decided not to go. Hooker wrote a book, *Survey of the Summe of Church Discipline*, stating his ideas on church structure to send back to England, but unfortunately, it was lost at sea. He died before he finished rewriting the book, so we only have an incomplete picture of his thoughts on the subject. Henry Whitfield did go back to England to assist the government in 1650—leaving his family in Guilford—but died in London a few years later, in 1657, and was buried in Winchester Cathedral. Hooker, who was important in the history of Connecticut and government ideals, died on July 7, 1647, at the age of 61, of an epidemic illness in Hartford and was buried there.[237]

Statue of Rev. Henry Whitfield, founder of Guilford, CT, (ancestor of Daniel B. Adlum) at the Henry Whitfield State Museum, Guilford, CT, source: cc by 4.0, 2016, en.wiki.org/wiki/file:Henry_Whitfield

Cotton Mather of the great dynasty of Puritan ministers—his father was the influential Increase Mather, one grandfather was Richard Mather, the other grandfather was John Cotton—wrote in his *Magnalia Christi Americana*, in 1702, about Thomas Hooker, "Tis he whom I may call, ...The light of the western churches." John Winthrop the Elder wrote in his journal of Hooker, "for piety, prudence, wisdom, zeal, learning, and what else might make him serviceable in the place and time he lived in, might be compared with men of greatest note; and he shall need no other praise: the fruits of his labors in both Englands shall preserve an honorable and happy remembrance of him forever."

A great man himself, and a most significant leader, John Winthrop died in 1649, the same year Charles I was executed in England. John Endicott, who was the very first governor of Massachusetts Bay Colony, became governor again. John Cotton, the influential teacher of the First Church of Boston, died at age 67 on December 23, 1652.[238]

Thomas Welles was serving as secretary of Connecticut Colony at the time his beloved minister Hooker died. After Welles' wife, Alice, died, he moved to Wethersfield in 1646, where he married Elizabeth Deming Foote, the widow of the founder of Wethersfield, Nathaniel Foote. His children were all from his first wife, Alice. Welles continued to be significant in the government of the colony, serving as deputy governor, 1654-55, 1656-57 and 1659-60. Welles became the seventeenth governor of the colony, 1655-1656, and served as deputy governor to John Winthrop the Younger while Winthrop was governor in 1657. He then succeeded John Winthrop the Younger as the twentieth governor of Connecticut Colony, 1658-1659. He had the unusual position of being governor while his eldest son, John was elected a magistrate and his youngest son, Samuel, was elected a deputy to the General Court. It must have seemed like a dynasty of the Welles family. The position Thomas held at his death in 1660 was deputy governor. He died suddenly. Winthrop wrote, "He was well at supper and then died suddenly that night." Welles' son John who had been magistrate and probate judge in the colony, died the year before just as suddenly.[239]

Great-grandson of Thomas, Captain Robert Welles Jr., of Wethersfield, would tie the Welles and Wolcott families together when he married Sarah Wolcott, daughter of Judith Appleton and Samuel Wolcott, on September 28, 1699, in Wethersfield. The ancestry of William Paine, Samuel Appleton, Henry Wolcott, and Governor Welles ran through the blood of the children of Robert Welles Jr., and his wife, Sarah. The families would continue to live in Wethersfield for generations.[240]

John Winthrop the Younger would miss his deputy governor as he was serving as governor of Connecticut Colony at a tumultuous time in 1660 when the Puritan Protectorate fell in England and the monarchy was restored. The arm of English law came to the colony as they looked for the judges who had decided that King Charles I must be put to death—the regicides—who fled to New England. Two of the judges who signed the death warrant, Edward Whalley and William Goffe, who both served as generals in Cromwell's army, hid in New Haven with Minister John Davenport. When the king's men came looking for them, William Leete, who was then serving as acting governor of New

Haven Colony, delayed them, saying he must consult with the magistrates of the colony. In the meantime, he sent a secret message to the regicides, allowing them to escape. He said to their pursuers, "We honor His Majesty, but we have tender consciences." One of the poems about Guilford at the time contains the verse:

> *And tell of Guilford's William Leete*
> *Who stretched the State's right arm to hide*
> *In many a wilderness retreat*
> *The vengeance hunted regicide*
> *And told the bearers of the ban,*
> *Signed and broad sealed 'that tender thing*
> *The conscience of an honest man,*
> *Is full as loyal as a king.*[241]

The colony charters were also in question with the Restoration. The colonies had supported parliament against King Charles I. John Winthrop the Younger, because of his close contacts among the lords and influential men in England, managed to negotiate for a more lenient charter for Connecticut than the other colonies. The new charter of 1662 absorbed New Haven Colony into Connecticut and confirmed the continuation of the Fundamental Orders and that it would remain a Puritan colony. John Davenport of New Haven resisted; his colony was a theocracy and less liberal than Connecticut, but with William Leete smoothing the way, New Haven finally agreed in 1664 to become part of Connecticut. Rhode Island received its own charter in 1663. Massachusetts had to accommodate a new charter as well.

All of the colonies had pressure put upon them, not only in government but also in religion. The first Quakers arrived to Massachusetts in 1656 and were promptly banished. Connecticut was somewhat more understanding of the Quakers, but the Congregational Church remained the official church. There was increasing pressure from Baptists over infant baptism, as well as other sects that disagreed with the official theology of the colony. Church attendance was a problem as people split into different Protestant sects. The Congregational Church Synod endorsed the Half-Way Covenant in 1662 which allowed baptism of the children of the elect—those already baptized in the church—to increase membership.[242]

John Winthrop the Younger continued to lead Connecticut Colony for seven years as governor, physician, and scientist. In 1663 he was made a fellow of the Royal Society, a scientific organization in England. At the start of King Philip's War, Winthrop was worn out and desperate to resign. He died in Boston on April 6, 1676, having gone there to attend a meeting of the commissioners of the United Colonies of New England. William Leete took over as governor of Connecticut. Leete had an active history in the government of Guilford and New Haven Colony and was most capable.[243]

William Leete was born in Dodington, Huntingdonshire (Hunts), England, in 1613, supposedly, just nine miles from the home of Oliver Cromwell, the future Lord Protector of England. At the age of twenty-three, on August 1, 1636, he married Anne Paine, the daughter of Rev. John Paine of Southoe in Hunts. Leete was an attorney and served in the Bishop's Court at Cambridge as registrar. As registrar, he saw firsthand the oppression and mistreatment of Puritans and was won over to their cause. On May 20, 1639, he and his wife, Anne, joined Rev. Henry Whitfield in immigrating to New England. Leete was one of the twenty-five signers of the Plantation Compact to establish a town they called Guilford in New Haven Colony. They arrived in Quinnipiac (New Haven) in July 1639, and after consulting with Rev. John Davenport, they decided to purchase land halfway between New Haven and Saybrook from the Menunkatuck Indians. William Leete was one of the "seven pillars" of the community and became secretary. As the only attorney in the community, he was active in all negotiations and held office the entire forty years he was in New England.[244]

Puritans believed that God calls every man and women to serve in a certain occupation. They did not divide the secular and spiritual life or prefer one over the other. As Professor Leland Ryken states, "The Puritan goal was to serve God, not simply *within* one's work in the world, but *through* that work." They believed all work had dignity, expressing love for God through service to one's neighbor, and thus, all work was sanctified. The Puritans praised duty and diligence but felt that seeking wealth for personal glory was wrong and that moderation in all was ideal. Puritan William Perkins said it this way: "The main end of our lives … is to serve God in the serving of men in the works of our callings."

William Leete, Esq. thought his calling was to serve in government. He served as magistrate after the founding of Guilford and then became deputy governor of New Haven Colony, governor of New Haven, and then, finally, governor of Connecticut.[245]

William Leete's first wife, Anne, died in 1668, and he married Sarah Rutherford, widow of Henry Rutherford, in 1670. All ten children of his children were with his first wife, Anne Payne. Some of them would become active in government as well. When his second wife died in 1673, he married twice-widowed Mary Newman. He was married to Mary when he took on the job of governor of Connecticut. He moved to Hartford when he became governor but maintained property in Guilford, as did his sons. Leete's Island, a popular resort area in Guilford/Branford is named for him. He took over for Winthrop in 1676 and served until he died in April 1683. His third wife died eight months later. His funeral apparently had full military honors with a gun salute. John Talcott, the treasurer of the colony, made an entry in the colony books: "To 11 pound of powder for the Great Guns at Gov'r Leet's funerall…£1:07:06."[246]

The decades that followed brought challenges to the colonies. Orders coming from the crown and divisions at home led to frustration. When Charles II died and James II, his son, became king, things came to a head in the colonies when Sir Edmund Andros was appointed royal governor of all of New England, including Connecticut. Samuel Appleton and others protested in Massachusetts Bay Colony.

Connecticut also gave Andros a hard time. When Andros came by horseback from Boston in 1686 to take back their precious charter, which would destroy their Fundamental Orders, the deputies delayed and tricked him. Andrew Leete, son of William Leete, was elected deputy to the court from Guilford and was in the court chamber on the second floor of the Hartford meeting house where all were gathered around the charter. He supposedly feigned a faint and the candle lights were extinguished, allowing Captain Joseph Wadsworth to grab the charter and hide it in a hollow tree on the property of the Honorable Samuel Wyllys. Andros was furious but left without the charter. Andrew Leete took the charter to Guilford and hid it at his house at the northwest corner of the Guilford Green for a season.

Meanwhile, in Massachusetts, prominent minister and president of Harvard, Increase Mather, slipped by Andros's men and sailed to England with grievances against the Andros rule. Leaders of protestants in England sent a message to the great protestant ruler of The Netherlands, William of Orange, to assert his claim to the throne of England. (He was married to James's daughter, Mary.) In the bloodless Glorious Revolution of 1688, James was overthrown. A year later, Andros was imprisoned by the rebellious colonists in Boston, while in England William and Mary became the new monarchs.[247]

The next few years were stressful in New England as the colonists adapted to new circumstances. The Connecticut charter was restored and brought out of hiding in 1690, while Rev. Increase Mather lobbied the English court for a new charter for Massachusetts. A new charter was granted that included the General Court, but also included a royal governor and blended Plymouth Colony into Massachusetts Bay in 1691.

The stress of changing governments, economic circumstances, and uncertainty of living on the frontier after Indian attacks led to a flare-up of superstitions and tensions about religion. In 1700 Rev. Increase Mather was pushed out as president of Harvard by a more liberal faction. In 1701 Yale University in Connecticut was founded as competition to Harvard. Cotton Mather, who never got along well with his father, Increase, encouraged Elihu Yale to donate money for the college. Andrew Leete was on the General Court of Connecticut that approved Yale's charter.

Francis Bremer, in his book *The Puritan Experiment*, points out that the growing influences of the Enlightenment led to an emphasis on man and morality and rational instruction rather than emotional inspiration in sermons. The Enlightenment of the Eighteenth Century, or Age of Reason as it was called, changed the way men looked at religion, human nature, and science. Enlightenment writers such as John Locke and Voltaire emphasized scientific method as the source of knowledge that would lead to better people and societies. They believed in individual liberty and constitutional government and sought to wipeout intolerance and superstition.[248]

Rev. Cotton Mather tried to rejuvenate the Puritan faith while also believing in scientific method. He wrote more than 400 books and encouraged second- and third-generation Puritans to return to their roots. He was one of the few who believed in inoculation during a smallpox outbreak in Boston in 1721. Despite his efforts to revive the Puritan faith, the colonies were dividing on religious lines. The Baptists were increasing in numbers, many of them believing that education was not necessary for their ministers. Other colonists lost interest in religion altogether. Samuel Johnson, a tutor at Yale, turned to Anglicanism, but first he taught Jonathan Edwards, who would become the most important Puritan minister in what would be called The Great Awakening, a revival of Puritan thought beginning in 1734. Jonathan Edwards rejected the new, rational lecturing style of sermons and tried to inspire followers with his passion.[249]

According to Francis Bremer, Edwards tried to present the essence of Calvinism and explain it in a way that was compatible with The Enlightenment. Edwards is thought by many to be the greatest theologian in American history. One of his most famous sermons was delivered at Enfield, Connecticut, on July 8, 1741. "Sinners in the Hands of an Angry God" was said by some to scare the grace of God into people. He preached with two main themes: that of the beauty of God's holiness and the absolute sovereignty of God.

Other preachers followed in his footsteps. George Whitfield in 1740 attracted large crowds by appealing to the heart. He was an associate of John and Charles Wesley, who started the Methodist movement. Likewise, Rev. Gilbert Tennent, an ordained Presbyterian minister, drew large crowds, which inspired believers to abandon their congregations and look for more effective ministers.

The religious in New England divided into what they called the "New Lights," supporters of the new emotionalism, and "Old Lights," traditional churches that opposed the revivals. The Great Awakening divided families and congregations. At the same time, it encouraged religious freedom and minimized the importance of denominations.[250]

By the time Jonathan Edwards died in 1758, the Puritan Age was past, but the lessons that they taught us remain. Their idea of "A City on a Hill" to inspire mankind was rekindled in a spirit of American exceptionalism and led us on the path to revolution. The Congregational Church remained important in New England, and its clergy were in the forefront of protesting unfair policies such as the Stamp Act. The idea of the value of the individual that the Puritans nourished became important as the rights of man and the right to choose those who govern us. Leland Ryken tells us that the Puritan interest in the health of society was based on their sense of duty and responsibility for the common good.[251]

The descendants of the Wolcotts, Welleses, and Leetes would go on to fight in the American Revolution for those very ideas. Oliver Wolcott, great grandson of Henry Wolcott and cousin of Sarah Wolcott Welles, was a signer of the Declaration of Independence and went on to become a brigadier general in the Revolution, fighting most famously in the Battle of Saratoga. One story about him tells how after militia troops toppled an enormous statue of lead and gold leaf of King George astride a horse, Wolcott carried the pieces home to Litchfield, Connecticut by ox cart. There he had his wife, children, and other ladies melt it down to make bullets that were then used in the Battle of Saratoga. More than twenty of Patricia's and Daniel's Congregational ancestors fought on the colonies' side in the Revolution.[252]

After the Revolution, families were forced to adapt as the ruins of war caused many to move from their homes and spread out in western Massachusetts, New York, and Vermont, again on the frontier. They took their values with them as they tried to start new towns in the wilderness. One of the Puritans' greatest achievements was that, in addition to social action as a community, they believed in individualism for the common man. They led us towards the development of democracy. Their practical structure of society, with an emphasis on doing good, left us with the ideas of the importance of education and good government, as well as charity towards our neighbors.

The Puritans of Massachusetts and Connecticut cast a long shadow that is still with us. Samuel Appleton's farm in Ipswich is still an operating farm, one of the oldest in the country. The Saugus Iron Works has been restored and is operated by the National Park Service. You can see the home that Samuel Appleton Jr. built there in 1681. Henry

House of Samuel Appleton Jr. at Saugus Iron Works, Saugus, MA built c. 1690, Source: Saugus Iron Works-House.Jpg-Wikimedia Commons

Whitfield of Guilford built a large stone house with three-foot-thick walls, used by the community in 1642, which still stands. It is the oldest stone house in Connecticut.

And what of energetic entrepreneur William Paine? His gift to the Ipswich Public Schools of thirty-six acres of land has stood the test of time. Through the centuries, this special peninsula, called Little Neck, has provided money for the schools. It started as pasture and eventually had summer houses built on it, the rents earning money for the schools. The Ipswich Massachusetts Grammar School Trust was established in 1652, with its most valuable asset added in 1660 through the will of William Paine. The trust lasted until 2012, when the Massachusetts Attorney General and Courts decided to dissolve the trust and sell the land due to poor management by the trustees (feofees.) Paine's vision lasted 360 years, the longest running charitable trust ever established in what is now the United States. William Paine's simple yet extraordinary gift was given in the Puritan spirit of providing for the common good.[253]

Chapter Six

Reaching for Zion

Family Cast of Characters

Grace Merriam Williams…(1867-1950) *daughter of Hyrum and Mary Ann; grandmother of Patricia Reese*
Sylvester Spenser Williams…(1872-1937) *a younger brother of Grace*
Hyrum Andrus Williams…(1843-1896) *father of Grace; great-grandfather of Patricia Reese*
Mary Ann Snyder…(1843-1876) *mother of Grace; great-grandmother of Patricia Reese*

Gustavus Williams…(1807-1887) *father of Hyrum; second-great-grandfather of Patricia Reese*
Hannah Maria Andrews…(1811-1901) *mother of Hyrum; second-great-grandmother of Patricia Reese*
Solomon Williams…(1783-1834) *father of Gustavus; third-great-grandfather of Patricia Reese*
Elizabeth Pool…(1780?-1872) *mother of Gustavus; third-great-grandmother of Patricia Reese*

Samuel Comstock Snyder…(1806-1866) *father of Mary Ann; second-great-grandfather of Patricia Reese*
Henrietta Stockwell…(1810-1888) *mother of Mary Ann; second-great-grandmother of Patricia Reese*
Isaac Snyder…(1787-1844) *father of Samuel; third-great-grandfather of Patricia Reese*
Lovisa Comstock…(1789-1856) *mother of Samuel; third great grandmother of Patricia Reese*

Jacob Rees(e)…(1865-1901) *husband of Grace Williams; son of Watkin and Jane; father of Grover and Cora*
Grover Williams Reese…(1888-1950) *son of Grace and Jacob; father of Patricia Reese*
Cora Reese…(1890-1977) *sister of Grover; aunt of Patricia Reese*

Frank Holladay…(1867-1952) *second husband of Grace Williams; father of Bonnie*
Bonnie France Holladay…(1900-1990) *married Donald Stewart; half-sister of Grover and Cora*

Watkin Henry Rees…(1830-1922) *emigrated from Wales, 1854; great-grandfather of Patricia Reese*
Jane Williams…(1837-1920) *emigrated from Wales, 1854; great-grandmother of Patricia Reese*

The Latter-day Saints

"Perseverance is the secret of all triumph"

~Victor Hugo

Panguitch, Utah, is surrounded by a dramatic and stark landscape. Nestled in the valley of the Sevier River, with the Markagunt and Paunsaugunt plateaus in the distance, its name means "Big Fish" in the Southern Paiute language, after the fish in the nearby lake. Located in Garfield County in south central Utah's color country, it is just twenty-five miles from Bryce Canyon National Park with its high mountain plateaus, steep mesas, gorges, hoodoos, red and yellow canyons, and dry, desert foothills. The town has an elevation of about 6,600 feet, brisk weather, and a very short growing season. It is said of the weather that *there are nine months of winter and three months of (darn) cold weather.*

Patricia Reese's great grandfather, Hyrum A. Williams, answered the call of his church to settle there in 1871 with his wife, Mary Ann Snyder, daughters Mary Adell and Grace, and infant son, Hyrum. Like his pioneer Puritan ancestors, the Welles, Wolcott, and Williams families in Wethersfield, Connecticut he was starting anew.

Hyrum's most recent move was from Parley's Park (now Park City) in Utah Territory, settled by his father-in-law, Samuel Comstock Snyder, with wife, Henrietta Maria Stockwell, and extended family. His parents and his wife's parents were some of the first converts to a new religion founded by fellow Yankee, Joseph Smith. In the years after the Revolution, the two families moved from the settled parts of New England to the western frontier. The Williamses moved to the Berkshires in western Massachusetts. The Comstocks, ancestors of Samuel Comstock Snyder, moved there as well and then moved on to western New York and Vermont in search of opportunity and land to farm. Their restlessness in the lonely frontier, and spiritual longing to be part of something bigger than themselves, led them to follow Joseph Smith and his new church, The Church of Jesus Christ of Latter-day Saints. The story of the Mormons is one of incredible hardship and perseverance as they moved west across the country and, eventually, out of the U.S. to the Great Basin of Utah to reach their Zion.[254]

The first attempt to settle Panguitch was made in March of 1864 with a group of Mormons from Parowan and Beaver, but the settlers suffered a crisis of hunger when their first crops were killed by frost. Seven men left the new settlement in the dead of winter to seek food from other communities. They were forced by heavy snow to walk with quilts put down in front of them as they slowly made their way for help. They survived the winter, but the Black Hawk War soon had the settlers abandoning the area in May of 1865.

Hyrum Williams was among the new settlers in 1871 who built a fort, a grist mill, and sawmills, harvesting lumber from the forests. Hyrum had worked as a logger in Parley's Park, where his father-in-law, Samuel Comstock Snyder, built the area's first sawmill. Hyrum was also experienced with horses and soon began a new career as a freighter. He and Mary Ann had more children, while the town grew larger with houses built from rose-colored adobe bricks made in a kiln in town. The workers were paid in bricks. At some point the Williams family established a home and store in the bleak John's Valley, about forty miles from Panguitch, according to nephew Rodney Williams. Terrible drought in the 1870s resulted in the loss of their house and store by fire. Son Sylvester Spenser was born in 1872, followed by daughter, Cora Lucy, in 1874, and Hyrum A. in March of 1876. On September 10, 1876, Hyrum's wife, Mary Ann, mother of a six-month-old baby and four other children, died at age thirty-three of the flu. Hyrum, also thirty-three, was left a widower. His two oldest daughters, Mary Adell, age twelve, and Patricia Reese's grandmother Grace, age nine, took over for their mother. A hard life became even harder for Hyrum.[255]

Hardships and constant pioneering were not new to the families of Hyrum and Mary Ann. They had been constant companions for two generations, forging a determined people. Hyrum's parents, Gustavus Williams and Hannah Maria Andrews, were both descended from Puritan families in New England. Gustavus was the son of Solomon Williams and Elizabeth Poole of Wethersfield, Connecticut. Gustavus' third-great-grandfather, Captain Jacob Williams, a sea captain, settled in the Rocky Hill district of Wethersfield in the early seventeenth century. Gustavus was a descendent of the Paine, Wolcott, Appleton and Welles families through his grandmother Hannah Robbins. His wife's family, the Andrewses, likewise had lived in Connecticut and Massachusetts since the seventeenth century.

The religious and economic turmoil of the early nineteenth century in upstate New York spilled over to the Berkshires in western Massachusetts, where they lived, and the Williams family became converts to a new religion that offered hope and purpose. They were disowned by their families, who did not understand their enthusiasm. The marriage of Gustavus and Maria took place on January 19,

Portrait of Mary Ann Snyder, (1843-1876) wife of Hyrum A. Williams, image Ancestry.com

1833, in West Stockbridge, Berkshire, Massachusetts. Maria was twenty-one and her new husband was twenty-five. Their early married life was filled with sadness.[256]

Maria's first child, Mary Ann, born when her mother was twenty-two, lived only a week. Their second child, Elizabeth Mary born in May of 1836, died just seven months later, in December. Son Gustavus was born in 1839 while western Massachusetts, as well as the rest of the country, was in the midst of an economic depression caused by the Panic of 1837. He died two years later. Gustavus and Maria joined the Church of Jesus Christ of Latter-Day Saints in 1840 with the hope of a better future. The church provided structure and emotional support for those tossed around by the unpredictable, chaotic frontier life many were experiencing at the time.

After Andrew Jackson was elected president in 1828 and the start of Jacksonian Democracy, there was a new focus on the common man and individualism. But there was also an increase in lawlessness and swindlers, as the new nation could not enforce laws to control the frontier. The Williams family left Massachusetts, intending to join the Saints in Missouri, where the founder and leader of this new religion, Joseph Smith, had built a new community, but church members were chased out of Missouri before Gustavus and his family got there.

The story of the Latter-day Saints is a violent one filled with conflict with non-Mormon settlers, whom they referred to as gentiles. To understand the turmoil, one has to understand the unusual life of Joseph Smith and his controversial beliefs.[257]

Joseph Smith Jr. and his family were drifters in the economically unstable New England frontier of the early nineteenth century. He was born in Sharon, Vermont, on December 23, 1805, to Joseph Smith Sr. and his wife, Lucy Mack Smith. Joseph's father was a peddler, sometime farmer, and money digger. (Money digging was a scam in which the digger, using "peek stones," or "seer stones," was supposedly able to find buried treasure.) Joseph Sr. had moved the family nineteen times throughout Vermont and New Hampshire in a ten-year period, finally ending up in Palmyra, New York, in 1816. Palmyra is in western New York near the site of the Erie Canal, which was under construction at the time.

The Smiths struggled financially; the plans of Joseph Smith Sr. usually ended in failure, and they were frequently at risk of bankruptcy. In Palmyra they put money down on a 100-acre farm—just three miles from the Erie Canal—but never properly farmed it or paid it off. The Smiths had eleven children, six of them sons. Because of Joseph Sr.'s alcoholism and ineffective support, the family depended upon the eldest son, Alvin, to bring money in, until Alvin died in 1823 at age twenty-five. Hyrum was the next oldest, followed by Joseph Jr., Samuel, William, and Don Carlos. Family members were only semi-literate and were enthralled with the supernatural, the miraculous, and revelations. Joseph's mother had visions, as did her husband, leading to arguments in the family over religion.[258]

Visions and folk magic were common undercurrents in the frontier society at the time, as well as an anti-Christian bent of lawlessness, including money digging, passing bogus money, and religious scams. Many of the most successful criminals of the nineteenth century passed themselves off as preachers, such as Steven Burroughs, the "Emperor of Counterfeiters," whose memoir was in the public library at Palmyra. Palmyra newspaperman Pomeroy Tucker claimed young Joseph Smith loved reading about Steven Burroughs.

Joseph's mother, Lucy Mack Smith, was filled with religious emotionalism. Both of Joseph's parents engaged in religious folk magic and were connected by family to a group of radical sects, as well as scam artists called "blacklegs." They were so poor that they were addicted to the idea of riches and fed into the superstitions and scams of the day, which included money digging, as well as timing the rising of the moon for gold finding. The Smiths were "gold seekers" who would go to different farms and convince the owner to pay them to dig for treasure. This was apparently their main means of support. Joseph practiced his craft from age fourteen on, perfecting the use of a seer stone to conjure up treasure, along with drawing magic circles and using the occult to outsmart the spirit guardians of whatever treasure they were seeking.

Joseph was arrested for fraud in his early twenties for his money digging activities in Chenango County, New York. He was charismatic and an incredible storyteller who held audiences spellbound. In the religious excitement of upstate New York in the 1820s, he began to have visions of angels, specifically, one angel, Moroni, who told him where the "Golden Bible" of the New World was hidden.[259]

Upstate New York from the 1820s through the 1850s was a center of religious fever during the Second Great Awakening. So many competing religious and social movements swept through the area that the revivalist preacher Charles Grandison Finney called it the "Burnt-Over District." Joseph's mother Lucy and her family, never really satisfied with traditional religion, attended many of these revival meetings and frequently changed their denomination. They were seekers, always questioning and wondering.

Not only were many of the people of these frontier towns carved from former Indian lands superstitious, but quite a few had limited schooling. Some traditional churches, such as the Congregational and Presbyterian churches, had educated ministers, but others such as the Baptists and Reformed Methodists did not. The Baptists did not require their ministers to be educated but depended on emotionality to move the faithful. Professors at Dartmouth College in New Hampshire influenced the area with new ideas on religion that moved away from Calvinism towards Arminianism—the theology of Jacobus Arminius, a sixteenth-century Dutch theologian—and Freemasonry.

As the Erie Canal was built, more people, mostly of Puritan heritage, enticed by the availability of cheap land, swept into the area. The new market economy left some—those who were trying to exist on subsistence farming—behind financially, wondering about the fairness of capitalism and struggling to find their place. The transplants brought their traditional values but had to adapt those values to fit the situation of the frontier. A huge push began to perfect man and society, with radically different ideas on how to do that.[260]

Experiments in religion ranged from the celibate Shakers and the semi-celibate followers of Jemima Wilkinson, the supposed female reincarnation of Christ, to the free love movement at the Perfectionist Oneida Community. Charles Miller, a local farmer in New York, began a movement in 1833 based on his prediction of the Second Coming of Christ, which was supposed to happen—among other dates—in October 1844.

Miller lived on the other side of the Burnt-Over District, about 250 miles from the Smith family. Miller had quite a following, with some followers abandoning their farms to wait for the millennium. After the end date came and went, the Millerite movement faded and turned into the Seventh Day Adventists, as well as spanning other, second-coming movements.[261]

There were secular movements as well. There was alarm over the secretive Masonic lodges and the political power they held, resulting in a strong, anti-Mason protest and thousands leaving their lodges. The Freemason Society, which had started in England, grew more powerful in the new United States. Their hierarchy and secret society were exposed in 1826 by member William Morgan, leading to furious condemnation from evangelistic Christians who felt the Masons were anti-Christian. Morgan was kidnapped by Masons and murdered. The Women's Rights movement began in Seneca Falls, New York, with Elizabeth Cody Stanton pushing for women's right to vote. Anti-slavery movements also began to rise up at the same time.

William Lloyd Garrison published the abolitionist newspaper *The Liberator*, starting in 1831, and with others formed the American Anti-Slavery Society in 1833. Economic and social stresses left people on the frontier searching for spiritual answers. They would follow anyone they thought provided answers and peace of mind.[262]

Joseph Smith claimed to have had a vision in his teenage years that would explain the lost tribes of Israel—thought to be American Indians—and the history of the New World, which involved Jesus coming to America. Western New York was a treasure trove of Indian archeological sites, with as many as eight Indian burial sites near the Smith farm. Joseph would tell stories about these tribes to anyone who would listen. After his vision he claimed the angel Moroni came to him to tell him of a book of gold plates buried on a hill near the town of Manchester, along with two stones set in a silver bow like spectacles that would help him translate the book. Joseph visited the hill several times but did not dig up the plates. He claimed the guardian spirit would not let him take the plates yet.

It was common among treasure seekers at the time to say "the treasure slipped away" into the earth to have an excuse why one could not retrieve it. Joseph continued his treasure-seeking activities, using his magic peep stone, for several years after his vision, leading him over the border to the town of Harmony in Susquehanna County, Pennsylvania, where he fell in love with Emma Hale, the daughter of the man he was staying with. Emma's father, Isaac Hale, had employed Joseph and others to find the supposed "lost Spanish silver mines" in Susquehanna County, until Hale came to the conclusion that he was being conned. Joseph convinced Emma to elope on January 18, 1827. Emma's father was furious because he believed Joseph to be incapable of supporting his daughter. When Smith promised to give up treasure seeking, Hale helped them get started in Harmony.[263]

On September 22, 1827, Joseph made his last visit to Hill Cumorah near Manchester, taking Emma with him in the dead of night, both dressed all in black. While Emma's back was turned, he unearthed the gold plates that were purportedly a religious record of the Native Americans, written in an unknown language he called "Reformed Egyptian." Smith was allegedly told by Moroni that only he could see the plates and only he could translate.

This was not the first time someone had suggested that the Native Americans might be the lost tribes of Israel; there had been stories since the days of the Puritans about the Native Americans and their possible origins. Rev. Ethan Smith published his story of the origins of the American Indians, *View of the Hebrews: The Ten Tribes of Israel in America,* seven years before the Book of Mormon. The Reverend lived just one hundred miles from Palmyra and speculated that the Indians descended from ancient Israelites. Scientists now hypothesize, through DNA testing, that Native American ancestry lies in East Asia and Eurasia.[264]

Joseph Smith took two years to translate the plates; sometimes, he would use the special spectacles—the Urim and Thummim—he said were left by Moroni, which allowed him to translate. He got tired of this and resorted to using the stone he had used for treasure seeking; he stared at it at the bottom of his hat, not looking at the plates. The plates were covered with a linen cloth and kept behind a screen some of the time, as his wife, Emma, wrote what he dictated. Joseph had not learned to write yet, so he needed someone to write the story for him.

Martin Harris, a wealthy farmer who was enthralled with Joseph, took over as scribe from Emma and started giving financial help to Smith. Harris' wife, who was not a believer and was furious at the bankrolling of Joseph by her husband, asked him to bring home the manuscript so she could see it. According to her family, she hid and then destroyed the first 116 pages that Joseph had dictated. There was no way for Joseph to duplicate them. He claimed that the angel took away the gold plates as punishment, and he took a break from his work.[265]

Joseph then had a revelation that allowed him to continue: the Lord told him he could not duplicate the book of Lehi, which might be in the devil's hands and corrupted, so the Lord provided a second set of gold plates—the plates of Nephi—which covered the same time period and told a similar but not identical tale. Joseph began to use Oliver Cowdery, a third cousin, as his scribe in April of 1829. (Cowdery was a native of Poultney, Vermont, and a member of its Congregational Church where Rev. Ethan Smith, author of the book on Indian origins, preached.)

After his translation was finished, Joseph found a printer that would print 5,000 copies of his work, called the Book of Mormon. The book was published on March 26, 1830, in Palmyra. The cost of publication was borne by Martin Harris, who also served as one of three sworn witnesses, along with Oliver Cowdery and David Whitmer, who claimed to have seen the plates. Martin Harris later slipped up and admitted to having "seen them in faith."

The angel Moroni took the plates back when Joseph was finished translating them, according to Smith. Later, Smith would add eight more witnesses, some from his family, most of whom would end up excommunicated from the church. The Book of Mormon was written in a combination of King James English—with many passages similar to the 1769 King James Bible that Smith owned—as well as the early-nineteenth-century vernacular of the semi-literate. In subsequent issues the sloppy grammar of the book was cleaned up.[266]

Although the Book of Mormon is largely described by non-Mormons as a poorly written work of fiction, it was captivating enough to hold the interest of a percentage of the population and convert them to this new religion. The Book of Mormon quotes a Nephite prophet, Mormon, and the story of two great civilizations. One civilization came from Jerusalem in 600 B.C. and separated into two nations, known as the Nephites, who were righteous people, and the Lamanites, who were an idle people full of mischief. The book focuses on the story of Lehi, leader of a Hebrew tribe, whose two sons, Nephi, the favored son, and Laman, the evil son, formed the two major tribes. After great battles involving horse-drawn chariots and steel swords—there are no archaeological signs of any horses or steel having been in the New World before the Spanish—all Nephites except Moroni were killed by the Lamanites, the ancestors of the American Indians. The Lamanites were cursed with dark skin as punishment until they repent.

The leader of the Nephites during their last battle was Mormon. Mormon's son Moroni, the last survivor of the tribe, engraved the plates to tell the story and buried them around 400 A.D. for Joseph to find in 1827 on the hill near Manchester, New York. Fawn Brodie, author of *No Man Knows My History*, calls the Book of Mormon a response to the religious and social questions of the time and the frenzied environment of upstate New York. Other historians suggest that the book is autobiographical in nature with Joseph's own conflicts with his brothers figuring into the story.[267]

After the book was written, Smith realized he had the start of a new religion, drawn mostly from the Old Testament with a uniquely American twist. He established the Church of Christ, later called the Church of Jesus Christ of Latter-day Saints or the Mormon Church. He predicted that the second coming of Christ—this time in America—would happen by the 1890s and that it was necessary to prepare a Zion on Earth for his return. To Mormons, this new sacred text was supposed to be the "sealed" book, described in the Book of Isaiah, which would signal the end times. Believers were the "New Israelites," called out from the gentiles to usher in the millennium.

Joseph Sr. is thought by some historians to have prior association with a radical sect in Vermont in 1801-1802 called the New Israelites, who were involved with counterfeiting. Since the millennium was supposed to be near, followers were called latter-day saints of the true church. All other Christian sects were called out by the Mormons as false. Cowdery and Smith baptized each other, as well as Smith's brother Hyrum, and established three small branches of the church in Manchester, Fayette, and Colesville, New York. Emma resisted being baptized for six weeks but finally consented. After the Book of Mormon was published, and Emma and Joseph left Harmony, Emma never saw her parents again. They did not approve of Joseph or his new church.[268]

Joseph's church had a few followers in New York, but the bad reputation of the Smith family in Palmyra and nearby towns led to strident resistance to his Book of Mormon and his new church. Smith Sr. was in jail in Manchester for a fourteen-dollar debt, and Hyrum was being hounded by members of the Masonic lodge he belonged to for debts he could not pay; the entire Smith family was in disarray. When Smith Jr. was arrested and brought to trial for being a disorderly person—a common charge for those thought to be con-men or blacklegs—Smith and his followers decided to leave New York and find another place for their church.

Daniel Adlum's ancestors, Gurdon Collins Johnson and Louisa Lee Johnson, lived in the town of Dryden, New York, not far from Colesville, where the Mormons had a small branch of their new church. They had to have heard the uproar over this new religion. They were on the move, as well. Their Episcopal faith took them to Coshocton, Ohio, via the Erie Canal. Many of Joseph Smith's followers also ended up in Ohio.[269]

Oliver Cowdery was assigned to find the perfect spot to build their New Jerusalem and bring new converts. Smith thought it should be on the western border of the United States near the Lamanites—Indian Territory—which at the time was western Missouri in Jackson County, around the town of Independence. While traveling to Missouri, Cowdery and other missionaries, including new convert Parley Pratt, passed through northeastern Ohio. There they met Sidney Rigdon and over a hundred of his Campbellite followers, who converted to Mormonism within three weeks. Smith decided Kirtland, Ohio, would be the eastern boundary of his New Jerusalem. Kirtland grew rapidly, with converts pouring in after Joseph Smith moved there in 1831. Church members from New York traveled on the Erie Canal to their new home in Kirtland. People were hungry for a new prophet, and by 1831 Joseph was calling himself one. Smith made promises to church elders that, if they obeyed him, they would receive endowments of heavenly power, and he introduced a priesthood hierarchy, including the Quorum of the Twelve Apostles.[270]

Meanwhile, things were not going well for the Mormons who settled in Jackson County, Missouri. As their numbers increased, the resentment by native Missourians increased against them for both political and religious reasons. Rumors of horse thefts and fraudulent activities began to circulate. The sheer number of Mormons in the county made it possible for them to prevent members of their group being convicted in court. Because the Mormons voted as a group, and traded among each other as a group, their power threatened to change the dynamics in Missouri for non-Mormons, Joseph's revelation in 1831, when he said, "God commanded the Saints to assemble yourself together to rejoice upon the land of Missouri, which is the land of your inheritance, which is now the land of your enemies," made things worse. Mormons felt if you weren't with them, you were against them, which was not taken kindly by the rough and ready Missourians. Mobs forced the Mormons out of the county. Smith frequently visited Missouri, travelling the long distance by horseback, but concentrated his efforts on Kirtland, Ohio, where he built a temple and established a church organization.[271]

By 1837 things began to unravel in Kirtland, as well. The building of the temple put the church heavily in debt. Smith decided shortly after arriving to try a communistic approach to obtain more money, and he formed the United Order. New converts were to sign over their property to the church, and they would be given back what was thought appropriate. Smith also decided to create a joint stock company, called the Kirtland Safety Society Anti-Banking Company, to act as a bank. It never had a legal charter. Smith was reckless with the money, kept very poor records, and would fill bank boxes with sand and a thin layer of gold on top. The bank failed within a month to back the paper money by specie but continued to try to spread the notes far and wide to places where residents did not know they were receiving worthless money. There was open rebellion when the fraud was realized.

Sidney Rigdon, the bank president, was brought into court. Six of the twelve apostles spoke against Smith and Rigdon. Many converts had lost all their money. "Thirteen different lawsuits were brought against Smith. He was arrested seven times in four months." Smith spent months hiding out. He was also accused of engaging in an affair with his teenage serving girl, Fanny Alger. Resentment and rumors went flying, as well as accusations of counterfeiting, horse thefts, and other crimes. Warrants were issued for Joseph Smith, his brother Hyrum, and some of his apostles for bank fraud, and they fled to Missouri, pursued by 200 men of the state militia. Citizens of Kirtland had to abandon their homes in 1838 and made their way to a new settlement in Missouri.[272]

Chapter Six: Reaching for Zion

Having been driven out of Jackson County in 1833, the Saints' new Zion in Missouri was a town they called Far West in Caldwell County. Mormon settlements spilled over into bordering Davies County as well. Smith proclaimed that Far West was the place of the original Garden of Eden, despite the Bible stating it was at the headwaters of the Tigris and Euphrates rivers in old Babylon. Rumors of Mormon lawlessness in Ohio preceded their arrival in Missouri, and there was opposition from non-Mormon settlers from the start. Violent rhetoric by Sidney Rigdon, in a speech given on the Fourth of July in Far West, led Missourians to believe this was a threat to take over Missouri. They tried to prevent Mormons from voting in the August 1838 election in the town of Gallatin in Davies County.

The Mormons had formed their own army, called the Danites—avenging angels sworn to vengeance by blood oath—in June of 1838. Tensions increased to the point that the governor called out the militia to fight the Danites in the 1838 Mormon War. Vigilantes raided and burned Mormon towns, while the Danites plundered non-Mormon towns. Governor Lilburn Boggs issued an extermination order: "Mormons must be exterminated or driven from the state." Three days later, 240 Missouri militia men attacked a Mormon settlement at Haun's Mill and killed eighteen residents there. Smith was only sixteen miles away at Far West, surrounded by militia troops. The next day the Saints surrendered and agreed to leave the state. Smith was brought before a military court, accused of treason, arson, riot, burglary, and receiving stolen goods and was sentenced to be immediately executed. Alexander Doniphan, an attorney and brigadier general in the Missouri Militia, refused to carry out the order because he thought it was cold-blooded murder. Smith was then sent to a state court and transferred to the jail at Liberty, Missouri, to await trial for treason, along with Sidney Rigdon and four others. While Smith sat in jail for more than four months, Brigham Young, president of the Quorum of the Twelve Apostles, arranged the removal of about 14,000 Mormons from Missouri to Illinois and Iowa.[273]

Daniel B. Adlum's second-great-uncle Peter Hardeman Burnett, along with Alexander Doniphan, were hired to defend Smith at his hearing in Davis County. Both attorneys were determined that the mob would not rule in Missouri and that a proper court would try Smith.

Burnett described the scene as very tense, with all the attorneys armed and surrounded by close friends to protect them from the angry spectators in the courtroom. He gave the opening speech; his friend and mentor Doniphan made the closing argument, pressing for a change of venue for trial. Burnett had his gun on the table within reach at all times. The judge agreed to a change in venue, and Smith and his associates were transferred by the sheriff and guards but escaped on the way back to jail—some say he bribed the sheriff—and fled Missouri.[274]

One wonders why Joseph Smith had so many followers. Peter Burnett tried to describe the power of Joseph Smith's personality:

"Joseph Smith Jr was at least six feet high, well formed, and weighed about one hundred and eighty pounds. His appearance was not prepossessing, and his conversational powers were but ordinary. You could tell at a glance that his education was very limited. He was an awkward, but vehement speaker. In conversation he was slow and would not go directly to the point. But with all these drawbacks, he was much more than an ordinary man. He possessed the most indomitable perseverance, was a good judge of men and deemed himself *born to command and he did command.* (author's emphasis) His views were so strange and striking, and his manner was so earnest, and apparently so candid, that you could not but be interested. There was a kind, familiar look about him that pleased you … He had great influence over others."

Jon Krakauer, writing about Smith in his book *Under the Banner of Heaven*, 120 years after Burnett, put it more bluntly: "He could sell a muzzle to a dog." And so Smith would use the power of his personality to start again, this time in Illinois in swampy woodland on the banks of the Mississippi River.[275]

The Saints called their new town Nauvoo. The rest of the country, especially Illinois, had sympathy for the Mormons and the way they had been treated in Missouri. They were welcomed as a persecuted people. The Saints bought 20,000 acres from Isaac Galland, as well as the town of Commerce (renamed Nauvoo), on credit in 1840. Galland was baptized into the church by Smith and chosen to be his chief land agent. Galland turned out to be a fraud and counterfeiter. Some historians have suggested that the Mormons knew he was a counterfeiter because, in more than one instance, they seemed to settle where known shady characters had settled. There is considerable evidence that there were counterfeiters in the church as well, including Joseph Smith, his brothers, Brigham Young, and some of the apostles.

Galland not only sold fraudulent land deals in Iowa to the church, but he was also a horse thief. It seemed that everyone was trying to get the better of the other. Despite these issues, Nauvoo was very successful and grew to be the second largest town in Illinois. Missionaries sent to Europe brought back thousands of converts who were glad to have a new start in America. After Smith attracted the wealthy Dr. John Bennett, Illinois' quartermaster general, to the cause, the state government gave Nauvoo a very generous charter that allowed them autonomy, including allowing their own militia. Lieutenant General Smith and Major General Bennett were put in charge of what would be the largest group of armed men in Illinois. The Nauvoo Legion was half the size of the U.S. Army at the time. Bennett became the first mayor of the rapidly growing town.[276]

Gustavus and Maria Williams and the Snyders were among those who built homes and successful lives there. Gustavus and Maria were settled by 1841. They built a house and quickly became involved in community projects. During the first couple of years, there was a lot of illness from malaria and other diseases that preyed on the new settlers. Work had to be done to drain the malarial swamps as well as build up the town. Gustavus worked on the temple while Maria assisted the poor through the Relief Society. They were hard-working and devoted to building a good society. Maria told her granddaughter years later that when they churned butter, they saved it for those working on the temple. Maria was a practical nurse and midwife at a time when giving birth was perilous. Joseph Smith's wife, Emma, shared Maria's sad experiences with childbirth, losing her first four children before the age of two. She lost a total of five children; in 1842 she gave birth to a stillborn son. Maria Williams experienced great joy when her son Hyrum was born in 1843 and was healthy. In all, Joseph's first wife, Emma, had four sons who lived to maturity. Maria Williams would bear ten children herself; seven would precede her in death.[277]

Mary Ann Snyder, the future wife of Maria's son Hyrum, was born in Nauvoo in 1843. Her family's journey to Nauvoo and Jobs Creek—outside of Nauvoo—started in Canada. Mary Ann was the daughter of Samuel Comstock Snyder and Henrietta Stockwell. The Snyders converted to Mormonism as a family, along with Samuel's parents, Isaac Snyder and Lovisa Comstock, in 1838. Their story also starts in the New England Puritan tradition. Lovisa Comstock, Samuel's mother, was a descendent, through her mother, Sarah Crippin, of Edward Fuller of the *Mayflower* and Rev. John Lothrop, the Puritan minister. Lovisa was born in the Berkshires of Massachusetts in 1789 and moved to Fort Ann, New York, in 1805 with her family, where her father died soon after. At age sixteen she married Isaac Snyder, a native of Vermont, in Fort Ann. She had her first child, Samuel Comstock Snyder, there on February 14, 1806. They moved the next year to Camillus, about 186 miles away. Lovisa's second son, Isaac, died the same year. Two years later, their son Robert was born, after which they moved on. They moved back and forth between New York and Ontario, Canada, for many years, with children born both in New York and Ontario.[278]

Samuel Comstock Snyder, photo Ancestry.com

Henrietta Stockwell, wife of Samuel Comstock Snyder, photo Ancestry.com

In 1816, "the year without a summer" as it was called, the Snyders were living in Ontario. There were massive crops failures throughout New England and Eastern Canada, with snow and freezing weather in June and August that year causing severe hardship. Some called it "Eighteen Hundred and Freeze to Death." Vermonters, including the Joseph Smith family, foraged for nettles, wild turnips, and hedgehogs. The terrible, thin, rocky soil of Vermont made farming difficult under the best of circumstances. The Smiths moved to Palmyra, New York, in 1816, hoping for better luck—they were asked to leave the town in Vermont where they were living—but western New York had such terrible fires from the drought that year that the smoke blinded the sailors on Lake Champlain.

The Snyder family was much more prosperous than the Smith family, but it was a hard time for all. Isaac and Lovisa Snyder moved frequently over the next fifteen years, depending on economic opportunity. The Snyders' last child, David, was born in Ontario in 1832. By 1837 the Snyders were living in Kington, Ontario, where they had been hearing about Mormon missionaries in the area for the last five years.[279]

There was a small group of Mormons in their town in Ontario. The Snyders' son Robert had a severe case of consumption for three years and was very ill. The Snyders turned to the Mormons, who were known for faith healing. Elder Page of the Mormon Church prayed over Robert. Everyone except Robert's sister Jane was convinced that Elder Page cured him, and they converted to the faith. Lovisa was a Methodist, but she wholeheartedly accepted this new religion, as did her husband and her grown children. Her son Samuel, married to Henrietta, lived nearby and was converted at age twenty-nine. The families quickly sold their extensive property, planning to follow the Saints to Far West, Missouri. By the time the Snyders reached La Porte, Indiana, in November 1839, only twenty miles from Lake Michigan, they were told by Joseph Smith to wait there because of the trouble in Missouri. Here Jane got very sick in the winter air and was healed by her brother Robert's faith. She was then baptized a believer. Some of the family went on to Nauvoo when they had word that it was the new gathering place. All of the Snyders were in Nauvoo by 1841.[280]

Jane Snyder was married to Franklin D. Richards, who would become one of the Twelve Apostles in Utah in 1849, as soon as they arrived at her brother Samuel's place at Job's Creek just outside of Nauvoo. Her brother became a good friend of both Joseph and Hyrum Smith and frequently visited them. Samuel's daughter Mary Ann met the prophet as a young girl when she ran out to feed the oxen in front of the Nauvoo Temple. According to family history, he remarked what a sweet nature she had. About the same time, Joseph Smith gave Samuel a patriarchal blessing dated March 5, 1842. Among the blessings was the promise that he would prosper at everything he tried in business.

Samuel's parents, Isaac and Lovisa, settled in, with several of their children living very close to them. They bought a lot at the corner of Hyde and Taylor in Nauvoo, as well as farmland. Isaac worked on the temple as well. All able-bodied men were expected to donate one day out of ten to the work site. Isaac died of pneumonia on February 28, 1844. It was a sad event for the family in what would turn out to be an eventful year.[281]

Joseph Smith seemed to be on top of the world in 1844. His town, with neat, trim houses and wide streets, had 12,000 residents who worshipped him. According to biographer Fawn Brodie, Joseph Smith was: mayor of Nauvoo, owner of the leading store, hotel keeper, official temple architect, trustee for all church finances, Lt. General of the Nauvoo Legion, with 4,000 men at his command, King of the Kingdom of God on Earth, and a declared candidate for the Presidency of the United States, as well as husband to as many as fifty wives.

Although Illinois had been welcoming to Smith and his followers in Hancock County at first, neighboring counties were alarmed at the growing theocracy and Smith's reach for power, as well as the persistent rumors of theft and fraud.[282]

According to Professor Donald Scott, Professor of History at Queens College and the Graduate Center of the City University of New York, Mormonism seemed to run counter to American democratic values. "Mormonism seemed a mysterious cult, cloaked in secrecy and bent on assembling illegitimate, almost monopolistic power that would prevent ordinary non-Mormons from fulfilling their dreams of democratic self-improvement and rise."

It appeared that Joseph Smith wanted to rule the world. Smith represented his views in a manifesto on February 8, 1844 published and distributed to President Van Buren, his cabinet, and leading citizens. Smith wanted the country to take him seriously, so he declared himself a candidate for president and sent many of the apostles out on the road, campaigning and collecting money. *General Smith's Views* was a combination of his theological and political opinions that he presented to the world. Secretly, he had himself declared the King of the Kingdom of God by the Quorum of Fifty, and his word was law, regardless of the laws of the United States.[283]

Despite the outward success of Nauvoo, there was growing unrest because of Joseph's actions both inside the church and out. Once he was established in Nauvoo, Joseph began to add to his religious tracts. He planned an elaborate, secret endowment ceremony, borrowing many of the symbols of the Masons for his church. He was fond of the secretive rituals of the Masons and began to rapidly establish Masonic lodges in Nauvoo. Joseph set up the hierarchy of the church and even a hierarchy to his Mormon heaven. Like the Masons, there were levels of priesthood and secrecy. If one was in the outer levels, there was no understanding of the secret privileges of the inner circle. In addition to the deacons, elders, priests, and bishops of the New Testament tradition, he added a "First Presidency" and two counselors, a high counsel, and a Quorum of Seventy, as well as the Twelve Apostles and a patriarch, ordaining his father as the first patriarch. He borrowed from other religions as well, including that of Mohammed, whom he admired for his military powers.

Joseph proclaimed that he had sole authority to receive revelations from God and set forth a series of new revelations that included baptism of the dead, the idea that God originally was a man—Adam—and the startling idea that men could become gods. Most startling of all was his revelation on "celestial marriage," commonly called polygamy, since the Book of Mormon spoke against polygamy.[284]

Joseph Smith had been secretly practicing polygamy for years and had a close group of the elect with whom he shared the idea. He vehemently denied the practice in public. This practice of denial of the inner workings of the church was called "lying for the Lord" and was repeatedly used by the Mormon elite for their advantage. When Dr. Bennett, early in 1841, carried "celestial marriage" too far, causing scandal, Joseph denounced him and excommunicated him to save his own reputation.

Bennett saw the whole thing as a charade and an excuse to womanize. Bennett exposed Joseph's whole plan in a series of exposés with lurid details of prostitutes, as well as telling of the exploits of the Danites, trained as Mormon assassins. When an attempt was made on the life of Governor Briggs of Missouri as retaliation for his extermination order, Bennett claimed it was Joseph's bodyguard Porter Rockwell who did the dirty deed.

Smith could not "put the oil back in the bottle," so on August 12, 1843, he revealed the "new doctrine" of plural marriage to his secret counsel. Let by his trusted advisor William Law, there was immediate fallout and outrage by a number of his counsel who were opposed to the idea. Law was aided by Joseph's wife, Emma Smith, who was very opposed to the celestial marriage doctrine. Joseph had tried to win her over but never could get her to accept or admit the practice of polygamy. She denied that he practiced it until the day she died.[285]

Joseph Smith's megalomania reached a peak in 1844. Fawn Brodie wrote in her book *No Man Knows My History* that he was literally drunk on power. As a candidate for president, some of his platform seemed reasonable enough. He called for prison reform and the gradual abolishment of slavery. He vacillated on the subject on slavery, sometimes supporting it and sometimes not. He demanded that the federal government and institutions protect his rights but secretly created a legislative body, known as the Council of Fifty, which would decide which federal and state laws the Mormons would obey.

Smith also had an increasing appetite for more wives. For years he had propositioned the daughters and wives of his associates, and then he tried to seduce the wife of William Law. It was his undoing. Law was enraged and called Joseph a "false prophet," as well as calling him out for dishonest business practices. Joseph responded by excommunicating Law.

Law retaliated by buying a printing press and distributing 1,000 copies of the premium edition of what he called the *Nauvoo Expositor*. Law explained in his newspaper, in the first and only issue, on June 7, 1844, that Joseph had contempt for the separation of church and state. He told Mormons they "were voting for a man who contends all governments are to be put down and the one established upon its ruins." He called out the practice of preaching and practicing polygamy and confirmed the prior confessional of Joseph H. Jackson, one of Smith's inner circle, who had previously been banished. Law sought to reform the church, not to demolish it, so his words had great meaning for those who read them.[286]

The Saints destroyed all copies of the newspaper they could find and per Joseph's order destroyed the printing press. This was too much for the citizens of Illinois. They were disgusted by the polygamy but more concerned about the destruction of private property and the destruction of the free press. Vigilantes howled treason. There was so much unrest that Joseph declared martial law in Nauvoo on June 18. The governor asked him to turn himself in to avoid a civil war, but Joseph and Hyrum ran for their lives, slipping across the Mississippi in a rowboat to Iowa. Emma wrote him a note asking him to come back, telling him that the Saints were calling him a coward, so he did. He said, "I am going like a lamb to the slaughter."[287]

Joseph, his brother Hyrum, and ten others charged with destroying the press surrendered to the authorities on June 24. Joseph and Hyrum were put in the Carthage Jail, which was about twenty-five miles from Nauvoo. On June 27, 1844, a group of about 125 militia men from the anti-Mormon town of Warsaw surrounded the jail and overpowered the guards, while Apostles John Taylor and Willard Richards were upstairs, visiting the prisoners and smuggling in two pistols for the Smith brothers to use. Hyrum was killed first and Joseph soon after as he tried to jump from the window after first killing two men with his pistol. Taylor and Richards survived. Joseph was thirty-eight years old. He had written the Book of Mormon only fourteen years before, at age twenty-four. The Saints mourned their prophet as they brought their bodies back to Nauvoo. Both the Snyder and Williams families remember seeing their dead bodies.[288]

The community was thrown into turmoil. Six weeks later they still had no church leader. Half the church leadership was out on the campaign trail, trying to get back from stumping for Smith's presidential campaign. The leadership of the Saints divided into pro-polygamy and anti-polygamy camps. Most of the faithful had no idea about the arguments of polygamy going on or of unlawful activities. They spent their time working hard and trying to follow a disciplined faith, while their leaders were conflicted.

William Law and Emma Smith were on the anti-polygamy side, while Brigham Young was very much pro. Emma and Brigham Young hated each other. Emma thought Brigham was responsible for the push for polygamy; she was blinded to her husband's actions. Brigham thought Emma was not meek enough. Joseph's younger brother Samuel was thought to have been poisoned by the Nauvoo police chief—a supporter of Brigham

Young—to keep him from assuming leadership. Anti-polygamist Sidney Rigdon stepped up, but the overwhelming support was for the determined, pragmatic Brigham Young, who was very different in temperament from Prophet Joseph Smith.[289]

The death of Joseph Smith left a huge hole for his followers. With his rare magnetism, he was one of the most astonishing men of the nineteenth century. A truly charismatic man, he was a religious genius, according to religion writer Harold Bloom. Others say he was an incredibly talented conman who used religion to hide his money-making schemes. He was in the right place at the right time to create a new religion. Fawn Brodie writes: "He threw off the Calvinism of America's early years and replaced it with a simple philosophy of promising good life, riches and even the chance of becoming a God if you followed the Mormon way." She continues: "It was no accident that his theology in the end discarded all traces of Calvinism and became an ingenious blend of supernaturalism and materialism, which promised in heaven a continuation of all earthly pleasures – work, wealth, sex and power." At the same time, because it was highly patriarchal and dismissed the Puritan idea of partnership in marriage, Mormonism destroyed the value of a true partnership with love and friendship for women with Smith's idea of polygamy, as well as any democratic freedom.[290]

Brigham Young believed in the teachings of Joseph Smith and in polygamy. He intended to continue Smith's legacy, but he knew the church must move out of the United States. Smith had been thinking of where to move before he died, exploring thoughts of settling in Texas, Oregon Country, or California. The unsettled political situation, the Mexican War, and the push by Americans to explore the west decided Young in favor of the Great Salt Basin of Utah, which was still Mexican territory and rejected by most as unlivable. They were hoping to settle where they could live by themselves without interference, and Utah seemed the logical choice.

Things were a mess in Illinois, with constant fighting between Mormons and gentiles, as well as infighting between splinter groups of Mormons breaking off from the main. In September 1845, Brigham Young sent a letter to Governor Thomas Ford, telling him the Saints planned to leave but would wait until the following spring so there would be grass along the way for their animals. On February 4, 1846, a warrant was issued for Young's arrest, as well as others, for harboring counterfeiters, and the Saints realized they needed to leave immediately.[291]

Nauvoo was known to be a haven for counterfeiters. Smith and Young had both shrugged off the idea that they were breaking the law. It was no problem to them that gentiles were given bogus money. Brigham Young was said to have passed off as much as $40,000 in bogus currency. Accusations of counterfeiting and passing bogus money plagued many of the principals of the Mormon movement, including Joseph and Hyrum Smith, Cowdery, Sidney Rigdon, and Brigham Young, following them through New

York, Missouri, Ohio, and Illinois. It was time to leave again. That day, the first platoon of Mormon emigrants started the exodus, crossing the Mississippi into Iowa, with the ground still frozen.[292]

Gustavus and Maria Williams were convinced that Brigham Young was the right man to lead the church and were resigned that they would have to leave their home and start over. The majority of faithful Mormons had no idea of the corruption of their leaders and faithfully followed them. Before leaving Nauvoo, they received their endowments in the Nauvoo Temple.

Maria had two very small children and was pregnant with another. They had their faith and determination, but it was a very difficult journey. They travelled slowly, their first stop Sugar Creek, Iowa, followed by Council Bluffs, Garden Grove, and Mount Pisgah, Iowa. At Winter Quarters (North Omaha), Nebraska, they planted crops for other companies that would come behind them.

Sites along the Mormon Trail, public domain, en.wikipedia.org

Young was a genius with details, and he assigned everyone duties in a quasi-military system. The Williams family spent the winters of 1847 and '48 there under terrible conditions. They built rough, sod-roofed cabins that offered little protection from the cold. They suffered greatly from hunger and rampant disease, including scurvy and consumption.[293]

Gustavus and Maria lost another child, their sweet, eighteen-month-old little girl, Ellen Aurelia, at Winter Quarters in July 1847. Sadness was part of their lives. Early in May 1848, they left for Salt Lake City, travelling in the Heber C. Kimball company. Averaging about fifteen miles a day, they finally finished the 1,300-mile journey, arriving in the Salt Lake Valley in September 1848.

Young had taken an advance party in 1847 to scout out the best spot for their Zion. Young and his party of 143 men and three women trekked over the mountains, through what was Indian and Mexican territory, to arrive on July 24, 1847, in the Great Salt Valley. When they went through Fort Bridger in Wyoming, Jim Bridger warned them not to try to settle in Utah, where none of the rivers ran to the sea and lakes turned to salt because of no outlet. Sick and exhausted, Brigham Young declared that Utah was the right place anyway.

When the city of Salt Lake was laid out, each family was allowed a ten-acre city lot and twenty acres outside the city for farming. Gustavus Williams owned the block where the future Walker Bank would stand, as well as farmland. Gustavus was known as a saddle maker. His wife, Hannah Maria, ran a boarding house, as well as tailoring men's suits at night, in addition to their farm chores as they struggled to survive in this new harsh environment.[294]

Gustavus Williams and wife Hannah Maria Andrews Williams, parents of Hyrum A. Williams, photo Ancestry.com

Like the Williamses, the Snyders had to leave Illinois suddenly in 1845, leaving livestock in their pens and their house and considerable property behind after being threatened by mobs. They travelled to the Mormon camp at Mount Pisgah, Iowa, where their son Isaac was born. They built temporary shelters and fenced off acreage for cultivation of crops. The next winter they spent at Winter Quarters, Nebraska, along with the Williams family and thousands of others. One of Samuel's daughters would be permanently crippled from black leg scurvy contracted there. Samuel's sister Jane Snyder Richards described the bitter cold conditions: "Clothes would be frozen stiff about my ankles, remaining so day by day that you could hear them rattle as they struck against anything." Hundreds died that winter, including some of Lovisa Snyder's grandchildren. The newborn son of Lovisa's daughter Jane died while they were camped at Mount Pisgah. Jane's three-year-old daughter then died at Winter Quarters, Nebraska. Jane said later of that terrible time: "I only lived because I could not die."[295]

Although most of those in Nauvoo followed Brigham Young and his plan to settle in the Great Salt Valley, hundreds split off and formed their own churches. Emma Smith and her sons stayed behind in Illinois. Emma didn't trust Young and was frightened of him. She married a man who was not a Mormon. Emma's son Joseph Smith III formed the Reorganized Latter-day Saints Church, which did not practice polygamy. Sidney Rigdon formed his own church. There are as many as 130 different offshoots of Joseph's church. The people who stayed with Young became closer and more determined to succeed because of their shared hardships, and they accepted his leadership without question.

One would not suspect from Brigham Young's childhood that he would become such a leader. Like Smith, he had a hardscrabble beginning. The ninth of eleven children, he was born to a poor family in Whittingham, Vermont, on June 1, 1801. He would later brag that he only had eleven days of schooling. Raised as a Reformed Methodist, which, along with many other evangelicals, preached an imminent apocalypse and damnation for those who ignored the message, he read the Book of Mormon in 1832 and became a convert and loyal lieutenant to Joseph Smith, doing missionary work for several years. The opposite in personality to Smith, who was emotional and impulsive but loving to his followers, Young was one of the great organizers of men—disciplined, ruthless, and determined to be obeyed. If he hadn't led the Saints to Utah and ruled with an iron hand, the story of the Mormons would probably be very different.[296]

The first couple of years in their new Zion were very difficult. They were plagued by crickets destroying their crops and much suffering and starvation. Young quickly focused the settlers on the task of erecting a new kingdom of God on Earth and laying out the city of Salt Lake, as well as assigning farmland outside the city in the New England style. They set up irrigation for crops in the Mexican style, using ditch irrigation and canals for the semi-arid climate.

The area was not completely unknown to them. They followed U.S. Army officer John C. Frémont's maps and his published articles on the area, which he had explored on the way to California in 1843 and back in 1845. Other explorers had seen the area as well, such as the ill-fated Donner party on the way to California in 1846. The pioneers of the Donner party cut a rough road through the Wasatch Mountains, coming through the later-named Emigration Canyon into the Salt Lake Valley on August 12, 1846. The Donner party would get stuck in the Sierras that winter, some resorting to cannibalism as a result of starvation until rescued.

Salt Lake City was within the territory of the Northwestern Shoshone when Young's settlers inhabited the area. Young tried to cooperate with the Indians because the Mormons believed that if they brought the fallen Indians (Lamanites) to the church, their dark skin would become "wholesome in whiteness again." The Ute as well as the Paiute and Goshute Indians also had roots in the area, and the Mormons struggled to get along with them for the first few years.[297]

The extended Snyder family left Winter Quarters on May 24, 1849. Samuel Comstock Snyder was a captain in Allen Taylor's company, which consisted of 246 people. Samuel had five wagons and numerous teams of oxen, and he furnished one team and wagon to apostle Parley Pratt. It was a difficult trip. One of the main problems seemed to be livestock stampedes, which were very dangerous. One such stampede killed a man when the cattle ran over him, breaking his back. The cattle were found scattered three miles from their camp a couple of days later. The company finally arrived in Salt Lake City on October 20, 1849. The Snyders settled there and built a house. The house of Samuel and Henrietta Snyder was located at 48 West 2nd South Street in Salt Lake City. Samuel's wife, Henrietta, was known for her hospitality and her sewing skills—she made gloves for Brigham Young as well as many others.[298]

Brigham Young, in his quest to settle the entire valley, sent Parley Pratt to explore the area now known as Park City to see if it was suitable for colonizing. Pratt soon turned over the rights to Samuel Snyder, trading them for a yoke of oxen in the spring of 1850. Samuel took his wife and family, as well as his brother George and family, to settle there on Spring Creek. They named it Snyderville and began to farm, as well as found the lumber industry there. Samuel's widowed mother, Lovisa, stayed in Salt Lake City near her daughters Jane and Sarah until she died of typhoid in 1856. Samuel Comstock Snyder became prosperous with his sawmill and other ventures. He died in 1866 in Park City, followed by his first wife, Henrietta, in 1888.

Both Samuel and his brother George added more wives when they came to Utah. Only about ten percent of Mormon men had multiple wives, usually, only the most wealthy and powerful. It is not known what Henrietta thought of her husband, Samuel, taking more wives, but it was quite distressing to the majority of women, who felt trapped in the system. Henrietta's daughter Jane Snyder Richards found the system miserable and "could never get used to it" as her husband took on more wives. Many women died young or lived lives of bitterness and heartache. Others said, "You have to make yourself indifferent to your husband." Brigham Young had cleverly closed heaven to women who did not have their husbands blessing. There were many excuses put forth for polygamy, one being that they needed to build up the Kingdom of God with more children, but the fact was that polygamist wives had less children and left less women for other men to marry.

Historian Kathleen Kimball Melonakos ties the idea of criminal behavior such as counterfeiting to polygamy with the idea that "family won't tell on family." Polygamy bound the Mormons together.[299]

Despite Brigham Young declaring a new state called Deseret—the Mormon's independent kingdom—the United States followed the Mormons to Utah. The election of James Polk over Henry Clay in the fateful 1844 presidential contest insured that the U.S. would push for expansion. (Henry Clay and the Whig Party thought the country was large enough.) At President Polk's request, Young had sent the 500-strong Mormon Battalion to California from Iowa in July 1846—the battalion marching the whole 2,000 miles—to aid in the Mexican War. Young hoped to win some favor from the U.S. government so they could settle in Utah unmolested. One of the Mormon leaders in California was none other than Sam Brannon, who became wealthy in the California Gold Rush and would end up being excommunicated by Brigham Young.

After the U.S. won the Mexican War, the treaty of Guadalupe Hidalgo, signed on February 2, 1848, gave California, one half of New Mexico, most of Arizona, Nevada, Utah, and Colorado to the U.S., as well as establishing the border of Texas at the Rio Grande.

The Mormons would not stay isolated for long. The California Gold Rush brought the '49ers through Salt Lake, and the Saints were able to profit by selling supplies to the miners. The Mormon settlement became part of Utah Territory in 1850. Brigham Young was appointed the territorial governor and superintendent of Indian Affairs by President Fillmore, as well as already being leader of the Mormon Church.

Mark Twain, writing about Brigham Young, said, "The petrified truth is that Utah is an absolute monarchy and Brigham Young is King." Young intended his colony to be successful by encouraging emigration brought from far flung missionaries in Europe, as well as encouraging Mormon colonization throughout Utah Territory and to California. Young was highly successful at encouraging colonization and established 250 small colonies, stretching throughout southern Utah, called Dixie, all the way to Bakersfield, California.[300]

The Snyder and the Williams families spread out from Salt Lake City, along with other pioneers, establishing smaller communities. Gustavus and Maria Williams were asked to settle in St. George, near the Arizona border, and also Teasdale, Utah. Gustavus died in 1887 in Teasdale, his wife in 1901. They had been devoted and faithful Mormons. The Williams offspring were instrumental in settling Utah's Dixie.

There was unrest with Indian tribes for many years in the south until the Mormons finally settled on a method of trade and cooperation, the Mormon settlers feeding the Indians when they would come asking. The Indian tribes were mostly hunters and gatherers, eventually starving and desperate for help from the settlers who had upended their way of life.

Brigham Young sent many more missionaries to Europe and established the Perpetual Emigrating Fund, requiring settlers to contribute to the fund to bring more Saints to Zion. The new immigrants would work to repay their journey. The fund ran out of money in 1856, and some new converts had to push handcarts across the plains, with disastrous consequences.

There were large numbers of converts in Scandinavia, England, and Wales. The social and economic structure in Scandinavia was feudalistic, and workers never had a chance to own their land. England and Wales had industrial workers suffering under a system which allowed them little recourse to change their economic situation. This new religion, with its chance to start over, was very attractive to them.

Fanny Stenhouse, in her book *Tell it All, A Woman's Life in Polygamy*, was one of these converts from England. She and her husband left England and came to their Zion in Salt Lake City. She became disillusioned with the church because the full extent of what was required by converts once they became members was not explained until they had left everything behind and were solid believers. The leaders of the church called it "milk before meat," leading to a grim realization for some converts when they reached Utah and had little recourse. Polygamy was just one of those revelations. Brigham Young came out and publicly proclaimed the doctrine of polygamy in 1852, which was not well received by the United States or by many European converts. Some 1,700 English Mormons left the church. Others did not believe the rumors or were convinced otherwise by elders.[301]

Watkin Rees and his wife, Jane Williams, were two such converts from the poor, coal mining area of South Wales. They immigrated to Utah in 1854 when the economic situation in Utah was still very shaky. After a 5,700-mile journey of six months and six days from Liverpool, England, on the ship *Golconda*, the Welsh-speaking, twenty-four-year old Watkin, his nineteen-year old wife, Jane, and infant daughter, Alice, arrived in New Orleans. They were transferred to a steamer that travelled up the Mississippi to St. Louis. There was a terrible outbreak of cholera on the steamer. Some of the new emigrants died; many more died at the landing place where they waited for a boat to take them up the Missouri to Kansas City. The cholera continued at the different camps there, which were located near the river bottoms. Finally, Watkin and Jane moved to land near Westport on the prairie, about eight miles from Independence, Missouri, where they worked and waited for three months before continuing to Salt Lake with cattle and wagons in the Daniel Garns company. Many in the group had never seen oxen or driven wagons before.[302]

Watkin and Jane and their baby girl arrived in Salt Lake City by wagon train on October 6, 1854, with nothing but their clothes and were left at the public square, where they waited for someone to help them. They were the last emigrants there, the others having friends to pick them up. They had no food or money and were not really fluent in English. Finally, a farmer came and asked them to get in his wagon, telling them he would take them to the town of Payson to work for him. About sixteen miles out, the infamous Porter Rockwell—former bodyguard of Joseph Smith, then current henchman for Brigham Young and member of the Danites—met them on the road and told them they would be working for him. He took them to his ranch, which was a very isolated, lonely place where there had been a lot of trouble with the Ute Indians the year before. Jane was miserable and frightened at the ranch; it was just the start of very hard times for the couple who had been raised in hardship in Wales.[303]

Watkin Henry Rees, son of Thomas Rees and Mary Jones of Merthyr Tydfil, Glamorgan, Wales, was born January 23, 1830. His father was an iron worker in a mill there. Glamorgan, with important access to coal and rivers, was the iron capital of the world at the time. The British developed their efforts to fight in the Napoleonic Wars with the iron works, where they made cannonballs for England's navy. The population exploded and the slums around the town of Merthyr Tydfil became known as "little Hell." By the 1830s and '40s, as many as four to five people would live in little stone huts of about 5 feet by 7 feet, with no toilets or sanitation. Epidemic disease was rampant.

Wales, on the west coast of Britain, was the home of the Celts—ancient Britons—and had its own culture and language. It was conquered by Edward I in 1290 but retained its Welsh language and customs. During the Industrial Revolution, workers had few rights anywhere but especially few in the iron works in Wales. Thomas made only £4 a month, which was not nearly enough to support his family. His son Watkin learned to read and write a few English words the few months he went to school, and then he went to work twelve hours a day—for sixpence a day—at age seven as a "pullup for the furnace man." Watkin would pull the chain that opened the oven door of the hot furnace from which workers with tongs would grab hot iron. It was an incredibly dangerous job for a child.[304]

Jane Williams, future wife of Watkin Rees, did not have it much better. Jane was born in Dowlais, Glamorgan, Wales, on April 23, 1837, to Jacob John and Margaret Cross. Her mother died when she was ten, and she had to take over her job and do all the chores for the family, including sewing every night to make some money. Her family converted to the Mormon Church after missionaries came to Merthyr Tydfil; Jane convinced Watkin to convert, as well. They married on Christmas Day 1852 and set out on their amazing journey to Utah eighteen months later.

Watkin and Jane moved frequently once they got to Utah. They were able to leave Rockwell's remote ranch due to the chance meeting of an acquaintance from Wales who stopped at the ranch and offered them work in Fillmore, 145 miles south of Salt Lake City, which had been designated by Brigham Young to be the new capital. Watkin worked on the new State House until they had no more work there. Later, the capital was moved back to Salt Lake City. Watkin and Jane moved south to Cedar City, and then Beaver, 243 miles from Salt Lake, and then settled in the lower Beaver Valley, moving from Minersville to Greensville and Adamsville, all along what was called the Mormon Road, which stretched south through Utah Territory. Watkin worked the iron works in Cedar City until the iron works eventually failed. The little family struggled to survive in a time of famine; their only source of income at times was butter from the one cow they owned. Watkin wrote in his diary how difficult it was to survive. The entire wheat crop failed all over Utah in 1856, except for Cedar City and one other town. The settlers were sometimes uncharitable to each other, especially, to the new immigrants.[305]

This was the time of the Mormon Restoration, with severe edicts and preaching coming from Brigham Young urging people to repent and follow his commands, including polygamy and blood atonement. Blood Atonement put a different value on the lives of gentiles or those who left the church. It was not an unforgiveable sin to kill gentiles; in fact, Mormons were encouraged to kill those who wanted to leave, and some followed his instructions. Brigham Young increased his rhetoric against the United States, leading the Mormon people to be afraid of outsiders.

John C. Frémont ran as a presidential candidate in 1856 with a platform against the two evils of slavery and polygamy. The fear on both sides increased, leading to President Buchanan appointing a new governor in 1857—Brigham Young had to step down—and ordering 2,500 troops to Utah to enforce martial law. This was the "Mormon War" or "Utah War" that, thankfully, did not lead to actual fighting. It did, however, lead to tragedy for California-bound pioneers who were caught in the fanatical religious fervor in southern Utah.[306]

Watkin was working in Cedar City when the Arkansas wagon train led by Captain Fancher and heading for California came through, wanting to buy supplies and rest their stock. The mood was angry in town toward gentiles, and they were refused supplies. The pioneers rested their wagons and oxen in Mountain Meadows, a pretty meadow filled with grass for their animals, about thirty-five miles away, where they defended themselves for five days against fierce Indian attacks while famished for water and food. Mormon men, including Bishop John D. Lee, Brigham Young's adopted son, rode out to meet the pioneers and convince them to give up and lay down their arms, telling them they would protect them from the Indians. They did so, and then they were brutally slaughtered—men, women and children, except for those too young to talk—by Indians and Mormon men dressed like Indians. One hundred and twenty bodies were stripped of valuables and clothes and left to nature on September 11, 1857.

It was a horrifying massacre and many blamed Brigham Young, although he was able to escape responsibility. Brigham Young visited the memorial for the tragedy years later and ordered it destroyed. He supposedly said, "Vengeance is mine."

Watkin wrote about the massacre in his journal and the sadness of not knowing exactly who was accountable, other than Lee, due to secrecy. Bishop Lee was the only one held accountable and was executed for the crime twenty years later, in March 1877. The Mountain Meadows Massacre was a stain on the Mormon Church and Brigham Young and an example of how fanaticism and fear can lead to tragedy.[307]

Brigham Young died a few months after Lee on August 29, 1877 and was succeeded by John Taylor as head of the Mormon Church. Young was called "the greatest colonizer in American history" by author John G. Turner. He was a "tribal chieftain" with all the negative and ruthless actions of total power.

Utah was settled with great effort by the Mormons, while the new Western Telegraph system and mining activity from the Rockies to the Sierras brought gentiles to the area. The race between the Central Pacific and Union Pacific railroads to complete the First Transcontinental Railroad—originally known as the Pacific Railroad—through to Sacramento, California, was completed in 1869, with the connecting spike in Promontory, Utah, north of Salt Lake. This guaranteed that the Mormons would no longer be self-contained: east and west coasts were connected through Utah and the railroad. Although Young was their leader, the real heroes of the settling of Utah are the dedicated, fearless Mormon pioneers. What the self-reliant and faithful Mormon settlers achieved under great duress in the desert is remarkable.[308] Watkin and Jane started over again and again, as did many colonists, when they were asked by their church to start a new settlement. They struggled to farm in many areas in southern Utah (Dixie) and lost two children out of their eight sons and two daughters and then two more sons as young adults. Their oldest daughter, Alice, who came from Wales with them, died at age six. One son tragically died after an accident with a pistol discharging while he was working on a ranch when he was seventeen. He shot

Watkin Rees and wife Jane Williams Rees on their 60th wedding anniversary, photo Family Search.org

himself through the bowel and died a slow, painful death over twenty-four hours. The local Indians, who had become friends with Watkin, cried with him, "Oh poor Watkin's papoose."

The Rees family worked very hard, and Watkin was respected for his work with the Church. During the Civil War, the family lived at Greenville, a tiny community in Beaver Valley, and Watkin served in the militia there. After moving to Adamsville, close by, Watkin became high priest and counselor to the Bishop of Adamsville from 1870 to 1890. He was justice of the peace, as well as a school trustee. Later, they lived in Escalante for four years, from 1891 to 1895, and then moved back to Beaver, where they stayed the rest of their lives. He was appointed high priest there as well.

Watkin was sent as a missionary back to Wales in 1890 and then was declared a patriarch of the church in 1914. He spent his later years writing his memoirs and poetry. Jane was always known for her cooking and loving manner, even in old age. Watkin and Jane were a devoted couple who were married almost sixty-eight years. Watkin teased that, "It was a really long time to be married to one woman."

Jane replied, "And what would you have done without me?"[309]

Hyrum A. Williams and his children, a few years after his wife died, c.1880, Utah Territory, children L-R, Hyrum, Mary, Cora, Grace and Sylvester, posted by Steve Karlson, Ancestry.com

The Hyrum Williams family moved around in Dixie as well. Hyrum took his family to Escalante in 1880, where he worked as a freighter, a most important job in the isolated town hemmed in by mountains. His daughter Grace was thirteen when they moved, her sister Mary Adell, sixteen, younger brother Hyrum, ten, Sylvester, eight, and baby sister, Cora, five. By age seventeen Grace's older sister was married to William Shurtz, and Grace became the daughter in charge. A few years later, Grace met Jacob Rees and fell in love. We don't know how they met; Adamsville is 121 miles from Escalante and a difficult journey in the 1880s. Perhaps, Jacob was one of the stage drivers for Hyrum's freighting business.

Grace and Jacob married on March 13, 1887, in Garfield County, Utah, when Grace was twenty and Jacob twenty-one. Nine months later, they had their first child, Grover Williams Reese, on January 9, 1888, in Adamsville, Utah. Their daughter Cora was born on March 28, 1890, in Beaver, Utah, just two months after the death of Grace's little sister Cora at age sixteen on January 27.

Hyrum was most displeased with Grace's marriage to Jacob. He did not think Jacob was a good choice for his daughter. The Rees family was well respected but poor by the Williams family standards. Perhaps, Hyrum just did not like Jacob. Hyrum turned out to be right.[310]

What happened to the marriage is a mystery. There are rumors that Jacob wanted another wife and Grace refused. In Watkin Rees' dairy there is a notation about a half-sister to Grover and Cora named Hope, but no date. Pressure against polygamy had come to a head, and there was no way that Utah could become a state unless they outlawed the practice, but there was reluctance by some men to give it up. Hyrum's nephew Rodney Williams reported that Jacob was rumored to be a horse thief. There is no proof of this, although, he did grow up beside one of the most famous horse thieves and outlaws of the age, Butch Cassidy. Cassidy, whose real name was Robert LeRoy Parker, was the son of a poor Mormon family in Beaver, Utah, and was the same age as Jacob.

Grace divorced Jacob and moved to Escalante with her young children. Jacob's children never knew him. He died on August 29, 1901, of typhoid in St. Mary Falls, Montana. He is buried in the Beaver Cemetery in Utah, along with his parents and other family.[311]

Grace's father, Hyrum, obtained the U.S. Mail contract for eastern Oregon in Harney and Malheur counties between the towns of Ontario and Burns. The stagecoach line was called a Star Route. It met the train—the Oregon Short Line—in Ontario, near the border of Idaho on the Snake River, and took the mail and passengers by stage to the scattered communities not on the train line. The high desert environment was sparsely populated with cattle and sheep stockmen, timbermen, and scattered gold mining towns. Harney County is the ninth largest county in the country and the largest in Oregon. Malheur, the adjacent county, is just as rugged and isolated.

Hyrum sold out in Escalante, Utah, and made the 660-mile journey to eastern Oregon with his son Sylvester to run the stages lines there. To take a stage from southern Utah to Ontario, Oregon, at that time would have taken more than a week, much longer with stock and horses. Utah finally became a state on January 4, 1896, having given up on polygamy and agreeing to abide by U.S. law. Grace had already left; she gave up on Utah as well as the Mormon Church and followed her father and brother to Oregon in 1894.

Grace's father gave her the job of running the stage station near Drewsey at the foot of Stinking Water Mountain—named so by the Indians because of the smelly sulfur water there. Drewsey was halfway between Ontario and Burns on the middle fork of the Malheur River, with only about fifty or so people in the surrounding area. The area was originally part of the Malheur Indian Reservation and, traditionally, the Paiute hunting grounds, but gradually, the Indians were pushed farther north as white settlers populated the area. Drewsey, founded in the mid-1880s, was originally called Gouge-Eye, a name typifying the violence of the Wild West, but the U.S. Postal Service refused to accept the name, so residents renamed the town Drewsey, after the daughter of a local rancher instead.

The Stinking Water Way Station was on Stinking Water Creek, near present Hwy. 20. Grace had six-year-old Grover and four-year-old Cora with her in this very isolated and harsh environment, but she was a capable and independent woman who did not let the atmosphere faze her. The station keeper fed the travelers. Grace was sure to include some johnnycakes, which were typical fare. The site included a hot-springs and a campground for travelers and horses for the stages to switch out, which the stages did every fifteen miles or so.

Grace's father, Hyrum, ran quite an operation, with hundreds of horses kept at a stock ranch and as many as eleven stage lines. Drivers would meet the train and transfer mail, newspapers, etc. to stages to deliver along the 150-mile rural route between towns, as well as transporting passengers. Ontario and Vale in far-eastern Malheur County, were first on the route, followed by small towns that included Drewsey in Harney County, Burns, which was the county seat, and back again. Gold was the preferred payment; greenbacks were frowned upon west of the Rockies.

In the 1890s it would have normally taken thirty-six hours to travel the distance. Hyrum Williams advertised that he could do it in twenty-four hours in summer. He rotated his drivers and horses, so they did only part of the route. Horses were rested and switched after twelve to fifteen miles and then later in the day did another twelve to fifteen miles back to their barn for the night. Stagecoach drivers were the captains of their coaches, with serious responsibility. They were under pressure to deliver the mail on time without penalties for lateness, as well as the threat from possible accidents and robberies in the isolated area.

The drivers were called Brother Whip or Whip and, sometimes, Charlie. They had rules for decorum on the coaches: no spitting or swearing or drinking. If the driver asked you to get off and walk, you did. The

Grover and Cora Reese, children of Grace Williams, Utah Territory c.1893, author's collection

mail was carried in waterproof canvas sacks locked with padlocks and carried under the box where the driver sat. Locked express boxes were kept there as well. The whip was an essential tool that drivers snapped in the air for attention from the horses. Drivers never struck the horses with the whip. If they needed a horse to listen, they tossed tiny pebbles at him. Drivers made about $40 a month plus room and board. Weather in the high mountain desert of eastern Oregon can be brutal and the stagecoach drivers were exposed to it all. [312]

Hyrum's son Sylvester was one of the drivers taking the U.S. Mail, seven days a week in all kinds of weather, no matter what. Stage companies used heavy Concord coaches—considered the Cadillac of coaches—on important routes and buggies and wagons most of the year on lesser routes. In eastern Oregon they mostly used a smaller version of the Concord called a mud coach or Celerity wagon with a two- or four-horse team. The two horses closest to the coach were the strongest and largest and were called the wheelers. The whip had to control his horses with a separate lead for each horse, up to six leads for the larger coaches. Winter was another story; sometimes, they sent mail by horseback or sled—wagons having difficulty in deep snow. Joseph MacDonald, in his book *MacDonald's Stage Coaches and Stations: Eastern Oregon*, claims that a mail contractor near the remote mining town of Sumpter used skis or snowshoes pulled by a horse to deliver the mail in deep snow.

Frank Holladay, stagecoach driver for the Williams Stage Line, (in fur coat) Drewsey, Oregon, c.1890s, curtesy Kathleen Stewart Baker

As well as being a driver, Sylvester also helped his father, Hyrum, with the hired hands and on the ranch where the horses were held. In 1896 Hyrum fell ill. His son Sylvester wrote to him in Ontario from New Station—somewhere in the area—hoping he would soon be better, but Hyrum died two weeks later at age fifty-three on October 4, 1896. Sylvester ran the Ontario-Burns Stage Company, Williams Line, after his father died. According to the postmaster in Drewsey, a Williams descendant still runs the route but with a van not a stagecoach.

Before Hyrum died he signed over a house and property in Burns to his eight-year-old grandson, Grover Reese, insuring his daughter Grace and her children could stay. *The Ontario News* printed his obituary on October 10, 1896:

> H. A. Williams, proprietor of Ontario-Burns Stage Line died at this place last Sunday. He had many warm friends in this part of the country. He was a member of the Masonic order and was buried by Washor Lodge of Payette, Idaho, on Monday afternoon. Rev. Clapp preached the funeral sermon, the deceased leaves several children who are all grown.

Hyrum had a sad and difficult life. He worked incredibly hard and tried to raise his children as well as he could as a widower. He loved his children and wanted the very best for them and instilled moral values and self-reliance in them. Hyrum had been a devout Mormon during his life, but he did not have a Mormon funeral.[313]

Grace Williams, about the time of her marriage to Frank Holladay, Burns, Oregon 1897, author's collection

Grace found it difficult to manage alone. She met a charming, funny man named Frank Holladay, who was a stage driver for her father, and they were married in Burns, Oregon, on March 8, 1897. Together, they managed the way station at Stinking Water Mountain near Drewsey. Grace had a photograph taken in Burns about the time of her marriage that showed her with a slender figure and beautiful, thick auburn hair almost long enough to sit on. She was happy and hopeful for the future.

Frank and Grace had a daughter, Bonnie, born in 1900. Grover and Cora now had a stepsister. Frank's younger sister Effie Holladay came out from Kentucky to visit and ended up marrying Grace's brother Sylvester in 1900. Effie and Sylvester bought a ranch near Drewsey, which by then was a booming place with three saloons and more than one hundred people.

Unfortunately, the marriage to Frank did not work out for Grace. Frank was an alcoholic and they divorced. Grace, a capable strong woman, managed to raise three remarkable children, mostly by herself, in the Wild West environment of eastern Oregon. The 1910 census shows her living with her three children, Grover, age twenty-two, Cora, age twenty, and little Bonnie, age nine, along with a hired hand/boarder at Drewsey.[314]

By 1912 Grace had moved 150 miles to the northeast to Baker County, Oregon. Much later in her life she would live in Baker County again, in Baker City, owning a restaurant near Baker High School and serving hamburgers to high school students.

On July 28, 1914, World War I started. Grover signed up when the U.S. entered the war in April 1917, serving in the cavalry. His sister Cora married Joseph Leonning, a Baker man, shortly before the end of the war, on July 15, 1918. She was married at Camp Lewis in Washington, where her fiancé was serving in the military. After the war they came home and settled in Baker City in Baker County. Grover worked as a rancher after the war at Silver Lake in central Oregon and then worked as a cattle merchant in Portland in 1920, always wanting to get back to Drewsey. His sister Bonnie went to Whitman College for two years, taught school, and then transferred to the University of Washington. Grace went with her and served as house mother to her sorority, Delta Gamma, at the University. Bonnie met her future husband, Donald Crawford Stewart, in Baker and married him on December 3, 1921, when she was twenty-one years old.

Grover was determined to be a cattle rancher again in eastern Oregon, and he moved back to Drewsey with his mother in the early 1920s. In 1926 he met a delightful, intelligent young woman who was visiting her Aunt Maggie, who lived in Drewsey with her husband Charles Dunten and four children. This young woman had travelled from Dexter, Oregon, in Lane County, about 300 miles to the south. Her name was Dorothy Parvin, and she was the granddaughter of Oregon pioneers. Grover had finally met the woman he wanted to marry. If his grandfather Hyrum had lived to see him grow up, he would have been extremely proud of his intelligent, hardworking grandson. Although Grover was not raised as a Mormon, he demonstrated the upstanding moral qualities that were taught by his grandfather. Hyrum surely would have been happy with his grandson's choice of bride.[315]

Grover Williams Reese, U.S. Calvary, WW I, 1918, Utah, author's collection

Chapter Seven

Wagons West

Family Cast of Characters

Dorothy Agnes Parvin…(1902-1998) *mother of Patricia Reese*
Hosea Morris Parvin…(1868-1954) *Dorothy's father*
Agnes Florence Templeman…(1873-1963) *Dorothy's mother*

James Parvin…(1831-1907) *came west in 1853; Dorothy's grandfather*
Selena Parker…(1834-1913) *came west in 1853; Dorothy's grandmother*
Joseph Parker…(1834-1921) *came west in 1853; Selena's twin brother*
Phoebe Parker…(1831-1885) *came west in 1853; older sister of Selena and James, married John Stoops*
James M. Parker (1833- 19?) *came west in 1853; older brother of Selena and Joseph*

Anna Elizabeth Matthews…(1851-1883) *came west in 1853, with parents; mother of Agnes Templeman*
David C. Matthews…(1840-1927) *came west in 1853; older brother of Anna*
Thomas Moffit Matthews…(1814-1880) *came west in 1853; father of David and Anna*
Elizabeth Cope…(1813-1898) *came west in 1853; wife of Thomas; mother of David and Anna*

William Dennison Templeman…(1841-1879) *from Kentucky; husband of Anna Matthews*
Elden Templeman…(1872-1945) *son of William and Anna; brother to Agnes and Maggie*
Maggie Templeman…(1877-1960) *sister to Elden and Agnes; married name Dunton*
Fielding Templeman…(1815-1893) *William's father; grandfather to Agnes, Elden, and Maggie*
Nancy Ann Dennison…(1820-1870) *wife of Fielding; grandmother to Agnes; Elden and Maggie*
Edward Reginald Templeman…(1708-1763) *born in Surrey, England; died Tackett's Mill, Stafford, VA*

Hosea Parvin…(1802-1882) *father of James Parvin; remarried; died in Collins County, TX*
Elizabeth France…(1805-1832) *mother of James Parvin; died when he was one*
Thomas Parvin…(1663-1743) *from Yorkshire, England; immigrated to Salem, NJ; sixth-great grandfather of Patricia Reese*

Charles Matthews…(1774-1840) *Scots-Irish descent; from Pennsylvania; father of Thomas Moffit Matthews*

Oliver Cope…(1647-1697) *Quaker emigrant from New Castle, DE/PA, seventh-great-grandfather of Patricia Reese*

The Parvin, Parker and Matthews Families

Eastward I go only by force, but westward I go free … This is the prevailing tendency of my countrymen. I must walk towards Oregon.

~Henry David Thoreau

Dorothy Agnes Parvin was born on her grandfather's beautiful farm nestled on Lost Creek just south of Dexter in Lane County, Oregon. She was the third child of Hosea M. Parvin and Agnes Templeman. Dorothy's grandparents, as well as her great-grandparents on the Matthews side, came west to Oregon on the wagon train of 1853 from Fulton County, Illinois. Dorothy was surrounded by pioneers and pioneer stories all her life. The 1853 wagon train from Illinois was an eventful trip: 1,000 people and 250 wagons with stock split off from their fellow travelers on the main trail through the desert country of eastern Oregon to take a shortcut to the Willamette Valley. They followed guide Elijah Elliot toward the unfinished Free Emigrant Trail—the Elliot Cutoff—over the Cascades and ended up lost and starving.

Map of Oregon with alternate Oregon Trail routes, from Settlement Settings, hugoneighborhood.org

Almost as soon as wagons started heading west to Oregon, pioneers began trying to find an easier route to the fertile Willamette Valley. In 1843 Peter Burnett and some of the Holman family took the original Oregon Trail to the town of The Dalles, Oregon, on the Columbia River and then floated the rest of the way down the Columbia. The desire to avoid the dangerous, frightening rapids of the river led to exploration of new routes across the formidable mountains.

The Barstow Road, blazed over the Cascades south of Mount Hood in 1845, was one difficult route. The Applegate brothers cut a rough, southern route which turned out to be very stressful for the pioneers of 1846, including some of the Holman family. Mountain man Stephen Meek tried to forge a central route through the Oregon desert. He led a wagon train through the Cascades over Willamette Pass to central Oregon in 1845—Meek's Cutoff—which turned into a disastrous trip when quite a few of his party died. They had to head back north to The Dalles. The Free Emigrant Road was started in 1853 at the initiation of a group of settlers in Linn, Benton, and Lane Counties. They intended to follow Stephen Meek's route to central Oregon. The Stoops, Matthews, and Parker families, along with James Parvin, did not take the new shortcut, but they were part of the story.[316]

The Illinois pioneers who headed west on the Oregon Trail were the sons and daughters of pioneers themselves. They had "itchy feet," a desire to better themselves, and a different personality type than those who stayed behind. They were filled with optimism, a sense of adventure, and were ready for a challenge.

The train that left on April 10, 1853, from Fulton County included Phoebe Parker, her younger twin siblings, Selena and Joseph Parker, Phoebe's husband, John Stoops, and their children, including oldest son, William Stoops—the son of John and his first wife—who turned eleven on the trip. Brother James M. Parker, a year older than Joseph and Selena, drove one of the wagons, along with James Parvin. Thomas Moffitt Matthews and his wife, Elizabeth Cope Matthews, came with their many children, including David C. Matthews—age thirteen, a buddy of William Stoops—as well as Dorothy Parvin's grandmother Anna Elizabeth Matthews, then age two. James Alexander Matthews, brother of Thomas Matthews, and his family were also among the group, as well as Welsh immigrant Thomas Williams and family. Elijah Elliot had met and married his wife, Polly, in Fulton County, Illinois, before staking a claim in Pleasant Hill, Oregon, in the newly established Lane County. His wife and children were on the train as well, in a wagon with a hired driver.[317]

Deciding to pull up stakes and head to Oregon was not for the faint of heart. Even though propaganda about the beauty, mild climate, and fertile soil of the Willamette Valley led to thousands catching Oregon Fever and making the trip, a great deal of planning and money was involved. Farms had to be sold, wagons outfitted with enough supplies to make the difficult journey, and difficult decisions about which heirlooms to take had to be made. Those who could not resist taking a beautiful piece of furniture that had been handed down more often than not had to discard it along the way. The trail to Oregon was littered with discarded treasured belongings among the wagon ruts. All that mattered in the end was enough flour and oxen to get you there. Peter Burnett and others such as Joel Palmer wrote guidebooks and offered advice about what to take. There were lists of food and supplies, instructions on what kind of wagons, and which beasts of burden could best get you there.

Map of Oregon Trail, image from Encyclopedia Britannica, www.cdn.britannica.com

The immigrants on their way to Oregon Country did not use the famous Conestoga wagons from Pennsylvania that were used on the easier Santa Fe Trail, but rather a lighter wagon called a Prairie Schooner. The Prairie Schooners, with their white canvas tops, looked like ships sailing across the grass of the Great Plains. Watkin Rees, writing in his journal about his trip west to Utah in a wagon train, was amazed at how much the waving grass on the high prairie looked like the sea to fellow British emigrants like him. Some pioneers used mules to pull their wagons west, but most preferred oxen.

Peter Burnett wrote of his admiration for the ox:

> One ox will pull as much as two mules, and in mud, as much as four. They are more easily managed, are not so subject to being lost or broken down on the way, cost less at the start, and are worth about four times as much here. The ox is a most noble animal, patient, thrifty, durable, gentle, and easily driven, and does not run off. Those who come to this country will be in love with their oxen by the time they reach here.318

The cost was substantial. To buy a wagon that would make it 2,100 miles with a team of oxen or mules cost around $600 for a wagon 6 feet wide, 12 feet long and 3 feet high with canvas top. Add another $300-$400 for supplies, including 200 lbs. flour, 150 lbs. bacon, 20 lbs. sugar, 10 lbs. coffee, and 10 lbs. of salt, as well as tar for waterproofing the wagon, extra wheels, rifles, and about $150 for tolls. The cost today would be nearly $40,000. Those with farms to sell could afford it. Others worked their way to Oregon.

The Matthews came from a family of farmers. Charles Matthews and Agnes Anderson left Pennsylvania for land in the far northeast corner of Ohio in Trumball County. They both died within three days of each other in August of 1840, no doubt victims of some epidemic of typhoid or cholera. Their sons Thomas and James Matthews then moved with their families to Clermont County in the far southwest of Ohio near Cincinnati on the Ohio River and, eventually, to Illinois. The Matthewses were descendants of Scots-Irish Presbyterians who had originally settled in Chester, Pennsylvania. Chester County was a predominantly Quaker area near the Delaware River outside Philadelphia.[319]

Thomas Matthews' wife, Elizabeth Cope, was a descendant of an old English family from Wiltshire in southwest England who settled in the Chester/Delaware area. The Cope family dates back to the 1400s and the family tree includes several high sheriffs and knights, as well as counselors to kings. They must have been early converts of the Society of Friends (Quaker) faith.

George Fox (1624-1691) was the founder of this extreme sect founded in 1651 in northwest England. Quakers took their criticism of the Anglican Church beyond the objections of the Puritans. They did not believe in churches or clergy, instead believing that the inner voice in all of us is the word of God. They were pacifists, didn't believe in loyalty oaths, and had strict ideas of Christian moral behavior. They held monthly as well as quarterly meetings in a meetinghouse, not a church. Quakers were the first to come out against slavery and believed in equality for all. They were heavily persecuted in England and by the Puritans, who thought they were a disruptive nuisance. By 1660 there were 50,000 converts to the Society of Friends in England.[320]

The talented William Penn, son of Admiral William Penn, is one of the most famous converts. In March of 1681, Penn was granted 50,000 square miles in the New World by Charles II as payment for a debt the king owed his father. In November 1682, Penn brought twenty-three ships full of Quakers to what is now Pennsylvania to create a Quaker colony.

Oliver Cope, son of John Cope and Elizabeth Deane of Wiltshire, England, was the first of his family to come to America. He was granted 250 acres of land from William Penn on Naaman's Creek near the Delaware River in 1681. Oliver Cope and his wife, Rebecca Crooke, were settled there by 1683. Many generations of Copes continued to stay in the area, according to Society of Friends records and probate records.

Quakers were highly successful at business with their thrifty, disciplined way of life. Elizabeth's father, David E. Cope, and mother, Elizabeth House, were still practicing Quakers when Elizabeth met and married Thomas Matthews. Quakers were usually expelled for marrying out of the faith. It's not known if Elizabeth kept her Quaker faith. After marriage, the Matthewses moved to Ohio and then to Fulton County, Illinois, to farm. Interestingly, there was a Quaker community in Fulton County at the time.[321]

Ohio, Indiana, and Illinois were part of the Northwest Territory, which opened to settlement in 1809. Fulton County, in the middle of the state about 160 miles due east from Nauvoo, was part of a military tract set aside in 1812 for compensation for soldiers. It was named after Robert Fulton, inventor of the steamboat. Lewistown, which became the largest town in the county, was located on the Spoon River. Some remarkable Indian mounds with artifacts from an ancient civilization, including evidence of cloth weaving, have been discovered nearby. The Indian Burial Mounds are now part of a state park.

The county was founded in 1823, with farming the main industry. It is still mostly rural farmland. The Parker, Parvin, and Matthews families who headed there were happy with the land that was more easily farmed than the hills of the East but were disappointed by the unhealthy conditions of disease that plagued the area along the Spoon River at the time.

By the 1850s the country was polarized and restless. *Uncle Tom's Cabin*, written by Harriet Beecher Stowe, was published in 1852, adding to the regional tensions about slavery. The giant orators of the age, Clay and Webster, had died, the Library of Congress had a massive fire which destroyed 35,000 books, and there were outbreaks of disease around the country, including a massive outbreak of yellow fever in New Orleans that killed almost 8,000 people. The outbreaks of disease in Illinois only encouraged those with restless hearts to move on to the possibility of a brighter future.

The Parker siblings were orphaned when their parents, James Parker and Nancy McCoy, died of cholera in 1847 in Duncan Mill, Illinois—close to Ipava—in Fulton County. The Parkers were descendants of a Scottish family who settled first in Virginia, then Pennsylvania, before pushing westward to Ohio and Illinois.

The cholera epidemic hit Fulton County hard. John Stoops lost his first wife and then married Phoebe Parker, who became stepmother to his children. They took in Joseph and Selena, Phoebe's younger twin siblings, as well as James Parker, Phoebe's younger brother by two years. The father of the Parker siblings, James Parker II, was born in Virginia on July 26, 1786; his father, also named James, fought in the American Revolution. James Parker II married Rachel Runyon and had seven children with her before she died. He married his second wife, Nancy McCoy—mother of four siblings who went west—in Wayne County, Ohio, at age thirty-nine and proceeded to have eleven more children, most born in Coshocton County, Ohio. The family lived in the Monroe Township on military tract land where James was the first justice of the peace. They then moved to Fulton County, Illinois. The Parker twins were twelve, James thirteen, and older sister Phoebe sixteen when their parents died. Six years later, they were all on the Oregon Trail, heading west.[322]

James Parvin, the driver of one of the Stoops' wagons, came from a family who had settled in America before 1696. The first Parvin in the country, Thomas Parvin, was born 1663 in Hornby, Great Smeaton Parish, Yorkshire, England. He immigrated to Sulfolk City, Long Island, New York, with his wife, Rebekah Holmes. By 1700 he was residing in Fenwick Colony in Salem City, New Jersey. He was a weaver as well as overseer of roads and surveyed the first road from the Cohansey area—where he lived—to Philadelphia. Enoch Parvin, James Parvin's grandfather and great-grandson of immigrant Thomas Parvin, began moving west from New Jersey to Clermont County, Ohio, after the Revolutionary War. Military tracts had opened up land for veterans, and they were eager to start new lives with new land.

Enoch Parvin's son Hosea met his wife, Elizabeth France, in Clermont County and married her on August 24, 1823. They had two daughters, born in Ohio, then a son, Michael, in Delaware County, Indiana, in 1828. They moved on to Marion County, Indiana, where Dorothy Parvin's grandfather James Parvin was born on May 2, 1831. A year later the family moved to Ipava, Fulton County, Illinois, where James lost his mother when he was only one year old. Elizabeth France Parvin died at the young age of twenty-eight, mostly likely of cholera, two days after arriving in Fulton County. A few months later, James' father, Hosea, enlisted to fight in the Black Hawk War.[323]

James and his two elder sisters, as well as his older brother, Michael, were taken in and cared for by an aunt. Michael, unfortunately, died at age ten. James' father, Hosea, eventually remarried and started another family, serving as justice of the peace in Fulton County, as well as working as a farmer and expert carpenter. Hosea considered moving west when there was talk of forming a wagon train in 1853 but decided to stay in Illinois for a few more years. He finally caught the bug to move on in 1857 and took his family to Collins County in northeast Texas in 1857. He worked as a cattle rancher there until his death in 1882.

Hosea's two oldest daughters, Rebecca and Hily Ann, had married and wanted to stay in Illinois. His son, James, had other plans. There were many romantic notions about going west to Oregon Country: Manifest Destiny, love of adventure, dreams of a new economic start. James had all of these notions, but most important of all, he was in love with pretty Selena Parker. He followed her to Oregon.

The typical jumping off place for the Oregon Trail, the California Trail, and the Santa Fe Trail was Independence, Missouri. As time went on, more towns on the Missouri River, such as St. Joseph, became starting points as well. For the first few hundred miles, all three trails followed the same basic direction across the "Big Muddy"—the Missouri River—and through the tall prairie grass of Kansas. It was mostly pleasant going and gave the emigrants a false sense of confidence as to the hardships ahead. William Stoops, who was a child on the trip, gave us his memories of the 1853 trip in a series of articles written in 1925 for the *Morning Register* in Eugene, Oregon.

Starting in Illinois, William's train crossed the Missouri at St. Jo's (St. Joseph). William said there was a traffic jam of 500 wagons waiting to cross the Missouri by ferry and no sensible way of telling who was there first. Hot tempers began to flare, as some emigrants had been waiting three days to cross. "After a few fist fights, guns came into view on both sides." Finally, the boss man of the ferry settled the fight, and they made their way across the river into Nebraska. "The road was dusty and dry and the wind blowing sand, followed that night by such a deluge of water so that there was a foot a water in camp, waking everyone up." It was discouraging to all and some of the women started to regret the journey. One pioneer said, "Once started on the journey, the problem was to finish. It was simply a desperate undertaking."[324]

Another wagon train from Indiana caught up with them and wanted to join together. They were joined later by yet more wagons, which made a very large train of almost 100 wagons and 250 men. Captain Frazier was an excellent leader who had taken a previous wagon train west. The thinking was that with a large train they would fear less from Indian attacks. Very few of the Indians attacked directly—they were more likely to steal cattle or horses and mules—but William had a frightening experience with some Sioux Indians along the Platte River. When the train passed Fort Kearney—built by the U.S. Army in 1847-48—a few miles from the south fork of the Platte, two men came up and wanted to join the train and said they would work their way across. One was an Army deserter from Fort Laramie named Sounder.

One afternoon William and two other boys were at the back of the mile-long wagon train with Sounder and the stock. William told the story of how Sounder stopped to buy some moccasins from some Sioux selling them by the side of the road. When he pulled out his money, the Indians saw the sack of money, and one grabbed it and turned to run, dropping a long-bladed knife. Sounder grabbed the knife and threw it, cutting the string that held the Indian's bow and arrows. He grabbed the bow and arrows and strung the bow, but the Indians would not give back the money. At this point some of the Indians strung their bows and pointed them towards William. "Sounder, speaking in the Sioux language, told them if they harmed the boy the men of the train would come back and kill every squaw and papoose."

Although the Indians hesitated, they were very upset, and Sounder told William and the other boys to run. One Indian threw a lariat and managed to catch William by the neck. William had the presence of mind to catch the rope and throw himself backwards on the ground with feet around the rope. He had a knife in a scabbard that he used to saw the rope in two, and then he ran toward the wagon train. About 150 men from the train got their guns and started back to save Sounder. "They met Sounder on the way back to the train: he said he had to give up all his money or be killed."[325]

The wide, shallow Platte River—said to be a mile wide and a foot deep—wound through the Great Plains with a thin ribbon of green on either side. This was the land of short grass and few trees but lots of buffalo. In the first years of the Oregon Trail, there were massive herds of buffalo roaming the plains. Francis Parkman, who wrote about his trip on the trail in 1846, described the terror of his horse when confronted by the thundering, massive beasts. "The sight of the buffalo filled my horse with terror, and when at full speed he was almost uncontrollable. Gaining the top of the ridge, I saw nothing of the buffalo; they had all vanished amid the intricacies of the hills and hollows … How many miles I had run, or in what direction, I had no idea."

The buffalo were, of course, of vital importance to the Plains Indians. The shrinking herds due to slaughter by increasing numbers of settlers led to desperation and hunger for the Indians. The emigrants shot buffalo for meat and also used buffalo chips (dung) for their fires because of lack of firewood in the area.[326]

The days on the trail started early, usually by 4 a.m. Many chores had to be done before they could start the day's journey. Women had the challenge of keeping children safe in a very dangerous environment where accidents happened constantly. Drownings, falling out of wagons, being injured by rolling wagons, or being trampled by livestock made motherhood a much harder job on the trail.

One surprising challenge came as they were passing through Pawnee Territory in Nebraska, when a Pawnee chief took a liking to dark-eyed Charlotte Rutledge and followed the train, which alarmed Charlotte's stepmother. The chief offered up to 100 ponies for Charlotte, which her father politely declined. There was much relief when the chief did not press the point. A few years later in Oregon, Charlotte would marry Selena's twin brother, Joseph.[327]

Women had new challenges every day due to weather and environmental circumstances. They found themselves driving wagons and doing men's work as well as their own. The challenge of feeding everyone was enormous. They found ways to save time by putting churns of cream on the back of their wagons so that the rocking motion would turn the cream to butter by the end of the day. Just the challenges of baking bread for fifteen people a day on an open fire, and creative use of whatever game was killed, were time-consuming chores. Most people walked the majority of the 2,000-mile trail. Selena Parker brought her beautiful, hand-tooled, leather sidesaddle to ride the trail, but she probably did not use it much. She walked with her good friend, instead. Selena's saddle is now in the Lane County History Museum.[328]

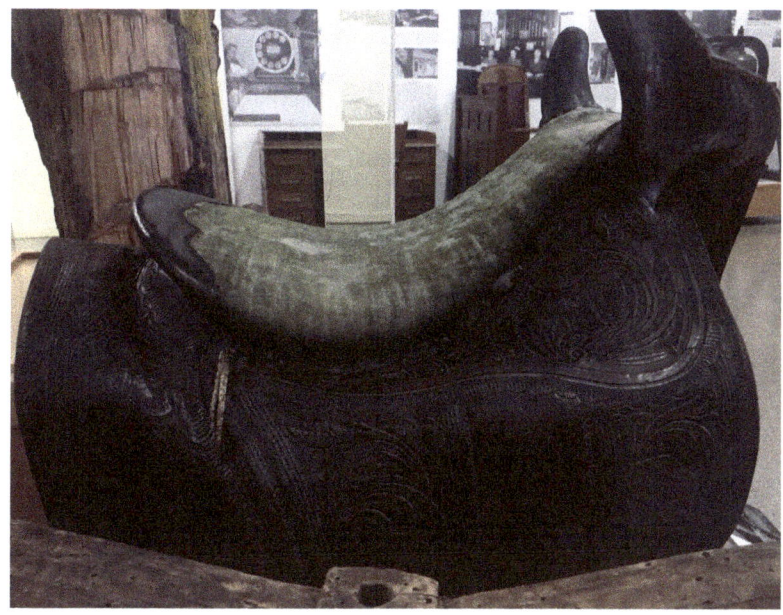

Selena Parker's side saddle brought on the Oregon Trail from Illinois, 1853, author's photo (2018) at the Lane County History Museum, Eugene, Oregon

Travelling along the Platte, the emigrants of 1853 saw evidence of tragedy of years past with bleached bones of dead cattle and even some graves of pioneers. Between 1849 and 1852, at the height of the California Gold Rush, the Oregon Trail was very heavily travelled. There are places along the trail where wagon ruts are still visible today. During the peak year, 1850, more than 55,000 people made their journey west.

Cholera hit the trail very hard, and some 5,000 died along the Platte in 1852. The emigrants always had the worry of death peeking around the corners of their minds. There was little to be done for cholera; contaminated water led to a severe stomachache, diarrhea, and, usually, death within twenty-four hours. They tried to bury victims under the trail so the rolling wagons would beat down the evidence of the grave so their bones would not be exposed by animals or marauders. There were few grave markers; families had to remember their loved ones in their hearts.

The trip was slow with a pace of about twelve to fifteen miles a day. On a very good day, they would travel farther, but many days were also lost with breakdowns and illness. Fording rivers was a major challenge. Ferries and toll bridges were thrown up by entrepreneurs over some of the many rivers and streams. One pioneer diarist of 1853, Charlotte Emily Stearns Pengra, wrote of "crossing an Indian toll bridge made of brush thrown into the stream," at the inexpensive price of ten cents a wagon to cross.

Sounder came to the rescue again when it was time to cross the dangerous South Platte River. It was shallow but treacherous, with deadly quicksand. Sounder told the pioneers to "cut blocks of wood about six inches long, then raise the wagon beds up and tie the blocks to the standards of the wagon. Each wagon had to be in a different track across the river or the wagons would sink." William Stoops said two men came close to drowning when the sand gave way beneath them and they were sucked in. The train lost many cattle to the quicksand but no emigrants. The year prior, nineteen emigrants drowned crossing the South Platte, along with many cattle. In 1849-50, forty-nine emigrants died crossing the North Platte near Fort Laramie.

The train continued on and saw the unusual rock landmarks in the plains that previous emigrants had named: first Courthouse Rock, then Chimney Rock, and finally, Scotts Bluff. When the train got within a half day of Fort Laramie—in present day Wyoming—Sounder took off, explaining that as a deserter he would be shot if found. William and the rest of the grateful train never saw him again, but they did not forget him.[329]

The emigrants had been on the road for months. They crossed the arid great plain of Indian and buffalo country onto the dry and dusty high plains and now pushed through the area covered with sagebrush west of Fort Laramie towards the Rocky Mountains. They passed Independence Rock, a major landmark a mile in circumference, 350 miles past Fort Laramie. They climbed towards Ice Slough, where it was possible to dig eighteen inches deep and cut out large chunks of ice. The air grew cooler and drier.

The Stoopses took the cutoff towards South Pass rather than go through Fort Bridger because of a shortage of grass for their teams. Fort Bridger, built by mountain man Jim Bridger, was a major stop on the trail. It was here that Mormon wagon trains left the main trail and turned south towards Salt Lake City, along with those wagon trains heading to California. Emigrants bound for Oregon continued towards the Rockies and the Continental Divide at South Pass. Although almost 8,000 feet in elevation, South Pass was a gradual ascent in a broad grassy valley and was used by both Indians and trappers to get over the Rockies. The South Pass was to emigration of the Far West as the Cumberland Gap over the Appalachians was to the first wave of pioneers to head for the first frontiers of Kentucky and Tennessee. Once through the South Pass, the wagon train crossed the Divide and headed downhill to Pacific Springs. Here, on the other side of the Divide, all the rivers ran to the Pacific.

Wagon trains often had advance parties, as well as parties that stayed behind due to wagon breakdowns or illness. At one point during this trip, William Stoops was part of an advance party near the Green River in present-day Wyoming; the party got separated from the main train for forty-two days. William wrote that he was filled with despair that he would never see his family again. When his father finally caught up with him, they were both filled with joy.

After the train passed Soda Springs, the next major stop was Fort Hall on the Snake River in what is now Idaho. The fort was a very important stop for supplies for trains before the hardest part of the journey. It was about 300 miles from Fort Laramie to Fort Hall. Fort Hall was abandoned two years later, in 1855, after an Indian massacre of settlers. By this point in the journey, everyone had dumped some belongings by the side of the road, had wagons break, animals die, or experienced illness of some sort. This was one of their last chances to get substantial supplies or do repairs.[330]

The Snake River was nothing like the rivers they had previously dealt with on the trip. It wound around and around, the very high cliffs at some points requiring chains and ropes to get their wagons down to the river of icy cold, swift-running water. It was quite dangerous to cross. The emigrants followed the Snake River for over 300 miles. Their livestock's feet were torn to shreds by the sharp rocks of the area. It was a trail of blood for the poor beasts of burden.

Although there was not really that much trouble with Indians along most of the trip—mostly, they came to beg—this area along the Snake was the most dangerous, and emigrants were on constant watch. The safest place to cross the Snake was a wide crossing called Three Islands. Three separate islands of land made it easier to prevent cattle from drowning and wagons from floating away. The emigrants of 1853 lost a great deal of cattle along the Snake that year. Whether from alkali water, contamination, or dust, many cattle died along the riverfront. Meanwhile, people were getting sick with dysentery.[331]

Finally, Oregon lay just ahead of them! They ate salmon from the river and, although exhausted and worried, felt they were within reach of their dreams. The train made it to Fort Boise near Parma on the present border of Idaho and Oregon. Ahead of them lay the massive Blue Mountains of eastern Oregon, which no one was eager to cross but which needed to be crossed before the first snows. The Willamette Valley they were heading for lay west of the Cascades, with rich, fertile soil, mild climate, and fir forests. East of the Cascades the mountains were thickly forested with pine. Little rain falls, and to the east, the mountains give way to desert and sagebrush, an arid and forbidding land that leads to the Oregon-Idaho line on the Snake River.

The Stoops family was desperately low on supplies at this point, as were many others. They had to sell two of their wagons to buy food for the rest of the trip. It was here at

Fort Boise that Elijah Elliot met up with the train and his wife, Polly, and children.[332]

Elijah Elliot was a thirty-five-year-old Kentuckian who had spent a lot of time on the frontiers of several states. He met and married his wife, Polly, in Fulton County, Illinois, then headed to California during the Gold Rush in '49 and ended up in Lane County, Oregon, which was just beginning to be formed, in 1851. Like Stephen Meek, he was a man of adventure. Stephen Meek was the older brother of famous mountain man Joe Meek, who blazed the first Oregon Trail in 1840. Like the Meeks, Elliot was full of confidence, which was necessary in such an environment. He knew Elliot Bristow, who staked his claim in Pleasant Hill in 1847. Pleasant Hill is just eight miles east of Eugene, near the middle fork of the Willamette River. Bristow claimed a spot with a beautiful view of the Cascade foothills in the distance. It reminded him of his native Virginia. Elliot stayed in the area with his brother-in-law, who had also settled in the Pleasant Hill/Rattlesnake Valley area.[333]

Plans for a road to central Oregon over the Cascades were developed by local commissioners in Lane and Benton counties to bring more population to the area. They raised close to $3,000 to build a road. Elliot himself donated $30. They thought twelve cents a mile would be sufficient, but it turned out to be woefully inadequate, as was the time allotted to complete the trail.

Dr. Robert Alexander was given the first two contracts for the road-building project. It took much longer than expected. Seven road viewers, including William Macy and John Diamond, planned to stake out a trail heading west to east in 1852. They would use an old Indian trail over the Cascades though Willamette Pass, up the middle fork of the Willamette past Indigo Spring, through the heavily forested mountain saddle now named Emigrant Pass between Summit Lake and Diamond Peak—John Diamond named it after himself—and cross the Deschutes River near present day Bend. Then they headed across the desert, planning to bring emigrants from the middle fork of the Malheur River through the desert of Harney Basin to cross the Cascades. They calculated it would cut 200 miles—really, it was 125—off the total trip and bring settlers closer to their area, rather than coming down through the upper Willamette Valley that had already been settled.

They were looking for Meek's wagon ruts from eight years past when they were attacked by Indians near Harney Lake in eastern Oregon. They lost their notes and abandoned the idea of tracing Meek's trail to Fort Boise. It was a risky idea to bring people through a waterless desert, as Stephen Meek found out when he was almost strung-up—Meek's wife begged for his life—by those emigrants who had faithfully followed and then abandoned him in 1845 over essentially the same route.[334]

Unfortunately, the new road was never finished, due to late snows in the mountains and abandonment by the contractor, who did not communicate to Dr. Alexander that the road was not finished. They managed to clear some of the trail up the Willamette, leaving many stumps and logs, but they never made it through to the other side of the mountains to clear the trail.

The commissioners were eager to have someone try their new road, and not realizing that it was unfinished, they asked Elliot to take it and lead other settlers that way. He agreed and set out, armed with enthusiasm and a few notes and confident the trail would be finished. But he didn't set foot on the new trail heading east; he took the old route on the Barlow Toll Road to meet the wagon train at Fort Boise.

Elliot was quite successful at Camp Boise and, later, near the site of the future town of Vale along the Malheur River in Oregon, in convincing emigrants to follow him on the new cutoff, according to Daniel Owen, a descendant of one of those pioneers, Benjamin Franklin Owen. Owen's ancestor, as well as Andrew Samuel McClure, kept a diary of the trip. The McClure train was about a day's ride behind the train led by Elliot. They were both later involved in a relief party sent ahead to try to bring help for the train that was running out of supplies. Elliot was very confident and told some people the cutoff would be far fewer miles to travel. He told others that they would get there three weeks ahead of the rest of the train that was following the traditional route. At Vale, on the banks of the middle fork of the Malheur River, the Willamette Valley lay due west of them through the desert and over the Cascades. The established Oregon Trail turned north and northwest at this point, following the Malheur across the Blue Mountains to the Columbia River.

Lea Menefee, in her article "Cutoff Fever," points out the reasoning: Why should they go north when they were headed west? This was very appealing to a large number of exhausted and sick emigrants with dwindling supplies but not to the families of John Stoops and Thomas Matthews. They were skeptical of taking an untried route.[335]

Daniel Owen, in his book *Lost Rescue*, relays the conversation about the route according to William Stoops. "As their fathers spoke to Elliot, eleven-year old William Stoops and thirteen-year old David Cleveland Matthews took it all in. 'Elliot told my father he would beat him into the Willamette Valley by three weeks,' said William 'but father said the new road had never been traveled.'" The cutoff sounded good to some of the others, including their friends, the Thomas Williams family. They could avoid the Blue Mountains, the dangerous Deschutes River crossing, and the Barlow Toll Road. Over 1,000 people with 250 wagons followed Elliot. At the small encampment at Vale, they separated themselves from the rest of the people going on the traditional route. This little town in Malheur County would be on the stagecoach mail route of Hyrum A. Williams forty years later.[336]

The Stoopses, the Parker brothers, James Parvin, and the Matthewses family headed north. When they reached the John Day River, they had a two days' drive ahead of them without water. They filled every container they had with water and travelled all day and night and the next morning. William Stoops relayed that when they got to within a half mile of the water, the teams started to go very fast, parched for water, as was everyone. When they finally reached The Dalles, everything had to be shipped down the Columbia *except* the cattle. "They had to be driven by the men down the pack trail to near the Cascade Locks and there had to swim to the north side." At the falls they went by a tram car pulled by mules for six miles and then by boat again to the mouth of the Sandy River. After reaching Oregon City, they started the trek south to Rattlesnake Valley (Trent) in Lane County, where they camped at William McCall's place. McCall was Elliot's brother-in-law.[337]

Rattlesnake Valley is a small valley between Pleasant Hill and Lost Valley, about fourteen miles west of Eugene, Oregon. The trip from Illinois took them about six months. It's not clear the exact day they arrived in the area just east of the middle fork of the Willamette River, but it was more than three weeks before those following Elliot arrived. James Parvin settled in Rattlesnake Valley on some land near Dexter—records show he arrived in September 1853—along with Joseph Parker, Selena's brother.

Selena's brother James Parker did not come all the way to Lane County with them. He stopped in The Dalles for four months and took a job. He was trained as a blacksmith, so perhaps he found work. He would settle a few years later in Lost Valley and run a gristmill with his brother, Joseph, just a few miles from James Parvin on Lost Creek. The mill was the source for flour in the valley. It was thirty feet by thirty-six feet and three stories tall, with a mile-long run down Lost Creek, used for waterpower. His son James would later become sheriff of Lane County. In October the Matthewses filed a claim for land just north of Lowell, right at the mouth of the Free Emigrant Trail.[338]

Friends following Elliot quickly found themselves in serious trouble. Elliot started out with an advance party of about forty wagons, followed by staged departures for the rest of the train. He led them from the Malheur River past the present-day towns of Westfall and Drewsey but then detoured south, where he lost the trail. Thomas Williams took leadership of the train as people lost confidence in Elliot. Elliot took one group and Williams another, and both groups tried to find their way in the desert. They misidentified rivers and mountains and found themselves going in a circle in the Harney Basin around the alkali Malheur and Harney Lakes for more than a week. They were desperate for water because the water in the lakes was undrinkable, and they constantly had to search for pockets of fresh water.

They then ran into a severe area of basalt rocks south of Westfall Butte that was torture to walk over for beasts and people alike. It seemed that some of the emigrants were ready to do away with Elliot. The strain on Elliot must have been considerable, considering the magnitude of their dilemma. Many of the emigrants could ill afford to lose a week of supplies, as they were already low on food. Elliot sent rescue parties ahead with seven days' rations, but it would be forty days before they found help.

The rescue groups included Charles Clark and Robert Tandy, as well as Frank Owen and Andrew McClure. The first group wandered through the harsh wilderness area of Three Sisters Mountains, mistaking South Sister for Diamond Peak, and suffered terribly. Another group went towards Diamond Peak, where they did find ax marks on trees near the Deschutes River. There was even a group of five boys and their dog that set out looking for help. They knew they would starve if they did not succeed.[339]

The emigrants' cattle were very thin, but there was no other option than to eat the stock that were not pulling a wagon. Families that did not have stock tried to shoot game. One starving family shot a squirrel and promptly ate him raw, brains and all, according to journals of the emigrants. One of the men on the train, Colonel Cline, had invested all his money into a small herd of cattle that he brought with him. He offered his cattle to anyone desperate for food and, in doing so, saved many lives.

The main group of emigrants started to clear the trail and struggle inch by inch through the tangled, thick underbrush of the heavily forested Cascade Mountains. Finally, they were so desperate that they abandoned the wagons their cattle were too weak to pull, and some kept going on foot. Elliot and his men, as well as the other parties sent ahead, were trying to rescue them, but the rescue parties needed rescue themselves. Elliot managed to mark the trail with red strings, but it was said that the Indians removed the strings and the trail was not clear. It was almost November by then, cold and rainy with some snowfall, and, in such depleted condition, the emigrants were not prepared for the weather.[340]

The main group was camped near present day Bend, Oregon, at this time. Two of the men who left the main group to get help were Ranson Kelly and Martin Blanding. At one point, Kelly sick with hunger and fatigue, could go no farther. Blanding left him somewhere above the present-day town of Oakridge on October 16 and continued on with no food. After his horse died, he walked on, carrying the still-born foal of his dead mare. He planned to eat it, but he was too exhausted to prepare it. He finally got a fire going near Disappointment Butte, near Lowell, where he stopped to rest.

Thirteen-year-old David Cleveland Matthews, whose family had been in the area for weeks, wondering where the rest of the wagon train was, and his companion George Penline, were herding cattle around the Butte. David saw the fire, and after searching, he and Penline discovered Blanding. They carried him to John Barkdull's cabin less than a mile away. They had to restrain him from eating too much because he was mad with hunger. He told his desperate story and men went off on horses in all directions to sound the alarm and gather supplies.

Settlers from all over Lane County, as well as Linn and Benton counties, loaded up horses and wagons with supplies. They did not sleep, because they knew time was of the essence. "They took twenty-three loaded wagons with 20,000 pounds of flour, bacon, potatoes, onion, salt, and sugar, as well as ninety-four pack animals and 290 head of cattle." It was an extraordinary effort by settlers, many of whom were new to the area themselves.[341]

There were twenty-seven river crossings and an uphill climb over the mountains to reach the emigrants, but the first group of rescuers managed to reach the first group of starving people within three days. Two days after Martin Blanding was discovered by David Matthews, part of the advance rescue party following the McKenzie River down to Springfield straggled into town, starving, shoeless, and torn up from brambles. They were followed the next day by the group of five boys. Sadly, nine died during this terrible ordeal, and the rest showed effects of starvation. Ordeals such as these, as well as death, were not uncommon. In 1845, on the train led by Meek, twenty-three people died, as well as most of the cattle, on the Meek Cutoff before the survivors struggled north to The Dalles.

The lost emigrants of 1853 were in terrible shape when the last of them reached their destination on December 1. Ranson Kelly was found near death where Blanding had left him and saved; it was two more weeks before his family was rescued. It took three weeks to bring in all the members of the train. Many of them spent the winter in the homes of their rescuers. The community had come together in an amazing way and lifelong friendships were made. These new emigrants doubled the population of the county. Poor Elliot died only three years later and is buried in the Pleasant Hill Pioneer Cemetery. He tried his best, but no doubt the strain of the trip shortened his life.[342]

The first winter was a struggle, even for those who had not been on the lost train. Rough log cabins were built and fences put up in the wilderness. The Stoopses had a hard time keeping their few cattle alive and had to cut boughs from trees so the cattle could eat the moss.

James Parvin and Selena Parker were the first couple in the valley to get married—on February 5, 1854, by minister Gilmore Calliston in the Stoops' log home, today known as the Hunsaker place. James was twenty-two and Selena was twenty. James couldn't have been more pleased. He had to travel more than 2,000 miles, but he married the woman he loved, and now they could start their new life together in a great adventure.[343]

The Parvins started the process of improving their 320-acre claim. James built a log cabin, but within a year—in 1855—he decided to trade for some land on Lost Creek, a mile south of Dexter. It was here that he built up his property into one of the prettiest farms in the area. He had a total of 667 acers. James farmed, and the land had stands of timber which he harvested as well. He was an excellent carpenter and built a very large barn, along with furniture for himself and others. He helped build a number of barns in the area. He often worked with Thomas Williams, whom he called "Daddy" Williams and who had brought along equipment for the first sawmill in the area as well as woodworking tools on the fateful wagon train of 1853.

The land in the area was not as fertile as that closer to Eugene, but the timber was valuable, especially, the stands of Douglas fir. Although they were in an undeveloped rural area, the properties of Selena's two brothers and her sister were close by and could be reached on horseback, which was a comfort to them According to the census of 1860, the Parvin, Parker, Stoops, Matthews and Williams families all owned farms where the future towns of Dexter and Lowell developed in Lost Valley, about sixteen miles from Eugene.[344]

Lane County and its principal town, Eugene—named after one of its earliest settlers, Eugene Skinner—continued to grow due to pioneers pouring into Oregon Country. On February 14, 1859, Oregon became the thirty-third state. John Whiteaker of Pleasant Hill was sworn in as the first governor. Joseph Parker, brother of Selena, was called upon to give the first nominating speech for his neighbor Whiteaker.

The boundaries of Lane County changed over time but were finally established with the Pacific to the west and the summit of the Cascades to the east, a hundred miles in length, bordered by Douglas County to the south and Linn and Benton counties to the north. It was about one third valley land, with rich soil for growing crops of grain and grass and the rest of the county rolling foothills, open prairies, and large stands of timber. The Willamette River and its tributaries, the Middle Branch, Coast Branch, and McKenzie River, were the main water sources, with the McKenzie having some of the coldest and purest water anywhere. The main industries were agriculture and timber, and the families worked in both areas.

When the Civil War started in 1861, Oregon was on the side of the Union, but there were some southern sympathizers in Oregon's Dixie, which included Douglas County, just south of Lane County. There were many settlers from Kentucky and other southern states there. Sometimes, tempers would flare as the strain of the war continued. Thomas Williams, the fiery Welshman and southern sympathizer who was a neighbor of James Parvin, broke up a meeting of Northern sympathizers at the Pleasant Hill school building.

Oregon did not have a large presence in the war but sent six companies of cavalry, called the First Oregon Cavalry, to serve in the Union Army until June of 1865. Oregon had to scramble to find volunteers, some coming from California to guard the Indian Reservations—mostly in eastern Oregon—as well as guard the influx of settlers drawn by discovery of gold from attack by Indians in central and eastern Oregon. There was Indian unrest in eastern Oregon but not much in Lane County, where the Kalapuya Indians were generally friendly.[345]

James and Selena Parvin saw Indians infrequently at their homestead near Dexter. There were no documented altercations between the different civilizations in Lost Valley, although the settlers retreated to a block house in Trent out of fear a few times in early years. However, the settlers had to constantly fight timber wolves that were killing their livestock. James and Selena had eight children, but due to the rough, pioneer environment, they lost five of those eight. Their eldest, Lillis, died at age three, their second born, Joseph, died at nineteen. They lost Hila and Edgar at ages one and two. One of them died from burns suffered from falling into the fireplace, which in those days was open to the room. Their daughter Bertha, born in 1863, married William Williams, son of Thomas Williams, but sadly, died at age twenty-one as a young mother of two in 1884. The children were taken in by the Parvin family until William married Bertha's younger sister Ida five years later in 1889. Ida and William went on to have seven children.

Ida, her sister Phoebe (Jeannie), and Hosea were the remaining children of the Parvins. Jeannie Parvin married A. L. Schaffler. Hosea, their remaining son, born in 1868, worked the homestead with his father. Hosea married Agnes E. Templeman, granddaughter of Thomas Matthews and Elizabeth Cope Matthews, in 1896.[346]

James Parvin and his wife were members and supporters of the Christian Church founded in the area by "Uncle" Gilford. James was a member of the Democratic Party, was active in public affairs, and served many years on the school board. He gave generously to the drive to establish the University of Oregon at Eugene, established in 1876 on the banks of the Willamette. James ran the Dexter Post Office from his property on Lost Creek after he took over the postmaster job from Hunsaker. He ran a thrashing machine for twenty-five years on his farm and a mercantile store in a building on his land for eleven years.

Thomas Moffit Matthews and his wife Elizabeth Cope Matthews, photo Ancestry.com

James bought the store in 1883; his wife ran the counter while he served as postmaster. There was a cast iron stove in the store with the name of O. Dexter on it, which later became the name of the town. The large hill that framed the edge of the town was named Parvin Butte. James' wife, Selena, was as hard working and kind, as was he, and always helped with those who were ill or short of food. Sometimes, Indians came to the farm, and she always fed them. As time went on, James felt the urge to go back to see relatives in Illinois and Texas, and he had a chance to do so in 1884.

In 1899 he turned over all his farm equipment to Hosea, and the store and post office were moved off the farm and run by his daughters Ida and Jeannie. Jeannie, who had taught school for a few years as well as clerked for the school district, then became postmaster for eight years. After Jeannie married August Schaffler, her sister, Ida, took over as postmaster for twenty-nine years. Ida's husband, William Williams, bought out Jeannie's portion of the store, and it became known as the Williams and Williams store.

James Parvin and his wife Selena Parker Parvin, author's collection

James Parvin went for another visit back East to see family in 1900. About this time, he consulted and helped his son Hosea build a new, large farmhouse on the property across the creek. The Parvin Bridge had already been built in the 1880s for ease of crossing Lost Creek and would become a historic site. James Parvin died on December 17, 1907, after a full and meaningful life. Selena lived in the original home across Lost Creek from her son Hosea's family until she died on October 3, 1913.[347]

In such a small community, everyone was family. The Thomas Matthews family lived not far away. Their children grew up with the Stoops, Parvin, and Williams families. David C. Matthews married John Stoops' daughter, Malinda. One of his younger sisters, Anna E. Matthews, who was only two when her parents came west, grew up and met a handsome man born in Kentucky, William D. Templeman. He was a pioneer from Calapooia in Douglas County, Oregon, south of Lane County, and was a son of Fielding Templeman and Nancy Dennison from Grayson, Kentucky.

The Templeman family origins were in Stafford County, Virginia. The Templemans migrated to Kentucky. The family left Kentucky with three sons and two daughters, stopping in Missouri, where their fourth son, Bailey, was born, before moving on to Oregon.

Anna married William in Pleasant Hill on July 2, 1871. They had three children, all born in Dexter, Lost Valley: Elden, born in 1872, Flora Agnes, born in 1873, and their younger sister, Margaret (Maggie), born in 1876. William Templeman died in 1879 at age thirty-eight of a sudden illness, leaving Anna a widow at twenty-eight. Anna and her three children moved in with her elderly parents, Thomas and Elizabeth Matthews. Her father Thomas died in 1880.

Anna Elizabeth Matthews (1851-1883) wife of William D. Templeman, Pleasant Hill, Oregon, author's collection

William D. Templeman (1841-1879) Pleasant Hill, Oregon author's collection

In October of 1883 Anna married a Mr. E. Wilson, but she died just two months later on December 23, 1883. The children were raised by their Quaker grandmother, Elizabeth Cope Matthews, with the help of her other grown children's families. Their paternal grandfather, Fielding Templeman, wrote them encouraging letters. Their grandmother Elizabeth Cope Matthews took care of them until she died in May of 1893.[348]

The small schoolhouse at Lost Valley (Dexter) was built in 1855 by the residents who organized the school, which included Thomas Matthews, Thomas Williams, and John Stoops. They paid Mr. Laughlin $30 a month to teach reading, spelling, writing, arithmetic, geography, and English grammar. One of the teachers in the 1880s, Ellis Parker, son of Joseph Parker, went on to have a distinguished career, teaching for sixty years and serving as principal of two Eugene schools. Ellis Parker Elementary in Eugene is named after him.

The three children of Anna Elizabeth Matthews and William D. Templeman, L-R, Maggie, Elden, Agnes, Pleasant Hill, Oregon, c. early 1890s author's collection

On the Lost Valley school rolls in 1875 were Hosea and Jeannie Parvin, the three Templeman children, and Lisa Matthews, one of the Matthews children. Hosea Parvin married his schoolhouse friend Agnes Templeman on November 22, 1896, at the home of the minister there, Edgar J. Candler.

Agnes' brother Elden was known in the area as the strongest man around and often challenged newcomers to tests of strength. Elden ended up tearing the tendons in his knees in one such contest and had to wear braces on his legs for the rest of his life. In spite of that fact, he was a successful and generous businessman. He opened the first general store in Oakridge, Oregon. Sister Maggie married a rancher and moved to Drewsey in eastern Oregon.

Hosea and Agnes started their married life on the farm in Dexter. They built a large, new farmhouse, complete with an egg room, cream room, and canning room. Agnes would clean the eggs and place them in cartons to sell in the egg room. Egg money was important to a farmer's wife. Hosea loved the land, as had his father, and was an industrious farmer. He also loved horses and was an expert horseman. His favorite horse, "Ol' Bess," once carried him 171 miles in two days and nights from Silver Falls to Dexter. She was so sure footed that she could carry him across the creek just on the bridge footings.[349]

Hosea and Agnes had five children: Alberta A., born 1897; Loris T., 1899; Dorothy Agnes, 1902; Selena Elizabeth, 1904; and Florence J., born in 1906. Living on a farm, they all had chores, of course, but also time for blackberry picking and playing in Lost Creek. When Dorothy was five, her grandfather James died. Her grandmother did not want to be alone at night, and Dorothy was picked to stay with her. Dorothy crossed the bridge to her grandmother's house every night. Often, her older siblings would hide under the bridge to jump out and scare her. Dorothy always had a sweet nature, but very late in life she remembered having to do this and thought it had been unfair. She was a bright and precocious child who was always helpful. Her father bought one of the earliest automobiles in the area, and she learned to drive at an early age, but not without mishaps. She discovered automobiles don't respond to "Whoa!" and she ran through a fence. Her father thought she could do no wrong and constantly encouraged her.

The Parvin Family- three generations, adults L-R, Hosea, Agnes, James, Selena, children L-R, Loris, Florence, Dorothy, Selenia and Alberta, Dexter, Oregon c. 1908, author's collection

In high school Dorothy boarded in town. She graduated from Springfield High in 1922. Dorothy then attended Monmouth Normal School to become a teacher. About this time, in 1921, the county decided to redo the Parvin Bridge. Covered bridges were rare in Oregon; the Parvin Bridge was one of only twenty in the state. The bridge was completely refurbished again in 1986 and dedicated, with Dorothy and her sister Florence in attendance. The Parvin Bridge is now on the National Register of Historic Places.[350]

Dorothy began teaching school in Edenvale, Oregon, and taught there from 1923-25. She was paid $80 a month plus $5 dollars a month for janitor work the first year, as well as $15 a month for room and board. The second year she received a raise, up to $100 a month. Her brother Loris took over the farm of his great-grandfather Thomas Matthews, and Dorothy's sisters spread out to work in Eugene. Dorothy was the first to get married, in 1926, followed by her sister Alberta, who married Cornelius S. Dillion on August 7, 1930. The Dillions had no children. Younger sister Selena Elizabeth was the next to get married, marrying George (Ted) Burian on July 7, 1934. They had two children: Wayne and Sharon. Loris Templeman Parvin married Georgia Brodus in 1936, but they were divorced in 1939. It was kept so quiet in the family that many thought he had never married. Florence Juanita Parvin married Martin Montgomery on May 15, 1937. They had three children: Caroline, David and Daniel.[351]

Dorothy Agnes Parvin, Springfield, Oregon, age 18, 1920 author's collection

Hosea and Agnes were wonderful grandparents and enjoyed visits from their children and grandchildren. The large farmhouse Hosea built burned to the ground in February 1948. They saved very little from the terrible fire but managed to save some of the downstairs furniture, including a child's rocking chair made by Hosea's father, James. It was a devastating loss for the elderly couple. A porcelain doorknob from the house was found years later by the author. Although they did not have much insurance money, Hosea and Agnes rebuilt a modest, modern house. Hosea, unlike many of his restless ancestors, was content to stay on the beautiful land on Lost Creek where he had been born. He died on August 26, 1954 and is buried in the Pleasant Hill Pioneer Cemetery. His faithful wife died nine years later on June 19, 1963 and is buried with her husband. The Parvin, Parker, and Matthews families, close in life, remained close in death. They are buried within sight of each other at the cemetery.[352]

The landmark of Dexter, Parvin Butte, was obtained by the railroad in 1952. The beautiful hill was surrounded by twenty small farms until 1973. The Parvin children sold their grandfather's homestead land after their parents died. None of them were able to take care of the land at that point. In 1973 Lane County zoned the area for quarry mining. The company, Lost Creek Rock Products, has been chipping away at the butte ever since. The company has been a less-than-good neighbor, according to the community organization—Save Parvin Butte—that sprang up in Dexter to save the butte. The only remaining signs of the Parvins in Dexter are the road leading to the Parvin Bridge, the beautiful, covered bridge which is a protected landmark, and what's left of Parvin Butte.[353]

Dorothy was close to her parents and missed them and the beautiful area around Lost Creek very much. Late in her life, she fondly remembered when she told her father, Hosea, that she was going to marry Grover Reese; he told her to go out and buy the prettiest dress she could find. She bought a beautiful, black silk dress in the 1920s flapper style. It had a dropped waist, a cream silk under-bodice, pearl buttons, and beautifully embroidered sleeves. She and Grover were married in the home of the minister in Dexter on December 17, 1926.

She was the first of the Parvin children to get married and a favorite of her father. Eastern Oregon was a long distance from Dexter, and Dorothy knew her parents would miss her. It would be hard for them to leave their farm. Dorothy noticed tears rolling down the cheeks of her father during the ceremony. He was happy for her but sad to see her go.[354]

Parvin Bridge rededication with sisters, Dorothy Parvin Reese and Florence Parvin Montgomery, source: Rhodes, The Springfield News, Wed. November 19, 1986

Chapter Eight

Unwavering Resolve

Family Cast of Characters

Grover Williams Reese…(1888-1950) *Patricia Reese's father*
Dorothy Agnes Parvin…(1902-1998) *Patricia Reese's mother*

Geraldine Reese…(1927-present) *daughter of Grover and Dorothy*

Patricia Reese…(1929-present) *daughter of Grover and Dorothy*

Grover Parvin Reese…(1933-2009) *son of Grover and Dorothy*

Kenneth Roy Pickett…(1924-2002) *husband of Geraldine Reese*
Daniel Bruce Adlum…(1921-1977) *husband of Patricia Reese*
Thelma Gulley…(1935-present) *wife of Grover Parvin Reese*

The Reese Family

Strength reveals itself through character

~Henry Rollins

Grover and Dorothy said their goodbyes after their wedding in Dexter, headed north to Seattle for a honeymoon, and then to the ranch at Drewsey. Dorothy was starting a new life as a rancher's wife. She knew it would be difficult to travel to see her parents very often, as a rancher's life was a busy one. She had grown up surrounded by family and many cousins and her life in this remote area would be very different. She would be sharing the ranch house with her mother-in-law, Grace, which was an intimidating thought, even for this very capable young woman. Dorothy's Aunt Maggie and family lived on a ranch in the area, and that was a comfort, but the landscape was dramatically different from Lane County.

The Drewsey Valley stretches several miles along the Malheur River in Harney County in the southeast, high-desert region of Oregon. The valley is about a mile wide, filled with grasslands, and surrounded by gentle hills covered with sagebrush, junipers, and lava rocks. The major focal point in this mostly flat landscape is Steens Mountain, a dramatic sight at 9,700 feet. Drewsey was and still is in a remote, isolated area, an hour's drive away from a town of a few thousand people, either Burns, the county seat, or Vale in Malheur County.

The town of Drewsey in the northeast part of the county had a population of 83 in 1920—part of 250 total in the valley, mostly ranchers, sheep herders, or timbermen. Harney County, with its 10,180 square miles, had vast open spaces that held a sparse population of 3,902 in 1920. Grover, having grown up there, loved the expansiveness of the land, but it was a harsh master.[355]

Grover and Dorothy were delighted to welcome their first child, Geraldine, on November 6, 1927, born in Burns. No doubt Dorothy's very capable mother-in-law, Grace, assisted her with her first child, but by the time she was pregnant with her second, Dorothy felt the strain of her mother-in-law overseeing everything she did. She went home to Dexter with Geraldine, then twenty-two months old, to be near her parents for the birth of her second daughter, Patricia. Dorothy asked her husband to find another place for his mother to live. Their daughter Patricia was born on September 15, 1929, at Sacred Heart Hospital in Eugene. Grover had his cattle in the back of his truck, ready to sell on his way to pick up his family in Eugene. He picked up a hitchhiker—common in those days—who threw his lit cigarette in the back of Grover's truck, starting a fire and killing the cattle.

Things only got more difficult from there. A little more than a month later, the stock market started its crash and the economic decline then accelerated for the Reese family, as well as the rest of the country. The town of Drewsey began to shrink: by the 1930 census, there were only 66 in town and about 200 in the area. There had been two lumber mills in Drewsey, as well as the Pacific Livestock Company, all of which went out of business during the Great Depression. Failure of the railroad to connect to the town, as well as the Central Oregon Highway bypassing the town by a few miles, helped in its decline, as well as the drought in eastern Oregon at the time. The Reeses held on to their ranch and Grace moved to her own house.

Dorothy Parvin Reese holding newborn daughter Patricia, Eugene, Oregon, 1929
author's collection

Dorothy became pregnant with her third child in 1932. Geraldine and Patricia's brother, Grover Parvin Reese, was born during a terrible blizzard on February 6, 1933. They were lucky to have a telephone on the ranch. It was a party line; each family had its own special ring, and no doubt, other families listened in on other families' calls! The telephone was certainly needed when Dorothy was ready to give birth.

The storm was so severe that the doctor was not able to come to the ranch. It was the coldest winter in eastern Oregon history. Snowplows cleared the road halfway from Burns to a neighbor's ranch, and the doctor was able to make it there—halfway to the Reeses—before the roads closed. Grover managed to get his wife to the neighbor's ranch but had to return in the bitter cold to their own ranch so they would not lose their cattle. Geraldine and Patricia, at five and three, were left in the ranch house alone by the phone while their father went out on the range to get the cattle. It was dangerous for them to be alone in the house but much more dangerous for them to be outside. They were good as gold, and it became quite a story to tell later.

It was the height of the Depression when Grover was born. The newly elected President Franklin Delano Roosevelt had a lot of work to do. Life was very difficult, but people persevered and had hope that things would improve.

Patricia recalls fond memories of the ranch in Drewsey. Her mother, Dorothy, told Patricia that when she received a new pair of shoes at age three, she planted them in the garden to grow another pair. When Patricia was five, she was allowed to go with her sister's class—even though she was not yet in school—to Steens Mountain to see the herds of antelope grazing there. Patricia was so astonished by the beautiful sight that she still remembers her amazement many years later. [356]

Dorothy Parvin Reese with daughters, Geraldine and Patricia on the Reese cattle ranch, Drewsey, Oregon, 1932, author's collection

Grover Williams Reese with his three children, Geraldine, Patricia and Grover, Drewsey, Oregon, 1933, author's collection

By September 1935, when Patricia was in first grade, the bank that held her parents' money failed, and they lost everything. Grover and Dorothy then lost the ranch through foreclosure. There was no money in cattle ranching during the Depression. This was about the same time that Patricia's future husband, Daniel, and his family lost their house in Portland. Grover, Dorothy, and their three children moved to a house in Adrian, Oregon, about twenty-five miles south of Ontario in Malheur County, for a year. Adrian is very close to the Idaho border at the convergence of the Owyhee and Snake Rivers on Hwy. 20. The area where Adrian was built was on the south alternate Oregon Trail route for those who did not want to cross the Snake River. It was a longer but safer route. When the Owyhee Dam was built thirty miles upstream from Adrian in 1932, people started moving in to farm and raise livestock. Grover and Dorothy tried to get a new start there.

Both Geraldine and Patricia rode the school bus to school in Adrian. Their brother, Grover, was still too young. There were two school buildings, one elementary and one for high school. Patricia remembers being terrorized by being held upside down out a second-story window by an eighth-grade boy and fainting from receiving shots. It was traumatic being in first grade! That same year Geraldine and Patricia were each given their own setting hen by their parents to care for. Ten baby chicks were hatched from Geraldine's hen, while Patricia's hen only had one chick. Patricia was so jealous that she accidently stepped on her one baby chick, learning a valuable lesson.

The Reese children lived very close to the Owyhee River and spent countless hours watching the river, catching catfish, and playing games. They played Kick the Can in the evenings after school. Patricia remembers always being It for hide-and-seek until her kind mother would come out and say someone else had to be It for a change. There were fierce snowstorms in eastern Oregon which were always a danger, and sometimes, the kids would get very anxious on the bus ride home, fearing they would be stuck in the snow.

When Patricia was seven and Geraldine nine, the family moved about 130 miles northwest from Adrian to a cattle ranch outside of McEwen, in Baker County, a few miles from Sumpter, the old gold mining town. When gold was first discovered in Oregon, Baker County was one of the hotspots in the eastern part of the state. In 1861 gold was discovered in Auburn, about ten miles from the present location of Baker City. Eastern Oregon was mostly Indian Country at the time, but that didn't stop prospectors from moving in.

Gold is a powerful motivator. A placer mine in Auburn started a trend, and hundreds of mines opened all over Baker County, as well as some in surrounding counties. Auburn faded, but Baker City grew very quickly, becoming the major town in the county. Baker City, located on the original Oregon Trail, sits at an elevation of 3,440 feet, with the Elkhorn Mountains to the west and the Wallowas on the east. It is a picturesque spot on the Powder River. The Oregon Railway and Navigation Company arrived in Baker in 1894, joining the Union Pacific at Huntington, giving Baker access to rail service, and attracting The Oregon Lumber Company to town. Baker became a boomtown with about 7,000 residents by 1900. There was a substantial downtown with a hotel—the Geiser Grand—with a dining room with seats for 200, as well as a theater where operas were performed. Baker was known as the "Queen of the Inland Empire" and was the third-largest city in Oregon at the time. In addition to cultural activities for the highbrow, there were slot machines and all-night saloons for the less-highbrow gold miners and loggers.[357]

Gold was discovered in nearby Sumpter in 1862 on Cracker Creek, and a town began to grow there as well. The Oregon Lumber Company, owned by Mormons from Salt Lake City, built the narrow-gauge Sumpter Valley Railroad, nicknamed the "Stump Dodger," which ran in its heyday eighty miles from Baker City to Prairie City in Grant County to the south. Ponderosa Pine logs from the great stands of pine in Grant County were hauled on the line.

When the railroad connected the town of Sumpter in 1897, the town prospered. By 1900 Sumpter had thousands of residents digging out millions of dollars of gold. A tragic fire in 1917 burned a large amount of the town, and it never recovered. By the time the Reeses moved nearby in 1936, Sumpter was a shadow of itself, but there was still gold to be found.[358]

McEwen is just six miles from Sumpter on the Sumpter Valley Railroad route. There was little there but a grange hall, schoolhouse, post office and store. The Reeses took a mortgage on a ranch called the Rockney place—named for the former owner—in the foothills of the Elkhorn Mountains, a subrange of the Blue Mountains, which were usually capped with snow ten months a year. Grover and Dorothy started again in the cattle business. This was such a remote area that they did not have a telephone or electricity the entire time they lived there. It must have been terribly lonely for Dorothy, but she never let her family see anything but purpose and cheerfulness. For Patricia and her siblings, it was a happy time.

Patricia remembers:

> We had a creek running by our house where my brother and sister and I played. There was a sort of box-like shelter on the bridge over the creek, and we would pretend that it was a restaurant. Christmas was a very big deal in those years. One winter my father made us skis for Christmas. We got to open our presents on Christmas Eve after dinner when Daddy had finished his chores. As I remember we always got a toy or a doll and got a new dress or something to wear. My mother made the most delicious cream caramel candy ever made. We always got an orange in our stocking Christmas morning, as well as hard candy and chocolate drop candy. One very special gift I received from Aunt Selena was a red, travel, doll trunk, which I really treasured and kept all my valuables in. I kept it until I was eighty-five years old, when I could finally part with it.[359]

There was no school bus to get to school in McEwen; Geraldine and Patricia rode a gentle old horse to school. When there were deep snowdrifts, as eastern Oregon is known for, Geraldine would feel sorry for the horse and get off and lead him. It's not likely that the two girls were too heavy—Geraldine reported that she was a skinny kid with the nickname of Jellybean. When their brother, Grover, started school in 1939, he rode another horse that Patricia reported was livelier. There was a barn near the one-room schoolhouse, where they would put the horses during the day. There were only about fifteen students total in the school. Patricia remembers that her sister's class, two grades ahead, held five people, and the class ahead of Patricia held four. She was in a class of her own for almost the entire time from second through sixth grade except for a few months in fourth grade when Kenneth Wilson was in the same grade. Kenneth must have been as thrilled as she was, because he gave her a beautiful diamond ring from a Cracker Jack box and considered them engaged, at least for the few months he was there.

They brought sleds to school in the winter and spent recesses sliding down the hill behind the school and playing a circle game in the snow, until one of the boys broke his arm. At lunch they would all gather around the big wood-burning stove in the classroom and eat their lunch together. There was no trash in those days—they simply folded up their paper sacks and waxed paper to take home to use again. Miss Adams was Patricia's favorite teacher; she lived in the house with her mother, the same house that Patricia's grandmother, Grace, would live in a few years later. When the teacher married one of the local ranchers and left, the new teacher was Mrs. Slaughter. Patricia doesn't remember being given a lesson at her grade level her entire time at the school. But she does remember that, when the weather was nice, she would listen to some of the younger children read outside on the steps of the school.

Despite the isolation, the Reeses managed to make a good childhood for their children. They were self-reliant and capable people, traits inherited from their pioneer ancestors. Although Dorothy and Grover must have been filled with doubt during those hard times, their children trusted their parents completely and had no thought of resisting what they said to do.

It was too far to go to church, so Dorothy sent for Sunday school lessons by mail and taught her children herself. She had a beautiful flower and vegetable garden and was a wonderful cook. Although they were poor, they had enough to eat. Dorothy canned and preserved all summer. They had venison and fried chicken, vegetables, fruits, and home-baked goods. In the bitterly cold winter, which usually had snow from October to April, Dorothy had the canned goods she'd put up in the summer to serve, as well as venison from deer they killed.

In winter the temperature never got much above the high 30s or low 40s, and the lows were in the teens. They had heat from two wood-burning stoves, but it was still extremely cold. The kids would take hot water bottles to bed to try to warm the sheets. One had to be very brave to get out of bed in the morning. Their father, Grover, got up first and fed the stove. On the ranch there were lots of animals, including many barn cats and two dogs—one named Joe Lewis, after the famous boxer. The Reese children's favorite pet of all was a scrawny chicken called Johnny Few Feathers.[360]

When Patricia was ten, she developed a large cyst on the lateral aspect of her knee. Medical help was scarce in the area, and the Reeses had little money to pay for it, but her father was good friends with Dr. Robert Pollack. The doctor lived and practiced in Baker and treated patients in the surrounding towns, and he charged a reasonable, small fee. Patricia's parents saved up for the hospital and surgery bill. Dr. Pollack performed the surgery, and Patricia was left with a five-inch scar on her leg but full function. Dr. Pollock went on to write a memoir, *The Education of a Country Doctor*, relaying his experiences in eastern Oregon treating miners, loggers, and ranchers in the community.[361]

The gold mining activities in Sumpter affected everyone in the area. Although Sumpter shrank in size, the gold mining activity never stopped. When the Reeses lived nearby, the third consecutive gold mining dredge was digging up the area twenty-four hours a day, seven days a week. The only days the dredge was quiet were Christmas and the Fourth of July. It was turning the Sumpter Valley into a big pile of rocks.

Grover Reese was very much opposed to the way the Sumpter Valley Dredge Company was proceeding. He felt that the environment should be protected, but it was the middle of the Depression, men needed work, and the company was very powerful. The dredge company put extreme pressure on ranchers to sell their land, to the point where they had a neighbor of the Reeses, Mr. Carlson, committed to a mental hospital in Salem when he wouldn't let them buy his land. Grover located Carlson's relatives back East and called them in an attempt to get him released. Patricia and Geraldine remember Mr. Carlson for his kindness and the beautiful, little log cabins he made for them to store their trinkets in.[362]

Sumpter Valley Dredge # 3 at work on the Powder River, Sumpter, Oregon, courtesy Baker County Library, Baker City, Oregon

The first of the dredges on the Powder River in Sumpter Valley started in 1913, chewing up the gravel base of the river, followed by the second dredge, called the Sumpter Valley Dredge, and then the third, simply called Number 3, built from parts of the first dredge. Number 3 weighed in at 1,250 tons, a huge floating "ship," with seventy-two massive buckets attached that churned up fifty cubic yards of river bottom an hour. It wasn't much more sophisticated than traditional placer mining: dirt was sifted, sorted, and washed with river water, allowing the gold to settle. The dredge then spit out the gravel tailings, leaving a scarred landscape along its track. Only three men were required to operate it, with another seventeen men in auxiliary roles. Between the three dredges, operating between 1913 and 1954, when Number 3 closed in debt, the gold dredges pulled out about $10 million of gold—at a time when gold was only worth $35 an ounce. The dredge chewed up more than eight miles of landscape along the Powder River, leaving ten-foot-high tailings of gravel and rock which are easily seen from space.[363]

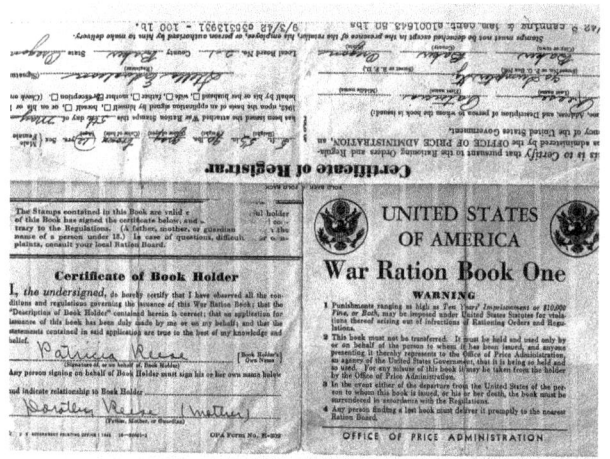

WW II ration card of Patricia Reese, author's collection

Despite Grover's best efforts, he and Dorothy could not afford the mortgage on the ranch, and after Geraldine graduated from eighth grade in 1941, the family left the ranch and moved to Baker for a few months. Patricia started junior high in Baker, and then a few months later, the family moved just outside of town, where her father could keep his cattle. In September of 1942 Grover and Dorothy leased a ranch halfway between Sumpter and Baker City, which were about twenty-nine miles apart. They leased it for three years and then one additional year.

By 1943 Grover was not feeling as strong as he had been. The family did not realize he was suffering from rheumatic heart disease, sometimes caused by untreated illnesses like strep throat. In the days before antibiotics, there could be significant damage to the heart with inflammation. Dorothy took a job teaching in the country school that her nine-year-old son, Grover, attended. The family all helped their father with the chores. World War II had already begun by this time, increasing anxiety for everyone.

The place they leased was called the Miles place. Again, the family was without a telephone or radio. Because they were so isolated, the war was not significant in their daily lives, except for rationing and price controls.

Some of the first items to be rationed were sugar and tires. Tires were rationed in January 1942 because of the shortage of rubber. The Japanese Imperial Army controlled the Dutch East Indies—present-day Indonesia—where most of the rubber came from. The first ration card issued in May 1942 was called the sugar book; the purchase of sugar was restricted to one half pound a week per person, which was half the normal usage. Dorothy had to restrict the amount of sugar she used for baking and canning. Gas rationing restricted the purchase of gas to three gallons a week, which limited any unnecessary driving. By 1943 there were ration cards with coupons for many items, such as meat, butter, cheese, coffee, sugar, clothing, bicycles, silk and nylon stockings, dried fruit, jams, and jellies. Everyone, including children, had to present their ration book to purchase these items. Since the Reeses lived on a ranch, they already provided much of their own food. People in the cities were encouraged to plant victory gardens. Factories stopped making automobiles and most household appliances, as all efforts at production went to the war effort. Rationing and price controls were an attempt to make sure limited items were available for all and to control inflation. Price controls were put on beef, limiting the amount ranchers could charge for their cattle, regardless of the cost to produce. This made life for a cattle rancher even harder. [364]

The focus of everyone was on the war effort. While Patricia's future husband, Daniel, was fighting the Japanese in the Pacific, the Japanese Americans on the west coast had their own battle. The vast majority were loyal, law-abiding citizens, but the fear caused by the war led the president to issue Executive Order 9066 on February 19, 1942, which set aside certain areas of the country as military zones.

The government enforced the Order selectively. It was meant to exclude the Japanese-Americans, both Issei—first generation—and Nisei—those with American citizenship by birth—but a few months later, the War Relocation Authority forced the Japanese Americans to quickly give up their homes and property and be interned in detention camps for the remainder of the war. Some Germans and Italians were interned as well. In Oregon, Germans were held in the Portland County Jail.

There were temporary camps thrown up in Oregon for the Japanese, while ten permanent camps were built in remote areas of the west. Those Japanese Americans who were able went to the East Coast, where they were not bothered. The Japanese American population of Hood River and southwest Oregon was sent to the camp at Tule Lake in northern California. There were a few spots in eastern Oregon with Japanese American residents; Baker City had a few, Ontario, in Malheur County, also had a small population. Because of a labor shortage, Amalgamated Sugar Company, ramping up production for the war, petitioned the government for Japanese Americans to be allowed in Ontario for farm labor to plant sugar beets. Some 400 Japanese Americans relocated and worked on farms, planting potatoes, onions, and celery, as well as sugar beets. By the end of the war, Ontario had a population of 1,500 Japanese Americans who stayed in the area and are known today as the most productive onion farmers. Today, Ontario has about a two percent Japanese American population.

The last camps closed in 1946, and the Japanese Americans worked very hard to regain the positions that had been ripped away from them in the war. Their stoic nature and determination allowed them to succeed in spite of their mistreatment. In college Patricia had a Japanese American friend, Mitzi, who had been through the experience. She said she preferred the camps as opposed to working all day as a farm laborer. She was a child at the time; no doubt, her parents were dramatically impacted by their experience.[365]

Patricia and her family lived out the war on the isolated ranch. The kids rode the school bus to Baker City, which took at least an hour and even longer in winter. Patricia lived here during eighth, ninth, tenth, and most of eleventh grade. One summer Grover decided his girls could make some money growing green onions, and he plowed up two acres. Everyone going by would stop with amazement, for they had not seen crops grown in the area. The two sisters, Tish and Deanie—their nicknames for each other—made some money on the project, and they saved every penny for their future expenses. Patricia said they made more money on fresh green onions than dried ones, but they sold both by leaving them by the road for the mail truck to pick up. They would also put out a five-gallon can full of cream to sell to the dairy co-operative in Baker. The mail truck took the green onions to Baker and then they were sent on the train to Portland to sell. The mail truck was very important in rural areas!

By September 1945 Grover was so ill with heart failure that he was unable to do any work at all on the farm. Dorothy wrote to her parents in Dexter:

> Dear Folks
> Grover is at the Veteran's Hospital in Portland. He has been feeling bad a long time. He got some medicine and was better for a while. Here the last 2 or 3 weeks-has been looking so bad seems like he can hardly get his breath. We decided he better go there and try to find out what the trouble was. We have had two letters, one telling us to send his Army Discharge papers ... I have been worried a long time – he looks so bad. I thought about putting my school off (teaching) til hear something definite. As I think more about it, guess I might just as well start. I would only be stewing.
> Grover said he had a hard trip to Portland with cattle, got there late Sunday night. There was a big run the day he sold, and the cattle sold slow. His cattle came to $2,395.06. I can't tell you much about them–I think 10 two-year-old steers, some heifer, part old cows, 25 head or so. Son Grover's steer brought $130, the girl's heifers $100. He seems to feel disappointed. There were 3 or 4 more he wanted to send but he could not find them ...
> Love Dorothy[366]

On Patricia's sixteenth birthday, September 15, 1945, she was left in charge of the ranch, along with her twelve-year-old brother. Her mother, Dorothy, left with Geraldine, who was starting college at the University of Oregon in Eugene. Dorothy took her daughter to the train, then returned and set out for Portland to pick up her husband from the Veteran's Hospital, where he had been hospitalized. Patricia knew there was so much her mother had to worry about; she was sure she had forgotten her birthday. But no, there was a pretty little bakery cake her mother had taken the time to buy and that she left for Patricia. That cake meant more to her than anything, and she realized she had the best mother in the world. Patricia and her brother, Grover, had to round up the cattle on the open range and bring them in and feed them. They could not find them all, but they got help from the cowboys on the big Burnt River ranches who would bring in any cattle they found with their brand—(R. Poachers would kill deer at night just across the river from the house, which was frightening to Patricia while they were staying alone.

When their parents returned home, their father was no longer able to do any physical work. One of the neighbors fed the cattle while Patricia and her brother were at school because they were gone so long, given their long bus ride to and from school. On the weekends, Patricia and her brother, Grover, took the wagon loaded with hay to feed the cattle. They tossed hay out as the horses slowly walked. That winter the ranchers were plagued by hungry elk herds, who were eating all their haystacks. Patricia killed an elk that winter, trying to scare the herd away from the hay; they could not afford to let them eat the hay. A neighbor took the elk for the meat.

By November 30, 1945, Dorothy wrote her parents another letter telling them they were out of the cattle business, not even having a milk cow. The cow Dorothy was milking "laid out on her" and disappeared. The Reeses sold nineteen head of cattle to a man from McEwen for $3,600. They wanted to sell their hay but weren't sure they should until the cattle were sold. Dorothy said so many ranchers were killing cattle because the cost of feeding them was prohibitive due to price controls limiting their profit. The price controls for cattle were taken off by the government the following year. Grover and Dorothy had to sell at one fourth the price they would have received a year later.

They had had hard luck for twenty years but were still looking forward. Dorothy wrote her folks: "I would give anything if we could buy a house." This brave, cheerful lady just wanted a home of her own.[367]

Dorothy got her house at 1095 Elm Street in Baker City. It was on the main road that had been part of the Oregon Trail. There was space for a garden, which she filled with flowers and vegetables. Grover and Dorothy bought the house from the Curfman-Ullman Real Estate Firm in April of 1946. Dorothy, after teaching four years in a country school, got a job teaching elementary school in Baker City to support the family. Geraldine was in Eugene, living with her mother's sister, Aunt Alberta. She lived with her for two years, working in a hardware store to pay her college expenses.

About a week after the rest of the family moved into the house on Elm Street, Patricia's shorthand teacher at Baker High School, Mrs. Romig, was asked to recommend her best student to the Curfman-Ullman firm for part time work. Patricia remembers:

> I was third best, not first, but my teacher felt I needed the job the most which was true. I worked in their office from 4-6 every day after school and four or five hours on Saturdays. It was a great opportunity. I worked full time both summers my junior and senior years. I saved all of my money and could pay my expenses at the University of Oregon the two years I was there.

Patricia's boss, Al Ullman, became a longtime U.S. Congressman from the area. He ended up becoming chairman of the powerful Ways and Means Committee in the House of Representatives.

All of the Reese family worked hard. At age fourteen, Grover Jr. took a job at the Grand Geiser hotel. One of his jobs was to hide the slot machines whenever the inspectors came around; Baker City still had a somewhat rowdy crowd. Grover made friends with the kids from the Lutheran church and ran around with them. Once he borrowed Patricia's bike, rode it too close to the raging Powder River, and almost drowned. His sister's bike was lost, but she was glad he made it out.

Patricia's senior year in high school was incredibly busy. In addition to working every day, she was editor of the high school newspaper, served as sportswriter, and had major roles in two plays, as well as involvement in many other activities. She received some

Geraldine Reese, Baker High School, Baker City, Oregon 1945

Patricia Reese, Baker High School, Baker City, Oregon 1947

Grover Parvin Reese, Baker High School, Baker City, Oregon 1950

scholarship money to both Linfield College and the University of Oregon, but she was suffering from measles the day she graduated high school and was so exhausted that she had no desire to go to college. Off she went anyway, in September, to the University of Oregon, majoring in journalism after her mother begged her to try it for a year.[368]

By now Geraldine and Patricia were Geri and Pat to most, but still Deanie and Tish to each other. They both lived in co-operatives at the University, and they both became engaged. Geri graduated with a degree in Business Administration in June of 1949 and then got married one week later on June 26 to Kenneth Pickett, whom she had met at the First Baptist Church in Eugene. Geri and Ken stayed in Eugene. Pat married her fiancé, Dan Adlum, later that summer in August at the First Christian Church in Baker City.

By this time their father was very frail. Pat was glad her father got to meet her fiancé, Dan. They bonded as they were both intellectual thinkers and shared an interest in politics. The Reeses were members of the Democratic Party and took civic duty seriously. Pat remembers that her father, who supported FDR in his first two terms, didn't vote for him for his third term simply because he thought no one should serve more than two terms. Other than that, her father strongly supported the values of the party. After their wedding Pat and Dan left for Richmond, California.

The two girls were married and gone. The following year, in June 1950, their brother, Grover Parvin Reese, graduated from Baker High, having just turned seventeen. He had signed up for the National Guard at sixteen. The Korean War started June 25, 1950. Grover scored high enough on the entrance exam to merit consideration for a scholarship to the Naval Academy at Annapolis, Maryland, but the Army would not let him out of his commitment. He served in the Army Airborne as a paratrooper in the Korean War.

Three months after Grover Jr. graduated from high school, the Reese children's formidable grandmother Grace Williams Reese died in Baker City on September 11, 1950. Grace had owned several businesses, including a hamburger place near Baker High School. She was a charter member of the Burns Order of Eastern Star, the female Masonic society, and received her fifty-year pin in 1947. Proper etiquette and tradition were important to this no-nonsense lady, and she instructed her grandchildren in manners, duty, and dedication to hard work. After her funeral, which was conducted by members of her Eastern Star Society, her ashes were buried next to her father, Hyrum, in Ontario, Oregon.[369]

Just three weeks later, at age 62, on October 3, 1950, Grace's son, Grover, died of heart failure in Baker City, causing his family great sadness. Dorothy became a widow at age forty-eight. Her kind, hard-working husband was gone, and her house was empty. Grover Williams Reese was buried in Baker City on October 5, 1950, at the Mt. Hope Cemetery. Rev. Joe Jewett, who had performed the marriage ceremony of Grover's daughter Patricia just the year before, officiated at the funeral.

Dorothy was a stoic, positive person whose motto was to "just make the best of things." She turned her sadness into work. She continued her teaching career, really enjoying her students and coworkers. Her teaching colleagues were an important part of her life, and she held several Thanksgivings at her house for her teaching friends. She loved to learn and was always ready for new experiences. She went on to receive her bachelor's degree from Eastern Oregon State College in 1956 and was noted several times for being an outstanding teacher in Baker City. She drew strength from her participation in her church, the First Christian Church of Baker City, Oregon..[370]

Dorothy's son, Grover, returned safely after the Korean War and married a girl from Indiana, Thelma Gulley. They made their life in Milan, Indiana, and raised their son, Paul, there. They were longtime members of the Lutheran church in Milan. Grover was a member of the AF & AM Masonic Lodge, a mason like his great grandfather Hyrum Williams, and was known for his community involvement in the American Legion, the Volunteer Fire Department, and the church.

Geri and Ken spent their lives in Eugene. Geri was secretary to the Dean of Education at the University of Oregon and then worked twenty-three years as the secretary of the English Department at Sheldon High School in Eugene. They had four children together—Ron, Judi, Bev, and Janet—whom they raised in the First Baptist Church where they were longtime, active members. Pat and Dan raised their three children in Southern California.

Wedding of Patricia Reese and Daniel B. Adlum, First Christian Church, Baker City, Oregon, August 21, 1949

Dorothy was the ideal grandmother to her grandchildren because she loved to have fun. She was always energetic and ready for action, had a yard filled with flowers, and a sparkling-clean house with fresh-baked cookies. In the summers when grandchildren made the long trek to Grandmother's house, whether from Eugene, Southern California, or Indiana, Dorothy always made it fun for them with tubing in Catherine Creek and picnics.

Later in life, when she retired from teaching in 1967, she had a chance to do some traveling. She traveled with the Montgomerys—her sister Florence and brother-in-law, Martin—on cruises and saw Hawaii and Alaska, among other places. She still loved gardening and entertaining, as well as studying pioneer history. She maintained her membership in the Retired Teachers Association and had an active interest in matters of education and public policy. In 1985, after one terrible eastern Oregon winter too many and being snowed in for weeks at a time, Dorothy sold the house she had lived for thirty-nine years and moved to a retirement home in Junction City, just north of Eugene. Even though she was older than many of the residents, as was typical of her spunky and youthful attitude, she thought "they were too old." When her health failed, she moved to a nursing home where she spent the remainder of her life, much loved by the staff for her sweet nature.

Dorothy Parvin Reese died on July 8, 1998, at the age of 96. All her siblings predeceased her; her sister Florence, the last, in 1994. Dorothy is buried in the Pleasant Hill Pioneer Cemetery. At her funeral on July 13 at the First Baptist Church of Eugene, one of her grandsons, Jeffrey Bruce Adlum, gave the following eulogy:

> We are here to remember Dorothy Parvin Reese, the woman whom all the forty-four years of my life I have called Grandma. We are here not for her sake, but for our own, so that we, the living, can take strength from remembrance – remembrance of the example this wonderful woman set through her long life, remembrance of her love, of her sweet unquenchable spirit. We are bereaved, yet relieved also, for her long wait at Eternity's gate is over at last. God had finally called her in. Hallelujah and Amen! Her long wait is finally past. Dorothy Reese is home at last.
>
> You youngsters should know this – with the wisdom of age comes bitterness as well, the bitterness of loss, of dreams dead and stillborn. What made my grandmother truly great was that regardless of loss, of sorrow and despair, she simply refused to drink from the cup of bitterness. She wasn't having any. She was a rock in every storm of life, and from the rock flowed a sweet stream of love, patience, forgiveness, and common sense that nourished us all.
>
> We can no longer look to her for strength, for reassurance, as we have done throughout our lives, but we can take strength from the example she set for all of us. When anger and frustration well up in us, how patient should we be? As patient as Grandma. How much love should we have for our family and friends? As much as Grandma had for all of us – a sweet, unconditional love, undiminished by age and disappointment. How long should we endure life's vicissitudes and sorrow? As long as she did, if we have the strength.
>
> Goodbye, Dorothy Parvin Reese, and Godspeed. You have shown us what it is like to live faithfully, to age courageously, and to die at peace with yourself. We are the fruit of your loins, the blood of your blood, and we'll never forget you."[371]

Chapter Nine
Still Restless After All These Years

Family Cast of Characters

Daniel Bruce Adlum…(1921-1977) *author's father*
Patricia Reese Adlum…(1929-present) *author's mother*
Pamela Adlum Vigil…(1953-present) *eldest daughter of Daniel and Patricia*
Jeffrey Bruce Adlum…(1954-present) *son of Daniel and Patricia*
Ellen Suzanne Adlum Pavlosek…(1965- present) *daughter of Daniel and Patricia*

Dr. Rodney D. Schmidt…(1952-present) *husband of Pamela Adlum, 1979-2001*
Joseph C. Vigil Jr.…(1956-present) *husband of Pamela Adlum, 2008-present*

Dr. Libor G. Pavlosek…(1968-present) *husband of Ellen S. Adlum, 1998-present*
Julia Suzanne Pavlosek…(2002-present) *daughter of Ellen and Libor*
Daniel George Pavlosek…(2004-present) *son of Ellen and Libor*

Kristin Paige Schmidt (Kadar)…(1981-present) *eldest daughter of Pamela and Rodney*
Nikolay M. Kadar…(2012-present) *son of Kristin, great-grandson of Daniel and Patricia*
Augustine Gray Decatur…(2017-present) *daughter of Kristin, great-granddaughter of Daniel and Patricia*

Katherine Karissa-Michelle Schmidt (Sasser)…(1988-present) *daughter of Pamela and Rodney*
Samuel Harris Sasser…(2020) *son of Katherine, great-grandson of Daniel and Patricia*

The Adlum Family

Curiosity is, in great and generous minds, the first passion and the last.

-William Samuel Johnson

My parents were married on a Sunday morning before church in my mother's hometown of Baker City, Oregon, on August 21, 1949. It was a beautiful, joyful ceremony; the worst mishap was the dropping of the ring by the ring bearer. The ring rolled merrily towards a grate in the floor before being rescued by the bride's mother. After a honeymoon that included Crater Lake and the California Redwoods, they proceeded to the San Francisco Bay area. My father was headed to graduate school at the University of California at Berkley, while my mother took a job to support them as secretary and bookkeeper for the CEO of Cyclone Fence.

In 1952 they set out for Los Angeles, along with thousands of other new residents. There was tremendous competition for teaching jobs in Los Angeles as former GIs poured out of college—my father got one of two available positions out of 500 applicants.

They were soon to be a family of three. I was born January 11, 1953, when Los Angeles was growing so rapidly that there was a waiting list for a telephone. My father had to send a telegram to his mother, Winifred, in Portland, as well as to his mother-in-law, Dorothy, to tell them that their first grandchild had been born. He had to do the same thing fourteen months later when my brother, Jeffrey Bruce, was born on March 11, 1954. They were still on the waiting list for a phone.

Los Angeles in the 1950s, '60s and early '70s seemed like the center of the universe. It *was* the center of popular culture, modern trends, and explosive population growth. Like his grandfather Will Turner, who had gone to Los Angeles during a real estate boom in the 1890s, and his father, Henry Bruce Adlum, who arrived during the 1920s' oil and movie industry boom, my father moved to L.A. as it was growing into a city of major importance. Writer Carey McWilliams, who was the longtime editor of *The Nation*, called the growth of L.A., "one continuous boom punctuated at intervals by major explosions." The post-war atmosphere in Los Angeles was that of a place where anything could—and did—get done.

In 1950 the population of Los Angeles was 1,970,358, making it the fourth-largest city in the nation. Los Angeles was a magical place in the '50s; with roots in agriculture, oil, and tourism, it expanded its major industries in large part due to the money the Federal government put into the area during World War II. Major aerospace companies were established during the war. Lockheed, Hughes, Teledyne, Rocketdyne, and Litton built factories in the San Fernando Valley—north of downtown—bringing engineers flooding in from all areas of the country to work. The television industry started in the 1950s in L.A., and along with the well-established movie industry, added even more jobs. Agriculture was still very strong, as was oil.

Although my father was born in Los Angeles, most residents were transplants. As my mother explained it, California was where forward-thinking people went when they didn't fit in at home. It was the land of great opportunity and dreams come true.[372]

When my parents moved to the San Fernando Valley in 1952, there were still orange and lemon groves, avocado orchards, and horse ranches, for which the area was famous. From 1910 until 1955, Los Angeles County had the largest agricultural output in the country. Real estate speculation changed that. Cheap land was rapidly bought up by real estate developers who filled the valley with ranch-style, one-story tract homes and pleasant neighborhoods for the new residents. Veterans were able to buy homes using the GI bill for help financing the mortgages.

Providing for public schools and universities became an important goal. The University of California at Los Angeles grew into an enviable institution. There was considerable effort to make the Los Angeles school system the best in the world. By 1959 twelve new elementary schools had opened up in the Valley, serving some 165,000 new students. There was also a push for a freeway system in Los Angeles, along with an excellent grid of surface streets. L.A. had the best civil engineers in the world and designed an incredible system that worked well until it became overwhelmed with too many cars.

Los Angeles also had an extensive rail system for years which included the "red car trolleys" that one could travel around town on. The rail line faded—the last of the trolleys was taken out of service in 1962—and L.A., all 470 square miles of it, became the city of the automobile. The Valley became "America's Suburb," where there was proof that the growing middle class could have a good life. Los Angeles was the most prosperous city in the most prosperous state in the most prosperous time the world had ever seen.[373]

In the 1890s, when Los Angeles was promoted for tourism and as a healthy place to live, it was advertised as a romantic place with a Mediterranean lifestyle, complete with Spanish and Italian architecture. Venice, Italy, was recreated, complete with canals, in one area of Los Angeles. Venice Beach is one of the more iconic sites in L.A. now. Fantasy and creativity were emphasized, leading to the creation of major art museums and entertainment parks. Oil magnate J. Paul Getty opened his first museum full of art treasures in Pacific Palisades in 1954. Today, the Getty Museum has grown into one of the richest in the world. Walt Disney built Disneyland just south of Los Angeles in Anaheim, and it opened to great fanfare in 1955. We were early visitors of this fabulous fantasyland, as well as Knotts Berry Farm when it opened nearby. Universal Studios Theme Park opened nine years later.

Los Angeles was full of ingenious, fanciful architecture in the Modernism style. Angelinos used innovative architecture to theatrical affect. The iconic Capitol Records Building in West Los Angeles, with its distinctive circular shape, echoes a stack of records. Custom homes such as Silvertop, in Silverlake, designed by John Lautner, and houses by Charles Eames, as well as Richard Neutra, sprinkled the urban landscape. My brother and I walked by the Von Sternberg House, designed for the movie producer Von Sternberg by Richard Neutra, on Tampa Blvd. in Northridge every day in junior high school on our way to and from school. The distinctive modern house made of steel, concrete, and glass had a dramatic, curved garden wall and was almost completely surrounded by a moat.[374]

In 1958 the Brooklyn Dodgers abandoned Brooklyn and came to L.A.. When they built Dodger Stadium in Chavez Ravine, my father took us to baseball games there to see the Dodgers play. There were endless cultural and social opportunities, as well as beautiful beaches and the famous Santa Monica Pier to visit. My brother and I learned to swim in the swimming pools at the local city parks and had an ideal suburban childhood. We spent the day outside, riding our bikes and creating elaborate games. We were never concerned for our safety and seldom locked the door.[375]

My parents were serious, hard-working people, but they believed in fun as well. They loved the outdoors and frequently took us on hikes and picnics and to visit Griffith Park, where we took horseback rides through the park and toured the observatory.

We had a black-and-white console TV set and a cat named Skipper who could turn the TV on and off with the push button. No remote control then. One of the favorite TV shows at the time was "Leave It to Beaver," with Jerry Mathers playing Beaver. Living in L.A., one could count on seeing the occasional movie star or movie sets. We once had a scene for a TV show filmed on our street. We were able to meet Beaver—Jerry Mathers— because his dad was a high school-principal friend of my father's.

Both my parents were handy and capable. When Mattel, which was based in Los Angeles, came out with the Barbie doll in 1959, of course I got one. My mother sewed many clothes for the doll, as well as my other dolls, in addition to making me a poodle skirt—the essential item for girls in the '50s—and all the curtains in the house. She and her sister, Deanie, learned to sew as children. My father was handy with construction and repairs.

My parents became members of the Congregational Church of Northridge, part of the United Church of Christ, and played an active role. Although my father had been raised in the Episcopal Church, he preferred the intellectualism of the church of some of his Puritan ancestors. Despite his busy life, my father was looking for new frontiers to conquer and ways to enrich his family's experiences.

He found a new challenge in a small company town called Westwood in the forests of Lassen County, California, that he and a friend had heard about. Westwood was a quaint lumber town established in 1913 by the Red River Lumber Company about 550 miles northeast of Los Angeles. About 110 miles northwest of Reno, Nevada, and at 5,128 feet elevation, Westwood was surrounded by hundreds of thousands of acres of forests, lakes, rivers and streams. The town was built on the distinctive, reddish-brown soil of a lava flow from the southern end of the Cascade Mountain Range. Mount Lassen, the largest plug dome volcano in the world, is about forty-five miles northwest of the town in Lassen Volcanic National Park. The mountain, county, and park are all named for the Danish-born fur trapper and early California explorer, Peter Lassen. The county seat of Lassen County is Susanville, a little over twenty miles from Westwood.

Two of the prettiest lakes in the basin between the southern end of the Cascades and the Sierra Nevadas are Lake Almanor, fifteen miles to the west of town, and Eagle Lake, some fifty-three miles north. Eagle Lake is the second largest natural lake in California with over one hundred miles of shoreline. It was known for its eagles and osprey, as well as its indigenous, large rainbow trout.

The town of Westwood depended on the lumber company for growth, and it was very successful for a number of years. In 1942 the lumber company hit the world record for number of board feet sawed. They advertised the town with a huge Paul Bunyan statue with an accompanying statue of Babe the Blue Ox. Even though the timber industry slowed down, they were still having lumber jack contests in the 1950s.

In 1944 the town was sold to the Fruit Growers Company—sister cooperative of Sunkist—and they operated a plant there until 1956. By 1958 the town had seen better days and real estate was very cheap. The company that owned the town planned to sell it off. My father bought a very inexpensive, sadly neglected, wood-frame house that backed up to fir and pine forests and decided the family project would be a "fixer-upper," a summer house in the woods.[376]

In the summer of '58, our family of four piled into our Ford sedan, with its wide bench backseat that would send my brother and me sliding when Dad turned a corner and drove the long way up the interior of California to Lassen County. When we saw our house in Westwood, it was not a pretty sight with its broken windows, peeling paint, a sagging porch, and a yard full of weeds and beer cans. Nevertheless, it was very exciting to my brother and me. We slept on cots and were amazed at the old wringer washer in the kitchen. We had never seen one before. We helped squeeze the wet clothes through the wringer before hanging them on a clothesline. I am sure our mother was less than amazed by the washer or the old wood-burning stove.

Our parents worked on the house all summer while my brother and I delighted in being small town kids who could walk to the five-and-dime. We relished going to see movies in the old-timey movie theatre. Jeff and I had pinecone wars in the woods with the neighborhood kids and spent many happy hours at the nearby lakes. Our entertainment at night was the record player; we listened while my dad played his 78-rpm records of classical music and Dixieland jazz.

We spent five summers in Westwood, having the best of both worlds: the city during the school year and the country in the summer. Meanwhile, our mother went back to school to finish her degree. Although her first love was journalism, she decided education was a better fit for her with young children. She received her Bachelor's Degree in Elementary Education from San Fernando Valley State College, now California State University, Northridge, and began to teach first grade in 1963. Mom was a reading specialist and brought home the most delightful children's books. The result of this was that she made me and my brother and, later, our sister, all bookaholics. We just could not stop reading and would often sneak books under the covers at night. In desperation my mom would sometimes hide books in the laundry basket under the dirty clothes in her many unsuccessful attempts to stop us from constantly reading.

My father's active and curious mind thought up a new adventure for the family in 1963. He had the restless energy and "go-ahead" spirit of his pioneer ancestors. He decided to take a sabbatical from his job as a history professor and take us all to Europe for the school year. He combined his desire to learn and explore new horizons with his desire to be the best teacher he could be by studying Western Civilization in the countries of origin. On sabbatical he only received fifty percent of his normal pay and affording travel in Europe for nine months was a challenge. My father met that challenge by meticulous planning and budgeting. He and Mom sold the house in Westwood and rented out our house on Gothic Avenue in the San Fernando Valley for nine months. We put our belongings in the attic. Our dog, a beagle named Dixie—after my dad's love of Dixieland jazz—was given to friends who took great care of him. Surprisingly, school officials gave my parents no trouble about us missing a year of school. My brother, Jeff, had already skipped third grade due to the realization by both my parents and the school that, otherwise, he would be bored, and they advanced him to fourth grade. (From then on we were in the same grade each year.) The principal of our school figured that, by travelling through Europe with teacher parents, we would learn more than staying in school that year. And we did.

My brother, Jeff, was nine and I was ten when our family flew to New York on TWA in August 1963. It was my first time on an airplane. What an adventure for this shy girl. We boarded the *Nieuw Amsterdam*, a ship of the Holland-American line, and crossed the Atlantic in six days. After getting our sea legs, my brother and I wandered all over the ship, including the bridge. The feeling of being on a ship on the ocean, so close to nature, is almost a spiritual experience. I have loved ships and boats ever since. We docked at Southampton, England, and took the train to London, where my father picked up a car he had arranged to buy while we were in California. It was a Helman Minx, a little white sedan with a red interior and *no* radio. For years afterwards we asked our dad why he did not buy a car with a radio in it. Although it was an English car, which would normally have the steering wheel on the right—since the British drive on the *wrong* side of the road—it was made for export, so the steering wheel was on the left, making it even more challenging for my dad to drive in the British Isles. There were a few close calls, but we survived to tell the tales. Once we took the ferry across to the "Continent," it was easier driving.

The next nine months were filled with castles, cathedrals, and art museums. Europe was not crowded like it is now. There were very few tourists, especially, in the off season. We saw ten-plus countries: England, Wales, Scotland, Belgium, the Netherlands, Germany, Austria, Italy, Spain, France, and the tiny principalities of Monaco and Liechtenstein, spending the most time in England, Germany, and Spain. We even went briefly to Morocco in North Africa. Through my father's network of professor friends, he arranged to rent a house in Bavaria, Germany. It was in a little town called Seeshaupt, just thirty miles from Munich. The house we rented backed up to the Starnberger See, where Mad King Ludwig—of Neuschwanstein Castle fame—allegedly drowned by his own hand . . . or someone else's.

Our house—half a house, really; it was a duplex—had its own name: *Haus Furst*. Jeff and I learned a little German, at least enough to count to ten and be able to order at the bakery there. The village was charming and friendly, with red roofs everywhere. The local church was built in the eighteenth century in the Rococo style. We made friends with some German children. Children are the same everywhere and can communicate without language. Our house had intricately carved, dark-wood, interior doorways. The original owner had copied the work of the late Gothic (1460) woodworking German artist Tilman Riemenschneider, whose work is in the Bavarian National Museum in Munich. The doorways were amazing—as was the curtained shower, which was just a shower head hanging from the ceiling and a drain in the floor in the middle of the kitchen.

October is beautiful in Bavaria, and we enjoyed every minute of it. In our backyard was the smooth-as-glass *see* (lake) with many swans, some of whom were aggressive and had us on the run once or twice. We had to watch our fingers.

After seeing as much of Germany as we could, including the shocking and sober sight of the concentration camp at Dachau, we headed to Vienna in late November. On November 22, 1963, we were staying in a small *pensionne* (guest house) in Vienna when we heard the news that President Kennedy had been assassinated. My father spoke a little German and French but not enough to get a full understanding of what had happened.

The next morning, he rushed out to the newsstand to get the *London Times* so he could read the story in English. The realization that something so terrible had happened while we were out of the country stunned all of us. Our gracious landlady let us watch JFK's funeral on her small TV in her tiny living room. She was very kind to us and the two other Americans who were staying there. Our family was profoundly saddened by the news.

By Christmas we were in Nice, France, and New Year's was spent at a beach resort on Spain's Costa Brava. Spain's Costa Brava—wild coast—is in Catalonia, an autonomous region on the northeastern coast of Spain that includes the city of Barcelona. We followed the local custom of trying to eat twelve grapes in the time it takes a clock to strike the last twelve seconds to midnight, ringing in the New Year. If one manages to swallow all twelve grapes, it insures good luck for every month of the New Year. Too late, I discovered the grapes all had seeds, and I didn't quite get them all down.

The coast is hauntingly beautiful there with rugged, pink clifftops and a variety of beaches ranging from wide expanses of sand to smuggler's coves. Jeff and I discovered fortifications from WWII on the beach near the hotel.

After the Costa Brava and the unique city of Barcelona, my father drove us on to the Costa del Sol in Andalusia to the province of Malaga. Malaga was an ancient city dating from Phoenician and Carthaginian times. The dominant landmark was the tenth-century Moorish fortress built by Abd al-Rahman III. The area surrounding Malaga, with the small fishing villages of Torremolinos and Fuengirola, was just opening up to tourism. Torremolinos, with its proximity to Malaga and its six beaches, was the first to be frequented by tourists.

In the early 1960s Spain was still under the grip of fascist dictator Francisco Franco. His infamous Civil Guards were very visible around the country. One day a very serious-looking guard, dressed in his uniform with heavy gray overcoat and carrying his rifle in his hands, motioned my father off the road and indicated he should stop, which alarmed us. It turned out he just wanted a ride, indicated by sign language since we did not speak Spanish. When he got into the back seat of our little English car, he took up more than half the seat. I was so frightened sitting next to him and his rifle that I practically pushed my brother out the other door.

My parents rented an apartment in a building called the Weltring in Torremolinos. It was a modern building, about five to six stories high, which backed up to the foothills behind the town. Later, Jeff and I would discover gypsies in the hills behind our apartment. My parents decided to stay a couple of months here to explore Spain. They found a private school in the town of Fuengirola, about ten miles away, called *The American School*, and they enrolled us for a couple of months. The school was very small but there were a few kids who spoke English: Jose and his sister from Cuba, Eddie, one very unhappy kid with American and Arab parentage, a couple of very bossy English girls, and a couple of others in our class. There were also about twenty-eight Spanish students in the school. We loved our teacher, Miss Brown, a young Englishwoman who had a Spanish boyfriend as well as a young daughter, Fina. Miss Brown and her daughter took the train with us every morning from Torremolinos, where we all lived, to Fuengirola to the school and back in the afternoon. The train was a green-colored, narrow-gauge, diesel train called Tren-Feve and it ran from Malaga to Fuengirola. It was very slow, incredibly crowded, and dirty, packed with workers taking their produce or animals on the train with them. Chickens and other fowl on the train were an everyday occurrence, as well as the old Spanish men smoking their hand-rolled cigarettes with the windows rolled up.

My brother and I loved the school. We had an amazing amount of freedom, including the ability to wander around town during the two-hour siesta break. The train tracks were right behind the school, and there was an empty field next door where local residents tied up their livestock. One harrowing day a pig got loose and fell asleep on the tracks. We spent our energy that afternoon shouting at and poking the pig in an attempt to get him off the tracks—just in time. We learned a great deal about life in that small fishing town and how desperate life was for these poor villagers if they lost an animal. And thanks to Miss Brown we learned an incredible amount of geography, far surpassing what kids at home had learned.

Gypsies had a significant presence in Andalusia, beginning in about 1425 when it was still under Arab rule. They probably migrated from India and brought their dance and music, history of trading at fairs, and sorcery to the area. They were always pushed to the periphery of society and mostly disapproved of. We noticed whenever they showed up the local residents chased them away. The gypsies were a closed society and had a reputation for theft. Once, we saw what appeared to be an entire Gypsy kingdom caravan moving down the main street of Torremolinos in French Citrons, one after another, with about 500 people in all. It was the most astonishing sight my brother and I had ever seen.

We were startled to discover gypsies up close when we went exploring in the foothills behind our apartment. There were a number of family groups camping out and cooking on wood fires. They were using the many caves as homes. To see people living in caves under such primitive conditions was a sobering sight for a girl who had grown up in a pristine L.A. suburb. An even sadder sight was that of lepers begging on the streets of Tangiers, Morocco.

Haus Furst, Seeshaupt, Bavaria, Germany, October 1963

Jeffrey Bruce Adlum and snake charmer, the Casbah, Tangiers, Morocco, 1964

Patricia Reese Adlum and son Jeffrey abroad the S. S. France, Spring 1964, photos collection of Patricia Reese Adlum

Author and her father Daniel B. Adlum, Caernarvon Castle, Wales, 1964

As we travelled on through Europe, we saw beautiful Italy, filled with spectacular scenery and art everywhere. I turned eleven and my brother Jeff ten on the trip. We have distinct memories of the incredible art we saw at that age. We followed our parents' lead. Since they were so interested and curious, we were as well. We spent hour after hour in the Prado in Madrid, the Louvre and other museums in Paris, the Uffizi Gallery in Florence, and the British Museum in London. Not only was my father gathering information for his class on Western Civilization, he was teaching his children about the history of the West at the same time. At the time, we just assumed our parents would always be capable under extraordinary circumstances, but now I realize we were incredibly lucky to have such an experience. It changed our lives and viewpoints, expanded our view of humanity, and let us see that all people in different cultures wish for the same things.

We headed home in late spring 1964 on the great ocean liner S.S. *France*. Only two years old, it was the epitome of nautical prestige and the fastest ocean liner on the water, with an Atlantic crossing taking only five days. It was said to have the finest French dining room in the world. To sail into New York Harbor on that magnificent ship and to see the Statue of Liberty was an unforgettable experience. Jeff and I had smuggled aboard the many Penguin children's books we had bought in London and read throughout the trip because we could not part with them, even though our parents told us to leave them behind to save space. Seeing we were determined to take the books; our parents just gave up with a smile.

After my mother, brother, and I crossed the country by Greyhound bus, we spent a month in Laguna Beach just south of Los Angeles, waiting for our renters to leave our house. My father joined us after waiting in New York for his car to be delivered. He had shipped his little English car back to the States and drove it for years.

The '60s that began in earnest in 1963 after the death of President Kennedy, were an exhilarating but exhausting decade. Cultural change began with dramatically different fashion, customs, and music. The British Invasion in music started. While we were in London in February 1964, the Beatles were in L.A., making their first appearance on the Ed Sullivan show. In addition to the British groups, the sounds of Motown went nationwide. California surf rock began to be very popular, and L.A. became the center of a great deal of popular music. The music was happy and fun for the most part and helped divert listeners from the current issues. Music was a big part of the '60s and a big part of our family life. My first record was the complete "Nutcracker Suite" by Tchaikovsky, given to me by my father. I continued to love classical music and sang in choir in school and at church. The first record I bought for myself was "I Want to Hold Your Hand" by the Beatles. Group after group in the '60s put out wonderful music. My brother, Jeff, loved Creedence Clearwater Revival, with their many songs centered on California. Anyone who has ever been to Lodi, California, would completely understand their song "Stuck in Lodi Again." Music helped us make it through the decade.

Problems in society started to bubble up, and in many cases, explode. Los Angeles had more than 500,000 additional residents by 1960 and a big smog problem. The Valley of Smoke, as the Native Americans had called Los Angeles, began to have unhealthy air the majority of the time, caused by automobiles, industry, and backyard incinerators. Surrounded by mountains, the inversion factor of the L.A. basin had to be dealt with. The environmental movement took flight, and great effort was made to limit smog, both on national and local levels. In 1962 Rachel Carson came out with her book *Silent Spring* about the danger from pesticides, and people realized they had to change their behavior, or they would destroy what had been built. My father was an environmentalist who became a member of the Sierra Club. He worked very hard to support open space and parks in the rapidly growing city by serving as the head of the Open Space and Parks Division of a citizen advisory organization, Destination Ninety. He learned so much about the field that he began teaching an environmental science class at Pierce College in addition to teaching history.[377]

Racial tensions started to show as well. In 1960 the majority of the population of Los Angeles was white and Protestant, with pockets of Jewish, some Hispanic and Asian residents—and a small, black population which began to grow. The black population increased from 500,000 to 1,500,000, mostly in South Central L.A. As the immigration quota system was changed in the '60s to allow more Asians in, the Asian population also began to rapidly grow. The Hispanic population dramatically increased as well. Los Angeles was a city of neighborhoods and ethnic populations that tended to stick together. The problem came when minorities tried to move out of those areas: housing discrimination, as well as other discrimination, caused tension.

The Civil Rights Movement was gaining prominence and was a major topic of discussion in our house. President Johnson had successfully pushed the Civil Rights Act through Congress in 1964, outlawing segregation, but there was great resistance, especially in the South. When about 600 civil rights leaders marched from Selma to Montgomery, Alabama, on March 7, 1965—a day which would become known as "Bloody Sunday"—and were severely beaten by law enforcement, the nation began to realize what a huge problem this was. Television brought the horror home to us.[378]

At the same time, activists in the farming communities in California were organizing for better working conditions for the workers. Filipino and Mexican American workers picked most of the grape crop in California, which was the supplier of the majority of the nation's grapes. The Filipino workers called a strike, followed by the United Farm Workers organized by Cesar Chavez and others in Delano, California, and called for a boycott of grapes. It took five years, but they were successful. My parents were in full support and we did not eat grapes during that time. Later in 1965, on August 11, the Watts Riots broke out in South Central Los Angeles after police pulled over a black man on suspicion of driving under the influence. The long simmering tensions between the police and the black community exploded. The riots, which lasted six days, were responsible for 34 deaths, 1,000 injuries, and over $40 million of property damage. The neighborhood went up in flames because the firemen could not get police protection as they tried to put out the fires. As California goes, so goes the nation, and Watts was followed by riots in major urban areas across the country over the next few years.[379]

Two weeks after the Watts Riots started, we had a new addition to our family. My sister Ellen Suzanne was born on August 26, 1965. The whole family was delighted. My parents had wanted another child for a long time. They moved to a bigger house in the Porter Ranch section of Northridge in the Valley. Porter Ranch, at the edge of the foothills of the Santa Susanna Mountains, was sold for development in 1962 and developed quickly. We had a brand-new house, a new sister, and a new puppy. My brother and I had read a book called *Greyfriars Bobby* about a Skye terrier in Scotland who had stayed on his owner's grave after he died. It was such a touching story that we decided we needed a Skye terrier. My dad found a Cairn terrier, a similar breed, and we named him Rob Roy after the Scottish bandit turned folk hero.

As soon as my sister was a little bigger, my parents started taking us camping to the great scenic spots in California. We went to Yosemite, Sequoia, Kings Canyon, Big Sur—as many national and state parks as my dad could get to—and always to the beach. The beaches in California are a joy because they are all different and all accessible. Whether it was La Jolla, Newport, Malibu, Pismo, or Carmel, there was no end of beaches to go to. Our favorite and closest beach was Zuma in Malibu, just thirty miles over Topanga Canyon to the wide expanse of beach on the Pacific Coast Highway. Nothing could have been better than being a California girl and listening to the Beach Boys sing about "California Girls" and the beaches I grew up with.

Politics in the '60s became a major focus for society because of all the dramatic events that were happening: Vietnam, civil rights, and women's rights. My parents always had an interest in civics and politics. They felt it was their duty as citizens. My earliest political memory was being on my dad's shoulders in 1959 at an Adlai Stevenson rally. We went on to support JFK when he won the Democratic nomination. When the Vietnam War came into focus in our living rooms on the nightly news, it caused anxiety for all. Our house was an intellectual house filled with books and a sense of purpose. My parents believed in a society that provides good schools for all, open space and parks, libraries, and laws that make a society work the best for most citizens. When we grew up, we were surprised to hear that most other families did not spend the dinner hour discussing current events. Because we were raised as idealists, sometimes, we were innocent about the world.

Nineteen sixty-eight was a year that really opened our eyes. I was fifteen and had a regular job cleaning house and babysitting for one of our neighbors and was on the job when I heard the shocking news that Martin Luther King Jr. had been assassinated on April 4, 1968. It was such a sad setback to civil rights and race relations. I was following the primaries for the Democratic nomination that year. I stayed up to watch Robert Kennedy's speech after he won the California primary and was very pleased. I had a quote from him on the wall of my bedroom and felt he would make a good president. I set my clock radio to wake me for school and went to bed. At 6 a.m. on the morning of June 5th, the radio woke me up to the news he had been assassinated as well. It was another devastating event in a tumultuous year. There were student protests about Vietnam, riots after MLK's assassination, and terrible violence in Chicago at the Democratic National Convention with Mayor Daley's very rough police forces fighting student protestors. Everyone was polarized. Hawks vs. doves, hippies vs. the establishment; society could not decide which way to go. Humphrey won the nomination, but Nixon won the presidency in a very close race.

Although there was polarization in society, there was not in our family. We had good parents who tried hard and provided a stable atmosphere. We always ate dinner together and my mom almost always cooked a full, well-balanced meal. We rarely went out to eat, just occasional trips to Mama Lucia's or The Pit BBQ, a casual place with sawdust on the floor. We always had breakfast, and from the time I can remember, we always read *The Los Angeles Times* every morning. My mother was a wonderful homemaker and hostess. Every year at Christmas she made gingerbread men that she decorated and hung on wide green ribbons in the kitchen. We always had a real Christmas tree and it was always a fir. My father would spend time making a delightful snow scene under the tree, complete with skating rink, while he played Christmas music. His favorite Christmas hymn was "O Holy Night," which I can't hear now without thinking of him. Our only family in California was my dad's cousin Patty and her husband, Ralph Holland and their three children, Lené, Kenny, and Patricia. They lived in Thousand Oaks, about thirty miles north of where we lived in L.A. We enjoyed many holidays with them. My father and Patty were close, more like sister and brother than cousins.

The Adlum Family, Northridge, California 1968, author's collection

In the summers my dad would drive us over the Fort Tejon Pass, the mountain pass that separated the Los Angeles Basin from the Central Valley on our long way north to Oregon. The long, steep grade was called the "the grapevine" and left many cars and trucks of the '50s and '60s stuck on the side of the road with overheated radiators in the summer. We then drove through the summer heat of the Central Valley, up through Nevada to eastern Oregon, to see our grandmother Dorothy in Baker City and cousins in Eugene. None of our other grandparents were alive, and Dorothy was special to us. Society seemed to be changing so fast and our grandmother's steady, calm nature was a comfort.

The summer of '69, when our sister, Ellen, was four, we took a major trip—some camping and some staying with family. We headed up the east side of the Sierras to our grandmother's, then over to Portland to see our Aunt Helen, to Eugene to see family, and then down the Oregon and California coasts. Near San Francisco we saw many flower children—"hippies"—hitchhiking, as well as in the VW buses the movement made famous. It was two years after the "summer of love" in San Francisco and the height of the hippie movement.

There seemed to always be something drastic happening on the news. In 1969 the civil war in Nigeria was raging, and the Nigerian separatists in Biafra were starving. We saw photo after photo of starving African children. When I heard about an organization to help the children, I signed up. They organized what was called "a walk for hunger." Sponsors paid participants a certain amount per mile to walk for a maximum of thirty miles. I had never walked even close to thirty miles in a day, but I gave a speech in front of my church congregation and sponsors signed up. My brother received sponsors as well, and we both walked the entire thirty miles. I could not walk afterwards, however, because my feet swelled up and my brother had to help me get into the car.

Jeff and I went to a very large high school, Chatsworth High, in northwest San Fernando Valley. When we graduated in 1971, there were 1,100 in our graduating class. During our senior year, on February 9, 1971, at 6 a.m., there was a tremendous earthquake (6.6), centered in Sylmar, twelve miles to the east of us. It was terrifying to see the room sway and things fall off shelves and break. Gas and sewer lines ruptured, water lines broke, freeway overpasses collapsed, and windows shattered. The San Fernando Veteran's Hospital was destroyed, killing forty-four in the building. Many other hospitals and buildings were damaged as well. All told there were 64 deaths, 2,500 injured and about $550 million of rubble created. We were lucky in that there was no major damage at our house other than the crumbling of the concrete bricks of the wall surrounding our yard. The aftershocks that occurred for days after the quake did more damage to our property. We had evacuated friends staying with us for days—we were without water—as the possibility that the lower and upper Van Norman dams would break and flood the homes of many neighborhoods necessitated an evacuation of large areas.[380]

Both my brother and I had jobs and hobbies in high school. I worked at a hamburger place making patty melts and endless fries. My brother worked for Ralph's Market. Ellen would get up early to eat Cheerios with Jeff before he went to work. Jeff was very active with his friends, fixing, riding, and racing motorcycles. He even raced the actor Steve McQueen in one dirt bike race. My main hobby was folk dancing. I ran around with an international crowd that met at a folk dancing place in Van Nuys called Zorba's. Jeff and I had both done roller skating, but our little sister, Ellen, beat us in ice skating. She loved ice skating, which neither one of her siblings could accomplish.

We lived in a very safe neighborhood, and Ellen had a best friend named Robbie whom she played with. One afternoon when Ellen decided she was thirsty, she and Robbie walked many blocks across a busy boulevard to get a Coca-Cola. They were both just six and everyone was frantically looking for them. That same year for Christmas, my father made Ellen a very special tree-stump house for all her stuffed animals. It was a memorable Christmas with Ellen having a part in the Christmas program and Jeff and I playing the parts of Joseph and Mary in the nativity scene.

My brother and I were active in our church youth group, while our mom took on a new role on the church finance committee. She was the first women to ever serve on the committee, at a time when women could not even have their own credit. Jeff and I went off to college when our sister was six. Ellen may have felt abandoned, but maybe, it was good to get all the attention for once! I left for San Diego State University to study nursing. My brother went to California State University, Northridge, to study economics. My parents' budget was tight with two kids in college at the same time, but they made it work. After we left for college, Ellen took many Saturday hikes with our father in the beautiful, natural canyon off Tampa Blvd. and Rinaldi Street near our house. This wild canyon with a stream, wildlife, and shaded hiking areas was one of the areas Dad was trying to preserve as open space for a future park through his work on Destination Ninety. Many years later, Ellen's former classmates are now taking their children for hikes in the canyon at Limekiln Canyon Park. The park that was established there has been an oasis for local residents.[381]

In 1974 tragedy stuck our family. My father became too ill to push the clutch down in his Helman Minx that he still drove to work every day. He had terminal cancer and was given only six months to live. I was living in West Los Angeles and working as a critical care nurse in a surgical intensive care unit at UCLA Medical Center. My brother, Jeff, was working for an antiques auction house. My sister, Ellen, was just eight years old when our father became so ill. She would go in and read to him after school and try to make him feel better while he was lying in bed. My mother was teaching but had to quit to take care of him.

Although my father was in a great deal of pain from the cancer that had spread to his bones, he was not a complainer. His optimistic attitude and love of life made him live every day to the fullest, even though he was in a wheelchair or in bed most of the time. His very strong will to live, and my mother's incredible care of him, allowed us to have him for three more years. She took care of him at home almost until the end, which amazed the doctors and nurses. When we finally had to put him in the hospital, we took turns staying with him. He died on March 28, 1977, just after his fifty-sixth birthday. My brother was at his side.[382]

My mother was now a widow at age forty-eight, just like her mother had been. She also had a young child still at home. Our family was very sad, and it took us a long time to recover from losing Dad. My mother was a tower of strength, but it was especially hard on her and my sister, who had a very different childhood from that of her older brother and sister. My mother kept the family together as only a strong matriarch can do. At the time, the Los Angeles city schools were working on integration, and they decided to send the teachers from the San Fernando Valley down to the inner-city schools. My mother worked at Second Street Elementary School in Los Angeles for a number of years, which necessitated a very long freeway commute. The majority of her students were immigrants, mostly Spanish speaking, but there were some Asian and Samoan students as well. She had a talent for identifying gifted kids, whether or not they could speak English, and spent time on home visits to help her students. She was the teachers' union rep for the school and started to become a leader in her own right.

I married in 1979 and gave her a first grandchild in 1981. I moved to Texas in 1982, and my brother moved to San Luis Obispo, California, in 1986. My sister, Ellen, graduated from Granada Hills High School in 1983. After she graduated from Cal Poly University in San Luis Obispo with a degree in Landscape Architecture, she moved to Seattle. The love and encouragement from our mother kept us all connected, even from afar.

My mother retired from teaching in 1991, and in 1992 moved back to Oregon to be near her mother, Dorothy, who died in 1998. In retirement my mother, Patricia, is active, with two book groups and the Newcomers Group, which she has stayed affiliated with for years after serving as president of the group. She is a member of the Congregational Church in Eugene. She loves art, especially, Asian Art, and worked as a docent at the Jordan Schnitzer Museum of Art at the University of Oregon. At age ninety she has kept her mind sharp, constantly reading about current events

Patricia Reese Adlum, September 15, 2019, Eugene, Oregon, Age 90.

and always having a new stack of library books at her house. Like the journalist she always wanted to be, my mother looks at events with a "who, what, when, where, and why" analysis. If you want to discuss politics or current events with her, you had better come with facts and well-thought-out, logical arguments. Her values have never wavered, and she can usually spot a dishonest person.

My mother loves nature, especially, having a picnic, which is one of her favorite things to do. She still supports the environmental causes that she and my father cared deeply about, as well as supporting her church. Her yard is filled with roses and perennial flowers; she has always loved flowers and flower arranging and has a collection of vases. If you are lucky enough to visit, there will always be a unique vase filled with roses in your room and other vases filled with flowers around the house. She is still a charming and gracious hostess. Her integrity and strong spirit have been an inspiration to her three children.

She and my father passed on their intellectual curiosity and their desire to see as much of the world as possible to their children, along with their faith and the values passed down through the generations. We value integrity, education, and good government and have an intense belief in working for good. We are a serious family, but one that loves travel, learning new things, and nature. We keep a very close eye on political affairs, not in a partisan way, but because we believe people's lives are too important to not guard our representative democracy. Our pioneer ancestors passed down the traits of self-reliance and individualism, as well as the importance of providing for the common good. They were optimists, with expectations of improving society and democracy, in addition to looking for economic opportunity.

The western movement across the country accelerated the move towards social democracy, even leading to approving women's suffrage in western states before states in the East. Historian Ray Billington stated. "The frontier set a high level of human expectation. It appealed to the restless, those men and women

The three children of Patricia Reese Adlum and Daniel B. Adlum, F-R, Ellen, Jeffrey, Pamela, Austin, Texas 1995 photo by Greer Evans

of action with a go-ahead spirit." My family still has that restless energy and belief in progress even though the frontier is long past. We are seekers, always looking to improve ourselves and the human condition.[383]

As I write this, 400 years since my family started their odyssey in America, we have continued our restless moves, but we have come full circle. Our mother, Patricia, is back in Eugene, the city of her birth, just a mile from her 92-year-old sister, Geraldine. They are both in their own homes and still very capable women. My brother, Jeff, is holding onto the Golden State, just two blocks away from his beloved Pacific Ocean in Shell (Pismo) Beach, California. My sister, Ellen, after living in Seattle, San Luis Obispo, the San Francisco Bay area, and Connecticut, moved with her family to a twenty-acre farm full of organic blueberry bushes in Pleasant Hill, Oregon, very close to her Parvin and Matthews ancestors' original homestead land. The Pleasant Hill Pioneer Cemetery, where four generations of Ellen's ancestors are buried, is just over the next hill. Her children, Julia and Daniel, have discovered that the place where the high school kids like to take homecoming pictures is none other than the Parvin Covered Bridge. My daughter Kristin and her family are in Stafford, Virginia, where her ancestors the Templemans got their start in America and are buried. My daughter, Kate, and her husband, Zach, live in Austin, Texas. Kate's cousins Bailey and Thomas Jones Hardeman—six generations ago—who were active in pioneering Texas, and responsible for naming the city Kate and Zach live in, are buried in the Texas State Cemetery just a few miles from their house. My husband, Joe, and I live in Round Rock, Texas, on Brushy Creek, within walking distance of the Chisolm Trail where some of my Hardeman ancestors splashed across Brushy Creek on horseback, driving cattle north some 150 years ago. Every once in a while, I close my eyes and imagine I am in Oregon and wish it were possible to live in two places at the same time. Yes, we are still a little restless, but we remain connected by love and history. We are an American family.

Pedigree Charts

Pedigree Chart for Daniel Bruce Adlum

Daniel Bruce Adlum
b: 31 Jan 1921 in El Monte, Los Angeles, California, USA
m: 17 Aug 1949 in Baker, Oregon, USA
d: 28 Mar 1977 in Los Angeles, Los Angeles, California, USA

- **Henry Bruce Adlum**
  b: 16 May 1889 in Iowa, USA
  m: 1911 in Multnomah, Oregon, USA
  d: 10 Feb 1955 in Los Angeles County, California, USA

  - **Daniel J. Adlum**
    b: 03 Feb 1860 in Altoona, Blair County, Pennsylvania, USA
    m: 19 Nov 1884 in Missouri Valley, Harrison County, Iowa, USA
    d: 14 Nov 1956 in Los Angeles County, California, USA

    - **Joseph Green Adlum**
      b: 09 Jul 1816 in Muncy, Lycoming County, Pennsylvania, USA
      m: Abt. 1846
      d: 13 Mar 1893 in Bellwood, Blair County, Pennsylvania, USA

    - **Evalyn Irwin**
      b: 31 Dec 1828 in Antis, Blair Co, Pennsylvania, USA
      d: 30 Oct 1908 in Fairview Cemetery, Altoona, Blair Co, Pennsylvania, USA

  - **Carrie A. McKain**
    b: 11 Dec 1863 in Springfield, Clark County, Ohio, USA
    d: 03 Jan 1956 in Los Angeles County,

    - **Henry B. McKain**
      b: 1818 in New Jersey
      m: Abt. 1857
      d: 19 Dec 1881 in Harrison County, Iowa, USA PROBABLE

    - **Lucy Mc Kain**
      b: Abt. 1832 in Pennsylvania
      d: Bef. 1930 in Nebraska

- **Winifred Beatrice Turner**
  b: 26 Aug 1890 in McMinnville, Yamhill County, Oregon, USA
  d: 02 Apr 1956 in Portland, Oregon, USA

  - **William B. Turner**
    b: 27 Jun 1860 in Vincennes, Knox, Indiana, United States
    m: 30 Jun 1881 in McMinnville, OR
    d: May 1924 in Sacramento, Sacramento, California, USA

    - **James H Turner**
      b: 21 Sep 1812 in ,Laffayette,Pennsylvania,USA
      m: 16 Sep 1852 in Granville,,Ohio,USA
      d: 01 Jan 1885 in Mcminnville,,Oregon,USA

    - **Esther Ann Johnson**
      b: 21 Feb 1825 in Dryden,,New York,USA
      d: 07 Nov 1910 in Portland,,Oregon,USA

  - **Mary Ellen Holman**
    b: 23 Oct 1856 in Polk Co. Oregon
    d: 29 Nov 1928 in Marshfield, Coos, Oregon, United States

    - **Daniel Sanders Holman**
      b: 15 Nov 1822 in Fayetteville, Lincoln County, Tennessee, United States of America
      m: 31 Dec 1847
      d: 15 Mar 1910 in McMinnville, Yamhill County, Oregon, USA

    - **Martha Elizabeth Burnett Holman**
      b: 11 Dec 1830 in Hardeman County, Tennessee, USA
      d: 27 Jun 1913 in McMinnville, Yamhill County, Oregon, USA

Pedigree Chart for Joseph Green Adlum

Joseph Green Adlum
b: 09 Jul 1816 in Muncy, Lycoming County, Pennsylvania, USA
m: Abt. 1846
d: 13 Mar 1893 in Bellwood, Blair County, Pennsylvania, USA

Joseph Adlum
b: 1767 in York Springs, York, Pennsylvania, United States
m: 07 Nov 1798 in Harford, Maryland, United States
d: 15 Jul 1846 in Muncy, Lycoming, Pennsylvania, United States

Anna McPhail
b: 1775 in Harford, Maryland, United States
d: 19 Apr 1851 in Muncy, Lycoming, Pennsylvania, United States

Joseph Adlum
b: 1732 in Ireland
m: 21 Jun 1758 in York Springs, York, Pennsylvania, United States
d: 1814 in Muncy, Lycoming, Pennsylvania, United States

Catherine Abbott
b: 1732 in Abbottstown, Adams County, Pennsylvania, USA
d: 1822 in Muncy Twp, Muncy, Pennsylvania, United States

John Adlum
b: 1701 in Ireland
m: 1724 in Ireland
d: 06 Dec 1773 in York, Pennsylvania, United States

Elizabeth Berwick
b: 1705 in Ireland
d: 21 Feb 1760 in York, York, Pennsylvania, United States

John Abbott
b: 1700 in England
m:
d: 1786 in Abbottstown, Adams Co. Pennsylvania, USA

Alice Berwick
b: 1702 in County Meath, Ireland Co. Meath, Ireland
d: 1742 in Abbottstown, Adams, Pennsylvania, United States

Pedigree Chart for Winifred Beatrice Turner

Winifred Beatrice Turner
b: 26 Aug 1890 in McMinnville, Yamhill County, Oregon, USA
m: 1911 in Multnomah, Oregon, USA
d: 02 Apr 1956 in Portland, Oregon, USA

- **William Burke Turner**
  b: 27 Jun 1860 in Vincennes, Knox, Indiana, United States
  m: 30 Jun 1881 in McMinnville, OR
  d: May 1924 in Sacramento, Sacramento, California, USA
  - **James Higgins Turner**
    b: 21 Sep 1812 in ,Laffayette,Pennsylvania,USA
    m: 16 Sep 1852 in Granville,,Ohio,USA
    d: 19 Jul 1885 in Portland, Multnomah County, Oregon, USA
    - **Nathan Turner**
      b: Abt. 1762 in Fayette,Pennsylvania,USA
      m: ,,Virginia,USA
      d:
    - **Jane Thompson Yates**
      b: 1780 in Hampshire,,Virginia,USA
      d: 1854
  - **Esther Ann Johnson**
    b: 21 Feb 1825 in Dryden,,New York,USA
    d: 07 Nov 1910 in Portland,,Oregon,USA
    - **Gurdon Collins Johnson**
      b: 11 Jan 1786 in Guilford, New Haven, Connecticut, United States
      m:
      d: 12 Feb 1860 in Indianapolis, Marion, Indiana, USA
    - **Louisa Lee**
      b: 11 Dec 1787 in Poutney, Rutland County, Vermont
      d: 11 Jul 1870 in Indianapolis, Marion, Indiana, USA
- **Mary Ellen Holman**
  b: 23 Oct 1856 in Polk Co. Oregon
  d: 29 Nov 1928 in Marshfield, Coos, Oregon, United States
  - **Daniel Sanders Holman**
    b: 15 Nov 1822 in Fayetteville, Lincoln County, Tennessee, United States of America
    m: 31 Dec 1847
    d: 15 Mar 1910 in McMinnville, Yamhill County, Oregon, USA
    - **John Holman**
      b: 16 Sep 1787 in Woodford County, Kentucky, USA
      m: 16 Oct 1810 in Woodford, Kentucky, USA
      d: 15 May 1864 in McMinnville, Yamhill, Oregon, USA
    - **Elizabeth Duval**
      b: 31 Aug 1792 in Virginia
      d: 12 May 1841 in Missouri
  - **Martha Elizabeth Burnett**
    b: 11 Dec 1830 in Hardeman County, Tennessee, USA
    d: 27 Jun 1913 in McMinnville, Yamhill County, Oregon, USA
    - **Glen Owen Burnett**
      b: 16 Nov 1809 in Tennessee, USA
      m: Jan 1830 in Hardeman, Tennessee
      d: 07 Jul 1886 in Santa Rosa, California, USA
    - **Sarah M Rogers**
      b: 28 Aug 1814 in Tennessee, United States
      d: 14 Jun 1889 in Santa Rosa, Santa Barbara, California, United States

Pedigree Chart for Esther Ann Johnson

Esther Ann Johnson
b: 21 Feb 1825 in Dryden,, New York, USA
m: 16 Sep 1852 in Granville,, Ohio, USA
d: 07 Nov 1910 in Portland,, Oregon, USA

- **Gurdon Collins Johnson**
  b: 11 Jan 1786 in Guilford, New Haven, Connecticut, United States
  m:
  d: 12 Feb 1860 in Indianapolis, Marion, Indiana, USA
  - **Gurdon Collins Johnson**
    b: 02 Feb 1759 in Guilford, New Haven, Connecticut, United States
    m: 08 May 1781 in Killingworth, New Haven, Connecticut, United States
    d: 22 Feb 1813 in Fair Haven, Rutland, Vermont, USA
    - **Samuel Johnson**
      b: 07 Mar 1727 in Guilford, New Hav…
      m: 20 Jun 1756 in Guilford, New Hav…
      d: 01 May 1808 in Guilford, New Hav…
    - **Margery Collins**
      b: 14 Mar 1732 in Guilford, New Haven, Connecticut, United States
      d: 13 Aug 1806 in Guilford, New Haven, Connecticut
  - **Esther Brainerd**
    b: 07 Aug 1757 in East Haddam, Middlesex, Connecticut, USA
    d: 10 Mar 1819 in Dryden, Tompkins, New York, USA
    - **Daniel Brainerd**
      b: 24 Feb 1722 in East Haddam, Mid…
      m: 15 Aug 1751 in East Haddam, Mi…
      d: 10 Jan 1777 in East Haddam, Mid…
    - **Esther Gates**
      b: 27 Jul 1727 in East Haddam, Middlesex, Connecticut, USA
      d: 11 May 1769 in East Haddam, Middlesex, Connecticut, USA
- **Louisa Lee**
  b: 11 Dec 1787 in Poutney, Rutland County, Vermont
  d: 11 Jul 1870 in Indianapolis, Marion, Indiana, USA
  - **Dr. Samuel Lee**
    b: 19 Nov 1754 in Canaan, Litchfield, Connecticut, USA
    m: 29 Sep 1774 in Salisbury
    d: 09 Apr 1813 in East Poultney, Rutland, Vermont, USA
    - **Samuel Lee**
      b: Abt. 1729 in Canaan, Litchfield, Connecticut
      m: 28 Mar 1754 in Canaan, Litchfield, CT
      d: 29 Aug 1779 in East Lyme, New London, Connecticut
    - **Silence Fletcher**
      b: 24 Dec 1731 in Westfield, Hampden Co, Massachusetts
      d:
  - **Mary Bingham**
    b: 03 Jul 1752 in Salisbury, Litchfield, Connecticut, USA
    d: 20 May 1791 in Poutltney, , Vermont, USA
    - **Jabez Bingham**
      b: 12 Apr 1724 in Norwich, New London, Connecticut, USA
      m: 29 Dec 1746 in Windham, Windham, Connecticut, USA
      d: 1784 in Norwich, New London, Connecticut, USA
    - **Mary Standish Wheelock**
      b: 28 Nov 1728 in Windham, Windham, Connecticut, United States
      d: 29 Jan 1809 in Athens, Athens, Ohio, United States

Pedigree Chart for Gurdon Collins Johnson

Gurdon Collins Johnson
b: 02 Feb 1759 in Guilford, New Haven, Connecticut, United States
m: 08 May 1781 in Killingworth, New Haven, Connecticut, United States
d: 22 Feb 1813 in Fair Haven, Rutland, Vermont, USA

- **Samuel Johnson**
  b: 07 Mar 1727 in Guilford, New Haven County, Connecticut, USA
  m: 20 Jun 1756 in Guilford, New Haven, Connecticut, United States
  d: 01 May 1808 in Guilford, New Haven County, Connecticut, USA
  - **Nathaniel Johnson**
    b: 17 Apr 1705 in Guilford, New Haven, Connecticut, United States
    m: 02 Aug 1727 in Guilford, New Haven, Connecticut, USA
    d: 06 Jun 1793 in Guilford, New Haven, Connecticut, United States
    - **Deacon Samuel Johnson**
      b: 05 Jun 1670 in Guilford, New Hav…
      m: 07 Nov 1694 in Guilford, New Ha…
      d: 08 May 1727 in Guilford, New Hav…
    - **Mary Sage**
      b: 15 Nov 1672 in Middletown, Middlesex, Connecticut, United States
      d: 13 Mar 1726 in Guilford, New Haven, Connecticut, United States
  - **Margery Morgan**
    b: 1705 in Groton, New London, Connecticut, USA
    d: 02 Oct 1752 in Guilford, New Haven, Connecticut, United States
    - **John Morgan Capt**
      b: 30 Mar 1645 in Roxbury, Suffolk,…
      m: 1689 in Preston, New London, Co…
      d: 12 Feb 1712 in Preston City, New…
    - **Elizabeth Jones**
      b: 28 Aug 1664 in New Haven, New Haven, Connecticut, United States
      d: 23 Aug 1711 in Preston City, New London, Connecticut, United States
- **Margery Collins**
  b: 14 Mar 1732 in Guilford, New Haven, Connecticut, United States
  d: 13 Aug 1806 in Guilford, New Haven, Connecticut
  - **Samuel Collins**
    b: 02 Nov 1704 in Guilford, New Haven, Connecticut, United States
    m: 20 Oct 1731 in Guilford, New Haven, Connecticut, United States
    d: 06 Dec 1784 in Guilford, New Haven, Connecticut, United States
    - **John Collins**
      b: 01 Mar 1665 in Guilford, New Haven, CT, USA
      m: 23 Jul 1691 in Guilford, New Haven, Connecticut, USA
      d: 24 Jan 1751 in Guilford, New Haven, CT, USA
    - **Ann Leete**
      b: 05 Aug 1671 in Guilford, New Haven, CT, USA
      d: 02 Nov 1724 in Guilford, New Haven, CT, USA
  - **Margery Leete**
    b: 08 Oct 1705 in Guilford, New Haven, Connecticut, United States
    d: 12 Aug 1796 in Guilford, New Haven, Connecticut, United States
    - **William Leete**
      b: 24 Mar 1671 in Guilford, New Hav…
      m: 12 Feb 1699 in Guilford, New Ha…
      d: 26 Jan 1736 in Guilford, New Hav…
    - **Hannah Stone**
      b: 27 Jul 1678 in Guilford, New Haven, Connecticut, United States
      d: 26 Feb 1724 in Guilford, New Haven County, Connecticut, United States of America

Pedigree Chart for Mary Standish Wheelock

Mary Standish Wheelock
b: 28 Nov 1728 in Windham, Windham, Connecticut, United States
m: 29 Dec 1746 in Windham, Windham, Connecticut, USA
d: 29 Jan 1809 in Athens, Athens, Ohio, United States

Ralph Wheelock
b: 12 Feb 1682 in Mendon, Worcester, Massachusetts, United States
m: 30 Sep 1726 in Windham, Windham, Connecticut, United States
d: 15 Oct 1748 in Windham, Windham, Connecticut, United States

Eleazer Wheelock
b: 03 May 1654 in Dedham, Norfolk County, Massachusetts, United States of America
m: 04 Aug 1672 in Rehoboth, Bristol, Massachusetts, United States
d: 24 Mar 1731 in Medfield, Norfolk, MA

Rev. Ralph Wheelock Sr. Sr.
b: 14 May 1600 in Dorrington, Shropshire, England
m: England
d: 11 Jan 1684 in Medfield, Norfolk, Massachusetts, United States

Rebecca Clark
b: 1610 in PRO, Norfolk, England
d: 01 Jan 1680 in Worcester, Massachusetts, United States

Elizabeth Fuller
b: 1645 in Salem, Essex, Massachusetts, United States
d: 11 Jan 1689 in Mendon, Massachusetts, USA

Robert Fuller
b: 1616 in Southampton, Hampshire, , England
m: of MA
d: 10 May 1706 in Rehoboth, Bristol, Massachusetts, United States

Sarah Bowen
b: 1616 in Weymouth, Norfolk, Massachusetts, USA
d: 14 Oct 1676 in Rehoboth, Bristol, Massachusetts, USA

Mercy Standish
b: 1685 in Duxbury, Plymouth, Massachusetts, United States
d: 04 Nov 1748 in Salisbury, Litchfield, Connecticut, United States

Josiah STANDISH
b: 1633 in Plymouth, Plymouth, Massachusetts, United States
m: 07 Mar 1656 in Duxbury, Plymouth, Massachusetts, United States
d: 19 Mar 1690 in Preston City, New London, Connecticut, United States

Captain Myles Standish
b: 1584 in Ellenbane, Isle Man, Lanca...
m: 03 Apr 1624 in Plymouth, Plymout...
d: 03 Oct 1656 in Duxbury, Plymouth...

Barbara Mullins Standish
b: 1584 in England
d: 06 Oct 1659 in Duxbury, Plymouth, Massachusetts, United States

Sarah ALLEN
b: 30 Mar 1639 in Braintree, Norfolk, Massachusetts, United States
d: 16 Sep 1690 in Preston City, New London, Connecticut, United States

Samuel Allen
b: 1607 in , Essex, , England
m: 30 1629 in Windsor, Hartford, Connecticut, United States
d: Apr 1647 in Windsor, Hartford, Connecticut, United States

Ann Whitmore
b: 30 Jul 1611 in England?
d: 13 Nov 1686 in Northampton, Hampshire, Massachusetts, United States

Pedigree Chart for Patricia Reese

Patricia Reese
b: 15/09/1929 in Eugene, Lane County, Oregon, USA
m: 17 Aug 1949 in Baker, Oregon, USA
d:

- **Grover W Reese**
  b: 09 Jan 1888 in Adamsville, Beaver, Utah, United States
  m: 17 Dec 1926 in Lane, Oregon, USA
  d: 05 Oct 1950 in Baker City, Oregon, USA

  - **Jacob Rees**
    b: 17 Oct 1865 in Utah Territory
    m: 13 Mar 1887 in Garfield, Utah, United States
    d: 1901 in Montana, USA

    - **Watkin Rees**
      b: 23 Jan 1830 in Merthyr Tydvil, Glamorgan, Wales
      m: 1853 in Merthyr Tydfil, Glamorgan, Wales
      d: 06 Aug 1922 in Beaver, Beaver, Utah, U.S.A.

    - **Jane Williams**
      b: 23 Apr 1836 in Dowlais, Glamorgan, Wales
      d: 04 Nov 1920 in Beaver County, Utah, U.S.A.

  - **Grace Merriam Williams**
    b: 03 Feb 1867 in Park City, Summit, Utah, USA
    d: 11 Sep 1950 in Baker, Baker, Oregon, USA

    - **Hyrum A. Williams**
      b: Abt. 1843 in Illinois
      m: 19 Jul 1863
      d: 04 Oct 1896 in Ontario, Malheur County, Oregon, USA

    - **Mary Ann Snyder**
      b: 31 Jan 1843 in Nauvoo, Hancock, Illinois, United States
      d: 10 Sep 1876 in Panguitch, Garfield, Utah

- **Dorothy Parvin**
  b: 21 Mar 1902 in Oregon
  d: 05 Jul 1998 in Eugene, Lane County, Oregon, USA

  - **Hosea M. Parvin**
    b: Sep 1868 in Dexter, Lane County, Oregon, USA
    m: 1897
    d: 26 Aug 1954 in Eugene, Lane, Oregon, USA

    - **James Parvin**
      b: 02 May 1831 in Marion County, Indiana, USA
      m:
      d: 17 Dec 1907 in Oregon, USA

    - **Selena Parker**
      b: 19 Dec 1833 in Coshocton, Coshocton, OH, USA
      d: 02 Oct 1913 in Lost Valley, Lane, OR, USA

  - **Agnes Florence Templeman**
    b: 06 Jul 1873 in Lane County, Oregon
    d: 19 Jun 1963 in Eugene, Lane County, Oregon

    - **William D Templeman**
      b: 09 Apr 1841 in Kentucky
      m: 02 Jul 1871 in Oregon, United States
      d: 14 Jun 1879 in Dexter, Lane, Oregon

    - **Anna Elizabeth Mathews**
      b: 29 Nov 1851 in Illinois, USA
      d: 23 Dec 1883 in Dexter, Lane, Oregon, USA

Pedigree Chart for Hyrum A. Williams

Hyrum A. Williams
b: Abt. 1843 in Illinois
m: 19 Jul 1863
d: 04 Oct 1896 in Ontario, Malheur County, Oregon, USA

- **Gustavious WILLIAMS**
  b: 11 Apr 1820 in New Berkshire, Berkshire, Massachusetts, USA
  m: 31 Jan 1833 in West Stockbridge, Berkshire, Massachusetts, USA
  d: 09 Oct 1889 in Teasdale, Wayne, Utah, USA
  - **Solomon WILLIAMS**
    b: 28 Aug 1783 in , Wethersfield, Hartford, Connecticut
    m: 29 Mar 1803 in , Boston, Suffolk, Massachusetts
    d: 1803
    - **Solomon Francis Williams**
      b: 27 Feb 1756 in Wethersfield, Hartf…
      m: 20 Nov 1777 in Wethersfield, Hartf…
      d: 10 Dec 1784 in Berkshire, Massac…
    - **Hannah Eunice Robbins**
      b: 20 Jul 1757 in Wethersfield, Hartford, Connecticut, USA
      d: 20 Oct 1804
  - **Elizabeth POOL**
    b: 1775 in , Roxbury, Suffolk, Massachusetts
    d: 13 Nov 1861 in Roxbury, Suffolk, Mass.
    - **John Poole**
      b: 11 Sep 1743 in Weymouth, Massa…
      m: 14 Oct 1769 in Weymouth, Norfol…
      d: 1798 or July 2, 1801 in Weymouth…
    - **Sarah Clark**
      b: 14 May 1749 in Braintree, Norfolk, Massachusetts, United States
      d: 1833 in Abington, Plymouth, Massachusetts, United States

- **Hannah Mariah ANDREWS**
  b: 12 Aug 1811 in New, Berkshire, Massachusetts, USA
  d: 12 Jan 1901 in Teasdale, Wayne, Utah, USA
  - **Oreb Andrews**
    b: 20 Oct 1785 in Cornwall, Litchfield, Connecticut, United States
    m: 15 Dec 1807 in Sheffield, Berkshire, Massachusetts, United States
    d: 13 Mar 1822 in Lenox, Berkshire, Massachusetts, United States
    - **Capt. Andrew Andrews II II**
      b: 19 Aug 1756 in Wallingford, New Haven, Connecticut, USA
      m: 06 Apr 1780 in Wallingford, New Haven, Connecticut
      d: 03 Jul 1834 in Sheffield, Berkshire, Massachusetts, USA
    - **Mary Moss**
      b: 28 Nov 1755 in Wallingford, New Haven, Connecticut, USA
      d: 09 Feb 1847 in Sheffield, Berkshire, Massachusetts, USA
  - **Diantha Willoughby**
    b: 27 Jun 1790 in Cornwall, Litchfield, Connecticut, United States
    d: 13 Mar 1822 in Marion, Wayne, New York, United States
    - **Solomon Willoughby**
      b: 22 Sep 1762 in Goshen, Litchfield, Connecticut, United States
      m: Bef. 1785 in Connecticut, USA
      d: 26 Jul 1837 in Cambridge, Lamoille, Vermont, United States
    - **Salome Jeffrey**
      b: 16 Jul 1762 in Cornwall, Litchfield, Connecticut, United States
      d: 08 Sep 1832 in Sheffield, Berkshire, Massachusetts, USA

Pedigree Chart for Hannah Eunice Robbins

- **Hannah Eunice Robbins**
  b: 20 Jul 1757 in Wethersfield, Hartford, Connecticut, USA
  m: 20 Nov 1777 in Wethersfield, Hartford, Connecticut, United States
  d: 20 Oct 1804
  - **Joshua Robbins**
    b: 30 Oct 1720 in Wethersfield, Hartford, Connecticut, USA
    m: 26 Aug 1742 in Wethersfield, Hartford, Connecticut, United States
    d: 30 Jul 1796 in Wethersfield, Hartford, Connecticut, USA
    - **Capt Joshua Robbins Jr**
      b: 21 Oct 1681 in Wethersfield, Hartford, Connecticut, USA
      m: 20 Nov 1707 in Wethersfield, Hartford, Connecticut, USA
      d: 30 May 1733 in Wethersfield, Hartford, Connecticut, USA
      - **Joshua Robbins Sr**
        b: 21 Oct 1652 in Wethersfield, Hartfo…
        m: 24 Dec 1680 in Wethersfield, Hartf…
        d: 15 Dec 1738 in Wethersfield, Hartf…
      - **Elizabeth Rose Butler**
        b: 15 Apr 1665 in Wethersfield, Hartford, Connecticut
        d: 24 Apr 1736 in Wethersfield, Hartford, Connecticut
    - **Sarah Bidwell**
      b: 19 Aug 1681 in Hartford, Hartford, Connecticut, USA
      d: 03 Dec 1744 in Wethersfield, Hartford, Connecticut, USA
      - **John Bidwell**
        b: 1641 in Hartford, CT
        m: 07 Nov 1678 in Colchester, New London, Connecticut, United States
        d: 03 Jul 1692 in Hartford, CT
      - **Sarah Welles**
        b: Apr 1659 in Wethersfield, CT
        d: 07 Mar 1708 in Hartford, CT
  - **Sarah Welles**
    b: 23 Jun 1719 in Wethersfield, Hartford, Connecticut, USA
    d: 16 Jul 1805 in Wethersfield, Hartford Co., CT, USA
    - **Captain Robert Welles Jr**
      b: 1684 in Wethersfield, Hartford Co., Connecticut Colony
      m: 12 Dec 1706 in Wethersfield, Hartford Co., Connecticut Colony
      d: Sep 1738 in Wethersfield, Hartford Co., Connecticut Colony
      - **Robert Welles**
        b: 22 Jun 1649 in Stratford, Fairfield Co., Connecticut Colony
        m: 1669 in Wethersfield, Hartford, Connecticut, United States
        d: 22 Jun 1714 in Wethersfield, Hartford, CT, USA
      - **Elizabeth Goodrich**
        b: 1658 in Wethersfield, Hartford, Connecticut, USA
        d: 17 Feb 1698 in Wethersfield, Hartford, Connecticut, USA
    - **Sarah Wolcott**
      b: 14 Aug 1686 in Wethersfield, Hartford Co., Connecticut Colony
      d: Sep 1738 in Wethersfield, Hartford Co., Connecticut Colony
      - **Samuel Wolcott**
        b: 16 Apr 1656 in Windsor, Hartford, Connecticut, USA
        m: 1677 in CT
        d: 14 Jun 1695 in Wethersfield, Hartford, Connecticut, USA
      - **Judith Appleton**
        b: 19 Aug 1653 in Ipswich, Essex, Massachusetts, USA
        d: 19 Feb 1741 in Wethersfield, Hartford, Connecticut, USA

Pedigree Chart for Sarah Wolcott

Sarah Wolcott
b: 14 Aug 1686 in Wethersfield, Hartford Co., Connecticut Colony
m: 12 Dec 1706 in Wethersfield, Hartford Co., Connecticut Colony
d: Sep 1738 in Wethersfield, Hartford Co., Connecticut Colony

- **Samuel Wolcott**
  b: 16 Apr 1656 in Windsor, Hartford, Connecticut, USA
  m: 1677 in CT
  d: 14 Jun 1695 in Wethersfield, Hartford, Connecticut, USA
  - **Henry Wolcott Jr Jr**
    b: 21 Nov 1610 in Taunton Deane Borough, Somerset, England
    m: 18 Nov 1641 in CT
    d: 12 Jul 1680 in Windsor, Hartford County, Connecticut, United States of America
    - **Henry Wolcott**
      b: 06 Dec 1578 in Tolland, Somerset, England
      m: MA
      d: 30 May 1655 in Windsor, Hartford, Connecticut, United States
    - **Elizabeth Saunders**
      b: 20 Dec 1584 in England
      d: 17 Jul 1655 in Windsor, Hartford, Connecticut, United States
  - **Sarah Newberry Wolcott ***
    b: 10 Apr 1620 in Windsor, Hartford, Connecticut, USA
    d: 16 Jun 1684 in Windsor, Hartford County, Connecticut, USA
    - **Thomas Newberry**
      b: 10 Nov 1594 in Yarcombe, Devon, England
      m: 1618 in Colony of Connecticut
      d: 01 Dec 1636 in Windsor, Hartford, Connecticut, United States
    - **Jane Dabinott**
      b: 1600 in Chardstock, Dorset, England
      d: 23 Apr 1645 in Norwalk, Fairfield, Connecticut, United States

- **Judith Appleton**
  b: 19 Aug 1653 in Ipswich, Essex, Massachusetts, USA
  d: 19 Feb 1741 in Wethersfield, Hartford, Connecticut, USA
  - **Col. Samuel Appleton**
    b: 02 Feb 1624 in Little Waldingfield, Suffolk, England
    m: 02 Apr 1651 in Ipswich, Essex, Massachusetts
    d: 15 May 1696 in Ipswich, Essex, Massachusetts, United States
    - **Samuel Appleton**
      b: 13 Aug 1586 in Little Waldingfield,,Suffolk,England
      m: 24 Jan 1615 in United States
      d: 10 Jun 1670 in Rowley,Essex,Massachusetts,USA
    - **Judith Everard**
      b:
      d:
  - **Hannah Paine**
    b: 11 Feb 1630 in Nowton, Suffolk, , England
    d: 08 Dec 1656 in Ipswich, Essex, Massachusetts, United States
    - **William Paine**
      b: 20 Feb 1596 in Lavenham, Suffolk, England
      m: 20 Nov 1616 in St Gregory by St Paul, London, England
      d: 10 Oct 1660 in Boston, Middlesex, Massachusetts, USA
    - **Anna North**
      b: 1595 in Lavenham, Suffolk, England
      d: 10 Oct 1660 in Ipswich, Essex, Massachusetts, USA

Pedigree Chart for Mary Ann Snyder

Mary Ann Snyder
b: 31 Jan 1843 in Nauvoo, Hancock, Illinois, United States
m: 19 Jul 1863 in Beaver, Beaver, Utah, USA
d: 10 Sep 1876 in Panguitch, Garfield, Utah

- **Samuel Comstock Snyder**
  b: 14 Feb 1806 in Fort Ann, Washington, New York, USA
  m: 26 Mar 1827 in Porta Ferry, St. Lawrence, New York
  d: 08 Apr 1866 in Salt Lake City, Salt Lake, Utah, USA
  - **Isaac Snyder**
    b: 15 Sep 1787 in Bennington County, Vermont, USA
    m: 18 Mar 1807 in Fort Ann, Washington, New York, USA
    d: 28 Feb 1844 in Nauvoo, Hancock County, Illinois, USA
    - **Jacob Uel-Guard SNYDER**
      b: 05 Feb 1745 in Poughkeepsie, Dutchess, New York, USA
      m: 01 Nov 1765 in Bennington, Bennington, Vermont, USA
      d: 15 Feb 1820 in Earnesttown, Ontario, Canada
    - **Nancy Nancie ISMAY**
      b: 1754 in Onondaga, New York, or Bennington, Bennington, Vermont
      d: 1826 in Earnesttown, , Ontario, Canada
  - **Louisa Comstock Snyder**
    b: 22 May 1789 in Egremont, Berkshire County, Massachusetts, USA
    d: 20 Mar 1856 in Salt Lake City, Salt Lake County, Utah, USA
    - **Samuel Comstock**
      b: 1749 in Providence, Providence, Rhode Island, USA
      m: 1764/1769 in Egremont, Berkshire, Massachusetts, USA
      d: 25 Dec 1805 in Fort Ann, Washington, New York, USA
    - **Sarah Crippen**
      b: 14 Feb 1748 in Egremont, Berkshire, Mass
      d: 07 Dec 1832 in Comstock, Washington, New York

- **Henrietta Mariah Stockwell**
  b: 04 Sep 1810 in High Gate, Chittenden, Vermont, USA
  d: 15 Oct 1888 in Salt Lake City, Salt Lake, Utah, USA
  - **Ephriam I. Stockwell**
    b: 12 Jan 1787 in Chittenden, Rutland, VT
    m: 1804 in Stockbridge, Berkshire, Massachusetts, United States
    d: 05 Jan 1855 in Michigan, United States
    - **Jesse Stockwell**
      b: 05 Jan 1759 in Templeton, Worces…
      m: 03 Apr 1782 in Athol, Templeton,…
      d: 1849 in Athol, Worcester, Massach…
    - **Annis Grout**
      b: 25 Oct 1763 in Petersham, Worcester, Massachusetts, USA
      d: 1847 in Athol, Worcester, Massachusetts, United States
  - **Ann Amy Hooker**
    b: 07 Apr 1790 in West Stockbridge, Berkshire, Massachusetts
    d: 17 Mar 1818 in Westfprd, Crottemdem, Vermont
    - **Capt Simeon Hooker**
      b: 14 Apr 1739 in Sturbridge, Worcest…
      m: 1772 in West Stockbridge, Berkshi…
      d: 21 Feb 1841 in Westford, Chittend…
    - **Mrs. Lydia Hooker**
      b: 1750 in West Stockbridge, Worcester, Massachusetts, USA
      d: Sturbridge, Worcester, Massachusetts, United States

Pedigree Chart for Sarah Crippen

Sarah Crippen
b: 14 Feb 1748 in Egremont, Berkshire, Mass
m: 1764/1769 in Egremont, Berkshire, Massachusetts, USA
d: 07 Dec 1832 in Comstock, Washington, New York

John Crippen
b: 20 Mar 1720 in Colchester, New London, Connecticut, United States
m: 10 Aug 1741 in Sharon, Windham, Connecticut, United States
d: 02 Jan 1776 in Weston, Middlesex, Massachusetts, United States

Mary Richmond
b: 1715 in Taunton, Bristol, Massachusetts, United States
d: 16 Oct 1739 in Alford, Berkshire, Massachusetts, United States

Jabez Crippen
b: 09 Jul 1680 in Plymouth County, Massachusetts, USA
m: 09 Jul 1707 in Colchester
d: 07 Jul 1785 in Manchester, Bennington County, Vermont, USA

Thankful Fuller
b: May 1689 in Barnstable, Barnstable County, Massachusetts, USA
d: May 1740 in Sharon, Litchfield County, Connecticut, USA

Benjamin Richmond
b: 10 Jan 1696 in Little Compton, Newport, Rhode Island, United States
m: 26 Jun 1685
d: 1776 in Sharon, Litchfield County, Connecticut, USA

Thomas Crippen
b: 1640 in Bristol, Gloucestershire, England
m: 1659 in East Haddam, Middlesex Co, CT, USA
d: 24 Jan 1709 in East Haddam, Middlesex, Connecticut, USA

Frances Bray
b: 1645 in Plymouth, Plymouth, Massachusetts, USA
d: 10 May 1705 in East Haddam, Middlesex, Connecticut, United States

John Fuller
b: 11 Jan 1656 in Barnstable, Barnsta…
m: 1678 in Barnstable, Barnstable, M…
d: 28 Feb 1726 in East Haddam, Mid…

Mehitable Rowley
b: 1660 in Barnstable, Barnstable Co., Massachusetts, USA
d: 1732 in East Haddam, Middlesex, CT

Edward Richmond
b: 1658 in Newport, Newport County,…
m: 1684 in New England, USA
d: 14 Feb 1743 in Little Compton, Ne…

Pedigree Chart for Thankful Fuller

Thankful Fuller
b: May 1689 in Barnstable, Barnstable County, Massachusetts, USA
m: 09 Jul 1707 in Colchester
d: May 1740 in Sharon, Litchfield County, Connecticut, USA

- **John Fuller**
  b: 11 Jan 1656 in Barnstable, Barnstable, Massachusetts, United States
  m: 1678 in Barnstable, Barnstable, Massachusetts, United States
  d: 28 Feb 1726 in East Haddam, Middlesex, Connecticut, United States

  - **Samuel Fuller**
    b: 1612 in Rendenhall, England
    m:
    d: 1683 in Barnstable, Barnstable Co., Massachusetts, USA

    - **Edward Fuller**
      b: 04 Sep 1575 in Norfolk, England
      m: Abt. 1594 in , Norfolk, , England
      d: 10 Apr 1621 in Plymouth, Plymout…

    - **Ann ? Fuller**
      b: 1581 in England
      d: 1621 in Plymouth, Plymouth County, Massachusetts, USA

  - **Jane Lothrop**
    b: 1614 in England
    d: 1658 in Barnstable, Barnstable Co., Massachusetts, USA

    - **Reverend John Lothrop**
      b: 1584 in England
      m:
      d: 1653 in Barnstable, Barnstable Co., Massachusetts, USA

    - **Hannah Howse**
      b: 1594 in Eastwell, Kent, England
      d: 16 Feb 1634 in London, London, England

- **Mehitable Rowley**
  b: 1660 in Barnstable, Barnstable Co., Massachusetts, USA
  d: 1732 in East Haddam, Middlesex, CT

  - **Moses Rowley**
    b: 1630 in Scituate, Plymouth, MA
    m: 22 Apr 1652 in Barnstable, Barnstable, Massachusetts, USA
    d: 08 Mar 1705 in East Haddam, Middlesex, Connecticut, United States

    - **Henry Rowley**
      b: 1598 in Bennington, Hartfordshire,…
      m: 1624 in Scituate, Massachusetts,…
      d: 15 Jul 1673 in Falmouth, Barnstabl…

    - **Sarah Ann Palmer**
      b: 1609 in Parham, Somerset, England
      d: 1633 in Barnstable, Barnstable, Massachusetts, United States

  - **Elizabeth Fuller**
    b: 04 Apr 1626 in England
    d: 07 Mar 1714 in East Haddam, Middlesex, Connecticut, USA

    - **Capt Matthew Fuller**
      b: 16 Oct 1603 in Redenhall, Norfolk,…
      m: 1625 in Plymouth, Plymouth, Mas…
      d: 22 Aug 1678 in Barnstable, Barnst…

    - **Frances Lyde**
      b: 1605 in Harleston, Norfolk, England
      d: 26 Oct 1678 in Barnstable, Barnstable County, Massachusetts, United States of America

Bibliography

Books

Adlum, John, *A Memoir of the Cultivation of the Vine in America and the Best Mode of Making Wine*, Davis and Ford Printers, Washington, DC, 1823, Reprint: Forgotten Books.com

———, *Adlum on Making Wine*, Davis and Ford Printers, Washington, DC, 1826, 2nd printing, 1828

———, *Memoirs of the Life of John Adlum in the Revolutionary War*, introduction and editing by Howard H. Peckham, Chicago, The Canton Club, 1968

———, *Memoirs of the Life of John Adlum*, The Pennsylvania Historical and Museum Commission for Microfilming, August 15, 1952, photocopy, includes childhood and history

Anderson, Robert Charles, *Puritan Pedigrees: The Deep Roots of the Great Migration to New England*, New England Historic Genealogical Society, Boston, MA, 2018

Andrews, Charles Mclean, *The River Towns of Connecticut: A Study of Weatherford, Hartford, and Windsor*, John Hopkins University Press, Baltimore, MA, 1899, reprint by Scholar Select

Banks, Charles Edward, *The Winthrop Fleet of 1630*, Heritage Books, 2008; first published 1930

Bailyn, Bernard, *The New England Merchants in the Seventeenth Century*, Harvard University Press, Cambridge, MA, and London, England, 1979

Baker City Chamber of Commerce, *The Gold Fields of Eastern Oregon*, printed by Baker City, 1899; intro by Kirby Jackson, 2014

Barber, John Warner, *Connecticut Historical Collections*, New England Historic Genealogical Society, Boston, MA, 2018, originally published 1857

Beck, Warren A. and David A. Williams, *California: A History of the Golden State*, Doubleday and Co., Garden City, New York, 1972

Bicknell, John, *1844: Religious Fervor, Westward Expansion and the Presidential Election That Transformed the Nation*, Chicago Review Press, 2015

Billington, Ray Allen and Martin Ridge, *Westward Expansion: A History of the American Frontier*, Macmillan Publishing Co. Inc., New York, 1982

Boorstin, Daniel J., *The Americans: The Colonial Experience*, Vintage Books/Random House, New York, 1958

———, *The Americans: The National Experience*, Vintage Books/Random House, New York, 1965

———, *The Americans: The Democratic Experience*, Vintage Books, New York, 1974

Bradford, William, *Of Plymouth Plantation 1620-1647*, edited with introduction and notes by Samuel Eliot Morrison, Alfred A. Knopf, New York, 1998

Brands, H. W., *The Age of Gold: The California Gold Rush and the New American Dream*, Anchor Books, New York, 2002

Bremer, Francis J., *The Puritan Experiment: New England Society from Bradford to Edwards*, University Press of New England, Hanover and London, 1995

Brodie, Fawn M., *No Man Knows My History: The Life of Joseph Smith*, Vintage Books, New York, 1995

Burnett, Peter H., *Reflections and Opinions of an Old Pioneer*, D. Appleton and Co., New York, 1880, Reprint Da Capo Press, New York, 1969

Campbell, Eugene E., *Establishing Zion: The Mormon Church in the American West 1847-69*, Signature Books, Salt Lake City, UT, 1968

Carson, Clarence B., *A Basic History of the United States: The Sections and the Civil War 1826-1877*, American Textbook Committee, Wadley, AL, 1985

———, *The Colonial Experience 1607-1774*, American Textbook Committee, Wadley, AL, 1983

Clarke, Ted, *Scituate Chronicles*, The History Press, Charleston and London, 2014

Cone, Joseph, *A Man Named Daniel*, publisher Text and Content, Corvallis, Oregon, 2010

Eisenhart, Willis W., *The Abbott-Adlum-Green Families*, Abbottstown, PA, 1957, University of Wisconsin, Madison, copy for Google books

Fagan, Brian, *The Little Ice Age: How Climate Made History 1300-1850*, Basic Books, New York

Faragher, John Mack, *Daniel Boone: the Life and Legend of an American Pioneer*, Holt Paperbacks, New York, 1992

Fitzgerald, David, *The Mormons*, publisher David Fitzgerald, 2013

Fraser, Rebecca, *The Mayflower: The Families, the Voyage and the Founding of America*, St. Martin's Press, New York, 2017

Gabler, James M., *Passions: The Wines and Travels of Thomas Jefferson*, Bacchus Press, Baltimore, MD, 1995

Gaskill, Malcolm, *Between Two Worlds: How the English Became Americans*, Basic Books, New York, 2014

Hall, David D., *Puritans in the New World*, Princeton University Press, Princeton and Oxford, 2004

Hardeman, Nicholas Perkins, *Wilderness Calling, the Hardeman Family in the American Westward Movement, 1750-1900*, University of Tennessee Press, Knoxville, TN, 1977

Hawke, David Freeman, *Everyday Life in Early America*, Perennial Library, Harper and Row, New York, 1988

Hinman, Royal Ralph, *A Catalog of the Names of the First Puritan Settlers of the Colony of*

Connecticut; With the Time of Their Arrival in the Colony, and Their Standing in Society, Together with Their Place of Residence, as far as can be Discovered by the Records, Vol. 4, from old catalog, published by the Andesite Press, Scholar Select

Hintzen, William, *Border Wars of the Upper Ohio Valley (1769-1794)*, Jess Stuart Foundation, publisher, Ashland, KY, 1999

Horn, Huston, *The Pioneers*, Time-Life Books, New York, 1974

Hunt, Douglas, *The Ohio Frontier: Crucible of the Old Northwest, 1720-1830*, Indiana University Press, Bloomington, IN, 1996

Johnson, Caleb H., *The Mayflower and Her Passengers*, Xlibris Corporation, 2006

Krakauer, Jon, *Under the Banner of Heaven A Story of Violent Faith*, Anchor Books, New York, 2003

Leyburn, James G., *The Scotch Irish: A Social History*, The University of North Carolina Press, Chapel Hill, NC, 1962

Love, William De Loss, *The Colonial History of Hartford*, originally published in Hartford, CT, 1914, reprint by Andesite Press, Scholar Select

Lucero, Donella J. and Nancy L. Hobbs, *The Long Beach Peninsula: Where the Columbia Meets The Pacific*, Arcadia Publishing, Charleston, SC, 2004

Macdonald, Joseph F., *Macdonald's Stage Coaches and Stations: Eastern Oregon, 1850-1920*, Western Places Publisher, Lake Oswego, OR, 2009

MacGunnigle, Bruce Campbell, *Mayflower Families Through Five Generations*, (Edward Fuller, Vol 4), General Society of Mayflower Descendants, Plymouth, MA, 2006

McCullough, David, *1776*, Simon and Schuster, New York, 2005

McFarland, Gerald W., *A Scattered People: An American Family Moves West*, Pantheon Books, New York, 1985

Melonakos, Kathleen Kimball, *Secret Combinations: Evidence of Early Mormon Counterfeiting 1800-1847*, Lyrical Productions, San Diego, CA, 2016

Morgan, Edmund S., *The Genuine Article*, W.W. Norton & Company, New York, 2004

Morgan, Ted, *A Shovel of Stars, The Making of the American West–1880 to the Present*, Simon and Schuster, New York, 1995

Morison, Samuel Eliot, and Henry Steele Commager, *The Growth of the American Republic*, Vol. 1, Oxford University Press, New York, 1962

Mourt's Relation: A Journal of the Pilgrims at Plymouth, from original text of 1622, intro by Dwight B. Heath, Applewood Books, Bedford, MA, 1963

Murphy, Dan, *The Oregon Trail – Voyage of Discovery – The Story Behind the Scenery*, KC Publications, Inc., 1993

Murphy, Jim, *An American Plague: The True and Terrifying Story of the Yellow Fever Epidemic of 1793*, published by Scholastic Books with Clarion Books, New York, 2003

New England Encounters, Indians & Euroamericans, ca. 1600-1850, Alden T. Vaughn, editor Northeastern University Press, The New England Quarterly, Boston, MA, 1999

Nokes, Gregory R., *The Troubled Life of Peter Burnett: Oregon Pioneer and First Governor of California*, Oregon State University Press, Corvallis, OR, 2018

Owen, Daniel, *The Lost Rescue – The Story of the Lost Wagon Train and the Men Who Tried to Save It*, Createspace Publishing, 2015

Parkman Jr., Francis, *The Oregon Trail*, Caxton House Inc., New York, originally published 1849

Parrington, Vernon Louis, *Main Currents in American Thought: Volume 2 – The Romantic Revolution in America 1800-1860*, University of Oklahoma Press, 1987, originally published 1927

Philbrick, Nathaniel, *Mayflower, A Story of Courage, Community and War*, Viking, published by The Penguin Group, New York, 2006

Pollack M.D., Robert W., *The Education of a Country Doctor*, Vantage Press, New York, 1978

Pope, Charles Henry, *Pioneers of Massachusetts 1620-1650*, New England Historical Society, Boston, MA, 1900

Ryken, Leland, *Worldly Saints, the Puritans as They Really Were*, Zondervan Publishing, Grand Rapids, MI, 1986

Rosenberry, Lois Kimball Matthews, *The expansion of New England: the Spread of the New England settlement and institutions to the Mississippi River 1620-1865*, Houghton and Mifflin Company, Boston and New York, 1909, reprint Forgottenbooks.com

Schiff, Stacy, *The Witches: Suspicion, Betrayal, and Hysteria in 1692 Salem*, Little, Brown, and Company, New York, 2015

Shawver, Patricia Turner, *Portrait of Mama*, P. K. Allen Printing, Portland, OR, 1965

Smith Jr., Joseph, The Book of Mormon, The Church of Jesus Christ of Latter-day Saints, Salt Lake City, UT, 1974; original 1830

Stenhouse, Fanny, *Tell it All, Woman's Life in Polygamy*, Hartford, CT, 1880; reprint 2019

Turner, Julia Clarissa, compiled and edited by Elizabeth L. Smith, *Esther Ann: All the Years of Her Life*, Bubba's Pal Publishing, Bryan, TX, 2010

Van Heukelem, Christy and Tom Fuller, *Images of America: McMinnville*, Arcadia Publishing, Charleston, SC, 2012

Wakefield, Robert S., complied by Russell L. Warner, *Mayflower Families through Five Generations*, (Vol. 14: Myles Standish), The Silver Book, Published by General Society of Mayflower Descendants, Plymouth, MA, 1997

Walker, George Leon, *Thomas Hooker: Preacher, Founder, Democrat*, Dodd, Mead and Co., New

York, 1891; reprint www.forgottenbooks.com

Weaver, Glenn, *Hartford, An Illustrated History of Connecticut's Capital*, Windsor Publishing, Albany, NY, 1982

Webb, Jim, *Born Fighting" How the Scots-Irish Shaped America*, Broadway Books, New York, 2004

Weidensaul, Scott, *The First Frontier, The Forgotten History of Struggle, Savagery, & Endurance*, Houghton Mifflin Harcourt, Boston, New York, 2012

Young, Alexander, *Chronicles of the First Planters of the Colony of Massachusetts Bay 1623-1636*, Da Capo Press, New York, 1970

Selected Articles and Pamphlets

A Short History of Guilford, The Guilford Keeping Society Archives, accessed February 7, 2019, https://gks.meka.net/about-the-gks

Altoona, PA (ALT) Great American Stations, https://www.greatamericanstations.com/stations/altoona-pa-alt/

Arrington, Leonard, *Pioneers and Cowboys – Colonization of Utah*, Utah History Encyclopedia, Utah History to Go, accessed March 31, 2019, https://historytogo.utah.gov/utahchapters/pioneers_andcowboys/colonizationofutah.html

Bledsoe, Lucy Jane, *Adventuresome Women on the Oregon Trail, 1840-1867*, Frontiers Vol. VII, No. 3 1984, University of Nebraska Press, https://www.jstor.org/stable/3346237

Brightwell, Eric, *California Fool's Gold – Exploring El Monte, the End of the Santa Fe Trail*, http://www.amoeba.com

Burch, Albert, *Development of Metal Mining in Oregon*, Oregon Historical Society Quarterly, Vol. 43, No. 2 (Jun., 1942) Published by the Oregon Historical Society, https://www.jstor.org/stable/206 11410

Butch Cassidy-Thief, Biography, accessed March 27, 2019, https://biography.com/people/butch-cassidy-9240908

Caleb Johnson's MayflowerHistory.com, http://mayflowerhistory.com

Chester, Ronald, *The Life and Death of the Ipswich Grammar School Trust: Is Enduring Dead Hand Control Possible?* New England Law/Boston Legal Studies Research Paper Series, Paper no. 14-09 Aztec Law Journal Vol. 39:201, https://ipswichtrust.org/2014/...the-life-death-of-the-grammar-school-trust

City of Drewsey Oregon, accessed September 19, 2019, http://www.oregoncities.us.drewsy/

Coquillette, Calvin W., *The Struggle to Preserve Iowa's State Banking System, 1920-1933*, Annals of Iowa, Vol 60, November/Winter 2001, https://ir.iowa.edu/cgi/viewcontents.cgi?article=10426

Deady, Lucy Ann Henderson, *Crossing the Plains in 1846*, Transactions of the Fifty-Sixth Annual Oregon Pioneer Association, Salem. OR, E. M. Waite, 1928

Destination Ninety Interview with Daniel B. Adlum, The Los Angeles Times, www.newspapers.com/clip/1478542/the_los_angeles_times/?xid=637

Defiant Samuel Appleton, Stories from Ipswich, https://storiesfromipswich.org

Early Roads in Vermont, The Vermont Historical Society, https://vermonthistory.org/journal/misc/EarlyRoads&Taverns.pdf

Finlay, Nancy, *Dr. Thomas Hooker*, Connecticut History.org, https://connecticutehistory.org/the-importance-of-being-puritan-church-and-state-in-colonial-connecticut

Frank, Michael, *Long Beach Peninsula, America's Last Coast*, May 08, 2009, www.travelandleisure.com

Franklin, William E., *A Forgotten Chapter in California's History: Peter H. Burnett and John A. Sutter's Fortune*, California Historical Society Quarterly 41 (December 1962)

Gahn, Bessie Wilmarth, *Major John Adlum of Rock Creek*, Records of Columbia Historical Society, Vol. 39, 1938, Washington DC, https://www.jstor.org/stable/40067536

Garfield County, accessed March 19, 2019, https://ilovehistory.utah.gov/place/counties/garfield.html

Governor Thomas Welles, http://wellesfamily.com

Gregory, James N., *The Shaping of California History*, originally published in the Encyclopedia of American Social History, Scribner's, New York, 1993, accessed October 16, 2019, https://faculty.washington.edu/gregoryj/Californina%20History.htm

Henry Whitfield House, https://en.wikipedia.org/wiki/Henry_Whitfield_House

Henry Wolcott: The Prominent Families of the United States of America, https://www.ancestry.com/interactive/48460/ProminentUSFam-0083309-152

Historic Baker City, Baker County, Oregon, http://www.oregongeneaology.com/baker/historicbc/bakercity.htm

Historic Ipswich: Arrival of the English, https://historicipswich.org/2019/01/07/arrival-of-the-english/

Historic Content of McMinnville, Oregon.gov, http://www.oregon.gov/oprd/HCD/100/yamhill_mcmhistoric_content_2011.pdf

History of the Puritans in North America, https://en.wikipedia.org/wiki/history_of_thePuritans_in_North_America

Holman, Frederick V., *Christmas on Baker's Bay*, The Sou'wester, Pacific County Historical Society, Winter 1970, Vol V, Number 4

Hooker's Most Famous Sermon-1638, Christian History Institute, https://christianhistoryinstitute.org/dailyquote/5/31

Isaac Snyder and Lovisa Comstock Snyder History, unknown author, Ancestry.com, accessed April 16,

2019, https://www.ancestry.com/mediaui-viewer/collection/1...905-4e76-8a66-7124bc9d91c3?

John Winthrop Jr., https://www.museumofcthistory.org/20/5/08/john-winthrop-jr/

Jungleers: 41st Infantry Division, Jungleer.com, http://jungleer.com/23honors/29-salam-aua-to-1st-battalion-162-infantry-regiment-july1945

Kent, Donald H., and Deardoroff, Merle H., *John Adlum on the Allegheny: Memoirs for the Year 1794: Part I*, the Pennsylvania Magazine of History and Biography, Vol. 84, No.3 (July 1960), Published by the Historical Society of Pennsylvania: University of Pennsylvania Press, https://www.jstor.org/stable/20089310

———, *John Adlum on the Allegheny: Memoirs for the Year 1794: Part II*, the Pennsylvania Magazine of History and Biography, Vol.84, No. 4 (Oct 1960), https://jstor.org/stable/20089336

Lehmann, Chris, *Young and Restless: On Brigham Young*, the Nation Magazine, Nov. 28, 2012, https://www.thenation.com/article/young-and-restless-brigham-young/

Levinson, N J., *Frederick V. Holman, An Appreciation*, The Oregon Historical Quarterly, Vol xxviii, No. 3, September 1927, www.jstor.org

Martin, John H., *Joseph Smith: The Angel Moroni and Mormonism in New York State*, from Saints, Sinners and Reformers, 2005, accessed March 20, 2019, http://www.crookedlakereview.co/books/saints-sinners/martin9.html

———, *The Burned-Over District Revisited*, Chapters one and nine, Saints, Sinners and Reformers, accessed March 20, 2019, http://www.crookedlakereview.com/books/saints-sinners/martin9.html

Melonakos, Kathleen Kimball, *Counterfeiting in Early Mormonism: The Historical Record*, The John Whitmer Historical Association Journal, Fall/Winter 2017, Vol. 37, No. 2

Menefee, Leah Collins and Tiller, Lowell, *Cutoff Fever*, Oregon Historical Quarterly, Vol. 77, No. 4. (Dec. 1976) published by The Oregon Historical Society, accessed July 30, 2019, https://www.jstor.org/stable/20613535, accessed 7/30/2019

———, *Cutoff Fever II*, Oregon Historical Quarterly, Vol. 78, No. 1 (May 1977), published by the Oregon Historical Society, accessed July 30, 2019, www.jstor.org/stable/20613558

———, *Cutoff Fever III*, Oregon Historical Quarterly, Vol 78, No. 2 (June 1977) Oregon Historical Society, www.jstor.org/stable/20613567

Minto, John, *Antecedents of the Oregon Pioneers and the Light These Throw on Their Motives*, Oregon Historical Society Quarterly, Vol. 5, No. 1(Mar., 1904) Oregon Historical Society, https://www.jstor.org/stable/20609602

Morrison, John, *Fundamental Orders*, https://connecticuthistory.orgthefundamental-orders-of-Connecticut/

Pace, Rebecca M., The History of Teasdale, Utah 1882-1982, Family Search.org, https://www.Familysearch.org/photos/artifacts/11658534?p=223905...2F%2Fwww.family

Pioneer Diaries in the Digital Age, published in The Artifact, Lane County History Museum, Eugene, Oregon, Fall 2018, No. 229

Rees, Watkin, *Watkin Rees Papers, Ca. [1880-1905]* LDS Church Archives, call no. MS16220, http://churchh istorycatalog.lds.org/primo_library/libweb/action/diSear...ield+lds02&vid

Rees, Watkin, *Watkin Rees Journal,* Church of LDS, https://history.churchofjesuschrist.org/overlandtravel/sources/17675/rees-watkin-reminiscences-8-12-in-watkin-rees-papers-ca-1880-1905

Reverend Cotton Mather, Notable biographies.com

Reverend John Cotton, https://historyofmassachusetts/reverend-john-cotton

Saugus Iron Works: Hammersmith, National Park Service, https://nationalparks.org/explore-parks/Saugus-iro n–works-national-historic-site

Saugus Iron Works: The Roland W. Excavations, 1948-1953, https://nps.gov/sair/learn/historyculture/robbins excavationbook.htm

Scott, Donald, *Mormonism and the American Mainstream,* Queens College/University of New York, National Humanities Center, accessed 6/8/2019, http://nationalhumanitiescenter.org/tserve/nineteen/nkeyinfo/nmormon.htm

Sharp, Gene and John G., *Adlum Defending the Native Americans,* http://geneaologytrails.com/washdc/biographies/adlumjohn.html#john_Adlum_Defend

———, *Major John Adlum and his Vineyard,* Genealogy Trails, Washington, DC, Genealogy Trails.com, 2006-2017, http://genealogytrail.com/washdc/biographies/adlumvineyards.html

Stoops, William, *By Ox Team to Oregon,* Eugene Morning Register, Eugene, Oregon, 1925, photocopy articles August 31, September 6, 13, 20 and 27

The Pilgrims Before Plymouth, Smithsonian.com, https://www.smithsonianmag.com/Travel/the-pilgrims–before–plymouth-111851259

The Plainfield Quakers: The Society of Friends in Fulton County, Illinois, http://illinois.outfitters.com/illinois/history/family/quakers/quakers.html

The Story of Wales: Life in Merthyr Tydfil 19th Century "Little Hell," BBC.com, March 12, 2013

Walls, Joseph F., *So-called Attempted Lynching of Judge Charles Bradley during the Farm Holiday Movement in Iowa,* "The Farmer in Crisis", 1920-1930, The Annals of Iowa, 47 (1983), http://ir.iowa.edu/annals-of-iowa/vol47/iss215

Wilkinson, Norman B., *Mr. Davy's Diary 1794 Part II,* Pennsylvania History: A Journal of Mid-Atlantic Studies, Vol. 20, No 3(July 1953) published by Penn State University Press, https://www.jstor.org/stable/27769431

———, *The "Philadelphia Fever" in Northern Pennsylvania,* Pennsylvania History: A Journal of Mid-Atlantic Studies, Vol.20, No. 1 (January 1953), Penn State Press, https://www.jstor.org/stable/27769282

Valauska, Edward J., *John Adlum and America's First Wines*, Chicago Botanic Garden, July 2015, https://www.chicagobotanic.org/library/stories/adlum

Other sources

American Ancestors, NEHGS, https://americanancestors.org

American Spirit Magazine-DAR, https://www.dar.org/americanspirit

Ancestry.com, Adlum Family Tree

Census records, vital records, land records, collection of personal family papers and records

Columbia Pacific Heritage Museum, Ilwaco, WA, https://columbiapacificheritagemuseum.org

Daughters of the American Revolution, https://www.dar.org

Family Search.org

Lane County History Museum, Eugene, OR, https://lchm.org

New England Historic Genealogical Society, https://library.nehgs.org

Newspapers.com

The State Museum of Pennsylvania in Harrisburg, statemuseumpa.org

Endnotes

1   **El Monte,** *Brightwell, Eric 2013 California Fool's Gold-Exploring El Monte, the end of the Santa Fe Trail,* http://www.amoeba.com.

2   **Census for Henry Bruce Adlum,** United States Federal Census in 1910 shows Henry Bruce and wife Winifred living in Portland and 1920, living in Seattle. Year: 1910; Census place: Portland Ward 4, Multnomah, Oregon, Roll T624-1286; Page: 18B; Enumeration District: 0144; FHL microfilm: 1375299. Year: 1920; Census Place: Seattle, King, Washington; Roll: T625-1927; Page: 4B; Enumeration District: 181; Image 1132.

U.S. City Directories put Henry Bruce and Winifred Adlum in several different locations in Portland between 1910 and 1918 and put them in Seattle in 1918. Source: U.S. City Directories 1821-1989, author, Ancestry.com Publisher, 2011, Provo; UT, USA. U.S. City Directories for HB Adlum, Residence year: 1922; 327 W. Main, El Monte, Residence Place: Alhambra, California, USA; Publication Title: Alhambra, California, City Directory 1922.

Birth Record Daniel Bruce Adlum, birth certificate of Daniel Bruce Adlum, January 31, 1921, El Monte, CA, California Vital Records.

Joseph Downs Adlum, Draft Card for Henry Bruce's brother Jack shows him living in Seattle in 1918. Source: U.S. World War I Draft Registration Cards 1917-1918 for Joseph Downs Adlum, 9/18/1918, Registration State: Washington; Registration County: King; Roll: 1991892; Draft Board: 06, U.S. City Directory shows Joseph D. Adlum in San Fernando, Los Angeles, California, in 1920s.

3   **Sources on Long Beach:** History links.org. Long Beach, Washington, Frank, Michael, "Long Beach Peninsula: America's Last Coast," May 08, 2009, www.travelandleisure.com>Trip Ideas> Washington, Lucero, Donella J. and Hobbs, Nancy L. *The Long Beach Peninsula,* 2004, Acadia Publishing, Charleston, SC, Chicago, Ill, Portsmouth, NH, San Francisco, CA.

Victor Hugo and Mildred Allen location, 1920, United States Federal Census for Mildred E. Allen and Victor H. Allen in Long Beach, Washington, source: Year 1920; Census Place: Long Beach, Pacific, Washington; Roll: T625_1932; Page: 1A; Enumeration District: 179.

4   **Adlum family location** 1930, U.S. Census for 1930 shows Henry Bruce Adlum, Winifred, Helen, and Daniel living in a house they own at 1345 E. Couch St., Portland, Oregon. Value of real estate is $4,500. U.S. Census: Year 1930; Census Place: Portland, Multnomah, Oregon: Roll 1952; Page 6A; Enumeration District: 0312; image: 1010; FHL microfilm: 2341686.

5   **Information on Depression and CCC in Oregon,** Oregon Blue Book: Oregon History: The Great Depression>cultural>history>1859-Present, https://Oregonhistoryproject.org/...history... oregon/a-new.../Thegreatdepression/.

6   **Daniel Adlum–High School,** U.S. School Yearbooks, 1880-2012 for Dan Adlum, School: Grant High School, Portland, Oregon, Year: 1940; Source: Ancestry.com, U.S. School Yearbooks, 1880-2012{database online} Provo, Utah.

Mildred Allen Residence, 1940 U.S. Federal Census shows her in Portland with daughter Patricia and house borders. Daniel joined them later that year. Source: Year: 1940; Census Place: Portland, Multnomah, Oregon; Roll: m-10627-03390; Page: 3A; Enumeration District: 37-323.

Additional information, interview with Patricia Reese Adlum, June 2017, background information.

7   **Quote "Old Dutch Ship" and background,** Adlum, Cpl. Daniel B., "Experiences Encountered in Southwest Pacific Duty," published in the U.S. Army newspaper, *Over's and Shorts*, Camp McQuaide, California, June 1944. Collection of Patricia Reese Adlum.

8   **WWII operations for Salamaua:** 41st Infantry Division Jungleer.com, http://jungleer.com/23honors/29-salamaua-to-1st-battalion-162nd-infantry-regiment-July-1945 Haugland, Vern, *Associated Press*, "162d Sets Battle Record, 76 days in Tropic Wilds," *Associated Press* article clipping describing the 162nd in Salamaua, unknown date. Collection of Patricia Reese Adlum, WWII operations>Salamaua, en.Wikipedia.org "41st Infantry Division" (United States) section 2.4 Salamaua.

9   **Fuzzy wuzzy angels:** Glover, April, "Photographs reveal how heroic tribes in Papua New Guinea carried injured Australian soldiers to safety during World War Two", *Daily Mail*, Australia, December 12, 2017, www.dailymail.co.uk/new//Photographs_reveal_tribes_helped_Aussie_troops_WWII.

10 **Quote about battle:** Adlum, Cpl. Daniel B, "Battle of Salamaua is described," third in series of articles written for Army newspaper, Camp McQuaide, July 29, 1944.

11 **Fear of Battle:** Adlum, Cpl. Daniel B., "Battle of Salamaua." **Medics:** ibid. **Courage of natives:** Ibid.

Native culture: Adlum, Cpl. Daniel B., "Novel Way of Boosting Average in Pig Hunting," second in series of articles written for Army newspaper at Camp McQuaide, Watsonville, CA, July 1944.

Airfield speech: Adlum, Corporal Daniel B. "Battle of Salamaua."

12 Daniel Bruce Adlum was discharged from the Army in August 1945 at Fort Bliss, TX, after serving two years overseas and two years serving in an Army hospital. Enlisted Record and Report of Separation, United Sates Army, Honorable discharge, Book 111, 307.

13 **Destination Ninety quote:** source *The Los Angeles Times* article 16, January 1967, 106, www.newspapers.com/clip/14785421/the_los_angeles_times/?xid=637, additional *Los Angeles Times* article quoting Daniel B. Adlum and his work, "Blight Threats to Van Nuys and Reseda," January 16, 1967, 106, newspapers.com.

14 **Daniel J. Adlum moves to Iowa,** *The Altoona Tribute*, June 24, 1880 Altoona, PA, www.newspapers.com/clip/147906241/daniel_J_adlum_moves_to_iowa_24_jun1880/?xid+637.

1880 Census, U.S. Federal Census for Daniel J. Adlum, Year: 1880; Census Place: Altoona, Blair, Pennsylvania; Roll: 1102; Family History Film: 1255102; Page: 67B; Enumeration District: 154; Image: 0469.

15 **Info about Missouri Valley and Harrison County,** Tamisiea, Hugh J. *Missouri Valley The First One Hundred Years*, 1971 http://iagenweb.org/harrison/directories/MoValley_Hugh_Tamisiea.htm. Hunt, Charles Walter, *History of Harrison County, Iowa, its people, industries and institutions*, 1915, https://archive.org/historyofharrison01.

16 . **Marriage,** Iowa Marriage Records, 1880-1937 for Daniel J. Adlum, age 25, married Carrie Mckain, age 19, November 19, 1884, Iowa State Archives; Des Moines, Iowa; Volume: 424 (Tana-Wright) Ancestry.com.

Birth Records, Joseph Downs Adlum, born January 16, 1886, Iowa, Births and Christenings Index: 1857-1947, name father: D J Adlum, FHL film 1513443; Ancestry.com; Henry Bruce Adlum, Iowa Delayed Birth Records, 1856-1940, Daniel Joseph Adlum, father, age 29, date of birth May 16, 1889, State Historical Society of Iowa; Des Moines, Iowa; DGS:101693731, Ancestry.com.

1920 Census, U.S. Federal Census for Daniel J. Adlum: Year: 1920; Census Place: Missouri Valley Ward 3, Harrison, Iowa: Roll: T625_943: Page: 2B; Enumeration District: 90; Image 432.

U.S. Postmaster Appointment of Daniel J. Adlum, Missouri Valley, Harrison, Iowa appointed March 22, 1898 source: Record of Appointment of Postmasters, 1832-1971, NARA microfilm Publication, M841,145 rolls. Records of the Post Office Department, Records Group Number 28. Washington, DC; National Archives.

17 **Bank Failures in Iowa,** Coquillette, Calvin W. *The Struggle to Preserve Iowa's State Banking System,1920-1933, Annals of Iowa*, Vol 60, Number 1 winter 2001 https://ir.viowa.edu/cgi/viewcontent.cgi?article=10426&content+annals_of_Iowa.

18 **Attempted Lynching,** Wall, Joseph F. *So- Called Attempted Lynching of Judge Charles Bradley during the Farm Holiday Movement in Iowa:"The Farmer in Crisis, 1920-1936."* The Annals of Iowa 47 (1983) 166-127. Available: http://ir.uiowa.edu/annals-of-iowa/vol47/iss2/5.

19 **1930 Census,** United States Federal Census for Daniel J Adlum: Missouri Valley, Harrison, Iowa, Ancestry.com.

Information about bank ownership, interview with Patricia Reese Adlum, June 2017.

20 **Adlum family history,** personal letters collection of Patricia Reese Adlum, Death Index 1940-1997 for Daniel J Adlum California Death Index 1940-1997 death date Nov 14, 1956, Carrie Adlum death date Jan 3, 1956, Florida Death Index 1877-1998 for Joseph Downs Adlum, death date 1951 Duval, Florida, USA, California Death Index 1940-1997 for Henry Bruce Adlum death date Feb 10, 1955 Los Angeles, source: Ancestry.com.

21 **Merle Daniel Adlum,** information from daughter Virginia Adlum Hauser, Archives West: Merle Daniel Adlum Papers, 1945-1986, at archiveswest.oriscascade.org/ark:/80444/XU04092, Merle Daniel Adlum: Social Networks, https://snaccop erative.org/ark:/99166/w62v3vh8.

22 **Joseph Green Adlum**, Clark, Charles B. *History of Blair County, Pennsylvania* 1896 source: https://wwwaltoonalibrary.org/sites/ default/blaircounty history. Additional; Evalyn Irwin Adlum Obituary Oct. 31, 1908 Altoona Times, page 9, Newspapers.com, First Methodist Church of Bellwood Records, Pennsylvania and New Jersey, Church and town Records 1669-2013 for Joseph G Adlum, United Sates Federal Census Records for Joseph Green Adlum, 1850, 1860, 1870, 1880, 1890.

23 **History of Pennsylvania,** https://en.wikipedia.org/wiki/History_of_Pennsylvania.

24 **Railroads, Altoona,** Altoona, PA, Great American Stations, http://www.greatamericanstations.com/stations/altoona-pa-alt/.

25   **Representative from Blair County,** Joseph Green Adlum is listed as representative from Blair County as a Republican (Union Party defunct) in the Pennsylvania Daily Telegraph Nov. 1864: Pennsylvania House of Representatives 1865, source: staffwebwilkes.edu Listed in Altoona Tribune Sept. 16, 1865, 2, Newspapers.com.

26   **Quote "English in character,"** Webb, Jim, *Born Fighting How the Scots-Irish Shaped America*, New York, Broadway Books, Penguin Random House, LLC, 2004, 72, background on Ulster Plantation, 67-75.

27   **History of Northern Ireland,** *The Plantation of Ulster*, taken from *A History of Ireland* by Eleanor Hull, libraryireland.com,

28   **Adlum Arrival in Pennsylvania,** Eisenhart, Willis W. The Abbott-Adlum-Green Families, Abbottstown, Pennsylvania 1957, Adlum, John, *Memoirs of the Life of John Adlum in the Revolutionary War*, ed. Howard H. Peckham Chicago 1968, as well as Photocopy of *Memoirs of the Life of John Adlum*, 2, The Pennsylvania Historical and Museum Commission for Microfilming, Aug. 15,1952, John Adlum states the family arrived in Pennsylvania in 1734. There is evidence of ownership of 300 acres of land near York by immigrant John Adlum in 1733 in Land Grant Records of York County. Simon Berwick was known to live in the Lancaster area in the 1730s.

29   **York Land Grant,** dated 1752 granted to Joseph Adlum, posted by John and Gene Sharp, Ancestry.com.

30   **John Adlum Sherriff York County,** *History of York County, Pennsylvania: from the earliest period to the present time*, 32, Photocopy of *Memoirs of the Life of John Adlum*, Adlum speaks about his grandfather's elected positions as well as his father Joseph's election to sheriff (he did not serve) and then coroner, obit, find a grave memorial John Adlum Sr., (1699/1700-1773)

31   **Joseph Adlum Coroner,** Eisenhart, Willis W. *The Abbott-Adlum-Green Families* Joseph Adlum elected coroner 1764-1780, 11.

32   **Marriage of Joseph Abbott and Catherine Abbott,** Eisenhart, The Abbott-Adlum-Green Families, 10.

    Quote, John Adlum's Memoir, 4.

33   **Stamp Act,** John Adlum's Memoir, 9.

34   **Militia,** Memoirs of the Life of John Adlum in the Revolutionary War, Ed. Howard Peckham. 2-4.

35   **John Adlum Quote,** McCullough, David, "*1776*," New York Simon and Schuster, 2005 pages, 242-243.

36   **New York experiences,** Peckham, Memoirs of John Adlum, 128-143,

    After, York during the American Revolution, https://yorkcountypa.gov/about-york-county/york-county-history.html Kent and Deardorff, John Adlum on the Allegheny: Memoirs for the Year 1794: Part I, source: The Pennsylvania Magazine of History and Biography, Vol 84. No 3 (Jul 1960) https://www.jstor.org/stable/20089310 page 272

37   **Need for surveying roads,** Lechner, Carl B. *The Erie Triangle: The Final Link Between Philadelphia and the Great Lakes*, source: *The Pennsylvania Magazine of History and Biography*, Vol. CXVI, No. 1 (January 1992) https:www.jstor.org.

38   **Start of career**, Major John Adlum's Memoirs, quote about Captain Lowden, 135-136.

Capt. John Lowden, Hannum, Lt. Col. Patrick H., *America's First Company Commanders*, Infantry Magazine, Oct-Dec 2013, 13.

39   **York Long Rifles,** History of Pennsylvania rifles, visithistoricallancaster.com/history_art/Pennsylvania_rifles, McDowell, Donald R. *Those Tall American Patriots and their Long Rifles*, source: revolutionarywararchives.org/longrifle.html.

40   **Surveying and speculation,** there are a number of sources I consulted about John Adlum's time in the wilderness of Pennsylvania, **Surveying, map** Gahn, Bessie Wilmarth, *Major John Adlum of Rock Creek*, source: Records of the Columbia Historical Society, Washington, DC, Vol. 39, 1938, https://www.jstor.org/stable/40067536 also Kent, Donald and Deardorff, *John Adlum on the Allegheny: Memoirs for the Year 1794* Part I and Part II, Wilkinson, Norman B. *The "Philadelphia Fever" in Northern Pennsylvania*, source: Pennsylvania History: A Journal of Mid-Atlantic Studies, Vol. 20 NO. 1 (Jan1953) https://www.jstor.org/stable/27769283 Wilkinson deals with Adlum's work for Bingham and others and compares the fever in land speculation to the yellow fever outbreak in Philadelphia.

41   **Philadelphia land office closed,** Wilkinson, *The "Philadelphia Fever" in Northern Pennsylvania*, 53

42   **Yellow Fever,** The story of the yellow fever epidemic is covered very well in Jim Murphy's book for Scholastic. Murphy, Jim, *An American Plague, The True and Terrifying Story of the Yellow Fever Epidemic of 1793*, Scholastic Inc., New York, 2003, in particular 21-23 and 27-31.

43   **Major John Adlum's Portrait,** Pennsylvania Historical Society, his portrait is now at the Pennsylvania State Museum in Harrisburg, Adlum's portrait is included in an article written about Charles Willson Peale. *Charles Willson Peale with Patron and Populace. A supplement to "Portraits and Miniatures by Charles Willson Peale" with a survey of His work in Other Genres*, authors Charles Coleman Sellers and Charles Willson Peale source: Transactions of The American Philosophical Society, New Series, Vol 59, NO. 3 (1969), 1-146, https://www.jstor.org/stable/1006131.

44   **Indian Situation,** Kent and Deardroff, *John Adlum on the Allegheny, Part I*, 267-269.

45   **Men Nervous, letters,** Kent and Deardroff, *John Adlum on the Allegheny, Part II*, 437, https://www.jstor.org/stable/20089336.

46   **House at Wolf Run,** John Adlum on the Allegheny, also Sharp, Gene Kerr and John G." *Major John Adlum and His Vineyard*, Genealogy Trails, Washington, DC, Genealogy Trails 2006-2017, http://genealogytrails.com/washdc/biographies/adlumvineyards.html.

Additional article by the Sharps about Adlum, *Defending the Native Americans*, Genealogy Trails, Washington, DC, Adlum house currently is at 424 Narber Fry Road, Muncy, PA, listed for sale Nov 2017. Pennsylvania, U.S. direct tax list for 1798 shows John Adlum paid tax on 400 acres and two dwellings in Muncy, occupied by his parents, Joseph and Catherine. Record: John Adlum County: Northumberland, Lycoming and Mifflin Location: Muncy. v **Surveying and speculation,** there are a number of sources I consulted about John Adlum's time in the wilderness of Pennsylvania, **Surveying, map** Gahn, Bessie Wilmarth, *Major John Adlum of Rock Creek*, source: Records of the Columbia Historical Society, Washington, DC, Vol. 39, 1938, https://www.jstor.org/stable/40067536 also Kent, Donald and Deardorff, *John Adlum on the Allegheny: Memoirs for the Year 1794* Part I and Part II, Wilkinson, Norman B. *The "Philadelphia Fever" in Northern Pennsylvania*, source: Pennsylvania History: A Journal of Mid-Atlantic Studies, Vol. 20 NO. 1 (Jan1953) https://www.jstor.org/stable/27769283

Wilkinson deals with Adlum's work for Bingham and others and compares the fever in land speculation to the yellow fever outbreak in Philadelphia.

47   **Quotes from Mr. Davy,** Wilkinson, Norman B., *Mr. Davy's Diary 1794* Part II, source: Pennsylvania History: A Journal of Mid-Atlantic Studies, page 266 and 267, **Background,** Kent, *John Adlum on the Allegheny*

48   **Move to Maryland,** Gahn, *Major John Adlum of Rock Creek*, Thomas Jefferson **letter,** October 7, 1809, to John Adlum Founders Online. https://founders.archives.gov/documents/Jefferson/03-01-02-0459.

49   **Father of American Viticulture,** Gabler, James M. *Passions, the Wines and Travels of Thomas Jefferson*, Bacchus Press Ltd., Baltimore, Maryland, 1995, 214.

50   **Vineyard,** Gahn, *Major John Adlum of Rock Creek*, Sharp, *Major John Adlum and His Vineyard*, Adlum, John, *A Memoir on the Cultivation of the Vine in America and the Best Mode of Making Wine*, Washington: Davis and Force, 1823, Valauskas, Edward J. *John Adlum and America's First Wines*, Chicago Botanic Garden, July 2015, https://www.chicagobotanic.org/library/stories/adlum.

51   Gahn, *Major John Adlum of Rock Creek*

52   **Letters, family relationships,** Adlum Family Letters, copies from collection of Virginia Adlum Houser, Daniel McPhail Obituary: find a grave.com/memorial/13953040408/daniel-mcphail.

53   **Joseph Adlum,** 1820 United States Federal Census for Joseph Adlum, Loyalsock, Lycoming county, Pennsylvania August 7, 1820. https://search.ancestry.com/cgi-bin/sse.dll?indiv=1&db=1 820usfedcenancestry&h=1068056, 1830 census shows Joseph and family, sister Elizabeth, brother Edward listed on same page in Muncy, Lycoming County, Pennsylvania, Ancestry.com, additional information from Eisenhart, Willis W. *The Abbott-Adlum-Green Families*, **Joseph Green Adlum** obituaries, Altoona and Bellwood papers, newspaper clipping from collection of Virginia Adlum Houser, unknown date.

Chapter Two

54   **Newspaper clipping** "*John Holman Honored*" Unknown Oregon newspaper dated Monday June 3, 1929, collection of Kay Holman Voth.

55   Much of the information about **Ella Holman Turner** is from her daughter's memoir of her: *Portrait of Mama*, Patricia Turner Shawver, privately printed by P.K. Allen Printing 1965 Portland, Oregon.

56   Ibid

57   **Holmans**, Ibid **Peter Burnett** and family, Burnett, Peter H., "*Reflections and Opinions of An Old Pioneer*" New York, D. Appleton and Company, 1880, 97-100.

58   **James D. Holman,** http://wwwrootsweb.ancestry.com/ormultno/History/Scott/BiogE-L/holman.htm, **Holman, Frederick V.,** "*Christmas on Baker's Bay*" The Sou'wester, Pacific County Historical Society, winter 1970, Vol V, Number 4.

Background on Pacific County and James D. Holman, Bailey, Bob, "*Notes on Early Pacific County,*" The Sou'wester, Pacific County Historical Society, Summer 2001, Vol xxxvi, Number 2.

59   **Holman**, Frederick V., "*Christmas on Baker's Bay.*"

60   **James D. Holman bio**, www.Rootsweb.ancestry.com.

Quote from Glen Holman, *The Oregon Daily Journal*, Portland, Oregon, 09 March 1922, Thursday, Page 10, Newspapers.com.

61   **Ella's Wedding**, *Portrait of Mama*, McMinnville, Historic Context of McMinnville, Oregon.gov, 2011, https://www.oregon.gov/oprd/HCD/.../yamhill_McMinniville_historiccontext_2011.pdf.

62   **Peter Burnett**, Burnett, Peter H., *Reflections and Opinions of an Old Pioneer*, 183-184. **Daniel S. Holman History**, Joseph Gaston and George H Himes, *The Centennial History of Oregon 1811-1912, Vol 2,* Deady, Lucy Ann Henderson, *Crossing the Plains in 1846*, Transactions of the Fifty-Sixth Annual Oregon Pioneer Ass. Salem, OR, E. M. Waite, 1928, 57-64.

63   **Holman, Frederick V.**, *Dr. John McLaughlin, the Father of Oregon*, The Arthur H. Clark Co., 1907, Cleveland, Ohio, 280.

64   **Glen Owen Burnett**, Pioneer Preacher Profile: Glen Owen Burnett, http://ncBible.org/nwh/proburnett.html, *Portrait of Mama*.

65   **Information on Peter Burnett's Oregon years** is from a variety of sources: Burnett, Peter H., *Recollections and Opinions of An Old Pioneer*, Hardeman, Nicholas Perkins, *Wilderness Calling: The Hardeman Family in The American Westward Movement, 1750-1900*, University of Tennessee Press, 1977, Nashville, TN;

Nokes, R. Gregory, *The Troubled Life of Peter Burnett*, Oregon State University Press, Corvallis, OR, 2018.

66   **Quote** from the *Spectator*, Oregon Secretary of State: "A New Territory and the California Gold Rush," http://sos.oregon.gov/archives/exhibits/constitution/Pages/before-gold.aspx. .

67   **Holman family history**, Burnett, Peter H., *Reflections*, 255-272.

68   **Applegate trail**: Nokes, R. Gregory, *The Troubled Life of Peter Burnett*, 80-84; Hardeman, *Wilderness Calling*, 192-200.

69   **Burnett, Peter H.**, *Reflections*, 272-273 and 286-287.

70   **Beck, Warren A. and Williams, David A.**, *California: A History of the Golden State*, Doubleday and Company, Garden City, NY, 1972, 123-124.

71   **Indians**: Beck, *California: A History of the Golden State*, 76.

72   **Sam Brannon**: Brands, H. W., *The Age of Gold*, Anchor Books, NY, 2002, 43.

73   **500 schooners:** Asbury, Herbert, *The Barbary Coast*, Alfred A. Knopf Inc., New York, 1933, 11.

74   **John Sutter and family**: Brands, H. W., *The Age of Gold*, Anchor Books, New York, 2002, 272-274

75   **Franklin, William E.** "A Forgotten Chapter in California's History: Peter H. Burnett and John A. Sutter's Fortune," California Historical Society Quarterly 41 (December 1962), 323.

76   **Hardeman, Nicholas Perkins**, *Wilderness Calling*, 206-214; Nokes, R. Gregory, *The Troubled Life of Peter Burnett*, 161-170.

77   **General information about Frederick V. Holman** from *Portrait of Mama*, and Levinson, N.

J., "Frederick V. Holman, An Appreciation," *The Oregon Historical Quarterly*, vol xxviii, number 3, September 1927, www.jstor.org; "1892 Frederick V. Holman House To Be Torn Down," staff writers, www.portlandchronicle.com, March 12, 2016.

78   **Information about Holman family origins** comes from census records and Holman Family History

79   **Squire Boone**: Faragher, John Mack, *Daniel Boone*, 29-30.

Holman family location to the Boones: Hoshorn, Ora Holman, "The Holman Branch," 1945, http://genform.genealogy.com/holman/messages/1687.html.

80   **Location of Holman properties**: census records and Holman Family History. Location of Daniel Boone's family from Faragher, John Mack, *Daniel Boone the Life and Legend of an American Pioneer*, Henry Holt and Company, New York, 1992, 65.

81   **Isaac Holeman** in the U.S. Revolutionary War Pension and Bounty-Land warrant application Files, 1800-1900, North Carolina Ancestry.com,

Holeman Brothers in Revolution: Holman Family History http://genforum.genealogy.com/holman/messages/1687.html.

82   **Stand at The Cumberland Gap**: Turner, Frederick Jackson, *The Significance of the Frontier in American History*, (1893): New York: Ungar, 1963.

Nancy Holman: Slagle, Mary Ella, "Records of Holmans and Crowleys, Ancestry.com. **Daniel Boone quote**: https://inspiringquotes.us/author/3483-daniel-boone.

83   Holman Family History: **Bryan Station siege**: https://en Wikipedia.org/wiki/Bryan Station.

84   **Tomahawking of Henry Holeman**: Holman Family History from http://genforum.geneal ogy.com/holman/ messages/1715.html. **Isaac Holeman Will** 1807, North Carolina, Ancestry.com.

85   **Daniel L. Holeman** census records and will, Ancestry.com.

86   **John Holman** census, war records, Ancestry.com.

87   **Lt Col. Isaac Holman quote**: "Ancestral Study of Four Families, Roberts, Griffith, Cartwright, Simpson: covering lineal and collateral relations of my child, https://books.goggle.com.

88   **John Holman** census and 1812 war records, Ancestry.com.

89   **Lt. Col. Isaac Holman**: "Ancestral study of four families, Roberts, Griffith, Cartwright, Simpson.

90   **Holman, James Saunders**: The Handbook of Texas Online/ Texas State Historical Association

91   **Holman, William Sandford**: A Guide to Sanford Holman Papers, 1839-1840, Legacy.lib.utexas.edu/taro/drtsa/00077/00077-P.html

92   **James Burnett** in the U.S., Revolutionary War rolls, 1775-1783, 6th Regiment, 2nd Lieutenant from Pittsylvania County, Ancestry.com.

Burnett, Peter H., *Reflections and Opinions of An Old Pioneer*, 1-3.

93   Ibid, 4-6.

94   Ibid, 7. **Will** of George W. Burnett, 1838, Ancestry.com.

95 **Exiled, Kicked by Racehorse**, Hardeman, Nicholas Perkins, *Wilderness Calling*, 5-6.

96 **Married, background**, Ibid, 6-7.

97 **Quote** is from Hardeman, Ibid, 9.

98 **The Battle of King's Mountain**: http://tngenweb.org/revwar/kingsmountain.html

Quote: "The Americans destroyed us," Neace, James Clell, *A Short History of the Kentucky Long Rifle*, Breathittcounty.com, 2001, *Wilderness Calling*, 12.

99 **Hardeman, Nicholas Perkins**, *Wilderness Calling*, 13-15.100 . Ibid, 18-19 and 24-25.

101 Ibid, 28-35.

102 **Thomas Jefferson quote**: Tn4me.org.*ns and Opinions of An Old Pioneer*, 1.

Hardeman, Nicholas Perkins, *Wilderness Calling*, 35-37.

103 Ibid, 35-38.

104 Ibid, 64-69.

105 Ibid, 35-38. **Elk Heaven quote,** 71.

106 **Quote from Peter Burnett about his Hardeman relations**: Burnett, Peter H., *Reflections and Opinions of An Old Pioneer*, 3.

John Hardeman: Hardeman, Nicholas Perkins, *Wilderness Calling*, 71-81.

107 **The Santa Fe trade**: Ibid, 95-117.

Thomas Jones and Bailey Hardeman: Hardeman, Bailey, The Handbook of Texas Online, Texas State Historical Association, https://tshaonline.org/handbook/online/articles/fha56 **Hardeman, Thomas Jones**, The Handbook of Texas Online, Texas State Historical Association, https://tshaonline.org/handbook/online/articles/fha57. **Hardeman County, Texas**: Texas History Notebook, https://texoso66.com/2015/12/03/hardeman-county/.

108 **Thomas Jones and Bailey Hardeman**, "The Handbook of Texas Online"

109 **Hardeman, Nicholas Perkins**, *Wilderness Calling*, 118-152.

110 **"Old Tom" Hardeman**, *Wilderness Calling*, 73.

Census and death records of George W. Burnett and Daniel L. Holman and families, Ancestry.com

111 **Burnett, Peter H.**, *Reflections*, 49-59; Mormons, 59-69. Nokes, R. Gregory, *The Troubled Life of Peter Burnett*, 10-18.

112 **Burnett, Peter H.**, *Reflections*, Mormons, 63-68.

113 Nokes, R. Gregory, *The Troubled Life of Peter Burnett*, 22-23.

Chapter Three

114   . **Info on move to McMinnville**: Shawver, Patricia Turner, *Portrait of Mama*,

1910 U.S. Census Records for **Winifred Turner** lists home in McMinnville Ward 2, Yamhill, OR, with grandmother Martha Elizabeth Burnett Holman, mother Mary Ellen Holman Turner, and her sister Patricia Turner, Year: 1910; Census Place: McMinnville Ward 2, Yamhill, OR; Roll: T624_1290; page: 2B; enumeration District: 0284; microfilm: 1375303, Ancestry.com, 1910 United States Federal Census (database online).

Winifred B. Turner in Oregon, Marriage Indexes, 1906-2009, marriage date: 16 June 1911, marriage place: Multnomah, OR, USA, Source: Oregon State Library; Salem, OR; Reel 2, Ancestry.com, Oregon Marriage Indexes, 1906-2009, (database online).

115   **Marriage of Mary Ellen Holman** and William Burke Turner, 30 June 1881, Yamhill, OR, source: Ancestry.com., Oregon County Marriage Records, 1851-1975, (database online).

History of pharmacy in the U.S., http://en.wikipedia.org/wiki/History_of_Pharmacy_in_the_United_States.

William B. Turner is working for Sanita Medical Co., Sierra Madre, CA, 1897, U.S. City Directories, 1822-1995 for William B. Turner: Ancestry.com. U.S. City Directories, 1822-1995 (database online).

Patricia Lee Turner born in Alameda, Los Angeles, CA, 7 March 1896: in the California, County Birth, Marriage and Deaths records, 1849-1980: Ancestry. Com. California, County Birth, Marriage and Death Records database online).

Additional information from Shawver, *Portrait of Mama*.

116   Information on **Los Angeles land boom** and mecca for those suffering from Tb: Boorstin, Daniel J., *The Americans: The Democratic Experience*, Vintage Books, New York, August 1974, 274-275

.117   **Voter Registration Record** for William B. Turner of July 1896 shows address of 2001 Toberman, Los Angeles, and occupation as pharmacist as well as a physical description: California, Voter Registers, 1866-1898 Ancestry.com

Additional information from *Portrait of Mama*.

Census records and city directories show Mary Ellen Holman and children as well as mother-in-law Esther Ann Johnson Turner and siblings of William living in Portland in 1899.

118   Portland: en.wikipedia.org>wiki>History_of_Portland_Oregon

119   **Cable car system in Portland**: History Blog: Portland's Cable-Car Adventure, Oregonlive.com post Nov 19, 2014; https:/www.oregonlive.com/multimedia/index…/history_blog_portlands_cable-car_adventure.html.

120   . **Patricia Turner's quote, recollection** of her childhood home: Shawver, Patricia L., *Portrait of Mama*.

121   **Description of Ella's gown**: Shawver, Patricia L., *Portrait of Mama*.

122 1910 Census records show **Ella Holman** living with mother in McMinnville

1910 Census Records for **Esther Ann (Johnson) Turner** show her at age 85 (widowed) living with her daughters Anna and Clarissa Turner at 525 16th Portland, Ward 5, Multnomah County, OR. Esther Ann had been a widow for 25 years. Her husband **James Higgins Turner**, born 21 September 1812 in Lancaster County, PA, died 1 January 1885 in McMinnville and is buried in the Masonic Cemetery there.

James Higgins Turner in the U.S., Find a Grave Index, 1600s-current, Ancestry.com

1910 Census record for **William B. Turner** shows him living on Pennsylvania Ave. NW, Precinct 3, Washington, District of Columbia, married 29 years at age 49, profession, clerk and out of work. Record: Year: 1910; Census Place: Precinct 3, Washington, District of Columbia; Roll: T624_150; Page:13A; Enumeration district: 0036; FHL microfilm 1374163, Ancestry.com 1910 United States Federal Census (database online)

Daniel Saunders Holman, born 15 November 1822 in Fayetteville, Lincoln County, TN, died 15 March 1910 in McMinnville, Yamhill County, OR. Record: Oregon, Wills and Probate records, 1849-1963 for Daniel S. Holman Source citation: Author: Oregon. County Court (Yamhill county); Probate Place: Yamhill, OR, Source Information: Ancestry.com Oregon. Wills and Probate Records, 1849-1963 (database online).

Esther Ann (Johnson) Turner born 21 February 1825 Dryden, NY, died on 7 November 1910 in Portland, Multnomah County, OR, and was buried in River View Cemetery in Portland. Record: U.S., Find a Grave Index, 1600s to current, Source Information: Ancestry.com U.S., Find a Grave Index 1600s-current (database online).

Mary Ellen (Holman) Turner born in Polk County, OR, on 23 October 1856, died 29 November in Marshfield, Coos County, OR, and is buried in the Masonic Cemetery in McMinnville with other members of her Holman family. Source: Mary Ella Turner in the U.S., Find a Grave Index, 1600s-current, Ancestry.com.

William Burke Turner, born 27 June 1860 in Vincennes, Knox County, IN, died 11 June 1924 in Sacramento, CA. William B. Turner in the California Death Index, 1905-1939, Source: Ancestry.com California, Death Index.

123 **Winifred Beatrice (Turner) Adlum** 1922 registered to vote in El Monte City Precinct 2, Los Angeles County, CA. Her address was 248 Granada St. and she registered as a Republican. Record: California, Voter Registrations, 1900-1968 for Winifred B. Adlum, Citation: California State Library; Sacramento, CA; Great Register of Voters, 1900-1968. Ancestry.com.

Winifred B. Adlum divorce record, maiden name Turner, State of Oregon, date of decree 7 November 1941 for desertion. Source: Vital Records, State of Oregon.

Winifred B. Turner certificate of death, State of Oregon: cause of death cerebral hemorrhage due to hypertension. Born 26 August 1890, died 2 April 1956 in Portland, OR. Roy G. Turner husband. Source: Oregon Vital Records.

124 **Trip to Oregon**: Turner, Julia Clarissa, *All the Years of Her Life: A Biography of Esther Ann Johnson*, edited and compiled by Elizabeth L. Smith, Bubba's Pal Publishing, Bryan, TX, 1997, 102-104.

125   **James H. Turner Postmaster**, Broad Ripple, Marion, IN, appointment date 26 Dec 1854:

James H. Turner in the U.S., Appointments of U.S. Postmasters, 1832-1971 Source: Ancestry.com.

James H. Turner, State Representative from Marion County: Southerland. James, "Biographical sketches of Members of the 41st General Assembly, 1861."

Major James H. Turner at Chattanooga: Turner, Julia Clarissa and Smith, Elizabeth L., *All the Years of Her Life*, 99b.

126   Information on medical situation and **diseases during the Civil War**: Brockett, L. P., *Women's Work in the Civil War: A record of Heroism, Patriotism and Patience,*. Philadelphia, PA: Zeigler, McCurdy & Co. Boston: R. H. Curran, 1867. Reprint, Bowie MD: Heritage Books, 1993, Burroughs, Wynell, "Teaching with Documents Surgeon General's Office." Social Education (January 1988), additional information from Turner, *All the Years of her Life*, 99-100.

127   **History of Indianapolis** in the Civil War: https://enwikipedia.org/wiki/History_of_Indianapolis.

128   **Esther Ann marriage to Peter Koontz**, 4 July 1850 in Marion County, IN:

Peter Koontz in the Indiana, Select Marriages Index, 1748-1993, spouse Hester (Esther) A. Johnson, FHL Film number: 499368, Reference ID: 212, Ancestry.com Indiana, Select Marriages Index, 1748-1993.

129   **Marriage of Esther Ann to James H. Turner**, 16 September 1852, Granville, OH, Turner, Julia Clarissa, *All the Years of her Life*, 94.

Letter from James to Esther Ann written on the canal at "The Falls of Ohio" a month after wedding 16 October 1852: Ibid, 95-96.

130   **Move from Dryden** to Ohio: Ibid, 20-22.

131   **History Ohio and Northwest Indian Wars**: Hintzen, William, *Border Wars of the Upper Ohio Valley (1769-1794)*, Jesse Stuart Foundation, Ashland, KY, 1999, and Rosenberry, Lois Kimball Matthews, *The Expansion of New England*, Houghton Mifflin Company, Boston and New York, 1909, reprinted by Forgotten Books.com.

132   Turner, *All the Years of Her Life*, 28-35.

133   **Information on move to Gambier** and Kenyon College, Ibid, 46-50.

Rutherford B. Hayes at Kenyon, Ibid, 51-52.

134   . **Indianapolis, epidemics**, death of Rev. Samuel Lee Johnson, Ibid, 70-75.

135   **Deaths from cholera and typhoid,** Ibid, 76-77, cholera epidemics: www.ohiohistorycentral.org/w/cholera_epidemic.

136   **Gurdon Collins Johnson, appointment as postmaster** in Granville, Licking, OH, 23 June 1849, West Newton, Marion, IN, 27 September 1858, Lawrence, Marion County, IN, 23 April 1856. U.S., Appointments to U. S. Postmaster, 1832-1971, Ancestry.com.

Gurdon Collins Johnson, one of first merchants in Broad Ripple (suburb of Indianapolis) Marion, IN, in "The History of Indianapolis and Marion County, chapter XXVII, Washington Township. Ancestry.com.

Gurdon Collins Johnson born 11 January 1786, Granville, Washington County, NY, married 08 October 1808, Poultney, VT, died 06 February 1864, Indianapolis, Marion County, IN.

Wife **Louisa Lee** born 11 December 1787, Poultney, VT, died 11 July 1870, Indianapolis, Marion County, IN.

137   **Gurdon Collins Johnson Sr. marriage record** shows marriage to Esther Brainerd of East Haddom, 8 May 1781, Guilford, CT. Source: Connecticut, Town Marriage Records, pre-1870 (Barbour Collection) for Gurdon Johnson.

Girden (Gurdon) Johnson, 33rd Regiment of Foot, Connecticut, 1775: U.S., Revolutionary War rolls, 1775-1783, Ancestry.com.

Information on Esther Brainerd and family, Turner, *All the Years of Her Life*.

138   **1790 census for Gurdon Johnson** shows home in Granville, Washington County, NY, Source Citation: Year: 1790; Census Place: Granville, Washington, NY; Series: M637; Roll: 6; Page: 193; Image: 242; Family History Library Film: 0568146, Source Information: Ancestry. Com. 1790, Unites States Federal Census (database online)

Service in militia, Turner, *All the Years of Her Life*, 13.

Gurdon in Fair Haven: Adams, Andrew Napoleon, *A History of the Town of Fair Haven, Vermont: in three parts*, 404-405, obtained from Ancestry.com.

Early roads in Vermont: The Vermont Historical Society, https://vermonthistory.org/journal/misc/EarlyRoads& Taverns.pdf

139   **Fulling**: https://www.britannica.com/technology/fulling

Quote from Gurdon: Adams, Andrew Napoleon, *History of the Town of Fair Haven, Vermont: in three parts*.

140   **Information on Reverend Samuel Johnson** comes from these sources: Genealogy of family from Ancestry.com and Turner's *All the Days of Her Life*;" Samuel Johnson's life: Beardsley, E. E., *Life and Correspondence of Samuel Johnson*, New York Hurd and Houghton, 1873; Bremer, Francis J., *The Puritan Experiment: New England Society from Bradford to Edwards*. University Press of New England, Lebanon, NH, 1995, Chapter Sixteen, 225-229; Samuel Johnson (American educator) http://en.wikipedia.org/wiki/Samuel_Johnson_(American_educator).

141   Information on **William Samuel Johnson**: American Ancestry vol. 4 p 166 Johnson, Samuel William available on Ancestry.com; William Samuel Johnson https://en.wikipedia.org/wiki/William_Samuel_Johnson; www.let.rug.nl/usa/biographies/William-Samuel-Johnson/.

142   **Dr. Samuel Lee death** in *All the Years of Her Life*, Samuel Lee (Deacon) birth record shows born 19 Nov 1754 in Canaan, VT; parents Samuell and Silence (Flecther), Samuell Lee in the Connecticut Town Birth Records, Pre-1870 (Barbour Collection) Source Information: Ancestry.com.

Samuel Lee (Deacon) **married Mary Bingham** (born 3 July 1752) Samuel Lee in the U.S. and International Marriage Records, 1560-1900, Source Information: Ancestry.com.

Mary Bingham in the Family Data Collections-Births, Father: Jabez Bingham Mother: Mary Wheelock, Birth Date: 3 July 1752, Salisbury, Litchfield, CT, Source Information: Edmund West, comp., Family Data collections - Births (database online) Ancestry.com.

Deacon Samuel Lee in the U.S., Find a Grave Index, 1600s-current: Birth Date: 19 Nov 1754, Birth Place: Canaan, Litchfield County, CT, Death Date: 9 April 1813, Death Place: Poultney, Rutland County, Vermont, Cemetery: East Poultney Cemetery. Source Information: Ancestry.com. U.S., find a Grave Index, 1600s-current (database online).

Samuel Lee, *Honor Roll of Litchfield County Revolutionary Soldiers*, Richards, Josephine Ellis editor, published by Mary Floyd Tallmadge Chapter Daughters of the American Revolution, Litchfield, CT, 1912, Town of Woodbury, Ancestry.com. Samuel Lee.

143 . **Jabez Bingham** in the U.S., Revolutionary War Rolls, 1775-1783, served in the Connecticut 06th Regiment 1777.

Source Information: Ancestry.com, North America, Family Histories, 1500-2000 for Jabez Bingham, Birth Date: 12 April 1724, Place: Norwich, CT, Marriage Date: 24 December 1746 at Windham, Father: Jabez Bingham, Mother: Bethia Woods, Spouse: Mary Wheelock, Child. Jabcz Bingham, Source Citation: Book title: *Spes Mea Christus: Ye Bingham Genealogy*, Ancestry.com.

Mary Wheelock marriage record shows she married Jabez Bingham 24 December 1746, Source Information: Connecticut, Town Marriage Records, pre-1870 for Mary Wheelock, Windham Vital Records 1692-1800 p 378, Ancestry.com.

Additional genealogy from Ancestry.com and Turner's *All the Days of Her Life*.

144 **Information on Rev. Ralph Wheelock** is from Ancesry.com, wheelockgenealogy.com; Mclure, David and Parish, Elijah, *Memoirs of the Rev. Eleazar Wheelock, D.D., Founder and President of Dartmouth College and Moor's Charity School*, published 1811, excerpts on Ancestry.com; *Puritans in the New World, A Critical Anthology*, Hall, David, editor, Princeton University Press Princeton and Oxford, 2004, Chapter 4: The Town of Denham Organizes a Gathered Church, Ralph Wheelock, https://en.Wikipedia.org/wiki/Ralph_Wheelock.

Chapter Four

145 The Courtship of Myles Standish is a famous 19th-century poem by Longfellow, a descendant of *Mayflower* passengers John Alden and Priscilla Mullins. It is the story of their romance and another suitor, Myles Standish; Johnson, Caleb H. *The Mayflower and Her Passengers*, Xlibris Corporation, www.Xlibris.com, 2006, 47-48.

Myles Standish origins, Moorwood, Helen, *Myles Standish-His Ancestry, Lands and Family Connections*, www.mylesstandish.com.info, Part Two, **will and background** Johnson, Caleb H. *The Mayflower and Her Passengers*, 210-231.

146 "**bred soldier**" Johnson, Caleb H., *The Mayflower and Her Passengers*, 211.

147 **John Robinson,** https://en.wikipedia.org/wiki/John_Robinson_(pastor).

148 **State of Anglican church in the time of the Puritans,** Fraser, Rebecca, *The Mayflower-The families, the Voyage and the Founding of America*, St. Martin's Press, New York, 2017, 9-10.

149 **John Robinson and Scrooby,** Ibid, 16-17, https://en.wikipedia.org/wiki/John_Robinson_(pastor).

150 **Information on Scrooby congregation,** Bradford, William, *Of Plymouth Plantation*, edited by Morison, Samuel Eliot, Alfred A. Knopf, New York, 1998, 9-10, Philbrook, Nathaniel, *Mayflower*, Penguin Group, New York, 2006, 7-13.

151 **Leaving England**, Bradford, William, *Of Plymouth Plantation*, 11-15.

   Leiden, Philbrick, Nathaniel, page 17

152 **Robinson**, Fraser, Rebecca, *The Mayflower*, 16-17, 23.

153 **Life in Leiden,** Ibid, chapter two; Leiden, Philbrick, *Mayflower*, 5, 16-17; Bangs, Jeremy, "Pilgrims in Leiden."

154 **Housing in Leiden**, Fraser, Rebecca, *The Mayflower*, 19-23; Bangs, Jeremy, "Pilgrims in Leiden" http://www.leidenamericanpilgrimmuseuem.org.

   Origins of the Fuller brothers, Mayflower Families Through Five Generations, (Mayflower Silver Books) Family of Edward Fuller, General Society of Mayflower Descendants, Plymouth, MA, 2006, Vol. Four, 1-8.

155 **women in the church,** Frazer, Rebecca, *The Mayflower*, 22.

   reasons to emigrate, Bradford, William, *Of Plymouth Plantation*, Chapter IV, "Showing the Reasons and Causes of Their Removal."

156 **University of Leiden descriptions of New England and Indians,** Philbrick, Nathaniel, *Mayflower*, 6.

   Negotiations, Frazer, Rebecca, *The Mayflower*, 27-30.

157 **William Brewster**, Frazer, Rebecca, *The Mayflower*, 27.

158 **Adventurers**, ibid, 29-31. **Billington family,** Ibid, 54.

159 **Farewell,** Ibid, 34, Philbrick, Nathaniel, *Mayflower*, 19-23.

160 **Mayflower,** Philbrick, Nathaniel, *Mayflower*, 24- 25.

161 www.mayflowerhistory.com Johnson Caleb H.

162 Frazer, Rebecca, *The Mayflower*, 35-40.

163 **Butter,** Bradford, William, *Of Plymouth Plantation*, 49.

   Samuel Morison estimates lbs. of butter, £100 due, Frazer, *The Mayflower*, 40.

164 **Mayflower conditions,** www.mayflowerhistory.com, Johnson, Caleb H.; Philbrick, Nathaniel, *Mayflower*, 27-29.

   Goods, Frazer, Rebecca, *The Mayflower*, 41.

165 **Death of other pilgrims**, Philbrick, Nathaniel, *Mayflower*, 19.

   Robert Cushman, Ibid, 19-20.

166 **Morison,** Frazer, Rebecca, *The Mayflower*, 46.

167 **Journey,** Caleb Johnson's MayflowerHistory.com, http://mayflowerhistory.com/voyage.

   Wet clothes, Frazer, Rebecca, *The Mayflower*, 49.

168 **Land,** Philbrick, Nathaniel, *Mayflower*, 38-42.

169   **Quote – Rebecca Fraser,** *The Mayflower,* 55.

        Quote – Nathaniel Philbrick, *Mayflower,* 41.

        Mayflower Compact, *The Mayflower,* 41.

170   **John Carver,** Bradford, William, *Of Plymouth Plantation,* 76; Hubbard, 66-7.

171   **William Bradford,** *Of Plymouth Plantation,* 78.

        Mourt's Relations, *A Journal of the Pilgrims at Plymouth,* Applewood Books, Bedford, MA, 1963, from the original 1622 text, 20.

172   **Little Ice Age,** Fagan, Brian, *The Little Ice Age,* Basic Books, New York, 2000, Chapter Six, "The Spector of Hunger."

        Dorothy Bradford, Johnson, Caleb, *The Mayflower and her Passengers,* 82.

173   **First winter,** Bradford, William, *Of Plymouth Plantation,* 76-77.

174   **Samoset,** Frazer, *The Mayflower,* 65-70; Philbrick, *Mayflower,* 92-97.

175   **Massasoit,** *Mourt's Relations,* 52-59, includes Edward Winslow's description of chief

176   **Indians,** Frazer, *The Mayflower,* 75-77.

        Language, Johnson, Caleb, MayflowerHistory.com, http://mayflowerhistory.com/Wampanoag-language.

177   **Mayflower fate,** Philbrick, *Mayflower,* 101.

178   **Dwelling houses,** *Mourt's Relations,* 81,

        Layout of Plymouth, Philbrick, *Mayflower,* 84.

179   The Fortune, Philbrick, *Mayflower,* 123-126.

        First Thanksgiving, Mayflowerhistory.com

180   **Massasoit,** Frazer, *The Mayflower,* 89-92.

        Hobbamock, Philbrick, *Mayflower,* 113-115.

181   **Indian Killings,** Bradford, *Of Plymouth Plantation,* letter from Robinson, 374-375.

182   **Ships,** www.Mayflowerhistory.com

183   **Size of community,** Gaskill, Malcolm, *Between Two Worlds, How the English Became American,* Basic Books, New York, 88.

        Broad-brimmed felt hats and fur trade, Weidensaul, Scott, *The First Frontier,* Houghton Mifflin Harcourt, Boston, New York, 2012, 123.

184   **Myles positions,** Johnson, *The Mayflower and her Passengers,* 210-231.

185   **Elizabeth Tully Howland,** *The Mayflower and her Passengers,* 175.

        Robinson quote, *The Mayflower and her Passengers,* 220.

186   **Josiah Standish,** The Wetmore Family of America and its collateral branches, www.ancestry.com.

187   **Quote from letter,** Massachusetts Historical Society Collection, VOL III, 76.

188 **William Morton's quotes,** Johnson, Caleb, *The Mayflower and Her Passengers*, 149, 222-223.

189 **Dr. Samuel Fuller,** The Truth About the Pilgrim's Ancestry, www.ancestry.com.

190 **Samuel Fuller marries,** Colonial Families of the USA, 1607-1775, for Samuel Fuller, www.ancestry.com.

191 **History Rev. Lothrop,** https://en.wikipedia.org/wiki/John_Lothropp.

192 **Lothrop quotes,** Hudson-Mohawk Genealogical and Family memoirs, vol 1, Hudson and Mohawk Valleys, 170; www.ancestry.com.

193 **Historian Jeremy Bangs,** Director of Leiden American Museum, Leiden, Holland.

194 . **Pequot War and Indian reaction,** Weidensaul, *The First Frontier*, 125-137.

195 **Standish and Massasoit,** Johnson, *The Mayflower and Her Passengers*, 227-228.

196 **Move to Barnstable,** https://en.wikipedia.org/wiki/John_Lothropp

197 **Matthew Fuller,** History of Barnstable, 228, American Fuller Genealogy, Captain Matthew Fuller line, North American Family Histories, www.ancestry.com,

198 **Death of leaders,** Johnson, *The Mayflower and Her Passengers*.

199 **Metacomet,** Bremer, Francis J., *The Puritan Experiment, New England Society from Bradford to Edwards*, University Press of New England, Hanover and London, 1995, 169.

200 **Quotes – David Brainerd,** *New England Encounters, Indian & Euroamericans*, ca, 1600-1850, Editor Alden T. Vaughan, Northeastern University Press, Boston, 1999, 77.

201 **Causes of King Philip's war,** Philbrick, *Mayflower*, The Trial, 199-225.

202 **"too ancient" Matthew Fuller, "Providence" Benjamin Church,** Philbrick, *Mayflower*, 246-250.

203 . **Destruction of war,** *History of King Philip's War*-History of Massachusetts Blog, http://historyofMassachusetts.org/what-was-King-Phillips-war

204 **Deaths of Matthew and Samuel Fuller, Death of Josiah Standish,** Genealogical Notes of Barnstable Families, 380, www.ancestry.com,, The Truth about the Pilgrims, 130-131; www.ancestry.com,

Josiah Standish, The Wetmore Family of America and its Collateral Branches, appendix H, Captain Myles Standish, www.ancestry.com.

205 **Quote of William Bradford,** *Of Plymouth Plantation*, 42.

Chapter Five

206 .**Persecuted minority,** Ryken, Leland *Worldly Saints, The Puritans as They Really Were*, Zonderman Publishing, Grand Rapids, MI, 1986, 13-14.

well educated, Historian Bruce C. Daniel: Puritans one of the most literate groups in the early modern world, https://en.wikipedia.org/wiki/history_of_the_Puritans_in_North_America

Family ties, Bremer, Francis J., *The Puritan Experiment*, 45.

207 **William Paine,** Boardman, William F. J., *The Ancestry of William Francis Joseph Boardman*, Hartford, CT, 1906, 317-318, Ancestry.com,

Sir Richard Saltonstall Jr., en.Wikipedia.org,/Richard-Saltonstall , Colonial Families of the USA, 1607-1775, for Richard Saltonstall, 410, Ancestry.com.

208   **Ipswich,** *Historic Ipswich.org,* Arrival of the English, Early settlers of Ipswich, https://hsitoric-ipswich.org/early-inhabitants-of-ipswich-massachusetts/

209   **.Paines in Ipswich,** Boardman, *The Ancestry of William Francis Joseph Boardman,* 317-318, Ancestry.com.

Education, Ryken, *Worldly Saints,* 158-170.

Harvard, Ibid, 96.

210   **Paine legacy in Ipswich,** Chester, Ronald, *The Life and Death of the Ipswich Grammar School Trust: Is Enduring Dead Hand Control Possible?* New England Law/Boston Legal Studies Research Paper Series, Paper No. 14-09, ACTEC Law Journal Vol. 39:201, https://ipswichtrust.org/2014/.../the-life-and-death-of-the-grammar-school-tru....

211   **John Winthrop Sr.,** https://www.britannica.com/print/article/645737.

John Winthrop the Younger, https://en.wikipedia.org/wiki/John_Winthrop_the_Younger

212   **New London,** New London was an important shipbuilding town. John Elderkin, ninth-great-grandfather of Patricia Reese, was a master builder who built the first merchant ship here in 1661, called the *New London Tryall,* at a cost of £200. He also built churches, mills, houses and bridges, including the first and second churches in New London and Norwich. Curland, Richard, *Historically speaking: John Elderkin and descendants helped build region,* Norwichbulletin.com June 24, 2018.

213   **Saugus Iron works – Hammersmith,** National Park Service, https://.nationalparks.org/explore-parks/saugus-iron-works-national-historic-site, *Saugus Iron Works: The Roland W. Excavations, 1948-1953,* https://www.nps.gov/sair/learn/historyculture/robbinsexcavationbook.htm, Regan and White, *Hammersmith through the Historical Texts* chapter two, https://www.nps.gov/sair/upload/03_chapter2.pdf.

Scottish Prisoners of War, Daniel B. Adlum's ninth-great-grandfather **Daniel Cone** (Mackhoe) was one of these prisoners used as indentured servants. He is alleged to have been captured and shipped to America on the *John and Sarah,* sold to Richard Leader at the Iron Works to make charcoal and then became indentured servant to John Winthrop the Younger by about 1656-7. He met his future wife, Mehitable Spenser, at the Hammersmith Iron Works Farm in 1657. Her father **Gerald Spenser** was a prominent citizen. By 1661 John Winthrop released Cone from servitude when he went back to England seeking a new colony charter. The next year Cone married Mehitable and became a founding member of Thirty Mile Plantation (Haddam), cited in *A Man Named Daniel, The Remarkable Life of Daniel Cone,* Cone Joseph, *A Man Named Daniel,* Text and Content, Corvallis, OR, 2010.

214   **Paine takeover of Iron Works,** Saugus Iron Works, https://nationalparks.org , Bailyn, Bernard, *The New England Merchants in the Seventeenth Century,* Harvard University Press, Cambridge, MA, and London, 1979, 71-72.

215   **Paine business and will,** Biography of William Paine, *New England, the Great Migration and the Great Migration Begins, 1620-1635,* 346, *The Pioneers of Massachusetts,* Ancestry.com

216   **Puritans and Wealth,** Ryken, *Worldly Saints,* 33,65l *On Robert Keayne and Rev. Cotton,* 69, 179.

217   **Appleton Family History,** Colonial Families of the USA, 1607-1775 for Samuel Appleton, *Memorial of Samuel Appleton of Ipswich, Massachusetts,* editor Jewett, Isaac Appleton, Boston, 1850, available Ancestry.com.

218   **Quote – Hubbard battle of Hatfield,** cited in The Ancestry of William Francis Joseph Boardman, Hartford, Connecticut, available at Ancestry.com.

219   **The Great Swamp Fight,** Ibid.

220   **Quote Andrew Marrell on Tyranny,** Gaskill, Malcolm, *Between Two Worlds: How the English Became Americans,* Basic Books, New York, 2014, 310.

221   **Appleton's Pulpit,** Jewett, Isaac Appleton, *Memorial of Samuel Appleton,* 19-20, Ipswich Historical Society, A Genealogy of the Ipswich Descendants of Samuel Appleton, 1906, Ipswich Historical Society.

222   **Defiant Samuel Appleton,** Source: https://storiesfromipswich.org/2014/04/11/the-defiant-samuel-appelton/.

223   **Spectral Evidence,** Schiff, Stacy, *The Witches, Salem 1692,* Little Brown and Co, New York, Boston, London, 2015, 8.

   Quote Cotton Mather, Ibid, 8. I leaned on Schiff's book for general background as well.

224   **Henry Wolcott, Magistrate at Witch Trial,** Ancestry.com.

   Numbers of accused and executed, Schiff, *The Witches,* 3-4.

225   **The Birthplace of American Independence,** from Defiant Samuel Appleton, https://storiesfromipswich.org.

226   **Judith Appleton and Samuel Wolcott,** A genealogical history of the Clark and Worth Families, Ancestry.com.

   Henry Wolcott, *The Prominent Families of the United States of America,* source: https://www.ancestry.com/interactive/48460/ProminentUSFam-0083309-152, *The Ely ancestry: lineage of Richard Ely of Plymouth, England, who came to Boston, Mass, about 1655,& settled at Lyme, CT,* https://www.ancestry.com/interactive/Print/10261/dvm.

227   **Rev. Thomas Hooker and Rev. John Cotton,** https://historyofmassachusetts.org/reverend-john-cotton/.

228   **Rev. Nathaniel Ward,** *The Simple Cobbler of Agawam in America,* https://historicipswich.org/.../nathaniel-ward-the-simple-cobbler-of-agawam-in-america

   Ann Hutchinson and Roger Williams, *Puritans in the New World, A Critical Anthology,* Edited by David D. Hall, Princeton University Press, Princeton and Oxford, 2004, chapter 20, "Roger Williams," chapter 21, "Anne Hutchinson."

229   **Hooker letter to John Winthrop,** *The Memorial History of Hartford County, Connecticut, 1633-1884 Vol 1,* edited by James Hammond Trumbull, Google Books, 1886, 28.

   Same Orb Quote, Walker, George Leon, *Thomas Hooker, Preacher, Founder, Democrat,* Dodd, Mead and Company, New York, 1881, 86, reprint by www.forgottenbooks.com.

230   **Hartford,** Weaver, Glenn, *Hartford, An Illustrated History of Connecticut's Capital,* Windsor Publications Inc.. 1982.

231   **Hartford founders**, a number of ancestors from both Daniel and Patricia have their names on the Founders Monument in Hartford that came with Rev. Hooker, including William Andrews, Thomas Welles, John Bidwell, William Clarke, James Olmsted, Thomas Selden, Richard Church and John Hopkins. http://josfamilyhistory.com/stories/founders-monument.htm.

William Andrew schoolteacher, New England, the Great Migration and the Great Migration Begins, 1620-1635 for William Andrews, Ancestry.com.

232   **Thomas Welles,** Governor Thomas Welles, http://wellesfamily.com, https://en.wikipedia.org/wiki/Thomas Welles, Welles settled in Wethersfield, as did many of Patricia's ancestors.

Nathaniel Dickinson-Wethersfield, Patricia's ninth-great-grandfather and the fifth-great-grandfather of poet **Emily Dickinson,** one of the two main founders of Wethersfield. Three of his sons were killed in King Philip's War, one was captured and taken to Canada, along with his daughter and later released. Nathaniel's grandson, the **Rev. Jonathan Dickinson** was the first president of **Princeton University** and a preacher, attorney and physician. He is considered second only to Jonathan Edwards in his abilities in religious study and argument.

233   **Hooker's famous sermon,** Walker, George, *Thomas Hooker*, 123-127.

234   **Fundamental Orders,** http://connecticuthistory.org/the-fundamental-orders-of-connecticut, "The birthplace of American democracy is Hartford" cited in Walker's *Thomas Hooker*, 118; Dr. Trumball translation of Henry Wolcott Jr. notebook, Ibid, 124.

235   **Massachusetts Body of Liberties,** Faith and Freedom, article at http://wwwleaderu.com/orgs/cdf/ff/chap 07.html.

236   **Rev. Henry Whitfield,** https://en.wikipedia.org/wiki/Henry_Whitfield_House_pp4-5, Guilford, Connecticut.org/towns-page/Guilford/, Ancestors of Patricia and Daniel that came to Guilford: Francis Bushnell is a grandfather on both sides, one daughter married into Daniel's family, another into Patricia's family. Gov. William Leete is the eighth-great-grandfather of Daniel. Patricia's ninth-great grandfather is **Benjamin Fenn**, whose granddaughter married into the Leete family, marrying Leete's son William.

William Chittenden is also tied by marriage to Rev. Henry Whitfield. Ancestry.com genealogy, Anderson, Robert Charles, *Puritan Pedigrees*, 108-110; *A Short History of Guilford*, The Guilford Keeping Society Archives, https://gks.omeka.net.

237   **Westminster Assembly 1643,** Bremer, *The Puritan Experiment*, 131,

Hooker's Book *Survey*, Walker, Thomas, *Hooker*, 141,

Whitfield return to England and burial, Rev. Henry Whitfield, minerdescent.com.

death of Rev. Hooker, Bremer, *The Puritan Experiment*, 143.

238   **Rev. Cotton Mather** from *Magnalia Christi Americana –The Life and Death of Master Thomas Hooker*, Bartley.com,

Winthrop Eulogy of Hooker, Walker, *Thomas Hooker*, 152.

death of great leaders, Bremer, *The Puritan Experiment*, 143.

239   **Gov. Welles,** English Origins of New England Families, Second Series Vol. III, Ancestry.com, 645-646.

240   **Capt. Robert Welles,** in the Hartford, Connecticut Probate Records, 1700-1729, Ancestry.com, Captain Robert Welles Jr. and Sarah Wolcott, Ancestry.com.

241   **William Leete and the regicides,** *The Historic Annals of Southwestern New York*, 414, Ancestry.com

242   **New charters,** Bremer, *Puritan Experiment*, 143; religion fragmenting, 139; Leete gov., 149; Halfway covenant, 160-162.

243   **John Winthrop the Younger,** https://www.museumofcthistory.org/2015/08/john-winthrop-jr/.

244   **Gov William Leete family history,** *Ancestry and descendants of Amaziah Hall and Betsy Baldwin*, reference cited from Chittenden Genealogy about being a neighbor of Cromwell. https://www.ancestry.com/interacyive/Print/18600/dvm_GenM, also *Founders and leaders of Connecticut*, https://www.ancestry.com/interactive/16211/dvm_LovHist004167-00066-1.

245   **Work as Calling,** Ryken, Leland, *Worldly Saints*, 24-28; quote, Ryken, 26, quote, William Perkins, cited by Ryken, 27.

246   **Guns at Gov Leete's funeral,** cited in Ancestry and Descendants of Amaziah Hall and Betsy Baldwin, 130, source: https://www.ancestry.com/interactive/Print/18600/dvm_GenM...12007874015748.

247   **Andrew Leete,** The descendants of William Leete, one of the founders of Guiford, CN, president of the Federation of colonies and Governor, 1-2, source: https://www.ancestry.com/interactive/Print/10367/dvm_GenMono0003D1.

   Orange Revolution, Bremer, 177.

248   **Establishment of Yale,** Bremer, *Puritan Experiment*, 221.

   Enlightenment, Bremer, *Puritan Experiment*, chapter Sixteen, 225-234.

249   **Rev. Cotton Mather,** www.Notable biographies.com.

250   Bremer, *Puritan Experiment*, chapter sixteen.

251   **Common Good,** Ryken, *Worldly Saints*, 174.

252   **Oliver Wolcott Sr,** Ancestry.com, also Mahoney, Patrick J., *Soldier, Patriot and Politician: The Life of Oliver Wolcott*, posted April 28,2015, www.connecticuthistory.org.

253   **Appleton Farm,** https://www.historicipswich.org/appleton-farms/.

   Saugus Iron Works and Samuel Appleton House, www.nationalparks.org.

   Henry Whitfield House, www.ctvisit.com/listings/henry-whitfiled-state-museum.

   William Paine Trust, Chester, R, *The Life and Death of the Ipswich Grammar School Trust*, https://www.ssrn.com/abstract=2450740.

Chapter Six

254   **Panguitch,** history https://Panguitch.com , www.visitutah.com/places-to-go/cities-and-towns/panguitch/.

Hyrum Williams and family, census, 1870, United States Federal Census for Hyrum Williams and family-Parley's Park, Summit, Utah Territory, birth records of Sylvester Spenser, Cora Lucy and Hyrum A., Ancestry.com.

Samuel Comstock Snyder, census, birth records and family history, Ancestry.com.

255   **Panguitch History,** https://Panguitch.com, Birth records of Williams children, Ancestry.com, Death of Mary Ann Synder Williams, "Billion Graves Index"- FamilySearch.org,

History of Summit County & Samuel Comstock Snyder's Sawmill, *A History of Summit County*, published 1998. 20, Ancestry.com.

256   **Ancestry of Hyrum Williams,** Adlum Family Tree, Ancestry.com.

257   Genealogy of Williams, Snyder, Comstock, Stockwell families, Adlum Family Tree, Ancestry.com, Family Search.org.

Gustavus and Maria Williams, early life, family story-by author unknown – possibly Rebecca Noyes, Ancestry.com, as well as census and birth records for the Williams family, Ancestry.com.

258   **Joseph Smith family,** Brodie, Fawn M., *No Man Knows My History,* Vintage Books, New York, 1995, chapter one.

Rodney Williams, notes from a conversation with Kathleen Stewart Baker, 1990s; Ancestry.com, Hyrum Williams.

259   **Joseph Smith early life and family origins,** Martin, John H., Joseph Smith: The Angel Moroni and Mormonism in New York State, *Saints, Sinners and Reformers, The Burned Over District Revisited*, Chapter 9, http://www.crookedlakereview.com/books/saints_sinners/martin1.html, Brodie, Fawn M., *No Man Knows My History, The Life of Joseph Smith,* Vintage Books, New York, August 1995, chapter 1-4, Fitzgerald, David, *The Mormons,* Publisher David Fitzgerald, 2013, chapters 1-3.

Burroughs, emperor of counterfeiters, Melonakos, Kathleen Kimball, *Secret Combinations- Evidence of Early Mormon Counterfeiting 1880-1847,* Lyrical Productions, San Diego, 2108,39-42; Library Memoirs, 39; blacklegs, 37.

260   **Finney "Burnt Over District",** Martin, *Saints, Sinners and Reformers,* Chapter 1.

religious revivalism, *The Burnt Over District,* en.wikipedia.org.

261   **Millerites,** ohiohistorycentral.org.

262   **Masons**, Melonakos, *Secret Combinations,* 158-165.

263   **Joseph Smith's first vision,** Brodie, *No Man Knows My History,* 405-412; Fitzgerald, *The Mormons,* 19-27.

Indian Burial sites, Fitzgerald, *The Mormons,* 18.

Nephi vs Moroni, fairmormon.org; Brodie, 411.

Marriage to Emma, https://en.wikipedia.org/wiki/Joseph_Smith.

Promise to Mr. Hale to stop fortune hunting, Brodie, 433, 438-439.

264   **Ethan Smith,** Brodie, *No Man Knows My History,* 46-47.

    Native American DNA, No Lost Tribes, https://www.theguardian.com/.../no-lost-tribes-or-aliens-what-ancient-dna-reveals-about.

    Dead of night, Krakauer, *Under the Banner of Heaven,* Anchor Books, New York, 2003.

265   **Translation of Book of Mormon,** Brodie, chapter four; *A Marvelous Work and a Wonder.*

    Martin Harris and his troublesome wife, Ibid, 54-55.

266   **Transcribing and publishing Book of Mormon,** Fitzgerald, *The Mormons,* 38-40.

    Witnesses, Ibid, 41-42; King James Bible, Brodie.

267   **Prologue to the book of Mormon,** Fitzgerald, 34.

    Description of Book, Brodie, 57-73.

    autobiographical, Vogel, Dan *Joseph Smith: The Making of a Prophet,* Signature Books, Salt Lake City, UT, 2004, xviii-xix; Krakauer, Jon, *Under the Banner of Heaven,* Anchor Books, New York, 2004, 68-69.

268   **The Book of Mormon,** translated by Joseph Smith, The Church of Jesus Christ of Latter-day Saints, Salt Lake City, UT, 1974 edition.

    New Israelites, Melonakos, *Secret Combinations,* 63-65.

269   **Starting the church,** Martin, *Saints, Sinners and Reformers,* chapter 9, 4.

    Arrested, Brodie, 82-87.

    Emma, Brodie, 89-90.

    Debts, Melonakos, *Secret Combinations,* 212.

270   **Cowdery Sent to Missouri,** Smith sent Cowdery and Parley Pratt to Missouri, stopping first in Ohio, Brodie, 89.

    Converting Sidney Rigdon, Brodie, 89-97.

    Kirtland eastern boundary of Zion, Brodie, 97.

    traveled on Erie Canal, The New York, Pennsylvania, and Ohio areas of the USA, https://www.churchofjesuschrist.org/study/scriptures/history-maps/maps-3?

271   **Joseph Smith quote on Missouri,** Fitzgerald, David, *The Mormons,* publisher David Fitzgerald, 2013, 54.

272   **Missouri,** Hamer, John, *Mapping Mormon Settlement in Caldwell County,* Mormonhistoricalsites.org, 16.

    Kirkland Banking fiasco, Fitzgerald, 49-53.

    Fanny Alger, Brodie, 181-182.

    Quote about lawsuits and arrests, Fitzgerald, 51.

    Smith quote, Krakauer, Jon, *Under the Banner of Heaven,* 100.

273 **Sources for Far West and Mormon War,** Hamer, Mapping Mormon Settlement in Caldwell County, 19; Fitzgerald, 53-59; Burnett, Peter Hardeman, *Reflections of an Old Pioneer*, 60-65; Brodie, chapter 9, *Expulsion from Eden*.

274 **Liberty Jail and Trial,** Burnett, Peter Hardeman, *Reflections*, 63-67.

275 **Description,** Burnett, 66; Krakauer, Jon, *Under the Banner of Heaven*, Anchor Books, New York. 2004, 57.

276 **Galland and purchase of Commerce (Nauvoo),** Fitzgerald, *The Mormons*, 64.

Dr. John Bennett, Nauvoo Legion, Fitzgerald, 66-69; Brodie, 266-268.

counterfeiters, Kathleen Kimball Melonakos in her book *Secret Combinations* shows evidence that the Saints picked spots to settle with known counterfeiters

277 **Gustavus and Maria Williams,** census and birth records, Ancestry.com, family story possible, author Rebecca Noyes, Ancestry.com,

Emma Smith, https://en.wkipedia.org/wiki/Joseph_Smith; Brodie, 54, 110, 120, 257, 327.

278 **Ancestry of Mary Ann Snyder, parents and grandparents,** Adlum Family Tree, Ancestry.com.

Mayflower descendants, Mayflower Silver Books for Edward Fuller.

279 **Snyder History,** Isaac Snyder and Lovisa Comstock Snyder History, *A Righteous History*, chapter 1, Ancestry.com, https://www.ancestry.com/medisui-viewer/collection/1...905-4e76-8a66-7124bc9d81c3?.

280 **Isaac and Lovisa History,** *Going Forth Boldly*, Chapter 2, Ibid.

281 **Isaac and Lovisa History,** Nauvoo, Ibid.

282 **12,000 residents in Nauvoo,** Fitzgerald, *The Mormons*, 63.

Roles of Smith, Brodie, 366.

283 **Reaction to Mormonism,** Scott, Donald, *Mormonism and the American Mainstream*, Queens College/City University of New York, National Humanities Center, article online http://nationalhumanitiescenter.org/tserve/nineteen/nkeyinfo/nmormon.htm accessed 6/8/19.

Candidate Smith, Bicknell, John, *America 1844*, Chicago Review Press, Chicago, 2015, 33-37.

284 **Revelations,** Krakauer, 116.

285 Fitzgerald, 68-71; Krakauer, 126-127; Brodie, 321, 327, 339, 341-3, 399, 475.

286 **Council of Fifty,** Fitzgerald, 71.

Law, Fitzgerald, 72-74; Bicknell, 167-168.

Law quote, Bicknell, 168.

287 **Destruction, martial law,** Krakauer, 130-131; Fitzgerald, 73-74.

Lamb to slaughter, Fitzgerald, 75.

288 **Death of Joseph and Hyrum,** Krakauer, 132-135.

289 **Succession,** Bicknell, 179-184.

Emma Smith, Law and Rigdon, Krakauer, 195.

290 **The prophet,** Krakauer, 112-115;

Bloom quote, Krakauer, 112

Brodie quote, cited 115 in Krakauer.

291 **Exodus,** Krakauer, 200-203; Fitzgerald, 89.

292 **counterfeiters,** Krakauer, 200-201; Melonakos, 297-300.

293 **Gustavus and Maria,** family story, Ancestry.com.

294 **Gustavus and Maria,** family story possible author Rebecca Noyes, Ancestry.com.

Death of Ellen, Winter Quarters Sexton's Records, June 25-July 13, 1847 -FamilySearch.org.

295 **History of Samuel Comstock Snyder,** Ancestry.com,

Quotes of Jane Snyder Richards, story in Centennial Birthday Anniversary Booklet on Jane Snyder Richards, Ancestry.com.

296 **Splitting of Mormons,** Melonakas, *Secret Combinations;* Fitzgerald, *The Mormons.*

Young's background, Lehmann, Chris, *Young and the Restless: On Brigham Young*, The Nation Magazine, November 20, 2012, online article, https://www.thenation.com/article/young-and-restless-brigham-young/.

297 Campbell, Eugene, *Establishing Zion the Mormon Church in the American West, 1847-1869*, Signature Books, Salt Lake City, 1988, chapter 1 and 2.

298 History of Samuel Comstock Snyder, Ancestry.com.

299 Ibid, **Women's experiences in Polygamy,** quotes from Jane Snyder Richards and others, Morgan, Ted, *A Shovel of Stars, the Making of the American West – 1800 to the Present*, Simon and Schuster, New York, 1995, 389-390.

300 **Mark Twain quote,** Morgan, *A Shovel Full of Stars*, 388.

Young and colonies, Campbell, *Establishing Zion*, chapters 4 and 5.

301 **Milk Before Meat,** Stenhouse, *Tell It All*, 58.

302 **History of Watkin Rees,** family letter by foster daughter, collection of author.

Journey to Utah, Watkin Rees Papers (ca. 1880-1905), Pioneer Overland Travel, https://history.church ofjesuschrist.org/overlandtravel/sources/17675/rees-watkin-reminiscences-8-12-in-watkin-rees-papers-ca-1880-1905.

303 Watkin Rees Papers.

304 Ibid, **History of Wales,** BBC.com, *The Story of Wales: Life in Merthyr Tydfil 19th Century,* "Little Hell," March 12, 2013.

305 Watkin Rees Papers

306 **Blood Atonement,** Stenhouse, *Tell It All;* Fitzgerald, *The Mormons.*

307 **Mountain Meadow Massacre,** Stenhouse, *Tell It All*, chapters XLV, XLVI, XLVII; Campbell, *Establishing Zion*, Lehman; *Young and Restless*, 12-15.

308 **Turner quote,** Lehmann, *Young and the Restless*, 3, 17.

309 **Rees Family History** – private letter.

310 **Williams Family history** – sources from Ancestry.com, Kathleen Stewart Baker, and Patricia Reese Adlum.

311 Notes from Rodney Williams as relayed by Kathleen Stewart Baker, as well as Ancestry.com.

312 Ibid.

313 Ibid.

Information on stagecoaches in eastern Oregon, MacDonald, Joseph F, *MacDonald's Stage Coaches and Stations: Eastern Oregon –1850-1920*, Western Places Publisher, Lake Oswego, OR, 2009.

314 Ancestry.com, oral family history from Patricia Reese Adlum.

315 Ancestry.com.

Chapter Seven

316 **Free Emigrant Road,** Menefee, Leah Collins and Tiller, Lowell, *Cutoff Fever*, Oregon Historical Quarterly, Vol. 77, No. 4 (Dec. 1976), 309-311, published by Oregon Historical Society, https://www.jstor.org/stable/20613545.

317 **Sources for emigrants on Illinois train, William Stoops,** Stoops, William, *By Ox Team to Oregon*, Morning Register, Eugene, Or, 1925, Aug. 31, Sept 6, 13, 20, 27; a clipping from Mrs. Henry Matthews of Dexter, OR; Williams, Mrs. C.C., "The Emigrants of 1853, Lost Immigrants of the Elliot Cutoff 1853,' typewritten story possibly by Catherine D. Williams.

318 **Watkin Rees quote,** Watkin Rees Journal, https://history.churchofjesuschrist.org/overlandtravel/sources/17675/rees-watkin-reminiscences-8-12-in-watkin-rees-papers-ca-1880-1905.

Peter Burnett, quoted in *Cutoff Fever*, Part III, 135.

319 **Cost,** Harrison, Lee, *Pioneer Diaries in The Digital Age*, (Charlotte Emily Stearn Pengra) published in *The Artifact*, Lane County History Museum, Fall 2018, No. 229, 6-7.

Matthews family history, Adlum Family Tree, Ancestry.com.

320 **History Cope Family,** Cope, G (1861) *A Record of the Cope Family*, as established in America by Oliver Cope, who came from England to Pennsylvania about 1682 with the residences, dates of births, deaths, and marriages of his descendants as far as ascertained, Philadelphia: King and Baird, Printers, Adlum Family Tree, Ancestry.com.

Quakers, Levy, Barry, *Quakers, the Delaware Valley, and North Midlands Emigration to America*, The William and Mary Quarterly, Vol 48, No. 2 (April 1991), 246-252, accessed through jstor.org.

321 **Marriage Elizabeth Cope – Thomas Matthews,** Adlum Family Tree, Ancestry.com.

Quakers in Fulton County, Calhoun, M.W. *The Plainfield Quakers: The Society of Friends in Fulton County, Illinois*, http://illinois.outfitters.com/illinois/history/family/quakers/quakers.html.

322   **Parker Family History,** genealogy by Wayne Burian, 2010 copy, Adlum Family Tree, Ancestry.com.

323   **Parvin Family History,** genealogy by Wayne Burian, 2010 copy, *The Centennial History of Oregon 1811-1912 Volume III*, Chicago, the S. J. Clarke Publishing Co. ,1912, 68, James Parvin.

324   **William Stoops,** "By Ox Team to Oregon, Part One," 1; *Eugene Morning Register*, Sunday __ 1925.

      Pioneer quote, Horn, Huston, *The Old West: the Pioneers*, Time-Life Books, New York, 1974, 18.

325   **William Stoops – Sioux Indians,** "By Ox Team to Oregon, Part One," *Eugene Morning Register*, Sunday __1925, (from a clipping of Mrs. Henry Matthews).

326   **Francis Parkman,** Parkman, Francis Jr. *The Oregon Trail*, Canton House, New York, quoted by Murphy, Dan, *Oregon Trail Voyage of Discovery: The Story Behind the Scenery*, KC Publications, 1992, 19.

327   **Women's Work,** Bledsoe, Lucy Jane, *Adventuresome Women on the Oregon Trail 1840-1867*, Frontiers Vol. VII, No. 3, 1984, 22-29; University of Nebraska Press, https://www.jstor.org/stable/3346237.

      Charlotte Rutledge, Williams, Mrs. C.C., *The Emigrants of 1853*, Lane County Historical Society, personal photocopy.

328   **Selena Parker's Saddle,** donated to the Lane County Historical Society Museum by the Parvin family.

329   **Indian Toll Bridge,** diary of Charlotte Emily Stearns Pengra, Harrison, Lee, "Pioneer Diaries in the Digital Age," 6-7, published in *The Artifact*, Fall 2018, NO. 229, Lane County History Museum, Eugene, Oregon.

      Crossing the South Platte, William Stoops, *By Ox Team to Oregon*, Part Two, 3.

330   **William Stoops separated from family,** *By Ox Team to Oregon*, Part Three.

331   **Cattle sickness on the Snake,** Owen, Daniel, *The Lost Rescue: The Story of the Lost Wagon Train and the Men who Tried to Save It*, CreateSpace Publishing, 2015.

332   **Stoops low on supplies,** Jeannie Parvin Schafler notes and letters, accessed at Lane County Historical Society Museum.

      Elliot meets train, *Lost Rescue*, 57-58.

333   **Elliot background,** *Lost Rescue*, 55-56.

334   **Planned route of Free Emigrant Trail,** Menefee, *Cutoff Fever*.

335   **Elliot convinces emigrants,** *Lost Rescue*, 56-57.

      Description of Oregon terrain and best routes, *Cutoff Fever*, 314.

336   **Elliot's Conversation with Matthews and Stoops,** *Lost Rescue*, 57.

337   **The Columbia and the Cascade Locks,** William Stoops, *By Ox Team to Oregon*, Part 5.

338   **Settling in Lane County,** the Parkers, James and Joseph, Walling, Albert, *Illustrated History of Lane County, Oregon*, AG Publishing, Portland, OR, 1884, 447; Williams, *Lost Immigrants of the Elliot Cutoff 1853*; Parvin obituary.

339   **Confusion of lost train,** *Lost Rescue,* 58-67.

340   **Col. Cline,** *Lost Rescue,* 83.

341   **David C. Matthews and rescue,** *Lost Rescue,* 89-95.

342   **Elliot dies,** *Lost Immigrants of the Elliot Cutoff.*

343   **James and Selena Marry,** Parvin family history, Adlum Family Tree, Ancestry.com.

344   **James Parvin,** history at Lane County Historical Society; newspaper clippings and family stories; 1860 census for Lost Valley; Ancestry.com.

345   **Thomas Williams southern sympathizer,** *Dexter Times,* published July 19, 1975, personal copy.

346   **Parvin Family History,** provided by Wayne Burian.

347   **Obits James and Selena Parvin, daughters Ida and Jeannie Postmasters,** Williams family history.

348   **Templemans,** *Adlum Family Tree,* Ancestry.com; Templeman family Bible; collection of Patricia Reese.

349   **Dexter Schoolhouse and Ellis Parker,** *Dexter Times* newspaper copy, July 19, 1975.

        New Parvin farmhouse, Parvin family history,

        history of Ol Bess, provided by Sharon and Larry Gilson Jr.

350   **Dorothy Parvin's childhood,** conversations with Patricia Reese and private letters of Dorothy Parvin.

351   **Dorothy teaching,** collection of author, teaching certificate and salary.

        Parvin sibs get married, genealogy done by Wayne Burian, 2010.

352   **Fire,** recollections of Jeannie Schafler and Reese girls, Patricia and Geraldine.

        Obituaries of Hosea and Agnes, *Eugene Register Guard.*

353   **Parvin Butte,** "A Plea for Parvin Butte," saveparvinbutte.org, DLUCA PO Box 89, Dexter, OR 97431.

354   Author conversation with Dorothy Parvin Reese, 1985.

Chapter Eight

355   **Drewsey,** http://www.oregoncities.us/drewsey/; Edgar, Leon, U.S. Bureau of the Census, pop. Vol 1, 910.

        Harney County, https://en.wikipedia.org/wiki/Harney_County_Oregon.

356   **Story of Reese Family,** Patricia Reese Adlum memoirs, March 2019.

357   **Baker City,** history of Baker County, http://www.oregongenealogy.com/baker/historybc/bakercity.htm.

358   **Sumpter,** *The Gold Fields of Eastern Oregon,* by the Baker City Chamber of Commerce, 1899, 39.

359   **Quote from Patricia,** Patricia Reese Adlum memoirs, March 2019.

360   **Story of ranch life,** Patricia Reese Adlum memoirs

361   **Dr. Pollock,** Pollock, Robert W., *The Education of a Country Doctor,* Vantage Press, New York, 1978.

362   **Pressure from Dredge Company,** Patricia Reese Adlum memoirs, 2019.

363   **Sumpter Valley Dredge,** https://westernmininghistory.com/1180/sumpter-valley-gold-dredge/; https://wikipedia.org/wiki/Sumpter_Valley_Gold_Dredge.

364   **Price controls and Rationing WW II,** *Food Rationing in Wartime America,* https://www.history.com>news>foodrationing-in-wartime-america; *The Two-Price System: U.S. Rationing during WW II,* https://fee.org>articles>the-two-price-sustem-us-rationing-during-world-war-two.

365   **Treatment of Japanese-Americans in Oregon in WWII,** *Japanese American Wartime Incarceration in Oregon,* https://oregonencyclopedia.org>articles>japanese-internment, *Oregon Town Was a Haven during WW II,* https://www.latimes.com>archives>la-xpm-1993-08-29-me-29008-story.

366   **Letter from Dorothy to her parents,** collection of Geraldine and Patricia Reese.

367   **Cattle Prices and quotes from Dorothy,** letter to her parents, private collection.

368   **Time in Baker and quotes from Patricia,** Patricia Reese Adlum memoirs.

369   **Death of Grace Williams Reese,** obituary September 9, 1950, Baker City, OR, newspaper, *The Record-Courier.*

370   **Death of Grover Williams Reese,** obituary October 4, 1950, Baker City, OR, Newspaper, *The Record-Courier.*

371   **Death of Dorothy Parvin Reese,** obituary Eugene, OR, newspaper, *The Register Guard,* Saturday. July 11, 1998; eulogy by Jeffrey Bruce Adlum, collection of author.

Chapter Nine

372   **Carey McWilliams quote,** McWilliams, Carey, *Southern California: An Island on the Land,* Gibbs-Smith Publisher, Peregrine Smith Books, Salt Lake City, 1946,

        Federal government and growth of L.A., Gregory, James N., *The Shaping of California,* 8, https://faculty.washington.edu/gregoryj/California%20History.htm.

373   **Greatest Agricultural Output,** Behrens, Zach, "Until the 1950s Los Angeles County was the Top Agriculture County in the Country," February. 11, 2011, https://www.kcet.org>socal-focus>until-the-1950s-los-angeles-county-was…,

        Red Cars, Chiland, Elijah, "Did a Conspiracy Really destroy LA's huge Streetcar system?" la.curbed.com, January 26, 2018.

        Finest public education, Gregory, James N., *The Shaping of California History,* 9, https://faculty.washington.edu/gregoryj/California%20History.htm.

374   **Mediterranean Fantasy Land,** Gregory, James N., *The Shaping of California History,* 7, https://faculty.washington.edu/gregoryj/California%20History.htm.

        Architecture, *1950-1960: Suburban Metropolis,* Los Angeles Conservancy, https://www.laconservancy.org/explore-la/curating-city/modern-architecture-la/history-la-modernism/1950-1960-suburban-metropolis.

375   **Brooklyn Dodgers move to L.A.,** Brownell, Richard, "Who's Really to blame for the Dodger's Leaving Brooklyn?" May 30, 2018, https://www.realclearhistory.com>2018/05/30>whos_really_to_....

376   **History of Westwood and Lassen County,** https://en.wikipedia.org>wiki>Westwood,_California

377   **Silent Spring,** this book by Rachel Carson was credited with starting the environmental movement, Carson, Rachel, *Silent Spring*, Houghton, Mifflin Company, original printing September 27, 1962, reprint October 2002.

378   **Increase in black and Asian population,** Gregory, James N., *The Shaping of California History*, 9.

379   **Watts Riots**, Queally, James, "Watts Riots: Traffic Stop was the spark that ignited days of destruction in LA," July 29, 2015, *Los Angeles Times*, https://www.latimes.com>local>lanow>la-me-In-watts-riots-expaliner-2.

380   **1971 Sylmar Earthquake,** Bartholomew, Dana, "Sylmar-San Fernando Earthquake," *Daily News*, February. 8, 2016, https://wwwdailynews.com>2016/02/08>sylmar-san-fernando-earthquake.

381   **Limekiln Canyon Park,** https://www.latimes.com/lifestyle/story/2019-08-08/la-walks-limekin-canyon-park.

382   **Daniel B. Adlum obit,** *Los Angeles Times* & *Valley News*, Van Nuys, March 31, 1977; burial at Oakwood Memorial Park, Chatsworth, Los Angeles, California; date of death March 28, 1977.

383   **Quote Ray Allen Billington,** Billington, Ray Allen and Ridge, Martin, *Westward Expansion: A History of the American Frontier*, Macmillan Publishing Company, New York, 1982, 683-684

Index

Symbols

41st Division 7
162nd Infantry 7
1905 World's Fair 72

A

Abbott, Catherine (Adlum) 1, 21
Abbott, John 1, 21, 31
Abbottstown, Pennsylvania 21
A City on a Hill 127, 148
Act Against Puritans, The 97
Adams, John 28, 29, 31
Adamsville, Utah 178, 179
A Description of New England 100
Adlum, Daniel Bruce 1, 3, 5, 6, 7, 9, 10, 14, 15, 18, 35, 75, 114, 115, 142, 209, 212, 218, 222, 225, 228, 230, 238, 240
Adlum, Daniel J. 1, 11, 12, 13, 14, 15
Adlum, Ellen Suzanne (Pavlosek) 11, 225, 237, 239, 240, 243
Adlum, Ellen twin of Joseph Green Adlum 31
Adlum family Bible 11
Adlum, Helen Lee (Moffitt) 1, 3, 5, 75, 239
Adlum, Henry Bruce 1, 3, 5, 13, 14, 70, 226
Adlumia Fungosa 30
Adlum, Jeffrey Bruce 11, 224, 225, 226, 230, 232, 239, 240, 243
Adlum, John (1701-1773) 2, 17, 18, 19, 20, 22, 24
Adlum, John (1725-1819) 2, 18, 21, 23, 29
Adlum, John (1759-1836) 1, 18, 22, 23, 24, 25, 26, 27, 28, 29, 30, 31
Adlum, Joseph (1727-1814) 1, 11, 15, 17, 18, 19, 20, 21, 22, 23, 24, 31
Adlum, Joseph (1732-1814) 14, 31
Adlum, Joseph (1767-1814) 31
Adlum, Joseph (1767-1846) 1, 29, 31, 32
Adlum, Joseph Downs 1, 3, 5, 13, 14
Adlum, Joseph Green 1, 15, 16, 17, 31, 32
Adlum, Margaret (Adlum) 29, 30
Adlum, Mary 14
Adlum, Merle Daniel 1, 14, 15
Adlum on Making Wine 30
Adlum, Pamela (Vigil) 225, 226, 240, 243
Adlum, Thomas 31
Adlum-Wallis Map 25
Adlum, Wilford Downs 12, 14
Adrian, Oregon 212
African American 54
Africans 136
agriculture 5, 13, 39, 189, 201, 227
Alaska Gold Rush 72
Albemarle County, Virginia 58
alcalde 45
Alden, John 113
Alderman, John 122
Alexander, Dr. Robert 196
Algonquian family of Indian languages 109
Allegations against Bishop Pilkington of Durham 95
Allegheny Mountains 15, 16
Allegheny Portage Railroad 16
Allegheny River 23, 30
Allen, Patricia (Holland) 6, 238
Allen, Philip 6
Allen, Richard 6
Allen, Sarah (Standish) 93
Allen Taylor's company 172
Allen, Victor 6
Allen, Victor Hugo 1, 4, 6
Allerton, Isaac 112
Allerton, Mary Allerton 102
Allin, Rev. John 92
Altoona, Pennsylvania 11, 12, 14, 15, 16, 17, 32
A Memoir on the Cultivation of the Vine in America and the Best Mode of Making Wine 30
America 18, 36, 66, 89, 90, 91, 92, 94, 98, 100, 101, 103, 108, 109, 122, 131, 132, 156, 159, 162, 168, 189, 190, 243
American Civil War 15, 17, 56, 77, 78, 178, 201
American Legion 223
American Restoration Movement 36
American Revolution 11, 20, 22, 23, 24, 26, 31, 52, 54, 56, 59, 81, 82, 83, 87, 149, 152, 190
American River 45, 46

Americans 59, 82, 83
American School, The 232
America's Suburb 227
A Model of Christian Charity 127
amputations during Civil War 78
Amsterdam, Holland 98
Andalusia, Spain 233
Anderson, Agnes (Matthews) 188
Anderson, Bailey Jr. Captain 55
Andrews, Hannah Maria (Williams) 151, 153, 163, 169, 170, 173
Andrews, Robert 129
Andrews, William, first schoolteacher of Hartford, Connecticut 140
Andros, Sir Edmund 135, 136, 137, 146, 147
Angel Gabriel 129
Anglican 18, 89, 115, 148
Anglican Church 51, 96, 97, 188
Anne 111
Antes, Col. 24
Antes, Henry 24
anti-Federalist 61
Apostle to the Indians, the 109
Appalachian Mountains 22, 50, 52, 82, 194
Applegate, Jesse 41
Applegate, Jesse and Lindsay 44, 186
Applegate trail 41, 44
Appleton, Hannah, 132
Appleton, John 133
Appleton, Judith (Wolcott) 125, 132, 137
Appleton, Samuel (1624-1696) 125, 127, 132, 133, 134, 135, 136, 144, 147, 149
Appleton, Samuel Jr. 132, 133, 149
Appleton, Samuel Sr 129, 133
Appleton's Pulpit 135
Arbella 127
Archbishop of Canterbury 115
Archbishop of York 98
architecture 228
Arminianism 155
Arminius, Jacobus 155
Army Airborne paratrooper 222
Assawompset Pond 121
Astoria, Oregon 4, 38
Auburn, Oregon 213
Augusta County, Virginia 50
Austin, Texas 64, 241, 243
Australia. 7
Austria 231

B

Babe the Blue Ox 229
Bacon, Francis 88
Baker City, Oregon 183, 213, 217, 220, 222, 226, 239
Baker County, Oregon 183
Baker High School 221, 222
Baker's Bay 37
Baltimore, Maryland 31
bank failures 13
bank fraud 160
banking 13, 65, 66, 212
Baptist 58, 61, 145, 148, 155
Barcelona, Spain 232
Barlow Toll Road 186 ,197
Barnstable, Massachusetts 113, 116, 117, 118, 119, 123
Barton, Clara 78
Bastrop County, Texas 64
Battle of Blue Licks 54
Battle of Dunbar 132
Battle of Fallen Timbers 27, 83
Battle of King's Mountain, The 59
Battle of New Orleans 55, 63
Battle of San Jacinto 56, 64, 65
Battle of Saratoga 149
Battle of Shiloh 78
Battle of Worchester 132
Bavaria, Germany 231
Beach Boys 237
Bean, William 52, 58, 59
Bear Creek Baptist Church 51
Bear Creek, North Carolina 51
Beatles 235
beaver fur trade 111, 117
Beaver, Utah 176, 178, 179
Beaver Wars 82
Becknell, William 64
beer 103, 104, 106, 107, 229
Belgium 231
Bell, John 16
Bellwood First Methodist Church 15
Bellwood, Pennsylvania 15, 32
Bend, Oregon 196, 199
Bennett, Dr. John 162, 166
Benton County, Oregon 199, 201
Berkley, Bishop George 90
Berkshires, Massachusetts, the 152, 153, 163
Bermuda Hundred, Virginia Colony 58

Berwick, Alice (Abbott) 22
Berwick, Alice (Adlum) 2, 31
Berwick, Elizabeth (Adlum) 2, 18, 22
Berwick, John 23
Berwick, Simon 18
Bethel College 42
Bible 42, 58, 92, 96, 97, 98, 101, 109, 110, 114, 129, 137, 141, 158, 161
Biblical laws 114
Bickerdyke, Mary 78
Big Harpeth River 62
Billington, John 101
Bill of Rights 142
Bingham, Jabez 69, 91
Bingham, Mary (Lee) 69, 91
Bingham, William 25, 26
Black Hawk War. 153, 190
blacklegs 159
Blair County, Pennsylvania 17
Blanding, Martin 199, 200
Block Island Indians 117
blood atonement 176
Bloody Sunday 236
Blue Mountains 50, 195, 197, 214
Blue Ridge Mountains 52
Bodega Bay, Sonoma County, California 45
Body of Liberties 142
Boggs, Lilburn 66, 161
Book of Mormon 157, 158, 159, 166, 167, 171
Boone, Alfonso 51
Boone, Benjamin 51
Boone, Daniel 24, 51, 52, 53, 54, 55
Boone, Israel 54
Boone's Creek 52, 59
Boone's Lick 63
Boone, Squire 51
Boone's Trace 56
Boston, England 98
Boston Harbor 136
Boston, Massachusetts 113, 116, 128, 129, 132, 135, 137, 138, 140, 147
bourbon whiskey 62
Braddock military road 15, 24
Bradford, Dorothy 102, 106
Bradford, William 94, 98, 99, 102, 105, 106, 107, 108, 111, 112, 114, 115, 120, 124, 134
Brainerd, Daniel 87
Brainerd, Esther 69, 87
Braintree (Quincy), Massachusetts 131

Brannon, Sam 46, 49, 173
Breckinridge, John C. 16
Brewer 100
Brewster Press, Pilgrim's Press, The 99
Brewster, William 94, 97, 98, 99, 100, 101, 102, 103, 105, 107, 108, 119
Bridewell Prison 23
Bridger, Jim 170
Briggs, Lilburn 166
Brigham Young is King 173
Bristow, Elliot 196
British 22, 23, 27, 29, 37, 39, 42, 45, 52, 54, 59, 87, 90, 175, 187, 231
British Museum 235
British prisoner of war ship 23
Bronze Star 7
Brown, Daniel 89
Browne, Robert 96
Brownists 96
Brushy Creek 243
Bryan's Station 53, 54
Bryan, Texas 56
Bryce Canyon National Park 152
bubonic plague 113
Buchanan, James 176
buffalo 192
Buffalo, New York 82
Burian, George (Ted) 206
Burian, Sharon (Gilson) 206
Burian, Wayne 206
Burnett, Constantia Dudley 56
Burnett Cutoff 44
Burnett, George William 33, 56, 57, 58, 63
Burnett, Glen Owen 33, 36, 42, 49, 56, 66
Burnett, Horace 44
Burnett, James 56
Burnett, Martha Elizabeth (Holman) 33, 35, 36, 40, 50, 64, 70
Burnett, Peter Hardeman 33, 36, 39, 40, 42, 43, 44, 45, 47, 48, 49, 56, 57, 63, 65, 66, 67, 68, 161, 162, 186, 187, 188
Burnett, Thomas 66
Burnham, Thomas 129
Burns, Oregon 179, 182, 210
Burnt-Over District 155, 156
Burroughs, Steven 155
Bushnell, Francis 143
Bushnell, Mary (Johnson) 86
Bushy Mountains 51

Butten, William 102
Buzzard Bay 111

C

cable cars, Portland, Oregon 72, 73
Cabrillo, Juan 45
Cairn terrier 237
Calapooia, Douglas County, Oregon 203
Caldwell County, Missouri 66
Calhoun, John 47
California 15, 35, 43, 44, 45, 46, 48, 49, 168, 173, 176, 194, 223
California beaches 237
California Gold Rush 49, 173, 193, 196
California grape boycott 236
California Legislative Assembly 48
California real estate 49
California state parks 237
California State University, Northridge 230, 240
California Supreme Court 49
California surf rock 235
California Trail 191
Cal Poly University 241
Calvinist 88, 94, 98, 115, 138, 155, 168
Calvin, John 96
Cambridge Agreement 128
Cambridge, England 127
Cambridge University 89, 91, 96, 97, 116
Camden, South Carolina 59
CA mission Indians 46
Campbell, Alexander and Thomas 36
Campbell, William 59
Camp Boise 197
Camp McQuaide 8
Canaan, Litchfield County, Connecticut 91
Canada 163
Canadian Rangers 54
canal boat 79
canals 15, 24, 25, 28, 79, 80, 81, 85, 98, 171, 227
candidate for president 166
Canoga Park, California 10
Cantrell, Ora 63
Cape Cod 104, 105, 106, 113, 118
Cape Disappointment 37
Cape Horn 35
Capitol Records 228
Captain Shrimpe 115
Carlisle, Pennsylvania 24

Carson, Kit 64
Carthage Jail 167
Carver, John 100, 101, 105
Cascade Mountains 41, 185, 186, 195, 196, 197, 199, 201, 229
Cassidy, Butch 179
Castleton River 87
Catalonia 232
Catawba grape 29
Catherine of Aragon 96
Catholic 17, 42, 66, 95, 96
Catholic Church 96
Catholic Spanish Empire 94
cattle 12, 45, 47, 53, 65, 87, 111, 117, 123, 139, 172, 174, 179, 183, 190, 191, 193, 194, 195, 198, 199, 200, 210, 211, 212, 213, 214, 217, 218, 219, 220, 243
Cayuse 40
Cedar City, Utah 176
Celerity wagon (mud wagon) 181
celestial marriage 166
Celts 175
Central Valley 239
Chagres, Panama 44
Champlain, John 100
Charles City, Charles, Virginia Colony 57
Charles River 128, 138
Charlestown (Boston),MA 114, 138
Charlestown, Virginia Colony 58
Chase, Philander, Episcopal Bishop of Ohio 83
Chatsworth High School, Chatsworth, California 239
Chaucer, Geoffrey 143
Chavez, Cesar 236
Chelmsford, England 128
Chenango County, New York 155
Cherokee 52, 53, 59, 65, 83
Chesapeake Bay. 29
Chester, Pennsylvania 188
Chicago, Illinois 12
Chichester, Sir Arthur 17
Chickamauga 53, 59, 83
Chickamauga Wars 83
Chief Concomly 38
Chief Ilwaco 38
Chimney Rock 194
Chinese 47, 50, 73
Chinook 38
Chisholm Trail 65, 243
cholera 43, 81, 85, 174, 188, 189, 190, 193

Christ Church, Indianapolis 84
Christ Church, Stratford, CT 89, 90
Christian Church 36
Christian Church, founded Barton Stone 202
Christianity 109, 121
Christian nation 66
Church, Benjamin 122, 123
Church of England 96, 97, 116
Church of Ireland 18
Church of Jesus Christ of Latter-day Saints 152, 154, 159
Cincinnati, Ohio 79, 82, 85
circuit preachers 42
Civilian Conservation Corps 6
Civil Rights Act 236
Clamshell Railroad 5, 38
Clark, Charles 199
Clarke, Rebecca (Wheelock) 91
Clarkson, Matthew 26
Clay County, Missouri 55, 57, 65
Clay, Henry 47, 55, 173, 189
Clemens, Samuel (Mark Twain) 65, 173
clerk of the senate 71
Clermont County, Ohio 188, 190
Cleveland Park, DC 29
Clifton, Rev. Richard 98
Clink prison, London 116
Coffee, John 63
Colesville, New York 159
Collins County, Texas 190
Coloma, CA 46
colonization of Utah 173
Colorado River 64
Colt six-shooter 65
Columbia River 4, 37, 38, 41, 42, 72, 186, 197, 198
Commissary Department of the Union Army 77
Commission on Inland Waterways of Pennsylvania, The 28
Company of Undertakers of The Iron Works in New England, The 131
compounding medicines 70
Compromise of 1850 47
Comstock, Lovisa (Snyder) 151, 163
Conestoga wagons 187
Conference of Northern War Governors 17
Congregational 89, 97, 115, 142, 155
Congregational Church 96, 145, 148, 158, 241
Congregational Church of Northridge, 11, 228
Congress of the Confederation 91

Congress of the Republic of Texas 64
Connecticut 153, 243
Connecticut Colony 86, 87, 88, 89, 90, 117, 121, 123, 124, 127, 128, 131, 136, 137, 139, 140, 141, 142, 143, 144, 145, 147, 148, 149
Connecticut Colony Record 141
Connecticut General Court 141
Connecticut Path 139
Connecticut River 117, 131, 137, 139
Connecticut River Valley 117, 133, 137, 139
Constitution 17, 34, 90, 91, 142
Constitutional Union Party 16, 17
Constitution of Tennessee 61
Continental Congress 23
Continental Divide 194
Cope, David E. 189
Cope, Elizabeth (Matthews) 184, 186, 188, 189, 202, 204
Cope, John 189
Cope, Oliver 184, 189
Corbitant 111
corn 12, 13, 51, 60, 62, 106, 107, 109
Cornplanter 25, 27, 28
Cornwallis, Gen. Charles 52
coroner 11, 19, 20, 21, 31
Coshocton County, Ohio 190
Coshocton, Ohio 81, 82, 83, 85, 159
Costa Brava, Spain 232
Costa del Sol, Spain 232
cotton 79
Cotton, Rev. John 127, 133, 137, 138, 143, 144
Council of Fifty 166
counterfeiting 160, 162, 168, 173
County Antrim, Ulster 17
Courthouse Rock 194
Court of Oyer and Terminer 136
Courtship of Myles Standish, The 94
Cowdery, Oliver 158, 159
Craig, Polly Hawkins 54
Creek War 62
Crippin, Sarah (Comstock) 163
Cromwell, Oliver 18, 132, 135, 144, 146
Crooke, Rebecca (Cope) 189
Crossing the Plains in 1846 41
CT colony agent for Indian affairs 90
Cumberland Gap 52, 53, 56, 60, 194
Cumberland River 52, 60
Cumberland River Valley 53
Curfman-Ullman Real Estate Firm 220, 221

Cushman, Robert 100, 101, 104, 110, 113

D

Dachau, Germany 231
Dalles, Oregon, The 41, 186, 198, 200
Daniel Garns company 174
Danites 66, 161, 166, 175
Dan River 58
Danville, Virginia 56
dark and bloody ground, the 52
Dartmouth College 92, 155
Dartmouth, England 103
Daughters of the American Revolution, The 30, 52
Davenport, Rev. John 127, 142, 143, 145
Davidson County, Tennessee 56, 61
Davies County, Missouri 161
Davy, William 28
Deady, William 41
Deane, Elizabeth (Cope) 189
death of Ellen Aurelia 169
Decatur, Augustine Gray 225
Declaration of Independence 22, 149
Dedham Covenant 92
Dedham, Massachusetts 92
deist 61, 66
Delaware 54, 82
Delaware River 188, 189
Delfts Haven, Holland 101
democracy 61, 124, 142, 149, 242
Democratic Party 10, 16, 202, 222
Dennison, Nancy Ann (Templeman) 184, 203
Deschutes River 196, 197, 199
Deseret 173
Destination Ninety 11, 236, 240
Deuteronomy 1.13 and 13 and 1.15

15 141
Devon County, England 17
Dexter, Oregon 198, 201, 204, 205, 207, 210
Dexter Post Office 183, 185, 202
Diamond, John 196
Diamond Peak 199
Dickinson, Emily 92
Dickinson, Rev. Jonathan 89
Disappointment Butte 199
Disciples of Christ Church, (Campbellites) 36, 66, 159
Disneyland 227

Disney, Walt 227
District of Columbia 28, 29, 30
Ditch That Brought the World to the Wilderness, The 81
Dix, Dorothea 78
Dodger Stadium 228
Dominion of New England 135
Doniphan, Alexander 161
Donner party 171
Dorkin chickens 102
Douglas County, Oregon 201
Douglas, Stephen A. 16
Dowlais, Glamorgan, Wales 175
Drewsey, Oregon 179, 182, 183, 198, 205, 210, 211, 212
Dryden, New York 76, 81, 159
dueling in California 48
Duke of Monmouth's rebellion 57
Duncan Mill, Illinois 189
Dunkhorn, Sarah 99
Dutch 80, 82, 94, 95, 99, 101, 110, 117, 139, 140, 141, 155
Dutch cheese 105
Dutch cheese and butter 103, 105
Dutch East Indies (Indonesia) 218
Duval, Elizabeth (Holman) 33, 55
Duxbury Hall, England 95
Duxbury, Massachusetts 95, 109, 113, 114, 120

E

Eagle Lake, California 229
Eames, Charles 228
earthquake 239
East Anglia, England 100, 129
Eastern Canada 164
eastern England 100
Eastern Oregon State College 223
Eastern Star 222
East Haddam, Connecticut 86, 87
Edenvale, Oregon 206
education 38, 62, 79, 83, 86, 88, 127, 129, 230, 242
Edwards, Dorothy 58
Edwards, Rev. Jonathan 90, 148
Eighty Year War 95
Elderkin, John 131
Elementa Philosophica 89
Eliot, John 91, 109, 121, 123
Elkhorn Mountains 213, 214

Ellicott, Andrew 27
Elliot Cutoff 185
Elliot, Elijah 185, 186, 196, 197, 198, 200
Elliot, Polly 186
El Monte, California 3
Elton, Rev. Edward 137
Emigrant Pass 196
Emigration Canyon 171
Endecott, John Captain 117
Endicott, John 114, 127, 128, 144
England 1, 17, 18, 21, 22, 50, 57, 79, 82, 87, 88, 89, 90, 91, 94, 95, 96, 97, 98, 99, 100, 101, 102, 104, 105, 107, 109, 112, 115, 118, 127, 128, 130, 131, 133, 135, 136, 137, 139, 140, 143, 144, 145, 146, 147, 156, 174, 175, 188, 231
English 17, 19, 20, 22, 57, 62, 63, 66, 70, 80, 82, 88, 89, 90, 94, 95, 96, 99, 100, 107, 113, 117, 118, 119, 120, 121, 123, 132, 135, 144, 147, 174, 175, 188, 223, 231, 232, 235, 241
English Civil War 18, 95, 131, 135, 143
English Common Law 114, 135
English folk songs 75
English Parliament 142, 145
Enlightenment 88, 90, 147
environmental movement 236, 242
epidemic 25, 64, 81, 85, 86, 106, 107, 143, 175, 188, 189
Episcopal (Anglican) Church of England 18
Episcopal Church 15, 20, 31, 83, 84, 86, 88, 89, 159, 228
Eppes, Frances II(Col) 58
Eppes, Frances Wayless 58
Eppes, Maria (Hardeman) 34, 57
Erie Canal 15, 80, 81, 154, 155, 159, 160
Erie Triangle, The 23, 25, 27
Escalante, Utah 178, 179
Eugene, Oregon 198, 201, 210, 223, 239, 243
Europe 43, 47, 96, 98, 99, 100, 102, 129, 136, 162, 173, 174, 230, 231, 235
excommunicated 166, 173

F

Fair Haven, Connecticut 91
Fair Haven, Vermont 87
famine 176
Far West, Caldwell County 161
Far West, Missouri 164
Far West, The 63, 65, 66, 68, 194

Father of American Library Classification 88
Father of American Viticulture 29
Father of Connecticut, The 141
Father of Oregon, The 41
Father of the Episcopal Church in America, The 89
Father of the Santa Fe Trail, The 64
Father Serra 45
Fayette County (Woodford) 54
Fayette, New York 159
Fayetteville, Lincoln County, Tennessee 55, 65
Feather River Canyon, California 51
Federal Deposit Insurance 13
Fenwick, George, founder of Saybrook Colony 143
feoffees, trustees 130
Ferguson, Patrick 59
Fighting Jungleers 7
Filipino 236
Fillmore, Utah 175
Finger Lake district, NY 81
Finney, Charles Grandison 155
first American Ranger Company, 122
First Baptist Church, Eugene, Oregon 222, 223
First Christian Church, Baker City, Oregon 222, 223
First Church of Boston 144
First Constitutional Convention of Tennessee 61
first elected governor of California 48
First Encounter 106
first mayor of Houston, Texas 56
First Oregon Cavalry, 201
First Presidency 165
First Thanksgiving 110
First Transcontinental Railroad 177
flatboat 60, 61
Fletcher, Silence 91
flower children 239
Folger, James 49
Foote, Elizabeth Deming (Welles) 144
Foote, Nathaniel 144
Fort Ann, New York 163
Fort Boise 195, 197
Fort Bridger 194
Fort Hall 195
for the common good. 150, 242
Fort Kearney 191
Fort Laramie 194, 195
Fort Le Boeuf 27
Fort Ross 45
Fort Saybrook 117, 131
Fort Saybrook, Massachusetts 128

Fort Tejon Pass 239
Fortune 110
Fortunes of Nicholas Nickleby, The 79
Fort Vancouver 37, 40
Fort Washington 22
Forty-niners 47, 173
Founder of American Philosophy, The 90
Fox, George 188
France 82, 231, 235
France, Elizabeth (Parvin) 184, 190
Franciscans 45
Franco, Francisco 232
Franklin, Benjamin 89
Franklin, Missouri 64
Franklin, Tennessee 57, 62
fraud 155, 162, 165
Frederick, Maryland 21, 23, 29
Free Adventurers 132
Free Emigrant Road 185, 186, 198
Freemasonry 155, 156, 159, 165, 182, 223
Freemason Society, The 156
freighter 153, 178
Frémont, John C. 45, 171, 176
French 22, 29, 63, 82, 96, 110, 112, 117, 231, 235
French and Indian War 22, 24
French Citrons 233
French fur traders 12, 82
French Lick 58, 60, 62
French, Rev. William 79, 84, 85, 86
frontier 12, 19, 22, 39, 50, 51, 53, 57, 58, 59, 60, 61, 62, 68, 82, 133, 147, 149, 152, 154, 155, 156, 242, 243
Fruit Growers Company 229
Fuengirola, Spain 232
Fugitive Slave Law 47
Fuller, Ann 93, 107
Fuller, Anne (Fuller) 119
Fuller, Bridget 111
Fuller, Dr. Samuel 93, 94, 99, 100, 102, 107, 111, 112, 114, 115
Fuller, Edward 93, 99, 102, 107, 163
Fuller, Edward and Samuel 105
Fuller, Elizabeth (Fuller) 93
Fuller, John 93
Fuller, Mary (Jones) 119
Fuller, Matthew 93, 102, 115, 118, 119, 122, 123
Fuller, Robert 99
Fuller, Samuel 122
Fuller, Samuel son of Dr. Fuller 115
Fuller, Samuel, son of Edward 93, 102, 107, 115, 117, 118, 123
Fullers, Matthew and Samuel 124
Fulling 86, 87, 88
fulling mill 87, 128
Fulton County, Illinois 185, 186, 189, 190, 196
Fulton, Robert 189
Fundamental Orders 141, 142, 145, 147
Fuzzy Wuzzy Angels 8

G

Galland, Isaac 162
Gallatin, Kentucky 55
Gallatin, Missouri 161
Gallitzin Tunnels 16
Gambier, Ohio 83
Garfield County, Utah 152, 179
Garfield, James A. 84
Garrison, William Lloyd 156
General Smith's Views 165
gentiles 154, 159, 168, 176, 177
gentry 96, 127, 133
Georgetown, DC 29
German 19, 22, 24, 51, 71, 81, 120, 231
Germany 136, 231
Getty, J. Paul 227
Getty Museum, Los Angeles 227
GI Bill 10
Glorious Revolution 147
gloves for Brigham Young 172
Golconda 174
Gold 8, 43, 44, 45, 46, 47, 49, 51, 66, 149, 155, 160, 179, 180, 201, 211, 213, 214, 216, 217
Golden Bible 155
Golden State 49, 243
gold mining cradle (rocker) 44
gold plates 156, 157
gold rush 8, 45, 46
gold seekers 155
Goochland County, Virginia 58
Goshute 172
government 42, 46, 48, 49, 56, 61, 71, 77, 90, 113, 114, 127, 128, 133, 140, 141, 142, 144, 146, 242
Government Experimental Farm 28
Granada Hills High School 241
Grand Geiser (Baker) Hotel 221
grand hotel in Pacific City 37
Grant, Ulysses S. 84

Granville Female Seminary 84
Granville, Ohio 79, 84, 85
Granville, Washington County, New York 87
grapevine, the 239
Graveyard of the Pacific 4
Grayson, Kentucky 203
Gray, William 42
Great Awakening, The 148
Great Depression 13, 15, 211, 212, 216
Great Migration of 1843 36, 46, 91, 128
Great Salt Basin of Utah 168
Great Swamp Fight, The 135
Great Warrior's Path 52
Greene, Gen. Nathaniel 52
Green Lawn Cemetery, Indianapolis 86
Green River 195
Greenville, Utah 178
Greenwich, Kent, England 142
Greyfriars Bobby 237
Griffin 116, 137
Griffith Park 228
grist mill 62, 153, 198
Groton Manor, England 130
Guilford, Connecticut 86, 88, 142, 143, 145, 146, 147
Gulley, Thelma (Reese) 209, 223
gypsies 232, 233

H

Hale, Emma (Smith) 157, 159, 163, 166, 167, 171
Hale, Isaac 157
Half-Way Covenant 145
Hamilton, Alexander 30
Hancock County, Illinois 165
Hannibal, Missouri 65
Hapsburgs, 98
Hardeman Academy 64
Hardeman, Bailey 34, 61, 62, 63, 64, 65, 243
Hardeman, Blackstone 62, 64
Hardeman County, Tennessee 64
Hardeman County, Texas 65
Hardeman, Dorothy (Burnett) 33, 44, 56, 57, 63
Hardeman, Dr. Glen Owen 44
Hardeman, John 62, 64
Hardeman, John (1654-1711) 34
Hardeman, John I 57
Hardeman, John II 63
Hardeman, John III 58
Hardeman, Julia 64
Hardeman, Nicholas Perkins 63
Hardeman, Owen Bailey 65
Hardeman, Peter 63
Hardeman's Station 61
Hardeman, Thomas 34, 56, 57, 58, 59, 60, 61, 62, 63, 65
Hardeman, Thomas Jones 34, 63, 64, 65, 243
Hardeman, Thomas Monroe 64, 65
Hardeman, William W. "Gotch" 65
Hardin, Bethenia (Perkins) 58
Harding, Warren B. 84
Harmony, Pennsylvania 157, 159
Harney Basin 196, 198
Harney County, Oregon 179, 210
Harney Lake 196, 198
Harris, Martin 157, 158
Harrison, Benjamin 84
Harrison County, Iowa 12
Harrison, William Henry 84
Hartford, Connecticut 10, 136, 137, 139, 140, 141, 142, 143, 147
Hartford County, Maryland 31
Harvard, John 129
Harvard University 89, 121, 129, 147
Hatfield, Massachusetts 134
Haun's Mill, Missouri 161
Haus Furst 231
Havre de Grace, Maryland 29, 31
Hayes, Rutherford B. 84
heart failure 219
Heber C. Kimball company 170
Hebrew 88
Helman Minx 231, 240
Henderson, Judge Richard 52
Henderson, Lucy (Deady) 41
Henrico County, Virginia 57
Hill Cumorah 157
Hobbamock 110, 111
Hogs 62
Holeman, Henry (Holman) 54
Holeman's Ford 51
Holladay, Bonnie (Stewart) 151, 182, 183
Holladay, Effie 182
Holladay, Frank 151, 182, 183
Holland, Kenneth 238
Holland Land Company 26
Holland, Lené 238
Holland, Netherlands 94, 96, 98, 99, 100, 102, 103, 106, 111, 127, 231

Holland, Patricia 238
Holland, Ralph 238
Hollidaysburg 16
Holman, Daniel 50
Holman, Daniel Boone 51
Holman, Daniel L. 33, 53, 54, 55, 65
Holman, Daniel S. 33, 35, 36, 37, 38, 39, 40, 41, 44, 49, 54, 55, 64, 74
Holman, Frederick V. 33, 37, 38, 41, 49, 50
Holman, Isaac Jr. 33, 55
Holman, Isaac Newton 55
Holman, James Duval 33, 36, 37, 38, 44, 47, 49, 55
Holman, James Saunders 33, 55, 56
Holman, John 33, 35, 36, 50, 55
Holman, Mary Ellen (Turner) 33, 35, 36, 39, 49, 50, 69, 70, 72, 73, 74
Holman, Rhonda (Henderson) 36
Holman, Thomas 51
Holman, Thomas Jefferson 55
Holman, Washington 38
Holman, William Sanford 56, 64
Holman, William W. 55
Holmes, Rebekah (Parvin) 190
Holston River 60
Honeyman Memorial State Park 6
Hooker, Rev. Thomas 127, 128, 137, 138, 139, 140, 141, 142, 143
Hopkins, Elizabeth 102, 104
Hopkins, Oceanus 104
Horseshoe Curve 16
horse thefts 160, 162
hospitals, Civil War 77
House, Elizabeth (Cope) 189
House, Hannah 116
House of Burgesses 58
House of Good Hope. 139
House of Representatives 221
Howard County, Missouri 57
Howland, Elizabeth Tilly 113
Howland, Stephen 104
Hudson River 81, 100, 104
Hudson's Bay Company 37, 39, 40, 41
Huguenots 96
Hungry Forties, The 66
Hutchinson, Anne 116, 137, 138

I

Ice Slough 194

Idaho 179, 195
Illinois 161, 162, 168, 186, 189, 198, 202
Ilwaco, Washington 37, 38
Increase 128
indentured servants 132
Independence, Missouri 66, 68, 159, 191
Independence Rock 194
India 233
Indian 22, 25, 27, 45, 46, 47, 59, 62, 82, 100, 106, 107, 108, 111, 115, 117, 118, 119, 120, 123, 133, 136, 138, 139, 147, 155, 156, 157, 158, 159, 170, 172, 173, 176, 178, 189, 191, 192, 195, 196, 202, 213
Indiana 71, 76, 77, 80, 85, 189
Indianapolis, Indiana 76, 78, 79, 84, 85
Indiana State Legislature 77
Indians (Lamanites) 172
Indian toll bridge 194
Indian Wars 54
individualism 149, 242
Industrial Revolution 12, 15, 175
inflation 66
influenza 85
Iowa 3, 11, 12, 13, 14, 15, 79, 161, 162, 167, 169, 173
Ipava, Fulton County, Illinois 190
Ipava, Illinois 189
Ipswich, Massachusetts 127, 128, 129, 131, 132, 133, 135, 136, 149
Ipswich Massachusetts Grammar School Trust, The 150
Ipswich, Massachusetts schools 132
Ipswich Post Office, Ipswich, MA 137
Ipswich Public Schools 150
Ipswich River 129
Ireland 17, 56, 105
Irish 80, 81
iron works 131, 175, 176
Iroquois Confederacy of Five Nations, The 82
Iroquois Nation 82
Irwin, Abraham 15
Irwin, Evalyn (Adlum) 1, 15
Isaac Holman 50, 51, 52, 54
Isthmus of Panama 44
Italy 231, 235
Ithaca, NY 82
It's a Wonderful Life 13

J

Jackson, Andrew 55, 61, 62, 63, 65, 154
Jackson County, Missouri 66, 160
Jacksonian Democracy 154
James River 58
Jamestown Colony, Virginia 58
Jamestown, Virginia 100, 108, 112
Japanese 7, 8, 9, 218
Japanese Americans 218, 219
Japanese Imperial Army 218
Jefferson, Thomas 12, 26, 29, 30, 58, 61
Jeffrey's Neck (Little Neck) Ipswich, Massachusetts 130
Jewett, Rev. Joe 222
Jobs Creek, Illinois 163, 164
John Adlum House 27
John Adlum's Memoirs for 1794 26
John Day River 197
Johnny Few Feathers 215
Johnson, Clarissa (Woods) 83, 84, 86
Johnson, Esther Ann (Turner) 69, 70, 72, 74, 75, 76, 78, 79, 83, 84, 85, 86, 92
Johnson, Gurdon Brainerd 83, 84
Johnson, Gurdon Collins 69, 76, 81, 83, 84, 86, 88, 91, 92, 159
Johnson, Gurdon Collins Sr. 69, 86, 87, 88
Johnson, Hirum Sobieski 84, 86
Johnson, Horatio 83, 84, 85, 86
Johnson, Lyndon Baines 236
Johnson, Mary Cordelia (French) 83, 84, 86
Johnson, Rev. Samuel 88, 89, 90, 148
Johnson, Rev. Samuel (1696-1772) 69
Johnson, Rev. Samuel Lee 81, 83, 84, 85
Johnson, Robert 87
Johnson, Samuel (1727-1808) 69
Johnson, Samuel, father of Gurdon Collins Sr. 87
Johnson, Samuel Sr. 88
Johnson, Vermont 91
Johnson, William 88
Johnson, William Samuel 90
Johnson, William Samuel (1727-1819) 69
Johnson, William Vittz 84, 86
John Sutter's Fort 44, 46
John's Valley, Utah 153
Jones, Master Christopher 101, 104, 106, 109
Jones, Ralph 119
Jordan, Elizabeth (Leete) 126
Jordan Schnitzer Museum of Art 241
journalism 230, 242
justice of the peace 15, 19, 130, 178, 190

K

Kadar, Nikolay M. 225
Kalapuya 201
Keanye, Robert Boston merchant 132
Keene, Ohio 83
Kelly, Ranson 199, 200
Kennebec River 111
Kennedy, John F. 231, 235, 237
Kennedy, Robert 238
Kent County, England 116
Kentucky 51, 52, 53, 54, 55, 56, 57, 62, 63, 65, 182, 194, 201, 203
Kentucky Legislature 55
Kentucky Militia 54
Kenyon College 76, 81, 83, 84
Killingworth, New Haven, Connecticut 87
Kimbro, William 56
King Charles I 115, 127, 135, 144, 145
King Charles II 18, 135, 146, 188
King Edward I 175
King Henry VIII 96
King James I 58, 97, 100, 105, 108
King James II 135, 146
King Phillip II 98
King Phillip's War 121, 122, 133, 145
King's College, Columbia University 90
King's Mountain 52, 59
Kington, Ontario 164
Kirtland, Ohio 159, 160
Kirtland Safety Society Anti-Banking Company 160
Klamath Falls, Oregon 44
Knotts Berry Farm 228
Knox, Henry 26
Knoxville, Tennessee 61
Koch, Robert Dr. 71
Koontz, Katherine 79
Koontz, Peter 79, 86
Korean War 222, 223

L

Lady of the Lake, The 79
Laguna Beach, California 235
Lake Almanor, California 229
Lake Champlain 164
Lake Erie 23, 24, 82
Lake Indians 54
Lake Michigan 164

Lamanites 158
Lancashire, England 95
Lancaster County, Pennsylvania 24
Lancaster, Pennsylvania 18
Landscape Architecture 241
Land speculation 25
land warrants 19, 25
Lane County, Oregon 196, 199, 201, 210
La Porte, Indiana 164
Lassen County, California 229
Lassen, Peter 44, 229
Lassen Volcanic National Park 229
Latin 88, 89
laudanum 41
Laud, William 115
Law, William 38, 90, 127, 130, 146, 161, 166, 167
Lazarus, Edgar M. architect 49
Leader, William 131
Leave It to Beaver 228
Lee, Bishop John D. 176, 177
Lee, Deacon Samuel 69, 91
Lee, Dr. Samuel 91
Lee, Dr. Samuel, brother of Louisa 81, 82, 83, 85, 91
Lee, Louisa (Johnson) 69, 76, 81, 84, 86, 91, 92, 159
Leete, Andrew 126, 147
Leete's Island, Connecticut 146
Leete, William 86, 126, 143, 144, 145, 146
Leiden, Holland 95, 96, 98, 99, 113
Lenape 82, 84
L'Enfant, Pierre Charles 73
Lewis and Clark 4, 12
Lewis and Clark Exposition 72
Lewistown, Illinois 189
Lexington, Kentucky 54
Liberator, The 156
Liberty, Missouri 66, 161
Library of Congress 91, 189
Limekiln Canyon Park 240
Lincoln, Abraham 16, 36, 53, 78
Lincoln County, Tennessee 55
Linfield College 70, 222
Linn County
Linn County, Oregon 199, 201
Linn, Missouri Senator 42
Linn, Senator of Missouri 67
Litchfield, Connecticut 149
Little Compton, Rhode Island 122
Little Harpeth River 60
little Hell 175

Little (Hog) River 139
Little Ice Age, The 106
Little James 111
Liverpool, England 174
Locke, John 61, 88, 90, 147
locks, (canal) 79, 81
London, England 58, 90, 98, 100, 101, 103, 111, 112, 113, 115, 116, 120, 128, 131, 142, 143, 231, 235
London Times 232
Long Beach, California 14
Long Beach car races 5
Long Beach Natatorium 4
Long Beach Peninsula 4, 5, 37, 38
Long Beach, Washington 4
Long, Dr. Benjamin 44
Longfellow, Henry Wadsworth 94
long hunters 51
Long's Bar 44
Longworth, Nicholas 29
Lord Brooke 131, 140
Lord Cornwallis 59
Lord Say and Sele 131, 140
Los Angeles, California 3, 10, 11, 14, 46, 71, 74, 226, 227, 228, 229, 235, 236
Los Angeles city schools 241
Los Angeles County 3, 71, 227
Los Angeles Times 11, 238
Lost Creek, Oregon 185, 198, 200, 203, 207
Lost Rescue 197
lost tribes of Israel, the 156, 157
Lost Valley 205
Lost Valley, Oregon 198, 201
Lothrop, Jane (Fuller) 93, 115, 118, 123
Lothrop, Rev. John 93, 115, 116, 117, 118, 163
Louisiana 63
Louisiana Purchase 12, 62
Louvre 235
Lovisa Snyder's grandchildren 171
Low Countries 94
Lowden, John 24
Lowell, Oregon 198, 199, 201
Ludlow, Roger 142
Lutheran 221, 223
Luther, Martin 96
lying for the Lord 166
Lynn (Saugus) Massachusetts 131

M

Mack, Lucy (Smith) 154, 155
Macy, William 196
Madison, James 30
magistrate 20, 140, 141, 146
Magistrate of Plymouth Colony 115
Magistrate of Windsor 136
magistrate, Winsor, CT 137
Magnalia Christi Americana 143
Main Line Canal 16
Main Line of Public Works, The 16
Major John Adlum of Rock Creek. 25
Malaga, Spain 232
malaria 7, 9, 38, 43, 57, 67, 85, 162
Malheur County, Oregon 179, 197, 210, 212
Malheur Indian Reservation 180
Malheur River 180, 196, 197, 198, 210
Manchester, New York 156, 158, 159
Manifest Destiny 66, 190
Manning, Mildred 142
Marion County 86
Marion County, Indiana 77, 79, 84, 190
Marshall, John W. 46
Marshfield, Massachusetts 113
Martin, Christopher 101, 103, 105
Martin Luther King Jr. 238
Mary and John 137
Maryland 28, 82
Massachusetts 127, 129, 136, 137, 153
Massachusetts Bay Colony 91, 92, 99, 113, 116, 117, 121, 123, 124, 127, 128, 131, 132, 133, 136, 137, 138, 142, 144, 145, 147, 149
Massachusetts General Court 133
Massachusetts Indian tribe 111
Massasoit 107, 108, 110, 111, 118, 120, 122
Matagorda County 64
Mather, Rev. Cotton 136, 143
Mather, Rev Increase 143, 147
Mather, Rev. Mather 148
Mather, Rev. Richard 143
Mathers, Jerry 228
Matthews, Anna Elizabeth (Templeman) 184, 186, 203
Matthews, Charles 184, 188
Matthews, David C. 184, 186, 197, 199, 200, 203
Matthews, James Alexander 186, 188
Matthews, Thomas Moffit 184, 186, 188, 189, 197, 198, 202, 204, 206, 243
Mayflower 92, 94, 101, 102, 103, 104, 105, 109, 110, 123, 163

Mayflower Compact 101, 102, 105
McBride, Charles W. 71
McBride, Dr. James 36, 42
McBride, George W. 42
McCall, William 198
McCarver, Morton 42, 48
McClure, Andrew 199
McClure, Andrew Samuel 197
McCoy, Nancy 189, 190
McEwen, Baker County, Oregon 213, 214
McGraw, Col. 23, 24
McGregor, Margaret, first wife of James H. Turner 79
McKain, Carrie (Adlum) 1, 13, 14
McKay, Thomas 44
McKenzie River 200, 201
McKinley, William 13, 84
McLoughlin, Dr. John 40, 41
McMillian, James 73
McMillian Plan of 1901, The 73
McMinnville, Oregon 35, 37, 39, 70, 74, 76
McPhail, Anna (Adlum) 1, 15, 31, 32
McPhail, Daniel 31
McQueen, Steve 240
McWilliams, Carey 226
Medfield, Massachusetts 92
medicine, field of 70
medics 8
Meek Cutoff 200
Meek, Joe 196
Meek's Cutoff 186
Meek, Stephen 186, 196
Mentzer, Carrie 14
Merchant Adventurers, The 101, 103, 104, 112
Meredith Miles Marmaduke expedition 64
Merrymount 114
Merthyr Tydfil, Glamorgan, Wales 175
Metacomet, King Philip 120, 121, 122, 129
Methodist 40, 148, 164
Mexican 45, 64, 170
Mexican American 236
Mexican style 171
Mexican War 45, 46, 168, 173
Mexico 45, 47
Miantonomo 118
midwife 163
Mifflin, Thomas 25, 26
Milan, Indiana 223
Miles place, the 217
militia 22, 54, 55, 58, 66, 87, 88, 90, 112, 118, 121,

122, 133, 149, 160, 161, 162, 167, 178
milk before meat 174
mill 86
Miller, Charles 156
Millerites 156
mills 86, 87
Milton, John 91
Mingo 82
Minnie ball 78
missionaries 40, 162, 164, 171, 173, 174, 175, 178
Missionary Baptists 51
missions 45, 46
Mississippi River 62, 63, 65, 66, 162, 167, 169, 174
Mississippi Valley 66
Missouri 36, 42, 44, 48, 63, 64, 65, 66, 154, 160, 161, 203
Missouri Militia 161
Missouri River 63, 65, 66, 191
Missouri Valley and Northwestern Railway Company. 12
Missouri Valley, Iowa 11, 12, 13
Mocksville, North Carolina 51
Mohammed 166
Mohawk 118, 121
Mohegan 90, 117, 118, 121, 134
Mohican 109
money digging 154, 155
Monmouth Normal School 206
Montana 179
Monterey, California 46
Montgomery, Caroline 206
Montgomery, Daniel 206
Montgomery, David 206
Montgomery, Martin 206
Monticello 29
Morgan, William 156
Mormon 46, 66, 154, 161, 165, 166, 168, 170, 171, 172, 173, 176, 177, 179, 182, 183
Mormon Battalion 173
Mormon Church 49, 159, 164, 175, 177, 179
Mormon Extermination order 66
Mormon, prophet 158
Mormon Restoration 176
Mormon Road 176
Mormons 45, 66, 152, 159, 160, 161, 162, 164, 165, 166, 167, 168, 169, 171, 172, 173, 174, 176, 177, 213
Mormon wagon trains 194
Mormon War 161

Morning Register 191
Morocco 231
Moroni 155, 156, 157, 158
Morrison, Mary (Burnett) 56
Morton, Oliver P. 77, 78
Morton, Thomas 114, 120
mosquitoes, 85
Mountain Meadows Massacre 176, 177
Mount Hood 186
Mount Hope 108
Mount Lassen, California 229
Mount Pisgah, Iowa 169, 170
Mr. Davy's Dairy 28
Mullins, Barbara (Standish) 93
Mullins, William 102
Muncy, Lycoming County, Pennsylvannia 31
Muncy, Lycoming County, Pennsylvannia 15, 25, 27, 28, 31, 32
Munich, Germany 231
muskets 22, 24, 105
Mystic, Connecticut 118

N

Narragansett 108, 109, 111, 118, 121, 134
Nashville, Tennessee 56, 60
Nassau Bay, Papua New Guinea 7, 8
National Mall 73
National Road 82
native customs New Guinea 9
Nauvoo Expositor 166
Nauvoo, Illinois 162, 163, 164, 165, 167, 168, 189
Nauvoo Legion 162
Nauvoo Temple 164, 169
Naval War of 1812 11
Nebraska 192
Nephites 158
Neptune, The 58
Netherlands 95
Neuschwanstein Castle 231
Neutra, Richard 228
Nevada 239
New College, Oxford University 143
New England 100, 113, 115, 119, 121, 122, 123, 127, 128, 129, 133, 137, 140, 147, 148, 152, 153, 154, 164
New England Indian tribes 109
New England style 171
New England Way 142

Newgate Prison, London 116
New Guinea 7, 8
New Haven Colony 86, 87, 121, 142, 143, 144, 145, 146
New Haven, Connecticut 88
New Helvetia 45
New Israelites 159
New Jersey 22, 190
New Jersey Plan 91
New Jerusalem 159
New Light Puritans 89
New Lights, 148
New London, Connecticut 123, 131
New Mexico 63, 64
New Orleans 62, 63, 64, 174, 189
New Plimouth 106
New Testament 165
Newton, Isaac 88
Newtown (Cambridge) MA 138
New World 18, 57, 90, 100, 101, 109, 116, 124, 127, 128, 131, 143, 155, 156, 158, 188
New York 15, 22, 23, 24, 30, 37, 80, 81, 82, 89, 149, 152, 153, 155, 156, 159, 163, 190, 230, 235
New York Harbor 235
Niantic 117
Nice, France 232
Nieuw Amsterdam 230
Nigerian Civil War 239
Nipmuc 121
Nobel Prize 1905 71
Norfolk, Virginia 7
North, Anna (Paine) 125, 128
North Carolina 50, 51, 52, 53, 54, 55, 59
North Carolina State Legislature 61
Northern Ireland 18
North Fork of the Yuba River 44
Northumberland County, Pennsylvania 27
Northumberland, Pennsylvania 24
Northwest Indian Federation 27
Northwest Indian Wars 83
Northwest Territory 82, 189
no taxation without representation 135
Nottinghamshire, England 96, 97
Number 3 Dredge 217

O

Oak Hill Cemetery, DC 30
Oakridge, Oregon 199, 205

Observations Divine and Mortal 113
Of Plymouth Plantation 98
Ohio 76, 79, 80, 81, 82, 85, 92, 159, 189
Ohio and Erie Canal 80
Ohio Country 82, 83
Ohio River 23, 60, 188
Ohio Territory 22, 82
Ohio Valley 83
oil. 227
old Dutch ship 7
Oldham, John 117
Old Hickory 63
Old Light Puritans 89
Old Lights 148
Old Spanish Trail 3
Old Testament 158
Oliver, Mary second wife of Major Samuel Appleton 133
Olmstead, Frederick Law 10
Olmstead, Nicholas (Captain) 10
Olmsted, Frederick Law Jr 73
Omaha 12
Oneida Lake, NY 81
Ontario-Burns Stage Company 182
Ontario, Canada 163
Ontario, Malheur County, Oregon 218
Ontario News, The 182
Ontario, Oregon 179, 180, 222
Oregon 40, 43, 49, 75, 185, 186, 191, 192, 195, 218, 239, 243
Oregon City 37, 72, 198
Oregon City, Oregon 37, 42
Oregon Country 36, 42, 43, 50, 67, 68, 168, 187, 190, 201
Oregon Fever 186
Oregonian, The 74
Oregon Indian Reservations 201
Oregon Lumber Company 213
Oregon National Guard 222
Oregon National Guard 6, 7
Oregon's first laws 42
Oregon Supreme Court Judge 43
Oregon's wine country 39
Oregon Territory 43, 46, 48
Oregon Trail 44, 50, 85, 186, 190, 191, 192, 193, 196, 197, 212, 213, 220
Overmountain Men 52, 59
Owen, Benjamin Franklin 197, 199
Owen, Glen 63

Owyhee Dam 212
Owyhee River 213
oxen 188
Oxford University 89, 90

P

Pacific Bank 49
Pacific City 37
Pacific Coast Highway 237
Pacific County, Oregon 37
Pacific Ocean 194, 201, 243
pacifists 188
Paine, Hannah (Appleton) 125, 132
Paine, John 125, 132
Paine, Robert 125, 129
Paine Street School, Ipswich, Massachusetts 130
Paine, William 125, 127, 128, 129, 131, 132, 133, 144, 150
Paine, William and Robert 129
Paiute 172, 180
Palmer, Joel 187
Palmyra, New York 154, 155, 158, 159, 164
Panama Canal 7
pandemics 85
Panguitch, Utah 152, 153
Panic of 1837 65, 67, 154
Park City, Utah 172
Parker, Ellis 204
Parker, James 189
Parker, James II 190
Parker, James M. 184, 186, 189, 198
Parker, Joseph 184, 186, 189, 192, 198, 201
Parker, Joseph and James 186, 197
Parker, Phoebe (Stoops) 184, 186, 189
Parker, Selena (Parvin) 184, 186, 189, 191, 193, 200, 201, 202, 203, 205
Parkman, Francis 192
Parley's Park (Park City), Utah 152, 153
Parvin, Alberta A. (Dillion) 205, 221
Parvin, Bertha (Williams) 202
Parvin Bridge 203, 206, 207, 243
Parvin Butte 202, 207
Parvin, Dorothy Agnes (Reese) 183, 184, 185, 205, 206, 207, 209, 210, 211, 212, 214, 215, 217, 218, 219, 220, 223, 224, 226, 239

Parvin, Edgar 202
Parvin, Enoch 190
Parvin, Florence J. (Montgomery) 205, 206, 224
Parvin, Hila 202
Parvin, Hosea 184, 190
Parvin, Hosea Morris 184, 185, 202, 203, 205, 207
Parvin, Ida (Williams) 202, 203
Parvin, James 184, 186, 190, 191, 197, 198, 200, 201, 202, 203, 243
Parvin, Joseph 202
Parvin, Lillis 202
Parvin, Loris T. 205, 206
Parvin, Phoebe (Jeannie) (Schaffler) 202, 203
Parvin, Selena Elizabeth (Burian) 205, 206
Parvin, Thomas 184, 190
patent medicines 70
patriarch 166, 178
patriarchal 168
patriarchal blessing 164
Paul Bunyan statue 229
Pavlosek, Daniel George 225, 243
Pavlosek, Dr. Libor G. 225
Pavlosek, Julia Suzanne 225, 243
Pawlett, Marie (Eppes) 58
Pawlett, Thomas 58
Pawnee 192
Pawtuxet, Massachusetts 107
Payne, Ann (Leete) 126
Peale, Charles Willson 26
Pearl Harbor 7
Pease Field Fight 122
Pengra, Charlotte 194
Penline, George 199
Penn, John 19
Pennsylvania 11, 14, 15, 16, 21, 22, 23, 24, 25, 26, 27, 28, 30, 31, 32, 50, 51, 52, 184, 187, 188, 189
Pennsylvania Brigade 22
Pennsylvania Canal 16
Pennsylvania House of Representatives 17
Pennsylvania long rifle 24, 51
Pennsylvania Militia 28
Pennsylvania Railroad Company 16
Pennsylvania Railroad, The 16
Penn, William 19, 188, 189
Pequot 109, 117, 118, 121, 140
Pequot War 117, 118, 140
Perfectionist Oneida Community 156
Perkins, Mary (Hardeman) 58, 60, 61
Perkins, Mary Hardin (Hardeman) 34

Perkins, Nicholas 58
Perkins, Susannah 62, 63
Perpetual Emigrating Fund 174
Petworth, DC suburb 73
pharmacy 70, 71
Philadelphia 15, 18, 19, 22, 23, 25, 26, 27, 28, 89, 188, 190
Philadelphia and Columbia Railroad 16
Philadelphia Constitutional Convention 91
Philadelphia Gazette 20
Pickett, Beverly 223
Pickett, Janet 223
Pickett, Judi 223
Pickett, Kenneth Roy 209, 222
Pickett, Ronald 223
Piedmont of the Carolinas 50, 51, 58
Pierce College 3, 10, 236
Pilgrim Hall Museum 102
Pilgrims 94, 98, 99, 101, 102, 103, 104, 105, 107, 108, 109, 110, 111, 112, 113, 114, 115, 116, 119, 120, 121, 123, 139
pillboxes 8
Piomingo, Chickasaw Chief 61
pioneer 230
pioneers 35, 36, 39, 40, 41, 42, 52, 53, 54, 61, 65, 76, 104, 171, 173, 176, 177, 183, 185, 186, 187, 193, 194, 197, 201
Piscataqua patent of lands 140
Pittsburg 15
Pittsylvania County, Virginia 56, 58
Pitt, William 56
plague of crickets 171
Plantation Compact 146
Platte County, Missouri 66
Platte River 191, 192, 193
Pleasant Hill, Oregon 186, 196, 198, 201, 204, 243
Pleasant Hill Pioneer Cemetery 200, 207, 224, 243
Plymouth Bay, Massachusetts 106
Plymouth Colony 113, 114, 117, 120, 121, 122, 123, 134, 139, 140, 142, 147
Plymouth Colony, Massachusetts 101
Plymouth, England 103
Plymouth Harbor, MA 106
Plymouth, Massachusetts 94, 99, 102, 110, 111, 113
pniese, counselor 110
Pocasset, Rhode Island 122
Pocumtuc 121
Pokanokets 107
Polk County, Oregon 37, 42

Polk, James 43, 47, 173
Polk, James K. 85
Pollack, Dr. Robert 215
polygamy 166, 167, 168, 172, 173, 174, 176, 179
Ponderosa Pine 213
Pool, Elizabeth (Williams) 151, 153
Pope Clement VII 96
Porter Ranch (Northridge) 237
Portland Heights, suburb of Portland, Oregon 73
Portland, Oregon 3, 4, 5, 6, 14, 35, 37, 38, 39, 42, 49, 50, 70, 72, 73, 74, 75, 76, 183, 212, 218, 219, 220, 226, 239
Portland Rose Society 50
Port Moresby 7
Port of Seattle Commissioner 14
postmaster 77, 86, 97, 202
Postmaster of Missouri Valley 13
Pottawattamie 12
Poultney, Vermont 91
Powder River 213, 217, 221
Prado 235
Prairie Schooners 187
Pratt, Parley 159, 172
Praying Indians 111, 121, 123
Predestination 138
Presbyterian 18, 36, 97, 142, 148, 155, 188
Presbyterian Scots 18
President Lincoln's cottage 74
presidios 45, 46
Presque Isle (Erie), Pennsylvania 25, 27
Price controls, beef 218, 220
Priestley, Dr Joseph 25
Prince George County, Virginia 58
Princess Pocahontas 108
Princeton University 89
Promontory, Utah 177
prophet 167
Protestant 18, 42, 98, 135, 145, 236
Protestant Reformation 96
Protestants 18, 51, 96, 97
Provincetown harbor 104
public school teacher 92
pueblos 45, 46
Puritan 18, 88, 89, 90, 91, 94, 95, 96, 97, 98, 99, 100, 113, 115, 116, 120, 124, 127, 128, 129, 130, 132, 135, 136, 137, 141, 143, 145, 146, 148, 149, 150, 152, 153, 155, 163, 168, 188, 228
Puritan Protectorate 144
Pynchon, William 133

Q

Quadequina 108
Quaker 19, 119, 137, 145, 188, 189, 204
Queen Ann of England 18
Queen Elizabeth I 95, 96, 97
Quorum of Seventy 165
Quorum of the Twelve Apostles 160

R

racial discrimination 236
rack-renting 18
railroad 233
railroads 4, 5, 11, 12, 14, 15, 16, 17, 38, 39, 43, 56, 72, 76, 79, 80, 85, 177, 207, 211, 214
Ralph Wheelock School 92
Ramus, Petrus 88
ranch 45, 175, 177, 180, 182, 183, 210, 211, 212, 213, 214, 215, 217, 218, 219, 220, 227
rationing World War II 218
Rattlesnake Valley (Trent) 198
razor clams 4, 38
Redenhall, Norwich, England 99, 102
Red River Lumber Company 229
Red Sticks 62
Reese, Cora (Leonning) 151, 179, 183
Reese, Geraldine (Pickett) 209, 210, 212, 213, 214, 217, 219, 220, 222, 223, 243
Reese, Grover Parvin 209, 211, 212, 214, 220, 221, 222, 223
Reese, Grover Williams 151, 179, 182, 183, 207, 209, 210, 211, 212, 214, 215, 216, 217, 219, 220, 222
Reese, Jacob 151, 178, 179
Reese, Patricia (Adlum) 115, 127, 128, 129, 140, 152, 209, 210, 212, 213, 214, 215, 217, 219, 220, 221, 222, 223, 225, 228, 230, 238, 240, 241, 242, 243
Reese, Paul 223
Rees, Watkin 151, 174, 175, 176, 177, 178, 179, 187
Reformed Methodist 155, 171
regicides 144
Relief Society 163
Reno, Nevada, 229
Reorganized Latter-day Saints Church 171
Republican Party 16
Republic of Texas 56
Restoration 145
Revised Encyclopedia of Philosophy 88

rheumatic heart disease 217
Rhode Island 108, 120, 121, 122, 138, 145
Richards, Franklin D. 164
Richards, Willard 167
Richmond, California 222
Riemenschneider, Tilman 231
Rigdon, Sidney 159, 160, 161, 168, 171
Riley, Gen. Bennet 48
Rittenhouse, Benjamin 25
Roanoke, Virginia 52
Robbins, Hannah 153
Robinson, Rev. John 94, 95, 96, 97, 98, 99, 100, 101, 105, 109, 111, 113, 116
Rock Creek Park, Washington DC 29, 31, 73
Rockwell, Porter 166, 175
Rocky Mountains 177, 194
Rogers, Harriet W. (Burnett) 33, 36
Rogers, John P. 44
Rogers, Peter 49
Rogers, Sarah (Burnett) 36, 49
Rogers, Sarah M. (Burnett) 33
Roosevelt, Alice 74
Roosevelt, Franklin D. 6, 211, 222
Roosevelt, Theodore 11, 73, 74
Rose City, The 50, 72
Round Rock, Texas 243
Rowan County, North Carolina 52
Rowan (later Davie) County 50
Rowley, Henry 116
Rowley, Massachusetts 133
Royal Proclamation of 1763 52, 82
run the gauntlet 118
Runyon, Rachel 190
Rush, Dr. Benjamin 25
Russia 47
Russian-American Company 45
Russian fur traders 45
Rutledge, Charlotte 192

S

Saconnet 122
Sacramento, California 44, 45, 48, 74, 177
Sacramento River 45
Sacramento Valley 45
Saint James Episcopal Cemetery 32
Salamaua 7, 8, 9
Salem Colony 127
Salem, Massachusetts 114, 124, 136

Salem witch trials 136
Salisbury, North Carolina 52
salmon 4, 38, 195
Salt Lake City, Utah 170, 172, 174, 175, 194, 213
Salt Lake Valley 171
Saltonstall, Richard son of Sir Richard Saltonstall Jr 129
Saltonstall, Sir Richard 125
Saltonstall, Sir Richard Jr. 125, 128, 140
Saltonstall, Sir Richard, Lord Mayor of London 128
Samoset 107
San Augustine Company 56
San Augustine, Texas 55
San Diego State University 240
Sandwich, Massachusetts 113
San Fernando Valley 10, 11, 227, 230, 239, 241
San Francisco 37, 44, 46, 47, 48, 73, 76, 226, 239, 243
San Gabriel Valley 3
San Juan Islands 14
San Luis Obispo, California 241, 243
Santa Fe trade 64
Santa Fe Trail 3, 65, 187, 191
Santa Monica Pier 228
Santa Rosa, California 49
Santa Susanna Mountains 237
Sassamon, John 121
Sasser, Samuel Harris 225
Sasser, Zachary 243
Saugus Iron Works, (Hammersmith) 132, 133, 135, 149
Saugus River 131
Saunders, Elizabeth (Wolcott) 125, 137
Saunders, James 53
Saunders, Nancy Anne (Holman) 33, 53
sawmill 37, 46, 62, 133, 153, 172, 201
Saxon name 17
Saybrook Colony 117, 131, 139
Scandinavia 174
scarlet fever 85
Scheafe, Dorothy (Whitfield) 126
Schmidt, Dr. Rodney D. 225
Schmidt, Katherine Karissa-Michelle (Sasser) 70, 225, 243
Schmidt, Kristin Paige (Kadar) 225, 243
school trust 130
Schuylkill River 25
scientific method 148
Scituate, Massachusetts 113, 115, 116, 117, 118
Scotland 18, 231

Scots-Irish 18, 19, 51, 188
Scottish prisoners of war 132
Scotts Bluff 194
Scrooby Manor, Scrooby, England 97
Scrooby, Nottinghamshire, England 96, 98
scurvy 78, 103, 104, 106, 169, 170
Sea Scout Manuel, The 11
Seaside, Oregon 5
Sea-Tac Airport 14
Seattle, Washington 3, 14, 72, 210, 241, 243
Second Bank of the United States, The 65
Second Great Awakening 36, 155
Second Street Elementary School in Los Angeles 241
seer stones, peep stones 154, 155, 157
Seeshaupt, Germany 231
seminary, 83
Seneca 25, 26, 27
Seneca Falls, New York 156
separation of church and state 111, 116
Separatist
separatists 94, 96, 97, 101, 123, 142
serge-weavers guild 99
sermon, Thomas Hooker's 141
Seventh Day Adventists 156
Sevier, John 59
Sevier River 152
Shakers 156
shallop 106
Sharon, Vermont 154
Shawnee 27, 52, 53, 54, 82, 83
Shawver, Patricia Turner 68
Sheaffe, Dorothy (Whitfield) 143
Shelby, Evan 59
Shelby, Isaac 59
Shell (Pismo) Beach, California 243
Shenandoah Old Cemetery in Shenandoah 50
Shenandoah, Page County, Virginia 50
Shenandoah Valley, Virginia 50, 51
Shepard, Rev. Thomas 127, 137
sheriff 19, 20, 45, 161, 198
shipbuilding 131
Shoshone 172
sidesaddle 193
Siege of Bexar 55
siege of Charleston 23
Sierra Club 236
Sierra Mountains 44, 46, 229
Silent Spring 236
Silver Falls State Park 6

Simple Cobbler of Agawam, The 138
Sinners in the Hands of an Angry God 148
Sioux 12, 191, 192
Six Nations 27
skin-dressing 21, 23
Skinner, Eugene 201
Slate Valley, The 87
slavery 16, 17, 42, 43, 47, 48, 51, 54, 56, 61, 64, 66, 118, 123, 156, 166, 176, 188
Smallpox 38, 85, 90, 114, 115, 148
Smith, Alvin 154
Smith, Hyrum 154, 159, 160, 164, 167
Smith, John 95, 100, 105
Smith, Joseph III 171
Smith, Joseph Jr. 66, 152, 154, 155, 156, 157, 158, 159, 160, 161, 162, 164, 165, 166, 167, 168, 171
Smith, Joseph Sr. 154, 159, 164
Smith, Rev. Ethan 157, 158
Smith, Samuel 167
Smith, William 89
smog 236
Snake River 179, 195, 212
Snyder family 170, 172
Snyder, George 172
Snyder, Isaac 151, 163, 164, 165
Snyder, Jane (Richards) 164, 170, 172
Snyder, Lovisa (Comstock) 164, 172
Snyder, Mary Ann (Williams) 151, 152, 153, 163, 164
Snyder, Robert 164
Snyder, Samuel Comstock 151, 152, 153, 163, 164, 172
Snyders, Isaac 162
Snyderville, Utah 172
Society of Friends 188
Somerset, England 137
South America 35, 43, 44
Southampton, England 231
Southern Paiute 152
southern Utah (Dixie) 177, 178, 179
South Pass 194
South, the 79
South Wales 174
Spain 45, 46, 48, 231
Spanish Civil Guards 232
Spanish Florida 62
Spanish, the 63, 95, 98, 99, 100, 102, 158, 233, 241
Specie Circular Act 66
Spectator, The 43
Speedwell 101, 103

Spoon River 189
Springfield, Massachusetts 133
Springfield, Oregon 200
Squanto 107
Stafford County, Virginia 203
Stafford, Virginia 243
Stagecoach 4, 76, 82, 179, 180, 181, 182, 197
Stamp Act 17, 22, 90, 148
Standish, Alexander 113
Standish, Barbara 111
Standish, Charles 113
Standish, John Myles 113
Standish, Josiah 93, 113, 114, 122, 123
Standish, Loara 93, 113
Standish, Mercy (Wheelock) 69, 92, 93, 114
Standish, Myles 69, 93, 94, 95, 102, 105, 106, 107, 108, 110, 111, 112, 113, 114, 115, 118, 119, 122, 124
Standish, Myles and Rose 102
Standish, Rose, first wife of Myles 102, 107
Stanton, Elizabeth Cody 156
Starnberger See 231
states' rights 16
St. Bartholomew's Day Massacre 96
steamboats 65
Steens Mountain 210, 212
sternwheeler 4
Stevenson, Adlai 237
Stewart, Donald Crawford 183
St. George, Utah 173
sticky Missouri bottoms 57
Stinking Water Mountain 180, 182
Stinking Water Way Station 180
St. John Episcopal Church 21
St. Joseph's (St. Jo's), Missouri 191
St. Louis, Missouri 63, 174
St. Mary's School, Indianapolis 84, 85
stock market crash of 1929 5, 13
Stockwell, Henrietta Maria (Snyder) 151, 152, 163, 164, 172
Stone, Barton 36
Stone, John 117
Stone, Rev. Samuel 138, 139
Stoops, John 186, 189, 197, 200, 204
Stoops, Malinda (Matthews) 203
Stoops, William 186, 191, 194, 195, 197
Stowe, Harriet Beecher 189
St. Paul's Episcopal Church, Washington DC 74
strangers, The 102, 104

Stratford, Connecticut 89, 90
Strauss, Levi 49
Stump Dodger 213
Sturbridge, Massachusetts 132
Suckiaug 140
Suffolk County, England 128, 133
Sugar Creek, Iowa 169
Sugar Hill 62, 63
Sumpter, Oregon 213, 214, 216
Sumpter Valley 217
Sumpter Valley Dredge Company 216
Supreme Court 90
surgery. 78
surveying 23, 24, 26, 27, 28, 30
Survey of the Summe of Church Discipline 143
Susanville, California 229
Susquehanna County, Pennsylvania 157
Susquehanna River 19, 24, 25, 27
Sutter, John Augustus Jr. (August) 45, 47, 48
Sutter, John Sr. 45, 46, 47, 48
Sutterville 48
Sweden 136
Switzerland 45
Sylmar, California 239

T

Taft, William Howard 84
Tambu Bay, Papua New Guinea 8
Tandy, Robert 199
Tangiers, Morocco 233
Tarleton, Col. 59
Taylor, John 167, 177
teacher's union rep 241
Teasdale, Utah 173
Tecumseh, Shawnee chief 62
Templeman, Agnes E. (Parvin) 202
Templeman, Agnes Florence (Parvin) 184, 185, 204, 205, 207
Templeman, Edward 243
Templeman, Edward Reginald 184
Templeman, Elden 184, 204, 205
Templeman, Fielding 184, 203, 204
Templeman, Maggie (Dunten) 183, 184, 204, 205, 210
Templeman, William Dennison 184, 203, 204
Tennent, Rev. Gilbert 148
Tennessee 52, 54, 55, 56, 58, 59, 60, 61, 62, 63, 65, 78, 194

Tennessee militia 62
Tennessee River 60
territorial governor 173
Territorial Legislature of Oregon 37, 43
Test Acts 18
Texas 63, 64, 168, 202
Texas Declaration of Independence 65
Texas Rangers 65
Texas Revolution 55, 56
Texas State Cemetery 65, 243
Texas State Legislature 64
Texas War for Independence 55
textile industry in Holland 99
Thames and Mystic rivers 117
The year without a summer 164
Thirty Year's War 100
Thomas Hardeman I 57
Thousand Oaks, California 238
Three Sisters Mountains 199
Tidewater of Virginia 51, 58, 65
timber 5, 200, 201
Timberline Lodge at Mount Hood 6
tobacco 51, 56
tomahawked 54
Tomes, Alice (Welles) 125, 140, 144
Tories 59
Torremolinos, Spain 232, 233
torture 100, 108, 118, 123, 198
Tower of London 116
transportation 5, 15, 23, 28, 79
Travis County, Texas 64
Treat, Robert 134
Treaty of Ghent 63
Treaty of Granville 83
Treaty of Guadalupe Hidalgo, The 46, 173
Treaty of Paris 22, 82
Tren-Feve 233
Trinity College, Cambridge University 130
Trinity College, Dublin, Ireland 131
Trumball County, Ohio 188
Trumball, Dr. J. Hammond 142
trustees (feofees.) 150
Tualatin County, Oregon 42
Tuberculosis, (consumption) 36, 49, 71, 85, 106, 164, 169
Turks 112
Turner, Ella Holman 68
Turner, Frederick Jackson 53
Turner, Horatio 70

Turner, Ida (Narver) 71
Turner, James H. 69, 71, 75, 76, 77, 78, 79, 80, 81, 86
Turner, Kate Pauline (Evans) 71
Turner, Mildred E. (Allen) 1, 6, 38, 71
Turner, Patricia Lee (Shawver) 70, 71, 73, 74
Turner, Roy G. second husband of Winifred 75
Turner, William B. 33, 39, 42, 69, 70, 71, 74, 226
Turner, Winifred B. (Adlum) 1, 3, 5, 35, 38, 69, 70, 71, 74, 75, 226
Twelve Apostles 165
typhoid 43, 79, 85, 86, 172, 179, 188
typhus 110
Tyrone's Rebellion 17

U

UCLA Medical Center 240
Uffizi Gallery 235
Ullman, Al 221
Ulster Plantation 17, 18, 19
Umpqua Canyon, Oregon 44
Uncas 117
Uncle Tom's Cabin 189
Underground Railroad 79
Union 79, 201
Union Army 77
United Church of Christ 228
United Farm Workers 236
United States 43, 173, 174
Universal Studios Theme Park 228
University of California at Los Angeles, The 227
University of California, Berkley 10, 226
University of Leiden 98, 100, 110, 114
University of Oregon 10, 202, 220, 221, 222, 223, 241
University of Pennsylvania 89
University of Washington 183
Urim and Thummim 157
U.S. Mail 181
U.S. Mail Star Route 179
U.S. senator from Connecticut 91
Utah 170, 171, 177, 179
Utah's Dixie 173
Utah Territory 152
Utah War (Mormon War) 176
Ute 172, 175

V

Vale, Oregon 180, 197, 210

Van Buren, Martin 165
Vere, Sir Horace 95
Vermont 149, 152, 163, 164
Victorian 73
Vienna, Austria 231
Vietnam War 237, 238
Vigil, Joseph C. Jr. 225, 243
Virginia 49, 50, 51, 52, 54, 55, 56, 57, 58, 65, 100, 104, 105, 189, 190, 196
Virginia Colony 100, 127
Voltaire 147
Von Sternberg House, Northridge, California 228

W

Wadsworth, Joseph 147
wagon train 185, 192
wagon train of 1843 41
Wales 174, 175, 177, 178, 231
Walker, Thomas Dr. 52
Wallis, John 25
Wallis, Samuel 25
Wallowa Mountains 213
Wampanoag 109, 111, 112, 118, 120, 121
Wampanoag Federation 107
wampum 108, 120
Wamsutta, Alexander 120
Ward, Rev. Nathaniel of Ipswich 142
War for Texas Independence 64
War of 1812 29, 35, 55, 62, 63, 83
Warsaw, Illinois 167
Wasatch Mountains 171
Washington County, North Carolina 59
Washington, DC 70, 71, 73
Washington, George 26
Washington state 14, 37
Washington State Ferry System 14
Watauga 52, 53, 59, 60
Watauga Association 52
Watertown, Massachusetts 91, 128
Watts Riots 237
Wayne, Gen. Anthony 27, 83
Webster, Daniel 47, 189
Welles, John 126, 144
Welles, Robert Jr. 126, 144
Welles, Samuel 144
Welles, Thomas 125, 127, 140, 141, 142, 144
Welsh 51, 57, 174, 175, 186

Index

Wesley, John and Charles 148
western Massachusetts 149
Western New York 156
Western Oregon University at Monmouth 42
Western Telegraph 177
Westfall Butte 198
Westfall, Oregon 198
West Indies 118, 120, 123
West Los Angeles 228
Weston, Thomas 101, 103, 110, 111
Westport, Missouri 174
West Stockbridge, Berkshire, Massachusetts 154
Westwood, California 229, 230
Wethersfield, Connecticut 137, 139, 144, 152, 153
Weymouth, MA 110
Wheelock, Mary Standish (Bingham) 69, 91
Wheelock, Ralph (1682-1748) 69
Wheelock, Rev. Eleazer 92
Wheelock, Rev. Ralph 91, 92
Wheelock, Rev. Ralph Sr. 69
Whig Party 16, 173
Whipple, Matthew 129
Whiteaker, John 201
White, Bridget (Robinson) 97
White, Dr. Elijah 37
White House 74
White River 84
White, Susanna 102
Whitfield House, Guilford, Connecticut 150
Whitfield, Rev. George 148
Whitfield, Rev. Henry 126, 142, 143, 146
Whitfield, Thomas 142
Whitman, Dr. Marcus 40, 41
Whitman, Narcissa 40
Whitmer, David 158
Whittingham, Vermont 171
Wilderness Calling 58
Wilderness Trail 53, 56
Wild West 180, 183
Wilkes (Rowan) County 52
Wilkinson, Jemima 156
Willamette Pass 186
Willamette River 42, 72, 196, 198, 201, 202
Willamette Valley, Oregon 39, 41, 44, 185, 186, 195, 196, 197
William and Mary, monarchs of England 147
William Brewster Steeg 99
William of Orange 147
Williams, Cora 178
Williams, Cora Lucy 153
Williams, Grace M. (Reese) 151, 152, 153, 178, 179, 180, 182, 183, 210, 215, 222
Williams, Gustavus 151, 153, 169, 170, 173
Williams, Gustavus and Maria 162
Williams, Hyrum 152, 153, 178
Williams, Hyrum A. 151, 152, 153, 163, 178, 179, 180, 182, 183, 197, 222, 223
Williams, Jacob 153
Williams, Jane (Rees) 151, 174, 175, 177, 178
Williams, Mary Adell (Shurtz) 152, 153, 178
Williamson County, Tennessee 57, 62, 64
Williamson County, Texas 64
Williams, Rodney 153
Williams, Roger 118, 120, 137, 138
Williams, Solomon 151, 153
Williams, Sylvester Spenser 151, 153, 178, 179, 181, 182
Williams, Thomas 186, 197, 198, 200, 201, 204
William the Silent 98
Wilshire, England 188
Wilson, James 25, 26
Wilson's Creek Baptist Church 64
Wilson, William 27
Wilton Farm 29
Wiltshire, England 189
Winchester Cathedral 143
Windsor, Connecticut 137, 139, 142
wine making 29, 30
Winslow, Edward 94, 99, 101, 105, 107, 108, 109, 110, 111, 120
Winslow, Josiah 120, 121, 134
Winter Quarters, Nebraska 169, 170
Winthrop, John the Elder 113, 117, 127, 128, 130, 131, 137, 138, 142, 143, 144
Winthrop, John the Elder Governor 138
Winthrop, John the Younger, 128, 129, 131, 132, 139, 144, 145, 146
Wise, John Reverend 137
witchcraft 136
Witches, Salem 1692, The 136
Wituwamat 111
Wolcott, Henry 144
Wolcott, Henry Jr. 125, 127, 137, 141, 142
Wolcott, Henry Sr. 125, 136, 137
Wolcott, Oliver Sr. 125, 149
Wolcott, Samuel 125, 137
Wolcott, Sarah 125
Wolcott, Sarah (Welles) 125, 144

Wolf Run, Muncy 28
Woodford County, Kentucky 54
Woods, Isaac 86
World War I 13, 183
World War II 7, 217, 227, 232
Worthy Saints 132
Wyandot 54, 82, 83
Wyoming 194, 195

Y

Yadkin River 51
Yale University 88, 89, 90, 147
Yamhill County, Oregon 39, 76
Yarmouth, Massachusetts 113
yellow fever 25, 26, 56, 64, 189
York County, Pennsylvania 11, 19
York, Pennsylvania 15, 18, 19, 20, 21, 22, 23, 24, 27, 31, 51, 89, 155
Yorkshire, England 190
Young, Brigham 161, 162, 167, 168, 169, 170, 171, 172, 173, 174, 176, 177

Z

Zion 66, 124, 152, 159, 161, 170, 171, 174
Zuma Beach 237

www.ingramcontent.com/pod-product-compliance
Lightning Source LLC
Chambersburg PA
CBHW061752290426
44108CB00029B/2972